Invitation to Cryptology

Invitation to Cryptology

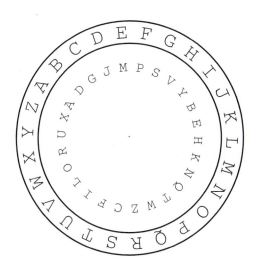

THOMAS H. BARR

Rhodes College

Supported by National Science Foundation Grant DUE-9555113

PRENTICE HALL, Upper Saddle River, New Jersey 07458

Library of Congress Cataloging-in-Publication Data

Barr, Thomas H.
  Invitation to cryptology/Thomas H. Barr
    p. cm.
  Includes bibliographical references and index.
  ISBN: 0-13-088976-8
  1. Cryptology. 2. Mathematics I. Title
Z103 .B34 2002
652'.8–dc21   2001036589

Acquisition Editor: *George Lobell*
Editor-in-Chief: *Sally Yagan*
Vice-President/Director of Production and Manufacturing: *David W. Riccardi*
Executive Managing Editor: *Kathleen Schiaparelli*
Senior Managing Editor: *Linda Mihatov Behrens*
Assistant Managing Editor/Production Editor: *Bayani Mendoza de Leon*
Manufacturing Buyer: *Alan Fischer*
Manufacturing Manager: *Trudy Pisciotti*
Marketing Manager: *Angela Battle*
Marketing Assistant: *Rachel Beckman*
Editorial Assistant: *Melanie Van Benthuysen*
Art Director: *Jayne Conte*
Cover Photo: *Onosato Toshinobu, "Three Blacks" 1958. Oil on Canvas, 162 × 132 cm,*
        Aichi Prefectural Museum of Art, Nagoya, Japan

©2002 by Prentice Hall, Inc.
Upper Saddle River, New Jersey 07458

Printed in the United States of America

10   9   8   7   6   5   4   3   2   1

ISBN   0-13-088976-8

Pearson Education Ltd., *London*
Pearson Education Australia Pty., Limited, *Sydney*
Pearson Education Singapore, Pte. Ltd.
Pearson Education North Asia Ltd., *Hong Kong*
Pearson Education Canada, Ltd., *Toronto*
Pearson Education de Mexico, S.A. de C.V.
Pearson Education—Japan, *Tokyo*
Pearson Education Malaysia, Pte. Ltd.

Contents

Foreword

Cryptology began almost as early as when humankind started communicating in writing. It developed slowly through the years, and even in ancient times, existed mainly as a tool for military and governmental covert actions. Much of its modern-day fame was gained during World War II with the cracking of the German Enigma code and the Japanese military cipher. The landmark discovery of cryptology's intimate connection to mathematics, and the rapid development of digital technology, have spawned an abundance of applications of this fascinating science in virtually all parts of today's society.

It is amazing to think that in this day and age most citizens of developed countries encounter cryptology every day! With the wide use of e-mail, credit cards, e-commerce, and automatic teller machines, people make use of cryptology, perhaps unknowingly, in many of their common transactions. With future advances in technology inevitable, the needs for and benefits of cryptology will expand dramatically.

But what about cryptology as a topic for a beginning mathematics student? Most of us have a natural curiosity about things secretive or hidden. As a child I remember making a cipher wheel and a code book and encrypting messages to send to a friend. The idea that only a friend (who held the common key) and I could know the contents of a message provoked a grand feeling of furtive power! This clandestine nature of cryptology, combined with its artful connection to all levels of mathematics, makes it an ideal topic for an introduction to mathematical reasoning. Moreover, the rich and lengthy history of cryptology makes it a natural topic in which to explore the development of linguistics and communication in different cultures and eras. I also submit that the many uses of electronic encryption today make it indeed a necessary topic for anyone desiring to learn how our technologically driven society functions at a very basic level.

This book, *Invitation to Cryptology*, fills a void in the literature on cryptology. The author creatively combines a history of the subject with its mathematical fundamentals. He introduces a variety of mathematical topics (statistical analysis, matrix manipulation, modular arithmetic, number theory, to name a few), then applies these topics to unravel the mysteries of this science. Moreover, he provides a source that not only highlights both classical and modern cryptology within the same binding, but makes doing both types of cryptology feasible. That is, the author presents the topics in such a way that the mechanics of enciphering and deciphering information is accessible to students. Students can truly get their hands dirty and learn the necessary skills to do and undo their own secret writing. This is achieved through the many clever examples, exercises, and computer programs.

For the novice searching for a mathematical topic that is accessible, practical, historically significant, and at the cutting edge of modern data manipulation, nothing could be more satisfying. For the instructor searching for a text to guide and nurture the learning of this material at an introductory level, this book is the potent, timely resource of choice.

Terri England Lindquester, Ph.D.
Associate Professor of Mathematics
Rhodes College
Memphis, Tennessee

Preface

In 1994, my colleague Terri Lindquester had a pedagogical inspiration: to teach cryptology. The lack of unified resources to teach an introductory course with mathematical themes, historical content, and current cryptographic relevance required her to piece together material from various sources. She had considerable success with the The Science of Secret Writing: more students requested it at registration time than could be accommodated, her own insights and teaching abilities made the course itself lively and appealing to the students enrolled, and students from a wide range of academic disciplines learned some mathematics and cryptology. The experience convinced her that there was a genuine need for an up-to-date introductory cryptology text, and this prompted her to seek National Science Foundation (NSF) funding to develop materials for such a course. A guiding principle was to introduce mathematics in the context of cryptology. This book is the result of Terri's application for that funding, of the foundation's awarding it, and of a great deal of work, teaching, and writing in the interim. Unfortunately for those who use this text, very little of it is Terri's writing. Almost coincident with the awarding of funding for the project, Terri was called to serve in an administrative capacity at Rhodes College. The demands of this post were such that it would be extraordinarily difficult for her to work on the cryptology project, and indeed its fate was, for a time, in question. In 1997, through conversations with and encouragement from Terri, I embarked on the project: teaching the second offering of Secret Writing, doing research, and writing materials based on her course notes from the first offering of Secret Writing. I became "Chief Staff Mathematician" on the project. With her continuing consultation and reviewing of early drafts, the book has evolved into its present form.

This book is directed toward those whose mathematical background includes college-preparatory courses such as high school algebra and geometry. In earlier drafts, I have used it as the basis for a course for which there were no formal mathematical prerequisites at the college level. Students majoring in areas ranging from Art History to Zoology took the course. Many had not taken mathematics in four or five years.

The purpose of the book is to introduce students to segments of history and current cryptological practice that have mathematical content or underpinnings. This is not a mathematics text in the strictest sense because it does not begin with a few definitions and axioms and build up a mathematical edifice on that. However, a variety of mathematical topics are developed here: modular arithmetic, probability and statistics, matrix arithmetic, Boolean functions, complexity theory, and number theory. In each case, the topic is germane to cryptology.

The concepts introduced in this book may also be a springboard for those who may not be drawn into technical careers but who instead may be headed toward careers in public service or industry where important policy or strategic decisions regarding information security will be made. The more technical background the policymakers and managers have, the better. With any luck, these pages may provide some of that background.

The treatment here is not comprehensive, but the concepts discussed cover a number of the current uses of cryptographic methods. The mathematical basis of cryptography has been a theme throughout this exposition, and what is here can provide an entrée to a range of mathematical areas. Readers may find their way into the general mathematical literature as well by following the links provided in the mathematical references in this book.

The academic and popular literature on cryptology is large and growing rapidly. It represents a considerable body of general knowledge about cryptology and specific information on implementations in hardware and software. In the bibliography of this book you will find a number of book and journal references on the subject. However, this merely scratches the surface. If you want to explore the literature more deeply, go to the references in these books.

A few words of advice about the book are in order. First, there is more material here than can be used in a one-semester course. One possible pathway through the material is this: Chapter 1, Chapter 2, Chapter 3 (possibly skipping 3.2), and Sections 4.1, 4.3, 4.4, 4.6, and 5.4. This sort of option covers conventional substitutions and transpositions, block ciphers and hash functions, public-key cryptography and related mathematics, applications of public-key cryptography such as key agreement and digital signatures, and finally a look at public policy issues relating to cryptography. Several mathematical topics arise naturally with this approach: modular arithmetic, functions, probability, matrix arithmetic, and number theory. In a more technically oriented course, a closer focus on 4.7, 5.1, or 5.3 may be appropriate.

There is a second caveat. An instructor is unlikely to be able to cover all this material at a uniform pages-per-unit-time rate: Some of the mathematical topics here are inherently more challenging than others to absorb. Consequently, while many sections can be dealt with effectively in one lecture, some may require more time to cover adequately. Instructors should be prepared to use their best judgment about this issue, taking into account the background of the students enrolled in the course.

In this material, opportunities abound for implementing encryption, decryption, and cryptanalytic methods on a computer. Depending on the method, students and instructors may wish to use a spreadsheet, computer algebra system, or compiled language such as C++ or Java. A few explicit examples and pseudocode and a range of hints throughout the text provide some indications how this can be done, though programming is not a focus in this text.

Acknowledgments

There are several people to whom I am greatly indebted. Elizabeth Teles, the program director at NSF, has been very supportive during the various turns the project has taken. My thanks go to John Planchon, former Dean of Academic Affairs at Rhodes, who had a role in the establishment of scholarly support funds for named chairs, and in particular for the one to which I currently hold an appointment—the E. C. Ellett chair in Mathematics. Also, my thanks go to the Rhodes College Faculty Development Committee, which provided additional summer support.

In the fall of 1998, a team of four mathematicians reviewed an earlier version of this manuscript, visited campus, interviewed students, attended the course, and drafted a report on their perceptions of various aspects of the project. To Joel Brawley (Clemson University), Stephen Davis (Davidson College), Larry Riddle (Agnes Scott College), and David Sutherland (Hendrix College) go my heartfelt thanks for their kindness, thoroughness, and constructive criticisms. I have tried very hard to incorporate their suggestions into my thinking and writing.

Andrew Simoson (King College) and Alan Durfee (Mt. Holyoke College) have used an earlier version of this text to teach cryptology courses. Their insights and correspondence have been enlightening, helpful, and heartening.

My student John Carpenter wrote a suite of applets for use by students. For his labors, I am grateful. My student Clara Cheung created pieces of art for chapter 1, and I am indebted to her for this work. Another student, Burke White, carefully read the entire manuscript in an earlier version, marked corrections, made suggestions, and worked the exercises. My thanks go to him for his careful work.

I am grateful to the students who enrolled in the Science of Secret Writing. It has been a pleasure to work with and learn from them. Their questions, insights, and comments have had a positive impact on this project.

Michelle McDaniel (the Rhodes Math and Computer Science secretary) TEX-ed a great deal of this manuscript. For her skill, patience, and good humor I am very grateful.

Several people reviewed the manuscript in earlier versions. In particular I thank Eric Bach (University of Wisconsin) and Stephen Greenfield (Rutgers University) for their careful reading and thoughtful criticisms. As usual, the editorial and production staff at Prentice Hall have been diligent and kind: My thanks go to George Lobell, Bayani De Leon, and Patricia Daly.

Figures 1.1, 1.5, and 1.6 are reproduced with the permission of the Center for Cryptologic History. Figure 2.2 is reproduced with the kind permission of S. Brent Morris.

Throughout this project, my family—Kathryn, Rebecca, Elizabeth, and Thomas—has been an abundant source of love and patience. My deepest thanks go for and to them.

Inevitably, imperfections in substance, infelicities of style, or just plain typing and production errors may become apparent to readers. In the interest of having any future editions of this book no less perfect than the first, readers should communicate their ideas, suggestions, corrections, or other comments to the author at the e-mail address shown below. Updates and resources related to this book will appear at the URL shown.

Tom Barr
Mathematics and Computer Science Department
Rhodes College
`tombarr@rhodes.edu`
`http://www.mathcs.rhodes.edu/~barr/crypto`

Chapter 1

Origins, Examples, and Ideas in Cryptology

In this chapter we look at a few of the contexts in which cryptology has arisen or played a role. This is only a glimpse of cryptologic history, but it is structured in order to draw out incidents, individuals, or writings that use or reveal new mathematical ideas. In the second section of this chapter, we delineate some of the broad concepts that are connected with secret writing. Informed by the examples of the first section, we will be able to understand the general definitions and maxims laid out in Section 1.3. We also take a glance at how cryptology has appeared in literature, both directly and as a story element.

There has never been a time prior to this juncture at the beginning of the twenty-first century when so many people deal directly with the benefits and challenges of making transmitted information secure from eavesdroppers and tamperers. Cryptology is ubiquitous, and in some forms, its workings are likely to be transparent to the casual user. In other cases, though, its workings may be mysterious. It is the purpose of this chapter to sketch some of the historical backdrop to the subject and to point out some of the contemporary applications of cryptology. There are fascinating human stories connected with the endeavor, and just as fascinating mathematical features of the subject as well.

1.1   A Crypto-Chronology

For millennia, people have invented and used methods of concealing the content of messages from those who are not the sender's intended recipients.

Some of the methods can be categorized as **cryptography**, the science and art of designing and using methods of message concealment. Writing itself is a form of cryptography in a time or place where the literate wish to communicate and conceal the content of their messages from the illiterate. Most of the time, however, the methods are designed to conceal messages from other, literate, individuals. Accounts of ingenuity in this area abound. There are stories of kings in antiquity tattooing messages on the shaved scalps of slaves and relying on subsequent hair growth to hide the message while the slaves traveled to the intended recipients. German spies in the United States during World War I corresponded using invisible inks. During World War II, Roosevelt and Churchill talked on a transatlantic telephone line where the signal was securely scrambled by an astonishing engineering feat of synchronizing two identical sound recordings on turntables a continent apart. Since the late 1970s, "DES-boards," specialized computers in automatic teller machines, have ensured that the financial information the automatic teller machines exchange over telephone lines with their banks remains obscured from eavesdroppers or tamperers. In this book, we will study the *mathematical* underpinnings of certain classical cipher methods and the way in which modern digitally based and public-key cryptography relies on mathematics for its design and security.

In this first section, we look at selected cryptological innovations of historical significance, especially those that contain or imply ideas of mathematical importance. For more complete accounts of cryptologic history, you can consult any of a range of references given in the bibliography.

Some of the historical accounts given here rely, to a considerable extent, on David Kahn's *The Codebreakers* and on a collection of lectures by William Friedman published under the title *The Friedman Legacy: A Tribute to William and Elizebeth Friedman* by the Center for Cryptologic History at the National Security Agency. Other references are given in the bibliography.

Throughout this book, we strive to use terminology consistently and in accord with practice in the literature. We have already indicated the meaning of the term *cryptography*. There are a few other terms that we will use, starting in this section, that need to be introduced at this point. **Cryptanalysis** is the activity of "breaking" a message concealment method, and a **cryptanalyst** is someone engaged in this activity. The term **cryptology** is applied to cryptography, cryptanalysis, and the interaction between them.

Proto-Cryptology:
Modified Hieroglyphics, c. 1900 B.C.

In some historical accounts of cryptology, notably Kahn's *The Codebreakers* and some of William Friedman's lectures, the modification of standard writing symbols counts as the first example of cryptography. In these works, however, the authors admit that the examples don't strictly fit the definition of modification with the intent to conceal content or meaning. Kahn says that writings on the tombs of some of the pharaohs were made different enough from the customary ways so that readers would be intrigued but not so different that the writing was impossible to read. The idea is much the same as that used by advertisers when they put mirror images of words in their products. "Madison Avenue in the Valley of the Kings" is Kahn's phrase. On the backs of the tee shirts issued to those attending Crypto '97—the annual conference of the International Association for Cryptologic Research—was a list of cryptological milestones through the years, and modified hieroglyphics was first.

Tenuous as this example might be, it points up a very basic idea in cryptology: substituting unusual symbols for those ordinarily used in writing.

Atbash, c. 500 B.C.

Biblical writers and scribes copied scripture using the only means available— writing by hand—and they sometimes used simple methods to detect errors in transcription. They also occasionally embellished their work.

In Jeremiah 25, the prophet chastises the tribe of Judah for not listening to his prophecies and tells them that the Lord will send the forces of King Nebuchadrezzar of Babylon to descend on their land and carry them into captivity for seventy years. After that, the prophet says that the Lord will punish Babylon too, sending them the wine of wrath. Recapitulating the names of all the tribes to receive retribution for their misdeeds, the writer says finally in verse 26, "And after them the king of Sheshach shall drink." *Sheshach* is code for Babylon, obtained in the following way: The Hebrew alphabet is shown in Figure 1.1, "doubled back" on itself. This provides a direct correspondence between the first letter *aleph* and the last letter *taw*, the second letter *beth* and the next-to-last letter *shin*, and so forth. Hebrew scribes used this correspondence to turn the word spelled *beth-beth-lamed* into the word spelled *shin-shin-kaph*, or, using the letter sounds and

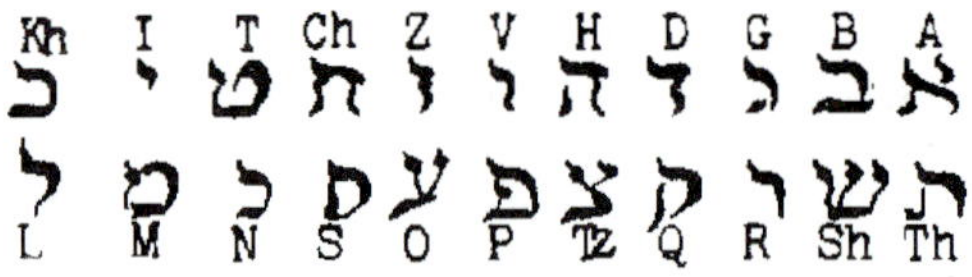

Kh I T Ch Z V H D G B A

כ י ט ח ז ו ה ד ג ב א

ל מ נ ס ע פ צ ק ר ש ת

L M N S O P Tz Q R Sh Th

Figure 1.1 The Hebrew alphabet (with English transliteration of the letter sounds). The first half of the alphabet is on the top line written in order, right to left; the second half is written in order, left to right.

interpolated vowels, B-A-B-E-L turns into Sh-E-Sh-A-Ch. The term **atbash** is used to designate this letter-for-letter replacement process. Its analog with the standard Roman alphabet would be to transform text by exchanging *A* with *Z*, *B* with *Y*, *C* with *X*, and so on. The word *atbash* itself is self descriptive: *aleph* and *taw* interchange, as do *beth* and *shin*. Perhaps the writer was playing on the story that Babel was the place where God had confused the speech of the people building the tower to reach heaven.

Atbash is an example of a **simple substitution cipher**, one in which letters of the alphabet substitute for one another in a designated way and are systematically replaced in this fashion throughout the message being enciphered.

Spartan Scytale, c. 500 B.C.

Figure 1.2 shows a **scytale** (pronounced si′-ta-lee), a device used by the mil-

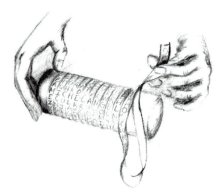

Figure 1.2 A Spartan Scytale

itary of Sparta for enciphering and deciphering messages. First, the sender wrapped a thin strip of parchment helically about a cylindrical rod and then wrote the message line by line parallel to the rod's axis so that successive letters went on successive turns of the parchment. Then he removed the parchment from the rod. A messenger carried the strip, which contained a jumble of letters, to the intended recipient who had a scytale of the same diameter. The message was then unscrambled by wrapping the parchment strip about his scytale and reading off the message. Such cryptographic methods, where the letters of the message are scrambled, are called **transposition ciphers**.

Polybius' Checkerboard, 205–123 B.C.

The **Polybius**[1] **checkerboard** cipher uses a form of substitution in which pairs of numbers substitute for letters. An adaptation of the Polybius checkerboard to the Roman alphabet is shown in Table 1.1. The first digit

	1	2	3	4	5
1	A	B	C	D	E
2	F	G	H	IJ	K
3	L	M	N	O	P
4	Q	R	S	T	U
5	V	W	X	Y	Z

Table 1.1 The Polybius checkerboard.

is the row in which the letter appears, and the second digit is the column. For example, 42 substitutes for R, and POLYBIUS is represented by 3534315412244543. This code was readily adapted to make a semaphore. A person standing on land could send a message to a ship off shore by holding in each hand as many torches as represented the numbers for the letter being transmitted. Figure 1.3 shows a person transmitting the letter C.

In the nineteenth century, the Polybius checkerboard idea was adapted to the cyrillic alphabet by Russian Nihilist political prisoners. To communicate in the prison, they tapped the numbers representing letters. In the Roman adaptation here, tap-tap—tap-tap-tap represents letter H, for instance.

Caesar Cipher, c. 50 B.C.

Gaius Julius Caesar (100 B.C.–44 B.C.), the general and politician who became dictator of Rome—and who was assassinated out of fear that he would

---

[1]Greek historian of c. 203–120 B.C.

Figure 1.3 The letter C represented using the Polybius checkerboard "semaphore."

make himself king—describes in his *Gallic Wars* a flimsy but easy to use method of encipherment. In a message, replace each A by D, each B by E, each C by F, ..., each W by Z; replace X by A, Y by B, and Z by C. For example, the message

OMNIA GALLIA EST DIVISA IN PARTES TRES

becomes

RPQLD JDOOLD HVW GLYLVD LQ SDWUHV

The Caesar cipher is one example of a **shift** cipher, where the entire alphabet is shifted (or rotated) to provide a rule for substitution. Some present-day text editors contain a similar sort of encryption function, called ROT13, which rotates the alphabet by 13 letters: A becomes N, B becomes O, ..., M becomes Z; N becomes A, O becomes B, ..., Z becomes M. This is still a weak form of encipherment, but at least it prevents a casual perusal of the enciphered document.

Nomenclators, c. 1400

A **nomenclator** is a codebook, usually in two parts: The first part shows how letters, syllables, words, and phrases translate into code; the second part shows how code translates back into the various pieces of ordinary language.

A telephone book is essentially half of a nomenclator: Names are listed in alphabetical order, and a code, the telephone number, is listed beside each name. Without another volume that lists telephone numbers in order along with the names of the people to whom they are assigned, it would be extraordinarily tedious to search the standard white pages for a person's name knowing only his or her telephone number. You can, of course, buy the other half from some organizations. The difficulty of going both directions is obviated by CD-ROM telephone directories that are searchable by computer.

Nomenclators came into considerable use in the early fifteenth century by trading states in southern Europe and by the Catholic Church. In the century or two following, the number of items in these came to be rather large—several hundred or a few thousand. In many instances, there were ways of representing high-frequency letters or words so as to make crypt-analysis more difficult than if there were a straight substitution.

Table 1.2 shows a toy nomenclator, completely unrealistic, but illustra-

A = 001	AND = 028
B = 002	THE = 027
C = 003	GENERAL = 029
$\vdots$	MEN = 030
Z = 026	WAR = 031
$\vdots$	NOT = 032

Table 1.2 A toy nomenclator.

tive nonetheless. It is so small that there is no need to make two parts. Using it, one enciphers the message MAKE LOVE NOT WAR as enciphered as 013 001 011 005 012 015 022 005 032 031.

Nomenclators have continued to be used into the twentieth century for commerce, military communications, and diplomatic communications. For instance, Thomas Jefferson compiled a nomenclator in 1785 and used it in correspondence with James Madison and James Monroe. Much military radio communication during World War II and later was conducted from codebooks —nomenclators.

Alberti's Cipher Disk

Italian Renaissance artist, architect, composer, organist, and scholar Leon Battista Alberti (1404–1472) wrote on many subjects, among them cryptology. Indeed, Kahn refers to him as the "Father of Western Cryptology," for he wrote on cryptanalysis and also developed a sophisticated combination of encipherment and encoding. He, along with such luminaries as Leonardo Da Vinci epitomized the term renaissance man. Among his inventions was a cipher wheel, shown in Figure 1.4. This cipher wheel implemented the first

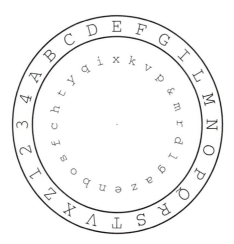

Figure 1.4 A model of the cipher wheel of Leon Battista Alberti

polyalphabetic substitution—where different substitution alphabets are used for various parts of the message—in the following way. The inner wheel, on which are written lowercase letters, could be turned so as to align with any of the 24 cells of the outer ring to permit an easy translation from plaintext (the letters on the outer ring) to ciphertext (the letters on the inner wheel). Two correspondents with identical disks first agree on a "pointer" letter on the inner wheel; Alberti chose k. The sender begins by selecting a letter on the outer ring with which to align the pointer; say it is F. Then the sender writes F as the first letter of ciphertext and proceeds to transcribe subsequent letters of the message as the letters indicated by the wheel in this position. After a few letters or words are enciphered, the sender then *changes* the position of the wheel so that the pointer aligns with a different letter, say Q. He writes Q in the ciphertext he is generating and then proceeds to translate some more message letters according to the new position of the cipher wheel. He continues this sort of pattern. For example, the message

A L B E R T I W A S A T R U E R E N A I S S A N C E M A N

would be enciphered using this method as

```
F t & y x a e p Q m m e p e & v m s G g i m h v a a h m y i A
                        a k z
```

Since W and U do not appear on the wheel, a double-V and V, respectively, are used to represent them. Of course, the choice and frequency of the inserted capital letters in the ciphertext were entirely up to the sender.

The omission of H, K, and Y on the outer ring, along with the inclusion of & on the inner one, allowed space for the digits 1, 2, 3, and 4 on the outer ring. Thus sequences of these digits could be enciphered as well. If the correspondents had agreed on a list of codes to represent commonly used words or phrases, then these representations could be enciphered as well. For instance, suppose that the correspondents had a small nomenclator in which the code for Pope was 12 and the code for Rome was 24. Then the ciphertext

```
L a x l x g D m l & c h m l X & r
```

deciphers as

```
VISITING 12 IN 24
```

which, by the nomenclator, is

```
VISITING POPE IN ROME
```

Though Alberti's polyalphabetic cipher, used properly, was considerably more sophisticated than letter- or nomenclator-substitutions, such approaches to cryptology were not taken until late in the nineteenth century.

Early Writings on Cryptology

Contemporaneous with Alberti was an Arab by the name of Shihab al-Din abu 'l-'Abbas Ahmad ben 'Ali ben Ahmad Abd Allah al-Qalqashandi—or Qalqashandi for short—who wrote an encyclopedia. A portion of that work was devoted to cryptology, and in particular to cryptanalysis of substitutions by examining letter frequencies.

Only after Johann Gutenberg invented printing by movable type, however, were books freed of hand transcription. One of the first printed works on cryptology was by a German who took the name Johannes Trithemius. In *Polygraphiae libri sex*[2] (Six Books of Polygraphy), published posthumously

---

[2]A first edition of this work is on display at the National Cryptologic Museum at the National Security Agency, in Ft. George Meade, Maryland.

in 1518, he discusses a form of polyalphabetic substitution that uses a rectangular table of letters to aid in encipherment. This "tabula recta" as Trithemius called it, was essentially what is now called the Vigenère square. His method is the direct precursor to such modern methods of encryption as the binary one-time pad, which we will study in this course.

Porta's Digraphic System, 1535–1615

Giovanni Battista Porta produced the earliest known **digraphic** cipher, one in which special symbols were used to represent *pairs* of letters. A digraphic substitution makes cryptanalysis harder by obscuring letter frequencies. This same basic idea reappeared in a refined and more mathematical form in a 1929 paper of Lester Hill entitled "Cryptography in an Algebraic Alphabet." In this instance, there is not a proliferation of special symbols, but instead pairs of letters substitute for other pairs. We will examine the Hill cipher later in this book.

In principle, there is there is nothing standing in the way of **polygraphic systems** where blocks of any number of letters are enciphered either as single special symbols or as other blocks of text. In modern parlance, such systems are called **block ciphers**. Since the mid-1970s, the **Data Encryption Standard (DES)** has been a widely used block cipher in commercial applications. The block size is 64 binary digits, so there is a total of $2^{64} = 18446744073709551616$ different "letters" in the DES "alphabet." Block ciphers are distinguished from **stream ciphers**, in which each single character of plaintext is transformed into a corresponding ciphertext character.

Blaise de Vigenère, 1523–1596

In 1585, the Frenchman Blaise de Vigenère wrote a treatise entitled *Traicté des Chiffres* that included magic, alchemy, speculation on the origins of the Bible, and cryptology. He discussed a cryptographic method very similar to Trithemius' except that instead of using a keyword or key phrase, he used the plaintext itself, shifted by one letter, as the key. One form of the tableau he used is shown in Table 1.3, adapted to the modern Roman alphabet. Plaintext letters label the columns, and key letters label the rows. Though this tableau might more properly be called the "Trithemius square," it is most often called the **Vigenère Square**.

We can easily illustrate Vigenère's **autokey** method. Suppose we want

	A	B	C	D	E	F	G	H	I	J	K	L	M	N	O	P	Q	R	S	T	U	V	W	X	Y	Z
A	A	B	C	D	E	F	G	H	I	J	K	L	M	N	O	P	Q	R	S	T	U	V	W	X	Y	Z
B	B	C	D	E	F	G	H	I	J	K	L	M	N	O	P	Q	R	S	T	U	V	W	X	Y	Z	A
C	C	D	E	F	G	H	I	J	K	L	M	N	O	P	Q	R	S	T	U	V	W	X	Y	Z	A	B
D	D	E	F	G	H	I	J	K	L	M	N	O	P	Q	R	S	T	U	V	W	X	Y	Z	A	B	C
E	E	F	G	H	I	J	K	L	M	N	O	P	Q	R	S	T	U	V	W	X	Y	Z	A	B	C	D
F	F	G	H	I	J	K	L	M	N	O	P	Q	R	S	T	U	V	W	X	Y	Z	A	B	C	D	E
G	G	H	I	J	K	L	M	N	O	P	Q	R	S	T	U	V	W	X	Y	Z	A	B	C	D	E	F
H	H	I	J	K	L	M	N	O	P	Q	R	S	T	U	V	W	X	Y	Z	A	B	C	D	E	F	G
I	I	J	K	L	M	N	O	P	Q	R	S	T	U	V	W	X	Y	Z	A	B	C	D	E	F	G	H
J	J	K	L	M	N	O	P	Q	R	S	T	U	V	W	X	Y	Z	A	B	C	D	E	F	G	H	I
K	K	L	M	N	O	P	Q	R	S	T	U	V	W	X	Y	Z	A	B	C	D	E	F	G	H	I	J
L	L	M	N	O	P	Q	R	S	T	U	V	W	X	Y	Z	A	B	C	D	E	F	G	H	I	J	K
M	M	N	O	P	Q	R	S	T	U	V	W	X	Y	Z	A	B	C	D	E	F	G	H	I	J	K	L
N	N	O	P	Q	R	S	T	U	V	W	X	Y	Z	A	B	C	D	E	F	G	H	I	J	K	L	M
O	O	P	Q	R	S	T	U	V	W	X	Y	Z	A	B	C	D	E	F	G	H	I	J	K	L	M	N
P	P	Q	R	S	T	U	V	W	X	Y	Z	A	B	C	D	E	F	G	H	I	J	K	L	M	N	O
Q	Q	R	S	T	U	V	W	X	Y	Z	A	B	C	D	E	F	G	H	I	J	K	L	M	N	O	P
R	R	S	T	U	V	W	X	Y	Z	A	B	C	D	E	F	G	H	I	J	K	L	M	N	O	P	Q
S	S	T	U	V	W	X	Y	Z	A	B	C	D	E	F	G	H	I	J	K	L	M	N	O	P	Q	R
T	T	U	V	W	X	Y	Z	A	B	C	D	E	F	G	H	I	J	K	L	M	N	O	P	Q	R	S
U	U	V	W	X	Y	Z	A	B	C	D	E	F	G	H	I	J	K	L	M	N	O	P	Q	R	S	T
V	V	W	X	Y	Z	A	B	C	D	E	F	G	H	I	J	K	L	M	N	O	P	Q	R	S	T	U
W	W	X	Y	Z	A	B	C	D	E	F	G	H	I	J	K	L	M	N	O	P	Q	R	S	T	U	V
X	X	Y	Z	A	B	C	D	E	F	G	H	I	J	K	L	M	N	O	P	Q	R	S	T	U	V	W
Y	Y	Z	A	B	C	D	E	F	G	H	I	J	K	L	M	N	O	P	Q	R	S	T	U	V	W	X
Z	Z	A	B	C	D	E	F	G	H	I	J	K	L	M	N	O	P	Q	R	S	T	U	V	W	X	Y

Table 1.3 The Vigenère Square.

to encipher some of Vigenère's own words: "All nature is merely a cipher and a secret writing."[3] We decide on a "priming key," a single letter to be remembered by sender and receiver, and append it to the beginning of the message to form the key. Take it to be P. Then we write the message on one line and the key on a second:

```
plain   ALL NATURE IS MERELY A CIPHER AND A SECRET WRITING
  key   PAL LNATUR EI SMEREL Y ACIPHE RAN D ASECRE TWRITIN
```

To encipher the first letter, we find in the Vigenère square the column labeled with A and then locate the letter in the row labeled by P: It is P. To encipher the second letter, we find the column in the square labeled by L and the

---

[3]Kahn, p. 146.

letter in that column that lies in the row labeled A: it is L. Continuing in this way to encipher the message, we obtain

```
 plain   ALL NATURE IS MERELY A CIPHER AND A SECRET WRITING
   key   PAL LNATUR EI SMEREL Y ACIPHE RAN D ASECRE TWRITIN
cipher   PLW YNTNLV MA EQVVPJ Y CKXWLV RNQ D SWGTVX PNZBBVT
```

A recipient of the message PUNHYOCGAAVFWGWLV would decipher it by first writing

```
   key   P
cipher   PUNHYOCGAAVFWGWLV
```

and then looking in row P for the cipher letter P. At the head of the column in which cipher P appears is the corresponding plaintext letter, A. Since this is also the second letter of the key, the recipient can now write

```
   key   PA
cipher   PUNHYOCGAAVFWGWLV
 plain   A
```

Next, the recipient looks in the row labeled A for the cipher letter U; it lies in the column labeled U, so the recipient can write

```
   key   PAU
cipher   PUNHYOCGAAVFWGWLV
 plain   AU
```

Continuing in this way, the recipient reconstructs the original message: AUTOKEY IS INSECURE. Can you explain why this statement is true?

While the autokey implementation of Vigenère is not much more secure than a Caesar-type cipher, the basic concept of using plaintext as key is used in modern implementations of some *block* ciphers, either for encryption or to generate **message authentication codes (MACs)**. A block cipher can be used in what is called **cipher block chaining (CBC)** mode, where plaintext blocks are enciphered or hashed using the previous cipher or plaintext block as key data.

Francis Bacon's Bilateral Cipher, 1623

English essayist, philosopher, and proponent of the scientific method, Sir Francis Bacon (1561–1626), wrote about cryptography along with grammar and rhetoric. He described various encipherment schemes, but one of the most ingenious and forward thinking is one to which he referred as a **bilateral cipher**. It relies, first of all, on a **binary** representation of the alphabet (Figure 1.5). Instead of the currently used symbols 0 and 1, Bacon uses *a*

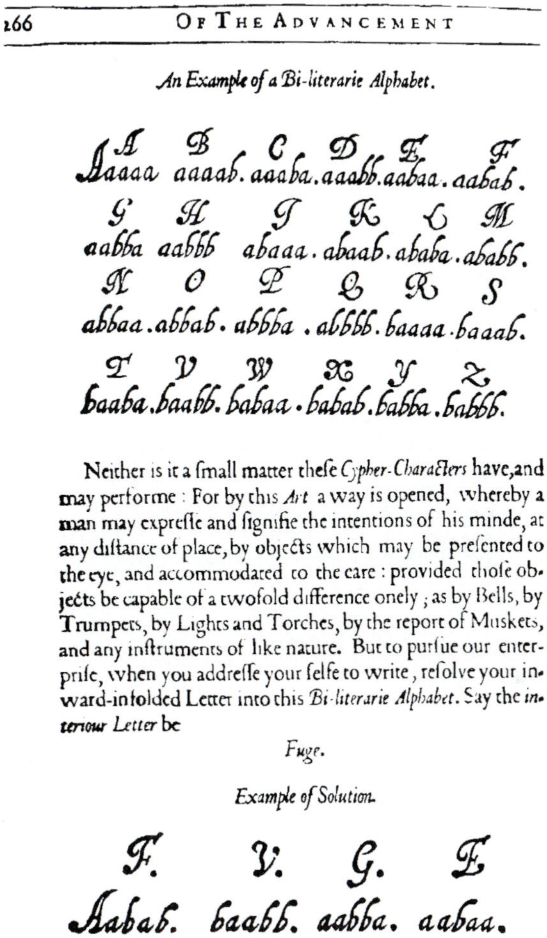

166 OF THE ADVANCEMENT

An Example of a Bi-literarie Alphabet.

A aaaaa. B aaaab. C aaaba. D aaabb. E aabaa. F aabab.
G aabba. H aabbb. I abaaa. K abaab. L ababa. M ababb.
N abbaa. O abbab. P abbba. Q abbbb. R baaaa. S baaab.
T baaba. V baabb. W babaa. X babab. Y babba. Z babbb.

Neither is it a ſmall matter theſe *Cypher-Characters* have,and may performe: For by this *Art* a way is opened, whereby a man may expreſſe and ſignifie the intentions of his minde, at any diſtance of place, by objects which may be preſented to the eye, and accommodated to the eare: provided thoſe objects be capable of a twofold difference onely; as by Bells, by Trumpets, by Lights and Torches, by the report of Muskets, and any inſtruments of like nature. But to purſue our enterpriſe, when you addreſſe your ſelfe to write, reſolve your inward-infolded Letter into this *Bi-literarie Alphabet*. Say the *interiour Letter* be

Fuge.

Example of Solution.

F. V. G. E.
Aabab. baabb. aabba. aabaa.

Figure 1.5 Binary representations for Francis Bacon's bilateral cipher. (Source: *The Friedman Legacy.*)

and *b* as the binary digits. These then are used to signify the use of two different fonts (Figure 1.6). A message is enciphered by first constructing an innocuous underlying text that is 5 times as long as the ciphertext. Then groups of five letters of the underlying text are put into the fonts *a* and *b* so that they encode the letters of the ciphertext. For example, suppose that font *a* is *slant* and font *b* is **boldface**. If the underlying text is

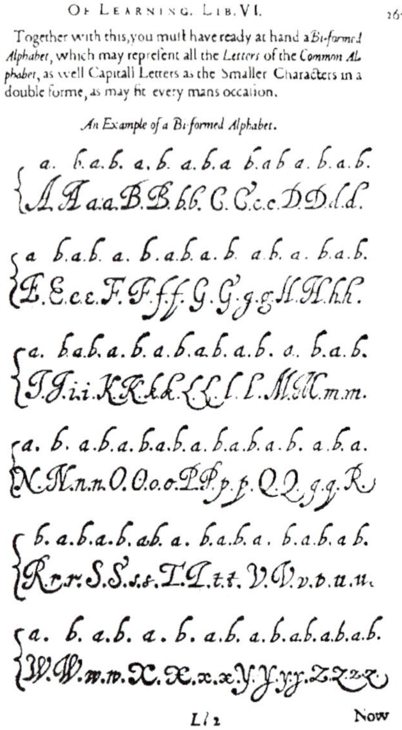

OF LEARNING. LIB.VI.   267

Together with this, you must have ready at hand a *Bi-formed*
Alphabet, which may represent all the *Letters* of the *Common Al-*
phabet, as well Capitall Letters as the Smaller Characters in a
double forme, as may fit every mans occasion.

An Example of a Bi-formed Alphabet.

Lℓ2   Now

Figure 1.6 The two fonts, labeled *a* and *b*, for the Bacon cipher
(Source: *The Friedman Legacy.*)

```
BACON DIEDA MONTH AFTER CONDU CTING HISFI RSTSC IENTI FICEX
PERIM ENTST UFFIN GACHI CKENW ITHSN OWTOD ETERM INETH EEFFE
              CTONT HERAT EOFDE COMPO SITIO N,
```

then we can encipher any message of 25 or fewer letters (just ignore the last
N). For instance, if the text to be concealed is DID BACON WRITE SHAKESPEARE,
we would write

```
aaabb abaaa aaabb aaaab aaaaa aaaba abbab abbaa
BACON DIEDA MONTH AFTER CONDU CTING HISFI RSTSC

babaa baaaa abaaa baaba aabaa baaab aabbb aaaaa
IENTI FICEX PERIM ENTST UFFIN GACHI CKENW ITHSN

abaab aabaa baaab abbba aabaa aaaaa baaaa aabaa
OWTOD ETERM INETH EEFFE CTONT HERAT EOFDE COMPO
```

and then produce the ciphertext by putting the various letters in the indicated font:

BACON DIEDA MONTH AFTER CONDU CTING
HISFI RSTSC IENTI FICEX PERIM ENTST UFFIN
GACHI CKENW ITHSN OWTOD ETERM INETH
EEFFE CTONT HERAT EOFDE COMPO

Of course, in this example the two fonts are chosen to contrast clearly with one another; Bacon shows, in Figure 1.6, the subtle differences between the two fonts that he proposed. To the casual reader, the slight variations between the two fonts would not be obvious, and so the very existence of a secret message would go unsuspected.

The bilateral cipher is actually a combination of substitution and **steganography**, the concealment of the very fact that there is a hidden message.

Thomas Jefferson's Wheel Cypher, 1790

One of the products of Thomas Jefferson's (1743–1826) imagination was a "wheel cypher," a mechanical device for encrypting and decrypting text (Figure 1.7). Though he gave a specific design for the wheel cypher, evidently

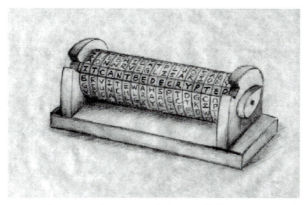

Figure 1.7 A cipher device modeled on Jefferson's wheel cypher.

he never used the device. His construction consisted of 36 concentric wooden disks, each about 1/6 inch thick and 2 inches in diameter, with a mix of the alphabet inscribed on the outer edge. Each disk was numbered; the correspondents who used the cypher agreed on a sequence of these numbers— their secret key. They then assembled their disks in this sequence on an iron spindle.

To encipher the first 36 letters of his message, the sender found the first letter on the first wheel, then found the second letter on the second wheel and lined it up with the first, then found the third letter of the message on the third wheel and lined it up with the first two, and so on. The 25 remaining parallel rows of letters at other positions about the disks constituted ciphertexts. The sender selected one and wrote it down. To complete the process, the sender repeated this process for the remaining blocks of 36 letters in the message.

To decipher, the receiver read off the first 36 letters of ciphertext and aligned them parallel to his spindle, as the sender had done with the plaintext. Then, at one of the other 25 positions about the circumference, he would find the corresponding plaintext. He repeated this process for the remaining ciphertext blocks to decipher the rest of the message.

The wheel cypher is essentially an implementation of polyalphabetic substitution with the message itself serving as the key! In the exercises, you are asked to criticize a special implementation of this device.

In about 1890, a Frenchman named Étienne Bazeries independently reproduced the wheel cypher. Around the time of World War I, the American Parker Hitt designed a "strip cipher" that was equivalent to Jefferson's cypher; after the war, Hitt's design was adapted, and the resulting metal cylinder device was used as a U.S. Army field cipher.

Wheatstone-Playfair Cipher, 1854

The eminent British scientist Charles Wheatstone invented the Wheatstone bridge—a device for measuring electrical resistance. He also invented a digraphic cipher which was popularized by Baron Lyon Playfair and used by British forces in the Boer War and World War I. The basis of the cipher is a 5×5 matrix that contains the alphabet and a set of three basic rules for using it to transform pairs of letters in plaintext to corresponding ciphertext letter pairs. The matrix consists of 25 of the 26 letters of the alphabet in some arrangement, agreed upon by the correspondents, that is easy to remember. Here we have written the letters in order in a counterclockwise spiral pattern that starts in the lower right hand corner:

I	H	G	F	E
J	U	T	S	D
K	V	Y	R	C
L	W	X	Q	B
M	N	O	P	A

To encipher, a sender first groups the plaintext into letter pairs; if a pair turns out to be a double letter, the sender inserts an X. Also, if the plaintext has an odd number of letters, the sender pads the end with X or other null. For example, if the plaintext is MERRILY WE ROLL ALONG, the sender will write ME RX RI LY WE RO LX LA LO NG. Then the sender uses the following rules:

1. If a pair of plaintext letters lies in the same row, the corresponding ciphertext pair is the two letters to the right, wrapping around to the left column if one of the letters is in the rightmost column. For example, IG enciphers as HF; XB enciphers as QL; UT enciphers as TS.

2. If a pair of plaintext letters lies in the same column, the corresponding ciphertext pair is the two letters below; we wrap around to the top row if one of the letters is in the bottom row. For example, FQ enciphers as SP; UN enciphers as VH; FS enciphers as SR.

3. If a pair of plaintext letters lies at the corners of a rectangle of letters in the matrix, the first letter enciphers as the letter in the corner in the same row, and the second letter enciphers as that in the corner on its row. For example, EK enciphers as IC; UR enciphers as SV; AI enciphers as ME.

Thus the plaintext given previously enciphers as

| plain | ME RX RI LY WE RO LX LA LO NG |
| cipher | AI YQ KF XK BH YP WQ BM XM OH |

The ciphertext MQOCEPFK, for instance, deciphers as PLAYFAIR.

If you think of the letters as being written on a torus as shown in Figure 1.8, two letters on a common "longitude" encipher by moving down one letter; two letters on a common "latitude" encipher by moving right one letter. The first and second letters of a pair not on a common longitude or latitude can be viewed as sitting, respectively, at the upper left and lower right corners of a rectangle of letters on the torus. Such a pair is enciphered by replacing the first letter with the one at the upper right corner of the rectangle and the second with the one at the lower left. Decipherment consists of reversing these replacements with pairs of ciphertext letters.

The Telegraph, 1844: A Glimpse of Error Correcting Codes

The invention of the telegraph marks one of the most significant turning points in communication security. Prior to that time, cryptographic methods

Figure 1.8 The Playfair cipher torus: the encipherment matrix written on a doughnut.

were implemented most often with pencil and paper, or possibly typewriter and paper. Moreover, an adversary to corresponding parties often had to go to some lengths and risk discovery of his efforts in order to get hold of enciphered correspondence. With telegraph wires strung for hundreds of miles across the countryside, correspondents—particularly military ones— had to assume that the lines were tapped. The American Civil War was one of the first in which a significant amount of military communication took place over telegraph lines, and both sides regularly tapped the other's lines. Of course, many of the classic cipher methods could be adapted directly to the telegraph. A monoalphabetic substitution would be easy, but easy for the enemy to crack as well. A polyalphabetic cipher, however, is very sensitive to errors in transmission, particularly if the errors involve dropping letters or having spurious extra letters introduced. Codebooks, or nomenclators, were used, and the designs of some accommodated to the possibility of the types of errors encountered in telegraphic transmissions.

During the Civil War (1861–1865), the U.S. Military Telegraph Corps (USMTC) used what were called **route ciphers**, basically word transpositions with a few added "arbitraries" to confuse potential cryptanalysts. Union telegraph operators had codebooks that contained lists of these arbitraries so that when they received transmissions and wrote them out, they would be able to strip out the arbitraries. Then they could follow the "route" of the transposition through the columns indicated by one of the code words received in the transmission. For example, suppose correspondents agreed on a five-column route: up 3, down 5, down 3 up 4, down 1. Then the message[4]

---

[4]Part of an actual telegram from Union Army General Halleck to General Buell. Quoted

```
HERE        AS      ELSEWHERE      YOU       MOVE
TOO       SLOWLY       THE      IMMOBILITY    OF
YOUR       ARMY        IS         MOST     SURPRISING
BRAGG       IN         THE        LAST       TWO
MONTHS      HAS      MARCHED      FOUR       TIMES
THE      DISTANCE      YOU        HAVE      HALLECK
```

is enciphered by transcribing words column by column in the specified order
and direction:

YOU MARCHED THE IS THE ELSEWHERE MOVE OR SURPRISING TWO
TIMES HALLECK AS SLOWLY ARMY IN HAS DISTANCE HAVE FOUR
LAST MOST IMMOBILITY YOU HERE TOO YOUR BRAGG MONTHS THE

Often "nulls," nonsense words, were inserted to confuse the enemy, and
also "arbitraries," that is, code words, might be substituted for people's
names and other critical words. The receiver deciphered by calculating the
column length from the message length and the number of columns and
then writing the received message on grid paper column by column in the
prescribed order and direction.

In Lecture IV of the collection contained in *The Friedman Legacy* [14],
William Friedman points out that these constituted one of the first examples of **error correcting codes**, codes that, by their very construction,
provided recipients a way to identify and fix portions of the message that
were corrupted during transmission.

> But what is indeed astonishing to note is that in the later editions
> of these cipher books, in a great majority of cases, the words used
> as "arbitraries" differ from one another by at least two letters (for
> example, LADY and LAMB, LARK and LAWN, ALBA and ASIA, LOCK
> and WICK, MILK and MINT) or by more than two (for example,
> MYRTLE and MYSTIC, CARBON and CANCER, ANDES and ATLAS). ...
> All in all, it is important to note that the compiler or compilers
> of these cipher books had adopted a principle known today as
> the "two-letter differential," a feature found only in codebooks
> of a much later date. In brief, the principle involves the use, in
> a given codebook, of code groups differing from one another by
> at least two letters. This principle is employed by knowledgeable

---

from p. 518 of James M. McPherson, *Battle Cry of Freedom: The Civil War Era*, Ballantine
Books, New York, 1989.

code compilers to this very day [1958], because it enables the recipient of a message not only to detect errors in transmissions or reception, but also to correct them. This is made possible if the permutation tables used in constructing the code words are printed in the codebooks, so that most errors can be corrected without calling for a repetition of the transmission.[5]

Nowadays, error correction is ubiquitous: music recorded on compact disks uses sophisticated mathematical techniques from finite field theory to correct for errors introduced by foreign material deposited on the disk; the very circuits of all digital computers incorporate error correction of an analogous type; transmissions over the Internet make use of error correction; Reed-Solomon codes were invented to allow Jet Propulsion Laboratory scientists to control and receive data from deep space probes. While we cannot go deeply into the details of error detection and correction, we can gain insight into how efficient redundancy is built into codes. Partly for this reason, we will briefly explore some elementary features of error detecting codes. A second reason for looking at these ideas is that, in a slightly different light they are precisely what one seeks in **message authentication codes**, strings of symbols appended to digital messages that allow the recipient to check whether the message was likely to have been altered in transit.

The Vernam One-Time Tape, 1917

By about 1917, telegraphy had advanced to the point where printing telegraph machines, or **teletypes**, had replaced telegraph operators. These operated by synchronized positive and negative electrical pulses, representing 1 and 0, sent over copper wires between telegraph company offices (e.g., AT&T, Western Union). Letters, digits, and a few **control characters**[6] were represented by 5-pulse groups in transmissions and by 5-digit binary codes in recordings on paper tape. A hole punched in the tape represented a 1, and no hole represented a 0. The standard collection of these 5-binary-digit codes was called the **Baudot code**. Gilbert Vernam, an engineer with American

---

[5]Lecture IV, in *The Friedman Legacy: a Tribute to William and Elizabeth Friedman*; see Bibliography.

[6]These were characters that *controlled* the teletype, for instance, to have it return the printing carriage to the left side of the paper or shift from lower- to uppercase. Some of these are evident in vestigial or modified form even on modern computer keyboards: shift, control, escape, carriage return, bell.

Telephone and Telegraph, invented a simple way of enciphering and deciphering Baudot-encoded messages online—that is, as the message was being transmitted or received. It amounts to nothing more than Vigenère encipherment on the "alphabet" $\{0, 1\}$ with a very long key, typically stored on one or more paper tape loops as described here.

This so-called Vernam one-time tape is precisely the basis for some modern stream ciphers in which a very long random-looking sequence of zeros and ones generated by a **linear-feedback shift register** or other electronic device is used by a computer as a key to encipher a binary message. We will examine these ideas under the heading of **binary one-time pads**, and we will have the opportunity to exploit a weakness in the shift register key generation method to perform a cryptanalysis of a message produced by these one-time pads.

ADFGVX, 1918

During World War I, the German military adopted a cipher known as AD-FGVX, simply the collection of letters that were used to represent all ciphertexts. Encipherment and decipherment took place in two phases: a substitution much like the Polybius checkerboard followed by a transposition, analogous to the Spartan scytale. The grid used was

	A	D	F	G	V	X
A	F	L	1	A	O	2
D	J	D	W	3	G	U
F	C	I	Y	B	4	P
G	R	5	Q	8	V	E
V	6	K	7	Z	M	X
X	S	N	H	⊘	T	9

The slash through zero is to distinguish it from the letter O. Plaintext could contain any of the 26 letters or 10 digits; plaintext characters were encoded by the labels on the row and column in which they appeared. For example, B enciphered as FG; 6 enciphered as VA. The second step of encipherment was a **columnar transposition** of the characters obtained in the first step, using a keyword. The sequence of As, Ds, Fs, Gs, Vs, and Xs was written across as many columns as there were letters in the keyword, and then they were transcribed column by column in the order determined by alphabetical arrangement of the keyword letters. For example if the plaintext is KAISER

W WILLING TO GRANT ARMISTICE and the keyword is BERLIN, then the first step of encipherment gives

```
VDAGFDXAGXGA DF DFFDADADFDXDDV XVAV DVGAAGXDXV
          AGGAVVFDXAXVFDFAGX
```

The second step is to write this in six-letter lines as

```
B E R L I N
1 2 6 4 3 5
-----------
V D A G F D
X A G X G A
D F D F F D
A D A D F D
X D D V X V
A V D V G A
A G X D X V
A G G A V V
F D X A X V
F D F A G X
```

and then transcribe the letters column by column in the numerical order determined by the keyword:

```
VXDAX AAAFF DAFDD VGGDD FGFFX GXVXG GXFDV VDAAA DADDV AVVVX
          AGDAD DXGXF
```

This composition or **product** of ciphers is, as you might guess, very difficult to crack. But in fact, French lieutenant Georges Painvin broke this cipher and aided in the effort to save his home country.

Two or more ciphers are composed to compute some modern cipher systems. For instance, DES combines precisely the two elements of substitution and transposition.

Cryptology and Mathematics Linked, 1920s

In 1917, the Riverbank Laboratory in Geneva, Illinois, supported by the wealthy and eccentric George Fabyan, began conducting a training program for U.S. government cryptologists. William Friedman(Figure 1.9), a geneticist trained at Cornell University, had joined the group as a researcher on

Figure 1.9 William Frederick Friedman (1891–1969).

Fabyan's pet question of whether Francis Bacon had been the author of the works that bear Shakespeare's name. (This claim about Shakespeare was later debunked by Friedman and his wife Elizebeth in a book called *The Shakespearean Ciphers Examined.*) He soon turned, however, to training cryptologists himself, and wrote several monographs on the subject. One of the most famous, number 22, *The Index of Coincidence and its Applications in Cryptography* is regarded as a landmark. Its significance lay not only in that Friedman presents in it a statistical tool for helping to break polyalphabetic ciphers but also in that he showed clearly that modern mathematics and cryptology are intimately linked. We will encounter Friedman's index of coincidence later in our course and use it ourselves to break polyalphabetic ciphers.

The appearance in 1929 of Lester Hill's "Cryptography in an Algebraic Alphabet" symbolized again the growing link between mathematics and the design of cryptographic methods. In this paper, Hill describes a mathematical basis for a digraphic cipher analogous to the one of Wheatstone-Playfair. The ideas he presents generalize directly to trigraphic and longer-block-length ciphers. Matrices play a central role in this cipher, as they do in many modern cryptosystems. We examine this method later in this book.

The World War II Era

It is a truism that, where there is war, there is cryptology. World War II was no exception. There were dramatic cryptographic and cryptanalytic feats—generally unknown to the public at the time—that had a tremendous influence on the outcome of the war. William Friedman and colleagues such as Solomon Kullback, Frank Rowlett, and Abraham Sinkov succeeded in breaking the Japanese diplomatic cipher called *Purple*. Devolving from this is the fascinating story of who-knew-what-when just before the sneak attack on Pearl Harbor. Lieutenant Commander Joseph Rochefort and his Combat Intelligence group worked fiercely with other Allied cryptanalytic groups to break the Japanese military code, known as JN-25. Their success at this helped directly to ensure a decisive Allied victory at the battle of Midway. This success in turn—some say—helped to shorten the war by a year or more. There are many historical accounts of these efforts as well as movies based on these stories.

In the European theater, the role of cryptology was no less important. During the 1930s, Marian Rejewski and others in Poland's Biuro Szyfrów (cipher bureau) had been recovering German military messages encrypted using the electromechanical Enigma machine. In 1939, after Germany had altered the machine so that they were no longer able to read messages, the Poles gave their allies Britain and France the information they possessed about Enigma in exchange for helping to defend them should Germany invade. The work of Alan Turing and many others at Bletchley Park built on the information provided by Poland and was crucial in the eventual Allied victory over Germany.

Enigma was but one of several cryptographic machines that came into manufacture and use in industrialized countries. These devices accepted letter input at a typewriter-like keyboard, implemented a polyalphabetic cipher by means of electrical contacts on rotors, and produced output by lighting electric lamps beneath lettered windows (Figure 1.10). Versions of the device were sold for commercial and government applications all over the world before the outbreak of the war. After that, the German military modified the device by adding additional rotors and plug-boards to increase the number of trial-and-error attempts necessary for an attack to astronomically large values. The Allies were able to improve on these unfavorable odds in various ways. First, the Polish and British cryptanalysts were able to exploit a basic understanding of the machine's operation—that it mechanized a polyalphabetic cipher akin to Vigenère and the Jefferson wheel cypher. Second, they took advantage of a few instances of carelessness in its use by German operators. Third, they had the sheer luck of capturing one of the machines from a sinking U-boat. On these topics there are many excellent and truly

Figure 1.10 A German Enigma machine

dramatic historical accounts, in books, films, and personal histories.

One of the first electronic computers, called Colossus, was constructed to aid in the British cryptanalytic effort. Other computers were built in the United States to assist in the enormous numbers of calculations needed to design the atomic bomb. At the end of the war, the first general-purpose stored-program electronic computer, ENIAC, was built. This marked the beginning of computer ascendancy.

Information Theory: the Mathematics of Language and Cryptology, 1949

In 1949, Claude Shannon, a researcher at Bell Laboratories, published a series of papers in the *Bell Systems Technical Journal* in which he took a general mathematical approach to all kinds of information that could be handled electronically. He defined and examined the notion of the **information capacity** of a digital channel and the **entropy** of a signal; he submitted natural languages such as English and French to statistical analysis and illustrated ways in which these could be simulated; and he defined the concept of **perfect security** in a cryptosystem. It is this last notion that provides us with a precise mathematical way of discerning when it is, in principle, impossible for an adversary who knows the cipher algorithm in use to do any better than pure guesswork at deciphering intercepts. Shannon's description of perfect security makes use of the language of probability, and we will encounter this idea in this book. It turns out that a Vigenère-type encipherment, in which the key is a random string of characters as long as the message and is never used to encipher any other messages, has the property of perfect security.

Data Encryption Standard, 1977

The use of computers—particularly in industry and commerce—had grown tremendously since the end of World War II, and the security of commercial data transmitted between computers in binary form, by telephone or other means, became a serious issue. In 1975, the National Bureau of Standards (NBS, the earlier name of what is now called the National Institute of Standards and Technology, NIST) solicited proposals for a standard method of encrypting nonmilitary data traffic. Mathematicians of IBM's Thomas Watson Laboratory submitted a method, termed in-house as "Lucifer," which was subsequently scrutinized and modified by the National Security Agency (NSA) and then set forth as the Data Encryption Standard by NBS in 1977. There was controversy over exactly what NSA's modifications had been: Perhaps, some claimed, NSA had constructed a "back door" into the standard. In spite of these concerns, banking, commerce, and industry began using the standard. Though it was set to be replaced by other methods within five years or so of its debut, there has not been any widespread acceptance of a standard to replace it. It is routinely used by banks all over the world to protect electronic funds transfers, such as automatic teller machine (ATM) and credit card transactions.

There have been estimates made on the computer resources necessary to crack DES's 56-bit key, but until the summer of 1998, no one had publicly announced a successful attack. However, a group, funded by the Electronic Frontier Foundation (EFF) and headed by Paul Kocher of Cryptography Research in San Francisco, custom-built a computer for roughly $250,000 and used it to identify a DES key from an encrypted message in 56 hours. The message read, "It's time for those 128-, 192-, and 256-bit keys."[7]

Public-Key Cryptography, 1978

About the time DES was on its way to becoming a standard, other researchers were looking for ways of solving a problem of every single cryp-

---

[7]Ivars Peterson, "Quick Cracking of Secret Code," *Science News*, 154, August 1998.

tosystem, up to and including DES: how to distribute the keys among the parties using the cryptosystem. It would be ridiculous to transmit keys over the very channels that would carry ciphertext; an eavesdropper could simply pick up the key and then use it to decipher subsequent transmissions. So keys typically were distributed by means that were less convenient than wire: printed on paper, recorded on floppy disks or magnetic tape, dictated by telephone. Even key generation methods such as shift registers still required the transfer of at least a small amount of information with which to "prime" the key stream.

Around 1976, Merkle and Hellman proposed a cryptographic algorithm whose details would be publicly available and by which a party wishing to receive encrypted messages published an encryption key for any sender to use. Unlike classical methods, in which knowledge of the key used to encipher a message could readily be turned into a decipherment key, the decipherment key for Merkle and Hellman's "Knapsack" could not be obtained in a computationally efficient manner by an adversary. This claim about the the inability of an adversary to produce the deciphering key in a reasonable length of time is based on the *belief* that the general case of solving a mathematical problem called the **knapsack** is inherently time-consuming. In principle, the problem is easily solved: Trying out all possible solutions to it will eventually lead to a solution. However, there is an enormous number of possible solutions, so this approach is not reasonable. No one has devised a general short-cut algorithm to solve it, and, moreover, there is other circumstantial evidence that suggests that no general short-cut algorithm can be found. While Merkle and Hellman's algorithm was shown to be insecure because it actually relied on a special category of knapsack problem, it was the first example of a public-key cryptosystem. Because of its simplicity, we will examine this method in our course.

The Merkle-Hellman Knapsack raised the possibility that the age-old key distribution problem might actually be solvable. Two parties who have never privately exchanged any information can establish encrypted communication in the following way. First, they both learn of a public-key algorithm, perhaps through some third party that disseminates its details. Party A (often referred to as Alice in the literature) selects an encryption key and a corresponding decryption key; she publishes the former and keeps the latter secret. Party B (often referred to as Bob in the literature) does the same. Alice can then send a message to Bob, using his encryption key, that says something like, "Bob, this is Alice. I want to communicate with you using private-key method X with key K." Bob can then respond with a message, encrypted using her encryption key, that says, "OK, Alice. I agree to use key K with method X." In order to know the content of either of their messages, an eavesdropping adversary E (often referred to as Eve) would presumably need to know either Alice's or Bob's secret decipherment key. But since the only method of obtaining either of those is effectively trial and error that is likely to take millions of years to complete, Eve's eavesdropping is stymied. Thus Alice and Bob have exchanged the key to a classical system, such as Vigenère, over the very channel that will convey their future correspondence. (You might wonder why Alice and Bob don't just use the public-key method directly for their communication. They can, but if their messages are very long, the calculations necessary for encryption and decryption can bog down the process. Typically, public-key methods are much slower to run than private-key methods.)

In 1978, the journal *Communications of the Association for Computing Machinery* (ACM) published a paper entitled "A Method for Obtaining Digital Signatures and Public Key Cryptosystems." The authors, Ronald Rivest, Adi Shamir, and Leonard Adelman, described a public-key method whose security rests on the apparent inherent time-consumption of factoring integers into their prime factors. This method, now known simply as RSA, has withstood tests of its security and is widely used in such applications as e-mail encryption and secure Web page transactions. The mathematical underpinnings that make this method work were developed in the eighteenth century by Fermat and Euler. We will study both the elegant mathematical results and exactly how they allow RSA to work.

The Beginning of the Twenty-First Century

Until about twenty years ago, information secrecy was largely the ken of military, diplomatic, and commercial concerns. That has changed with the advent of such conveniences as automated teller machines, cellular telephones, World Wide Web search engines, and smart cards. Individuals use **personal identification numbers (PINs)** to authenticate themselves at ATMs, encryption is sometimes used on wireless telephones, secure Web pages use public-key cryptography to ensure that credit card information travels securely from a personal computer to the site from which an individual is buying something, and smart cards use sophisticated authentication protocols when they are used to dispense electronic cash at a point of sale. While users are not always aware of the cryptographic protocols carried out, it is clear that cryptography is now "everybody's" business.

As a user of a wireless telephone phone, you are in some sense on a world-wide party line. It is possible for anyone with a few hundred dollars for the purchase of the requisite radio equipment to listen to cellular telephone conversations that are not scrambled in some way. Of course, one has no way of being certain who might be listening to standard telephone conversations either, but in that instance it is less likely that someone can casually pick up your conversation; some effort must be exerted to tap a standard wire telephone line.

As a user of electronic mail, you have no idea whose eyes see your messages. It is a simple matter for a "packet sniffer" to pick up e-mail messages in transmission on router computers. Some e-mail users employ such packages as **Privacy Enhanced Mail (PEM)** and **Pretty Good Privacy (PGP)** to help guard against unauthorized reading of their e-mail. Both of these employ public-key cryptography for key exchange and digital signature generation.

If you use a Web browser such as Netscape or Internet Explorer to order merchandise and pay for it with a credit card, you have encountered so-called **secure** pages. These make use of RSA or similar public-key cryptosystems to encrypt your credit card number.

There are many nonprofit organizations, such as the EFF, mentioned earlier, and young companies that specialize in various sorts of data security. In the academic arena, there is a great deal of research on new modes of cryptography. There are research journals in the public domain devoted exclusively to cryptology. Of course, long-standing government agencies such as NSA continue to do research and development on projects about which outsiders can only speculate.

In both research and applications, attention has focused on cryptographic **protocols**, procedures that employ cryptographic algorithms as components and provide three basic features of secure communication:

- **Integrity**, determining whether a message between parties has been altered by intermediaries. Example: Short MACs (see earlier material) appended to messages that depend on the content in a way known only to the correspondents permit the recipient to detect with high probability whether the integrity of the correspondence has been breached. MACs, in essence, are error detecting codes.

- **Authenticity**, determining whether a message claiming to be from a party is, in fact, from that party. Example: A public-key algorithm can be applied to a message's MAC to generate a **digital signature** that is intimately tied to the message's content and to the sender's published encipherment key. A receiver of a message claiming to be from Alice and affixed with a digital signature can verify whether the message is likely to have come from Alice by applying public-key encryption using Alice's published key.

- **Nonrepudiation**, ensuring that a party that enters into an agreement with another through electronic means does not later repudiate the agreement, claiming, for instance, that the agreement was forged. This amounts to a sort of electronic notarization.

As electronic commerce becomes even more prevalent, the last two features become especially important. In 1994, NIST published the **Digital Signature Standard (DSS)**, which established a uniform federal standard for signing nonclassified documents. The standard includes two parts: the **Secure Hash Algorithm (SHA)**, by which MACs are to be generated from documents, and the **Digital Signature Algorithm (DSA)**, a public-key algorithm for producing signatures from MACs generated by SHA. Since so many private companies do business with the federal government, such standards tend to be adopted in the private sector, much as DES has been.

The Future: Y2K[8] and Beyond

The **Advanced Encryption Standard (AES)** will be the replacement for DES. In 1997, NIST issued a call for submissions from around the world for a new encryption algorithm that would meet the following requirements:

- It would use symmetric (secret-key) cryptography.

- It would be a block cipher.

- It would operate on 128-bit blocks of plaintext and allow for three sizes of key: 128-, 192-, and 256-bit.

In the summer of 1999, there were five finalists: MARS (developed in the United States by a team at IBM), RC6 (developed in the United States by RSA Security, Inc.), Twofish (developed in the United States by Counterpane Systems, Inc.), Serpent (developed by cryptographers in the United

---

[8]Y2K stands for year 2000.

Kingdom, Israel, and Denmark), and Rijndael (developed by two Belgian cryptographers). Each of these demonstrated resistance to such powerful cryptanalytic attacks as **differential cryptanalysis** and **linear cryptanalysis**. They also were shown to be fast in implementations. This last requirement is crucial because encryption and decryption of such large-volume data streams as high-definition television signals and voice communication cannot be a bottleneck. In fall 2000, NIST announced the winner of the AES competition: Rijndael, the entry by Joan **Dae**men of Proton World International and Vincent **Rij**men of Katholieke Universiteit Leuven. The move to replace DES is now underway worldwide.

Number theory, ancient and long regarded as inapplicable, plays a prominent role in various cryptographic protocols being considered in the research community. So-called **zero-knowledge protocols** are good examples. Rather than rely on a cryptosystem to encipher a bank PIN, for example, it is possible to convince the bank that you know the PIN without ever transmitting it, encrypted or in plaintext! The protocol relies on the bank initially issuing a PIN consisting of two 100-digit prime numbers, which only you and the bank possess. You convince the bank that you possess the primes by repeatedly sending certain products of your primes with random numbers through an **oblivious transfer channel**, a channel over which you send two messages at a time and which in effect flips a coin to decide which of the two messages to transmit to the receiver. From the bank's perspective, at each successful round of the protocol, the probability that you don't have the PIN primes decreases by a factor of 2. So by the time you have carried out the protocol n times, the probability that you don't know the primes is $1/2^n$, a very small number when n is large. A complete description of the protocol relies on a bit of knowledge about modular arithmetic and modular square roots. See Ian Stewart's *Scientific American* article in the bibliography for more detail. There are variations on this theme, one of which is the **Fiat-Shamir protocol**, which we discuss later in this text.

Elliptic curve cryptography (**ECC**) is a type of public-key cryptography in which there is currently a great deal of research taking place. Proposed in 1985 by Neal Koblitz and Victor Miller, it is based on mathematics concerned with algebraic abstractions of certain types of geometric curves. Encryption based on ECC has properties that would make it preferable in some instances to RSA.

Quantum cryptography is a term applied to the possibility of exploiting quantum mechanical properties of subatomic particles to provide encryption or messages authentication. Photon attributes such as up or down spin can be used to encode information. Moreover, the general principle that an observation of a photon's spin permanently alters that attribute means that if a transmission over a quantum channel is intercepted, the communicating parties will automatically know about it. Some of the theoretical issues of implementing quantum cryptography have been worked out, but no one has constructed physical devices that carry out the processes. It is not yet clear that any will actually be possible. For a nice readable account of this intriguing possibility, see Simon J. D. Phoenix's article [63] listed in the references.

Biometrics offer the possibility that some forms of authentication can be performed by machines that recognize unique characteristic features of individuals, such as fingerprints, patterns in the iris of the eye, or the voice. Such technologies may well replace computer passwords and bank PINs. See Corinna Wu's article [89] for further detailed information.

Summary

The preceding subsections provide only a cursory account of a few cryptological methods and stories related to them. The intention here is to draw out some of those that are closely connected with the mathematics we will be studying. You should consult the bibliography for a number of general references on cryptology. In particular, David Kahn's book [39] is the granddaddy of cryptological history. If you are interested in details of current cryptosystems and protocols, you should consult such encyclopedic treatments as Menezes, van Oorschot, and Vanstone [52] or Schneier [71] and its extensive (1653 items) bibliography of the research literature.

Exercises

1. Use the atbash cipher to encipher the plaintext AND AFTER THEM THE KING OF SHESHACH SHALL DRINK.[9]

2. Use the atbash cipher to decipher GSRHDSLOV OZMW HSZOO YVXLNVZ IFRM ZMW Z DZHGV.[10]

---

[9]From Jeremiah 25.

[10]From Jeremiah 25.

3. Use the Atbash method to decipher[11]

```
QFHGZ   HDZGV   IIVUO   VXGHG
SVUZX   VHLLM   VSFNZ   MSVZI
GIVUO   VXGHZ   MLGSV   I
```

4. Suppose a message was written on a Spartan Scytale in six lines and that the letters on the parchment strip were those shown in Figure 1.11. Decipher the message. (The quote is from Aristotle.)

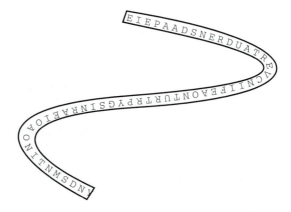

Figure 1.11 Figure for Exercise 4.

5. The following message was enciphered on a scytale in five lines with ten turns of the strip around the cylinder:

```
TWETIHAXROESAANSAMNCCNPSIYELPPTAEOHAROSELLFIREYAT
```

Decipher the message.

6. (a) Use Caesar's cipher to encipher FRIENDS, ROMANS, COUNTRYMEN, LEND ME YOUR EARS.[12]

   (b) Use Caesar's cipher to decipher EHZDU HWKHL GHVRL PDUFK.[13]

---

[11]Proverbs 27:19.

[12]William Shakespeare, *Julius Caesar*, 1599.

[13]ibid.

(c) Use ROT13 encipherment to encipher `CAN WE EVER HAVE TOO MUCH OF A GOOD THING.`[14]

(d) Use an 8-shift to decipher `JMQVO QAJMB BMZBP IVAMM UQVOB WJM`

7. Use Alberti's cipher disk to encipher

   `JOAN OF ARC WAS A CONTEMPORARY OF ALBERTI`

   by changing cipher wheel positions after every eight message letters, using the sequence of letters I-T-A-L-I as indicators.

8. Use Alberti's cipher disk to decipher the message

   `E y m q k z n & Z i i t f q a f s R i o k v i o n p c & o`
   `                    M i v e o b o`

9. Use the Vigenère autokey method, with priming key B, to encipher `WALTER RALEIGH BRINGS TOBACCO TO ENGLAND FROM AMERICA.`[15]

10. Use the Vigenère autokey method to decipher `ZGLTTPS UGLTTPM WPTWVMZW HTRQXFFG BTVZWRV`, assuming the priming key T.

11. The following is an encipherment by the Vigenère autokey method with a one-letter priming key:

    `AMIVSFYOMB`

    By trial and error or systematic search, obtain the three-word message.

12. Use Bacon's bilateral cipher to decipher the message contained in the following text: *READI NGMAK ETHAF ULLMA NCONF ERENC EAREA DYMAN ANDWR ITING ANEXA CTMAN.*[16]

13. A **homophonic substitution** cipher is one in which the syllables of the plaintext are replaced with those of other words that sound like the plaintext. For instance, `ALL'S WELL THAT ENDS WELL` can become `AWLS WEALTH ATTEND SWELL`. Sometimes the encipherment and decipherment require a little imagination. Decipher the following homophonic encipherments of two quotes from Samuel Johnson.

---

[14]Miguel Cervantes, *Don Quixote*, Modern Library, New York, 1930.

[15]This occurred almost exactly at the same time Vigenère was writing his *Traicté*, in 1586.

[16]Frances Bacon, *Of Studies*.

(a) NOLL EDGES MIRTH ANY QUIVER LENT TWO FOURS.[17]

(b) KNOW WON BUTT ABE LOCKET EVA ROTE ACCEPT FORM HONEY.

14. The **pigpen cipher** relies on its users memorizing the diagrams shown in Figure 1.12. It has been used through the centuries by diverse groups

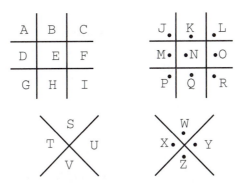

Figure 1.12 Diagrams for remembering the pigpen cipher.

such as the Freemasons and school children. Decipher the message in Figure 1.13.

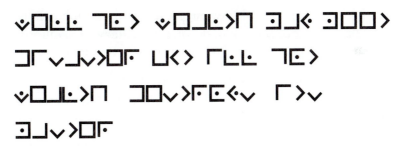

Figure 1.13 The quote is a statement by Sancho Panza in Miguel Cervantes's *Don Quixote*.

15. Suppose that each disk of Jefferson's wheel cypher had the alphabet

---

[17]Samuel Johnson (1709–1784) English lexicographer, critic, and author. The first quote is from *The History of Rasselas, Prince of Abissinia*, A. L. Burt Co., New York, c. 1910. The second is in James Boswell, *The Life of Samuel Johnson, LL.D.*, Curwen Press, London, 1938.

written *in order* around its circumference. What cipher would be implemented? How secure would it be? Explain.

16. Encipher THE QUICKEST WAY OF ENDING A WAR IS TO LOSE IT[18] by using the Wheatstone-Playfair table given in this section.

17. Decipher the following, which was enciphered using the Wheatstone-Playfair table given in this section:

BHPCHAGYHMDGCFDSDCHMUGFAPT
JFLEMJJGFDPGCDEIOD[19]

18. The following[20] is a route encipherment of an actual telegram from Abraham Lincoln.

1863 WOULD RELIEVED MEADE SINCE HAVE THE WITHOUT ME
WAS WHO THE SATURDAY HEVY A WAR FIGHTING CORPS KNOW
PLEASE THE TO OF AND IMPRESSION TO CAMERON 15 I BE
THAT ALL GETTYSBURG GET RIVER TELL WHO COMMANDER IN
ON LINCOLN SIGNED OF FOR ONE YOU FIGHT OVER ONLY BATTLE
SMITH THE MUCH SIMON WASHINGTON FOR GIVE OF COUCH THE
STRIVEN ENEMY ANOTHER IF THE WAS COUNCIL NIGHT

Treating numbers and abbreviations as words decipher it using the following route: down 5, up 3, down 4, up 2, down 1. Null words have been inserted to fill out the last short line in the encipherment. These are some of the nulls used in the original telegram.

19. Encipher the message ARMY MOVES 6 DECEMBER by using the ADFGVX method and the keyword BERLIN used in the example on page 22.

20. Decipher the message GVGGF XVXXD GGGXD DFVGD XAAVV XFXAX by using ADFGVX and the keyword BERLIN.

21. Suppose that a cryptanalyst suspects that the ciphertext

---

[18]George Orwell (1903–1950), "Second Thoughts on James Burnham," *Polemic*, 1946.

[19]Queen Victoria (1819–1901), queen of England from 1837 to 1901, on the Boer War in South Africa.

[20]See page 87 in [14]. The route cipher we use here is a simplification of the one actually used on Lincoln's telegram.

KNCFNNW OARNWMB CQNAN RB

WX WNNM XO SDBCRLN[21]

was produced by applying a shift encipherment of some (unknown) number of letters and then applying a second shift encipherment (by a different number of letters) to that. How will the work to obtain the plaintext in this case compare with the work to find it if the cryptanalyst suspected a single shift encipherment? Decipher this message.

22. A **permutation cipher** is one in which the letters of the message are reordered according to some method agreed upon by the correspondents. The scytale is one sort of permutation cipher. Another, more suited to pencil and paper, is what we will call a *rotation*. Encipherment consists of grouping message letters into blocks and then rotating the letters in each block by some specified number of letters. For example, if the block size is 5 and the rotation is 2, then LOVE IS BLIND; FRIENDSHIP CLOSES ITS EYES becomes VEILO LINSB RIEDF SHIND LOSPC ITSES ESEY.

   (a) Describe the decipherment algorithm for a rotation with block length b and rotation r.

   (b) The message

   UNITH ESEIV ERDEO SMAOR IFSTO TOESN OMSFA T[22]

   was enciphered with a block length of 6 and rotation 3. Decipher it.

   (c) Suppose

   IVGTH EPEEP LONEA WWERD ONDAH ETTHY NKIHE THAYE AVEWN

   ACFT[23]

   is an encipherment by a rotation. Describe a systematic approach to breaking the cipher and use it to recover the message.

   (d) Suppose a cryptanalyst suspects that

---

[21] Aristotle (384 B.C.–322 B.C.), *Nicomachean Ethics*.

[22] Muriel Rukeyser (1913–1980), U.S. poet, in *The Speed of Darkness*, Random House, New York, 1968.

[23] Willa Cather (1876–1947) U.S. Novelist, *On Writing: Critical Studies on Writing as an Art*, Knopf, New York, 1949.

```
SECEC SYHRI IRFET SSETE INLST AFNIA FSOAI HFSRT
TEATE24
```

was obtained by a succession of two rotations with different block lengths and rotation amounts. Compare the amount of work the cryptanalyst is likely to require under this assumption with what she is likely to require under the assumption of a single rotation. Try to do the cryptanalyst's work.

23. A crude form of error detection is employed by the United States Postal Service in the address bar codes that are often printed on pieces of mail. The address bar code represents twelve digits: The first five constitute the zip code, the second four the "+ four" zip-code digits, the next two the "destination code" (typically the last two digits of the street address), and the last one a check digit that is chosen so that the sum of it with the eleven digits preceding it is divisible by 10. For example, the barcode shown in Figure 1.14 translates into the 12 digits

Figure 1.14   A USPS zip-code bar code.

$$38112\ 1624\ 00\ 2$$

You can verify that the sum of these digits is divisible by 10. If, for instance, a machine reader scanned the bar code as

$$38111\ 1624\ 00\ 2$$

then the reader would compute a digit sum of 29, which is not divisible by 10. This fact would alert the reader that an error had occurred in the scan and cause the machine to attempt a reread. This scheme will catch all single-digit errors, but it may or may not detect errors in more than one digit.

(a) Assuming that at most one digit is in error in the scanned postal code 02284 5904 03 8, determine whether there is an error in this code.

---

[24]Cardinal de Richelieu (1585–1642), *Testament Politique*, 1641.

(b) Let $d_1\, d_2\, d_3\, d_4\, d_5 \quad d_6\, d_7\, d_8\, d_9 \quad d_{10}\, d_{11} \quad c$ be the correct values for a postal address code. Suppose that a scanner reads a bar code for it and that there may be an error in the first digit but not in the others. Explain why the check sum would determine or not the first digit is in error.

(c) Give an example of a postal address code with two erroneous digits such that the check sum is divisible by 10.

24. In [42], Neal Koblitz presents a toy public key cipher system, which he calls "Kid Krypto." It works in this fashion. To be able to receive enciphered messages from others elsewhere, Ursala chooses any four positive integers a, b, A, and B and calculates

$$
\begin{aligned}
M &= ab - 1 \\
e &= AM + a \quad (e \text{ for encipherment}) \\
d &= BM + b \quad (d \text{ for decipherment}) \\
n &= \frac{ed - 1}{M}
\end{aligned}
$$

She then publicizes e and n with instructions that a numerical message x in the range 0 to $n - 1$ is to be enciphered as

$$y = e \cdot x \text{ MOD } n$$

($e \cdot x$ MOD n denotes the remainder when $e \cdot x$ is divided by n; more about this later in the book). Ursala deciphers a received message y by computing

$$d \cdot y \text{ MOD } n$$

(a) If Ursala chooses $a = 47$, $b = 22$, $A = 11$, and $B = 5$, calculate her values of M, e, d, and n.

(b) Gustav, a customer at Ursala's bank, is accessing his account online and wants to encrypt his PIN 1958. Compute the encipherment of his PIN, and verify that when Ursala receives this value she deciphers it correctly by the formula given.

(c) Suppose that Ursala had used other choices of a, b, A, and B to generate the values $n = 1722629$ and $e = 41996$. Further suppose that Rhonda intercepts an enciphered PIN 1305808 belonging to another bank customer, Walter, and would like to decipher it in order to gain access to Walter's account. If Rhonda knows the relationship among e, d, and n, what can she do to find d? What alternative approach might she take to find Walter's PIN without finding d? See if you can find Walter's PIN.

1.2   Cryptology and Mathematics: Functions

In 1941, at a meeting of the American Mathematical Society in Manhattan, Kansas, A. Adrian Albert made the following statement in an invited address[25]:

> We shall see that cryptography is more than a subject permitting mathematical formulation for indeed it would not be an exaggeration to state that *abstract* cryptography is *identical* with abstract mathematics.

Perhaps one of the main reasons for this broad claim is that the concept of **function** is fundamental and pervasive in mathematics, and that cryptology is concerned with defining, evaluating, and inverting functions. The function concept provides a way for us to think clearly and abstractly about encryption and decryption, and the standard function notation is elegant and effective in expressing cryptographic ideas. Moreover, an understanding of such function classes as polynomials and exponentials will help us to see why some modern cryptosystems seem to be secure. We will make use of the ideas and notation throughout the rest of this book.

Definition 1.2.1   A **function** is a rule by which each element of one set, called the **domain** of the function, is associated with exactly one element of another set. We often use a letter such as f to represent a function, and if x is an element of the domain of the function, we write $f(x)$ for the **value** of the function at x. The collection of all values of f is called the **range** of f. See Figure 1.15 for a schematic representation.

The domain of a function can be a set of numbers (such as $\{1, 2, \ldots\}$), a set of pairs of numbers, events (such as "rolling a 3" with a die), strings of

---

[25]This quote appears in [75].

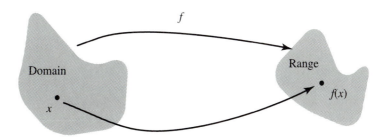

Figure 1.15   A schematic diagram of a function, its value at a point, its domain, and its range.

characters (such as encrypted messages), or even a collection of functions. The function rule itself can be specified by a precise verbal description, a formula, or an **algorithm**,[26] which is a list of steps for computing the value of the function at any given element of its domain. And the value of a function can be a number, an event, or a string.

Example 1.2.1 If x represents a plaintext string and $g(x)$ is its encipherment by a 5 shift, then, for example,

$$g(\texttt{FORM}) \quad = \quad \texttt{KTWR}$$
$$g(\texttt{SUBSTANCE}) \quad = \quad \texttt{XZGYFSGHJ}$$

The domain of this function consists of all finite strings with letters drawn from the Roman alphabet.   ◇

Example 1.2.2 If x represents a plaintext string with an even number of letters and $s(x)$ represents its encipherment by exchanging the position of adjacent letters, then for instance,

$$s(\texttt{NOENDINSIGHT}) = \texttt{ONNEIDSNGITH}$$

Any string with an odd number of letters is not in the domain of s, so in such cases one way of adapting is to pad the plaintext with an extra arbitrary letter before applying s.   ◇

Example 1.2.3 A function can have more than one variable. For instance, let $m(x, k)$ stand for the ciphertext obtained when plaintext string x has a

---

[26]For a specific example of an algorithm, think of the steps you use to obtain the quotient of two integers by long division.

k shift applied to it. Then, for instance,

$$m(\texttt{WECONCUR}, 4) = \texttt{AIGSRGYV} \quad \text{and} \quad m(\texttt{WECONCUR}, 7) = \texttt{DLJVUJBY}$$

If we apply a shift of k to a ciphertext and then apply another shift of l to that, in effect we have performed a shift by $k + l$. We can express this fact using function notation:

$$m(m(x, k), l) = m(x, k + l) \quad \Diamond$$

Sometimes a function may depend on two variables but we are more interested in its dependence on one than the other. In such a case we sometimes write the less important variable as a subscript. It is often the case that if a function designates encipherment, then the subscript is the key.

Example 1.2.4 The shift of k letters in Example 1.2.3 could be written $m_k(x)$. Then, for instance,

$$\begin{aligned} m_2(\texttt{LETSTALK}) &= \texttt{NGVUVCNM} \\ m_3(m_2(\texttt{LETSTALK})) &= m_3(\texttt{NGVUVCNM}) = \texttt{QJYXYFQP} \end{aligned}$$

and

$$m_5(\texttt{LETSTALK}) = \texttt{QJYXYFQP}$$

This corroborates what we observed in the example, namely $m_k(m_l(x)) = m_{k+l}(x)$. $\Diamond$

A function is called **one-to-one** if each element of the range is associated with precisely one element of the domain. For instance, the functions in Examples 1.2.1 and 1.2.2 are one-to-one. If x is a string of uppercase letters and $t(x)$ is the truncation of x to its first four letters, or the entire string if x has four or fewer letters, then, for instance, $t(\texttt{SUN}) = \texttt{SUN}$, $t(\texttt{THUNDER}) = \texttt{THUN}$, and $t(\texttt{THUNDERSTORM}) = \texttt{THUN}$. The latter two values of t show that t is not a one-to-one function.

Any function f that is one-to-one has an **inverse**, a function denoted f^{-1} that is computed by this rule: if y is an element of the range of f, then $f^{-1}(y)$ is the element x in the domain such that $f(x) = y$. This rule gives rise to a pair of very important formulas relating a function and its inverse:

$$\begin{aligned} f(f^{-1}(y)) &= y \quad \text{for all } y \text{ in the range of } f & (1.1) \\ f^{-1}(f(x)) &= x \quad \text{for all } x \text{ in the domain of } f. & (1.2) \end{aligned}$$

Example 1.2.5 The inverse of the function g in Example 1.2.1, you can verify, is the 21 shift, which we represent by h. Starting with a string x, each letter is 5 shifted to obtain $g(x)$; then each letter of $g(x)$ is 21 shifted to obtain $h(g(x))$. Since a 5 shift followed by a 21 shift is a 26 shift, each letter in $h(g(x))$ is the same as the corresponding letter in x; that is, $h(g(x)) = x$ for all x. Similarly, $g(h(y)) = y$ for all strings y.

The inverse of $s(x)$ defined in Example 1.2.2 is s itself: $s(x)$ swaps adjacent letters in x, and to put the letters back in their original order, we swap adjacent letters in $s(x)$. This means that s satisfies $s(s(x)) = x$ for all strings x with an even number of letters. So $s^{-1} = s$ in this case. ◇

Here is the fundamental connection between mathematics and cryptology:

> For each key, an encryption method defines a one-to-one function, and the corresponding decryption method is the inverse of that function. The process of encrypting a message is simply the evaluation of the encryption function for a given key; decrypting a message is the evaluation of the inverse of the encryption function for a given key. Cryptanalysis constitutes attempts either to determine (1) plaintext from ciphertext with incomplete key information or (2) key information from ciphertext and its corresponding plaintext.

The **composition** of two functions f and g, where the range of f is contained in the domain of g, is defined by

$$(g \circ f)(x) = g(f(x))$$

See Figure 1.16 for a schematic diagram of composition.

Example 1.2.6 Let $s(x)$ be the encipherment function of Example 1.2.2, and let $c(x)$ be the Caesar cipher. Then, for example,

$$c(\texttt{DINNERFORTWO}) = \texttt{GLQQHUIRUWZR}$$

so

$$
\begin{aligned}
(s \circ c)(\texttt{DINNERFORTWO}) &= s(c(\texttt{DINNERFORTWO})) = s(\texttt{GLQQHUIRUWZR}) \\
&= \texttt{LGQQUHRIWURZ}
\end{aligned}
$$

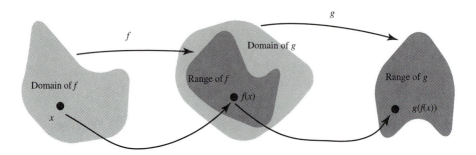

Figure 1.16   The composition of two functions: x is carried to $f(x)$ and then $f(x)$ is carried to $g(f(x))$.

and

$$(c \circ s)(\texttt{DINNERFORTWO}) \;=\; c(s(\texttt{DINNERFORTWO})) = c(\texttt{IDNNREOFTROW})$$
$$=\; \texttt{LGQQUHRIWURZ}$$

Explain why we get the same result no matter the order in which these two particular functions are applied.   ◇

Example 1.2.7   Recall the ADFGVX cipher discussed in Section 1.1. If x is a plaintext string and k the keyword used in the transposition phase, let $A(x, k)$ be the resulting ciphertext. For a given plaintext x of letters, let $s(x)$ represent the ciphertext obtained by applying the substitution defined in Table 1.4 and let $t(x, k)$ represent the keyword transposition of a string of

	A	D	F	G	V	X
A	F	L	1	A	O	2
D	J	D	W	3	G	U
F	C	I	Y	B	4	P
G	R	5	Q	8	V	E
V	6	K	7	Z	M	X
X	S	N	H	⊘	T	9

Table 1.4   Table for the ADFGVX cipher.

symbols x using a keyword k. Then $A(x, k) = t(s(x), k)$, and we can write the encipherment steps in the example on page 21 as

$A(\texttt{KAISER W WILLING TO GRANT ARMISTICE, BERLIN})$
   $=\quad t(s(\texttt{KAISER W WILLING TO GRANT ARMISTICE}), \texttt{BERLIN})$
   $=\quad t(\texttt{VDAGFDXAGXGA DF DFFDADADFDXDDV XVAV DVGAAGXDXV AGGAVVFDXAXVFDFAGX}, \texttt{BERLIN})$
   $=\quad \texttt{VXDAX AAAFF DAFDD VGGDD FGFFX GXVXG GXFDV VDAAA DADDV AVVVX AGDAD DXGXF}.$ ◇

Notice in the last example that the cipher A obtained as the composition of the subsidiary functions s and t would be harder to break than a cipher given by t or s individually. This illustrates one way of obtaining stronger ciphers from weaker ones: Compose the weaker ones. However, Example 1.2.4 illustrates that some compositions are no stronger than the separate ciphers used to obtain them.

Permutations

A **permutation** of n ordered objects is a way of reordering them. In mathematical language, it is one type of **function**, a concept that we will define and illustrate more fully in Section 2.4. For instance, the table

x	1	2	3	4	5	6	7
$p(x)$	7	3	5	6	4	1	2

specifies a permutation p of the ordered list 1, 2, 3, 4, 5, 6, 7. We write, for instance, $p(2) = 3$, $p(6) = 1$. An **inverse** of a permutation p is a permutation q such that $q(p(x)) = x$ and $p(q(x)) = x$ for each of the objects. For example, the permutation q given by

x	1	2	3	4	5	6	7
$q(x)$	6	7	2	5	3	4	1

is an inverse of the permutation p given previously. You can verify this by checking that $q(p(1)) = q(7) = 1$, $q(p(2)) = q(3) = 2$, ..., $q(p(7)) = q(2) = 7$ and $p(q(1)) = p(6) = 1$, ..., $p(q(7)) = p(1) = 7$. In more practical terms, you can see that the table for q is obtained from that for p by switching the columns of the table for p and then sorting the rows by the entries in the left column.

It does not take too much effort to see that this process can be applied to find the table for the inverse of a permutation of any number of objects. Moreover, this sorting process will never lead to more than one inverse permutation. So we refer to *the* inverse of p and use the special symbol p^{-1} to represent it. Thus

$$p^{-1}(p(x))) = x \text{ and } p(p^{-1}(x)) = x$$

for all x.

Summary

The concept of **function** is central in mathematics. Because cryptology involves the selection, computation, and analysis of functions of two variables (plaintext x and key k) that are invertible in x for each choice of k, function theory is useful in discussing cryptology. A permutation is an invertible function from a finite set back into itself.

EXERCISES

1. The table

x	A	B	C	D	E	F	G	H	I	J	K	L	M
$f(x)$	M	I	X	T	U	P	A	W	H	O	L	E	B

x	N	O	P	Q	R	S	T	U	V	W	X	Y	Z
$f(x)$	C	D	F	G	J	K	N	Q	R	S	V	Y	Z

   defines a function f.

   (a) Evaluate $f(\text{A})$ and $f(\text{V})$.

   (b) For which values of x is $f(x) = x$?

   (c) Explain why f is one-to-one and find a table for its inverse.

   (d) Find the table for $f \circ f$.

2. Pig Latin is a "language" sometimes spoken by children. To translate English to Pig Latin, there are two rules: (1) If an English word begins with a consonant sound, move the letters for that sound to the end of the word and append the letters "ay," and (2) if an English word begins with a vowel sound, append "ay" to the word. For instance, TOP OF THE MORNING TO YOU translates as OPTAY OFAY ETHAY ORNINGMAY OTAY OUYAY. Let $L(x)$ be the function that translates English to Pig Latin.

   (a) Evaluate $L(\text{MATHEMATICS IS THE LANGUAGE OF SECRET WRITING})$.

   (b) Is L a one-to-one function?

   (c) Evaluate $L \circ L(\text{COMPOSE YOURSELF})$.

3. Let $A(x)$ be the Atbash (see page 3) encipherment of a text string x. That is, A $\to$ Z, B $\to$ Y, and so on. Show that A is its own inverse. Such a function is called an **involution**. Give another example of a simple substitution that is an involution.

4. Let $e(x)$ be the string of uppercase letters obtained from a string x by replacing each letter in x (plaintext) with the letter given in the following table.

plain	A B C D E F G H I J K L M N O P Q R S T U V W X Y Z
cipher	B C D A F G H E J K L I N M P Q R O T U V S X Y Z W

   (a) Calculate $e(e(e(e(\mathtt{AMAZING}))))$.

   (b) Explain why the result of part (a) holds for any text string x.

   (c) If $d(x)$ is the decipherment function, find a formula for $d(x)$ in terms of $e(x)$.

5. Let $S(x)$ and $T(x)$ be the ciphertexts obtained by applying two different simple substitutions to the plaintext x. Explain why the encipherment function $U(x) = (T \circ S)(x)$ is no more secure than S or T.

6. Let $P(x)$ be the Polybius checkerboard (see page 5) encipherment of a plaintext string x, and let $s(x)$ be the function defined in Example 1.2.2.

   (a) Show by an example that, in general, $(P \circ s)(x) \neq (s \circ P)(x)$.

   (b) By looking at two similar plaintexts such as TEST and PEST, show that $s \circ P$ is not a substitution. Is $P \circ s$ a substitution?

   (c) Explain why, in contrast with the composition of two simple substitutions, this composition is a stronger cryptosystem than either substitution or transposition.

1.3   Crypto: Models, Maxims, and Mystique

General Concepts and Terminology

Cryptography is the science and art of concealing the content of communications between parties where the channel between them is controlled in some way by an unfriendly third party. The basic problem that cryptography is supposed to solve is represented in Figure 1.17. To help in thinking

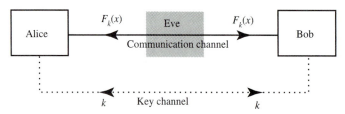

Figure 1.17 A diagrammatic representation of the central problem of classical cryptography.

about the activities of various entities in cryptography, we anthropomorphize a bit. Alice and Bob are the names often used in modern literature for correspondents (even though these "people" may be computers), and names such as Eve or Oscar are used for the **opponent** (also adversary, enemy, eavesdropper). In this book, we may—for variety—use other names as well. Bob and Alice employ a **cipher** or a **cryptosystem**, a method of message concealment where knowledge of shared secret information, the **key**, permits efficient **encipherment** (or **encryption**) of **plaintext** (a message in "readable" form) and **decipherment** (or **decryption**) of **ciphertext** (the form of a message after it has been enciphered). Eve's general activity is **cryptanalysis**: Without the benefit of the key information shared by Alice and Bob over the secure channel, she attempts to recover plaintexts or deduce the key from intercepted ciphertext. Her role may be passive in that she only eavesdrops and does not change any of the transmissions. Or her role may be active, in which case she may alter messages sent over the channel. We apply the term **cryptology** in general to the combination and interaction of cryptography and cryptanalysis.

In this book and generally in the cryptological literature, there is a distinction between a cipher and a **code**. Codes (for instance, ASCII codes, Morse code, International product codes, JPEG encoding of photographs) are ways of representing information in forms that are not readily human readable. The reason for encoding information is not to conceal its content or existence but to have it amenable to the type of channel over which it is transmitted, the sort of processing it may undergo, or the medium on which it is stored.

The term **steganography** is applied to the activity of hiding the very existence of a message. For example, German spies in the United States during World War I used disappearing inks. Messages could be written with these on the backs of pages with innocuous text on the front side. Then the recipient could—in a fashion analogous to photographic processing—develop the invisible message. This idea in simple form can be carried out by children writing on paper with with a toothpick dipped in lemon juice. Once the juice has dried, the message is invisible until the paper is heated, say over a candle. Some modern-day cryptographic experts have discussed digital steganographic schemes. One such method hides a message in a digital photograph by encoding it in the high-order bits of the bytes representing the picture. The alteration of this single bit might slightly alter the coloration of the pixels when the image is viewed, but not in a way that the human eye could detect. This sort of steganography has been termed the "Mona Lisa method" because it would be possible to hide a message in a digital copy of Da Vinci's painting *Mona Lisa*. As long as an opponent was not thinking to look at these bits, the message would be safe. This technique can also be used by the creator of a piece of digital work to hide ownership or permission information.

It is important to realize that when cryptographic methods are applied, that fact will be evident to anyone intercepting the message. Thus encryption draws attention to itself and can have the effect of raising not only the curiosity of an intermediary but the determination of that intermediary to figure out the concealed message. When that intermediary is well financed and feels it necessary to obtain the information, then the correspondents would be wise not to underestimate the likelihood of their secrets being uncovered. Indeed, an intermediary might circumvent cryptographic measures altogether by gaining access to the correspondents' computers or conducting espionage on them at their workplaces.

The term *cryptanalysis* gets extended to other contexts where messages are hidden (or suspected to be hidden) in texts, pictures, or music, but the motivation is not to conceal communication with another party. It is more an expression of cleverness on the part of the writer or artist, and at best an oblique sort of communication with the astute reader, interpreter, or

listener. One can take the idea to an extreme and regard such endeavors as
the human genome project as a form of cryptanalysis: there is an encoded
message—how to make a person—in human DNA that researchers are busy
decrypting. Taken in such a sense as this, almost any form of research is
tantamount to cryptanalysis.

Symmetric (or **classical** or **secret-key**) cryptography is represented
in Figure 1.17; its security relies on the correspondents agreeing on key
information through the key channel. **Public-key** (or **asymmetric**) **cryptography** is a development of the twentieth century that in some ways
solves the key distribution problem and simultaneously provides a way of
affixing "signatures" to documents that are intimately knit up with both
the document's content and the signer's identity (see Figure 1.18). While

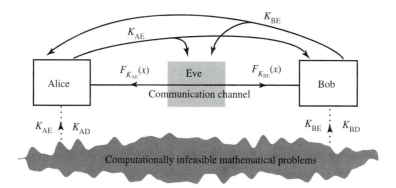

Figure 1.18 Schematic representation of public-key cryptography. K_{AE} and K_{AD} are Alice's encipherment and decipherment
keys, respectively; K_{BE} and K_{BD} are Bob's encipherment and decipherment keys respectively. F_K is the encipherment function;
Bob applies it with $K = K_{AE}$ to encipher a message for Alice;
Alice applies it with $K = K_{BE}$ to encipher a message for Bob.

it was known to British cryptographers as early as the 1960s, there was no
discussion of it in the "public" cryptographic community until the 1970s.
Generally, a public-key cryptographic algorithm is one that requires one key
for encipherment and another key for decipherment. The algorithm is such
that it is not feasible, with the current state of knowledge in mathematics
and current computational technology, to deduce the decryption key from
the encryption key in a reasonable amount of time. Moreover, it is generally
thought that the difficulty of obtaining plaintext from ciphertext alone is
equivalent to that of finding the decipherment key. Each entity using the

algorithm generates its own encryption/decryption key pair and publicizes the encryption key to all the other participants. If Alice is a participant with a message to send to Bob, she looks up Bob's public (encipherment) key, applies the algorithm, and transmits the encrypted message. If Eve intercepts the ciphertext and wishes to read it, then her only recourse is to calculate the decipherment key from the publicly-known encipherment key. However, this is thought to be intractable.

A Maxim of Cryptography and Methods of Attack

The very existence of cryptography is, in some ways, an indictment of human nature. If people were not inclined to spy, eavesdrop, borrow, or steal information to which they are not entitled, then there would be no need of message concealment methods. The reality, however, is that people's capacity to engage in these activities is almost unlimited. A moment's reflection makes it clear that it would be exceedingly difficult to run a national government without measures to keep sensitive information from the "other side." As another example, consider running a web site to which tens of thousands of people will be sending their credit card numbers to pay for the things they purchase. Since the electronic pathways that such information follows are accessible to computer system administrators all over the globe, and to many who hack their way into systems to play system administrator, this information is much more at risk than when it is, for instance, read over the telephone to a sales representative. Cryptography is one prudent measure to help ensure that this information does not fall into the wrong hands. Or consider the situation in which medical information (a chart, prescription, or x-ray, for instance) is sent by a hospital to a doctor at his or her office. Such information is generally regarded as private, and some form of cryptography is one way of helping to make sure that it stays that way while it is transmitted. Finally, consider banking records that are stored in files on magnetic media and that are supposed to be accessed only by certain bank employees. If an unauthorized person gains access to the system, then encryption of the files helps to make sure that such persons cannot immediately read the information recorded in them.

The Flemish philologist and author Auguste Kerckhoffs[27] (1835–1903), wrote about cryptography and its use in *La Cryptographie Militaire* (1883).

---

[27]His full name was Jean Guillaume Hubert Victor François Alexandre Auguste Kerckhoffs von Nieuwenhof

In it he articulated several pieces of advice to users of encipherment, one of which is now often called Kerckhoffs' maxim, which is paraphrased here:

> The opponent is not to be underestimated. In particular, the opponent knows the encryption (and decryption) algorithm. So the strength of a cipher system depends on keeping the key information secret, not the algorithm.

The wisdom of Kerckhoffs is borne out repeatedly in cryptographic history. Analogous caveats come from contemporary individuals to those who may think that fancy public-key algorithms and block ciphers with huge keys solve all modern-day cryptographic problems. Susan Landau in [47] says this: "Theorems do not establish a cryptographic algorithm's strength; surviving cryptanalytic attack does." Indeed, the designer and user of a cryptosystem that is actually supposed to work must play the role of the cryptanalyst. There are some general types of attacks on cipher systems, and these will come up from time to time throughout this book.

Ciphertext-Only Attack

The cryptanalyst knows the methods of encipherment and decipherment and possesses a portion of ciphertext. She hopes to recover plaintext and perhaps partial key information. For example, solving a "cryptoquote" using no hints is a ciphertext-only attack.

Known-Plaintext Attack

The cryptanalyst knows the methods of encipherment and decipherment and possesses a portion of ciphertext along with the corresponding plaintext. Such information is sometimes referred to as a **crib**. She hopes to recover the key and use it to decipher future encrypted messages.

In 1799, the discovery of the Rosetta stone in Egypt allowed a known-plaintext "attack" on hieroglyphics, which had remained undeciphered until that time. The basalt tablet was inscribed with a decree made by Ptolemy V in 196 B.C. written in Greek, Egyptian hieroglyphics, and Demotic. Since antiquities scholars of the time could read the Greek, this provided information for reading hieroglyphics.

Here is a second, more contemporary example. Someone has sensitive computer files on a Unix system that she wants to encrypt. To test the software, she uses it to encrypt an innocuous file, and then she inadvertently leaves the file along with the encrypted copy in her directory. She goes on to encipher the sensitive information using the same key, saving only the encrypted copies. Assuming that this took place, say, before the 1990s, the computer user is open to a known-plaintext attack: in earlier times, on Unix systems, the default protection set on a user's files allowed read access to others on the system. A nefarious person could see the encrypted sensitive information as well as the plain and encrypted versions of the test file. Depending on the encryption algorithm, this person could infer information about the key and potentially recover information from the sensitive files.

The cryptanalysis that concluded in the summer of 1998 with the recovery of a DES key in 56 hours was a known-plaintext attack.

Chosen-Plaintext Attack

Once again, the cryptanalyst knows the methods of encipherment and decipherment. She chooses a plaintext that, when enciphered by one of the correspondents with a key that is unknown to the cryptanalyst, provides information about the key. She then gets one of the correspondents unwittingly to encipher this chosen plaintext and intercepts the resulting ciphertext.

A classic example of a chosen-plaintext attack played a pivotal role in the U.S. victory at the battle of Midway Island in World War II. Interceptions of radio transmissions in the Pacific theater had made it clear that the Japanese were planning a major attack, but that location could not be ascertained because the coordinates of the site were represented by a code group "AF." The U.S. fleet was not big enough to be placed in more than one location, so it was essential for the naval command to be certain of the location and meet the threat with all of its ships. One of the likely targets was the garrison at Midway Island, which happened to rely on a distillation plant for fresh water. Naval communications personnel arranged for a radio transmission to be sent *in clear* from Midway saying that the distillation plant had broken down. This transmission, of course, was picked up by the Japanese, who subsequently radioed their fleet, in code, that Midway was low on fresh water. In turn, the Japanese transmission was picked up by the U.S. and partially decoded for its general contents, which were, in effect, "... AF is low on water ...". The target was definitively identified, and the U.S. fleet was dispatched to Midway. There it surprised the Japanese fleet and accomplished a decisive victory that changed the course of the war.

Cryptography in Music and Literature

In this brief subsection we look at a few examples in which people—either purportedly or obviously—have placed messages in written material simply for others to stumble upon and be astonished, both at the creator's and finder's cleverness. We also point out a few instances in which cryptography or cryptanalysis played a significant part of a story, novel, or movie.

The German composer Johann Sebastian Bach (1685–1750) occasionally inserted musical elements with extra-musical meaning. In Figure 1.19 you see a portion of the score of his F-major toccata. Beginning with the fourth measure, the bass line is a "shift encipherment" of the composer's last name. In German musical usage, the note B-flat is called B, and B-natural is called H. Thus the note sequence B-flat, A, C, B-natural spells the composer's last name. Any shift of this note pattern sounds the same, so, for instance, the note sequence shown in Figure 1.19, A-flat, G, B-flat, A, also sounds the name Bach. Other composers have knit Bach's name into compositions in

Figure 1.19 J. S. Bach signs his name in the F-major Toccata for organ. (Source: J. S. Bach, *Complete Organ Works*, vol. III, Edwin F. Kalmus, Music Publisher, 1947)

less subtle ways. For instance, Max Reger wrote *Fantasy and Fugue on the name BACH* in which the theme appears prominently throughout the piece.

The British composer Edward Elgar (1857–1934) made cryptic references to individuals he knew in the titles of movements in his orchestral composition *Enigma Variations*. It is also thought that Elgar wrote the composition first with the theme on which the variations were based an explicit part of the composition. Then he systematically removed the theme itself from all the variations, leaving only the accompaniments. The listener is then put in the position of trying to infer or "decipher" the theme from the musical setting in which it was originally placed. Of course, the composition can be heard and appreciated without knowing or even suspecting this.

It is straightforward to assign letter interpretations to various notes and then encipher a message directly by some form of substitution. The principal difficulty with such an approach is that a composition produced in this way would obviously not be "real" music. Anyone with a knowledge of musical notation would be able to identify it as serving a purpose besides listening pleasure.

Edgar Allan Poe (1809–1849), an American writer and newspaper editor, made a name for himself as a cryptographer. He wrote in *Alexander's Weekly Messenger*, a Philadelphia newspaper, on topics related to cryptography. Later, in *Graham's Magazine*, he accepted enciphered submissions from readers, solved the cryptograms, and published his feats. His short story "The Gold-Bug," in which a character named Legrand solves a substitution-type cryptogram by studying letter frequencies, was popular reading in various newspapers. Since then, it has made its way into anthologies of his stories. Some claim that, in his day in the United States, Poe was among the most knowledgeable about cryptographic matters.

In Arthur Conan Doyle's *Adventure of the Dancing Men*, Sherlock Holmes solves a cryptogram in which human stick figures represent messages. He uses his decipherment to send a fake message to a gangster named Slaney, which leads ultimately to Slaney's arrest for murder.

Many novels and movies, particularly those involving espionage, have codes and ciphers as part of the story. The mystique of these elements can be an effective embellishment and help contribute to the sense of challenge or conflict experienced by the protagonists. In *The Cryptographic Imagination: Secret Writing from Edgar Poe to the Internet* [69], Shawn Rosenhiem attempts to explicate some of the psychology behind this.

Chapter 2

Classical Cryptographic Techniques

In this chapter we examine classical methods of cryptography and cryptanalysis, along with underlying mathematical concepts. By **classical cryptography** we mean methods of encipherment that have been used from antiquity through the middle of the twentieth century and that are generally based on pencil-and-paper work. The goal in all of these methods is to keep secret from intermediaries the content of messages in ordinary human language.

One of the essential ideas throughout the course is **modular arithmetic**, which we introduce in the context of shift ciphers. We illustrate how some forms of typographical transformations can be performed by calculations that use modular arithmetic. Broadly speaking, there are two basic approaches to cryptology: **substitution**, where plaintext symbols are replaced by other symbols to produce ciphertext, and **transposition**, where plaintext symbols are rearranged to produce ciphertext. We will encounter these basic ideas in various forms, separately and in combination.

Elements of **probability** provide tools for **cryptanalysis**, or breaking ciphers. Natural languages have characteristic letter frequencies, and these often show up directly in ciphertexts. Such characteristics can be exploited to break various types of substitution ciphers. While it is not the intention to teach you how to break into information to which you do not have legitimate access, this material is intended to provide an understanding of what is involved in breaking a cipher. This will help you to understand the limitations and pitfalls of methods that may seem secure when they are viewed only from a legitimate user's point of view.

2.1   Shift Ciphers and Modular Arithmetic

Shift Ciphers

Virtually every introductory account of cryptology begins with the Caesar cipher. This is natural from both historical and mathematical perspectives. The emperor Julius Caesar, who ruled the Roman Empire for part of the first century B.C., is said to have used the following method to conceal military messages: replace A by D, B by E, C by F, ... , W by Z, X by A, Y by B, and Z by C. So, for instance, the (Latin) message

ET TU BRUTE

would be concealed as

HW WX EUXWH

The intended recipient of this message would decipher it simply by reversing the substitution or, equivalently, by counting back three letters in the alphabet from each letter in the text. Of course, any unintended recipient who could read and happened to suspect this to be the method of concealment could also decipher the message. A table such as

plain	A B C D E F G H I J K L M N O P Q R S T U V W X Y Z
cipher	D E F G H I J K L M N O P Q R S T U V W X Y Z A B C

would be helpful to senders and receivers. This table constitutes the **key** to the cipher.

There is nothing special about the number 3 (except that it designates the third letter of the alphabet, which is also the first letter of Caesar). We and an intended correspondent could privately agree, for instance, on the table

plain	A B C D E F G H I J K L M N O P Q R S T U V W X Y Z
cipher	H I J K L M N O P Q R S T U V W X Y Z A B C D E F G

The alphabet has been shifted seven letters to the left. Then, for example, the message

AOL JHLZHY JPWOLY PZ LHZPSF IYVRLU

is easily deciphered.

Now suppose we are walking down the street and find an apparently lost note that says

```
TO: SMITH
FROM: WESSON
JR EBO GUR ONAX NG ZVQAVTUG
```

Suppose further that we suspect this is a message in English enciphered by a shifted alphabet as above. How do we go about deciphering it? One way would be systematically to try out possible shifts. We would start with 1: J becomes I, R becomes Q, etc. This gives

IQ DAN FTZ NMZW MF YUPZUSTF

which is not English. Then we would try 2: J becomes H, R becomes P, etc. We can reject this possibility after the first two letters: There is no English word HP. Continuing in this way, we eventually find that an alphabet shifted by 13 letters deciphers the message into a message that we might want to forward to the police.

Alternatively, we could use facts about letter frequency in English to find a highly likely substitution for one letter. This substitution would determine the shift for all the other letters, and we could quickly check to see if the message is intelligible. In more or less decreasing order of frequency, the most frequently occurring letters in ordinary English are E, T, N, O, R, I, and A. See Table 2.1.

Letter	Frequency	Letter	Frequency
A	0.0663	N	0.0747
B	0.0116	O	0.0895
C	0.0263	P	0.0137
D	0.0316	Q	0.0021
E	0.1284	R	0.0547
F	0.0211	S	0.0842
G	0.0232	T	0.0979
H	0.0368	U	0.0421
I	0.0684	V	0.0063
J	0.0011	W	0.0189
K	0.0095	X	0.0032
L	0.0326	Y	0.0200
M	0.0337	Z	0.0021

Table 2.1 Letter frequencies from a 950-letter sample of English.

The letter G occurs three times in the message, and each of N, O, R, U, V and A occurs twice; all the other message letters occur once. So it is reasonable that the collection of cleartext letters E, T, N, O, R, I, A corresponds to the ciphertext letters G, N, O, R, U, V, A. Note that J does *not* occur among the frequent ciphertext letters. So it is unlikely that J corresponds to any of the vowels A, E, I, or O, which are in the collection of frequent cleartext letters. Since the only two-letter English words beginning with U are UP and US, neither of which is likely to be the first word of a sentence, we tentatively assume that J does not correspond to U. Thus, the cipher text J corresponds to a consonant and therefore ciphertext R corresponds to a vowel. Which vowel? Ruling out slang and onomatopoetic words, we find that R corresponds either to E (in which case IQ becomes BE, HE, ME, or WE or to O (in which case IQ becomes GO, NO, SO, or TO). We have reduced as many as 25 possible trials to two, which we can easily check. If ciphertext R corresponds to plaintext E (*and* if this is a shift cipher, which is an underlying assumption), then the key is

> plain A B C D E F G H I J K L M N O P Q R S T U V W X Y Z
> cipher N O P Q R S T U V W X Y Z A B C D E F G H I J K L M

from which we obtain

WE ROB THE BANK AT MIDNIGHT

By taking a mathematical view of shift-type ciphers, we can enlist a computer spreadsheet in solving shift ciphers. First, a little background.

Modular Arithmetic

If a 24-hour clock presently reads 14:00 (1400 hours or 2:00 P.M. on a 12-hour clock), what time will it be 53 hours from now? The passage of each 24-hour period brings the clock back to 14:00; two of these account for 48 hours, and the remainder of 5 hours added to 14 gives 19:00 or 7:00 P.M. Another way to think of the question is this: 14:00 plus 53 gives "67:00," that is, 67 hours after 0:00 (the starting time of today). Since 67 divided by 24 gives 2, there are two whole days in these 67 hours; the remainder of 19 is the number of hours into the third day the clock will have run. Thus, by the 24-hour clock, 14 plus 53 equals 19. In mathematical terms we would say this as

$$14 + 53 \equiv 19 \pmod{24},$$

or we might suggest the step of finding the remainder when dividing 67 by 24 by writing

$$14 + 53 \equiv 67$$
$$\equiv 19 \pmod{24}.$$

The integers are "modulated" by 24.

Because we will frequently use this idea and build on it in our study of cryptology, we make a general definition.

Definition 2.1.1 Let m be a positive integer (the **modulus** of our arithmetic). We say that two integers a and b are **congruent modulo** m if $b - a$ is (evenly) divisible by m and we write

$$a \equiv b \pmod{m}.$$

The symbol "$\equiv$" works in much the same way as the more familiar equal sign "$=$".

Example 2.1.1 Let the modulus be 10. Then, for instance, $3 \equiv 3 \pmod{10}$, $1 \equiv 11 \pmod{10}$, $143 \equiv 8723 \pmod{10}$, $\quad -6 \equiv 4 \pmod{10}$, $\quad$ and $68270 \equiv 0 \pmod{10}$. $\quad \diamondsuit$

Example 2.1.2 Let the modulus be 2. Then, for example, $-6 \equiv -4 \equiv -2 \equiv 0 \equiv 2 \equiv 4 \equiv 6 \equiv 8 \pmod{2}$ and $-5 \equiv -3 \equiv -1 \equiv 1 \equiv 3 \equiv 5 \pmod{2}$. Indeed, with this modulus there are just two classes of numbers: those congruent to 0 (the even numbers) and those congruent to 1 (the odd numbers). $\quad \diamondsuit$

Example 2.1.3 What are the numbers that are congruent to 39 modulo 8? Certainly 39 is one of them. Also, $39 + 8 = 47$, $39 + 2 \cdot 8 = 56$, $39 - 8 = 31$, and $39 - 2 \cdot 8 = 23$ are. An exhaustive list is generated by the formula $39 + 8k$ as k ranges through the integers:

k	$\cdots$	-6	-5	-4	-3	-2	-1	0	1	2	$\cdots$
$39 + 8k$	$\cdots$	-9	-1	7	15	23	31	39	47	55	$\cdots$

Notice that 7 is the smallest *positive* value of $39 + 8k$ and that 7 is also the remainder when 39 is divided by 8. In some sense, it is the simplest representative of this list. $\quad \diamondsuit$

Generally, we regard the simplest representative of a number n modulo m to be the remainder when n is divided by m. What are the possible remainders when a number is divided by m?

It is worth our stating a fundamental and familiar principle about the integers.

Division Principle: Let m be a positive integer and let b be any integer. Then there is exactly one pair of integers q (the **quotient** of b divided by m) and r satisfying $0 \leq r < m$ (the **remainder**) such that

$$b = qm + r.$$

The numbers q and r, of course, can be calculated by hand using the long division method you learned in elementary school. In this book we will use the notation b MOD m to represent the remainder r. You should think of MOD as an operation like $+$ or $/$. For instance, 17 MOD $5 = 2$, 5 MOD $17 = 5$, and (-8) MOD $3 = 1$. In other words,

$$b \text{ MOD } m = \begin{pmatrix} \text{Remainder when } b \text{ is} \\ \text{divided by } m \end{pmatrix}.$$

The connection between the "$(\bmod m)$" notation and the "MOD" notation is this:

$$b \text{ MOD } m = \begin{pmatrix} \text{Smallest} \quad \text{nonnegative} \\ \text{number} \quad a \quad \text{such that} \\ b \equiv a \, (\bmod m) \end{pmatrix}.$$

Also we sometimes use the notation b DIV m to represent the **integer quotient** when b is divided by m. That is, b DIV m is the q from the division algorithm. For instance, 17 DIV $5 = 3$, 5 DIV $17 = 0$, and (-8) DIV $3 = -3$.

Another way to think of division is as repeated subtraction. Suppose b is bigger than m (see Figure 2.1), and imagine the number line marked off in

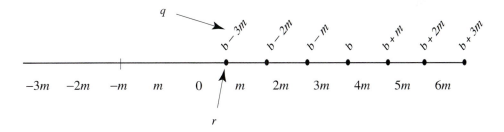

Figure 2.1 A number line representation of finding quotient q and remainder r when b is divided by m.

units of m starting at 0. Subtracting m from b gives the point $b - m$ on the number line, which is still bigger than m. Subtracting m from $b - m$ gives $b - 2m$, which is still bigger than m. Finally, subtracting m from $b - 2m$

gives $b - 3m$, which is less than m and no smaller than 0. This number is the remainder r, and the quotient q is 3 in this case.

Suppose we have two integers a and b such that $a \equiv b \pmod m$. Then $b - a$ is a multiple of m. If we select a third integer c and calculate the integers $a + c$ and $b + c$, what relationship exists between these two numbers? The difference is $(b + c) - (a + c) = b - a + c - c = b - a$, which is a multiple of m. So

$$a + c \equiv b + c \pmod m;$$

we can add a number to both sides of a modular equation. Another way to express this algebraic fact is that if we form a sum of two integers, $a + c$, and we know that $a \equiv b \pmod m$, then we can replace a by b and have a number that is congruent to $a + c$.

Example 2.1.4 Calculate a table of values for $y = (x + 2)$ MOD 9.

Solution The only possible values y can take are 0, ..., 8, so we only need to consider the values 0, 1, 2, 3, 4, 5, 6, 7, and 8 for x.

x	0	1	2	3	4	5	6	7	8
$(x + 2)$ MOD 9	2	3	4	5	6	7	8	0	1

$\diamondsuit$

Notice that the values of $(x + 2)$ MOD 9 are just the remainders shifted left by 2 and "wrapped." This is exactly what we were doing with the Caesar cipher, except the symbols were the 26 letters of the alphabet and the shift was 3. When we identify each letter by a number according to the table

A	B	C	D	$\cdots$	X	Y	Z
0	1	2	3	$\cdots$	23	24	25

(2.1)

then we see that the Caesar cipher can be represented by the formula $y = (x + 3)$ MOD 26. Any other shift-type cipher can be represented by $y = (x + k)$ MOD 26, where k is a key agreed upon by the correspondents.

Example 2.1.5 Use a formula for a 7 shift to encipher the message

MEET ME AT DINOS

Solution Translate the message first into numerical equivalents according to (2.1):

$$12, 4, 4, 19 \quad 12, 4 \quad 0, 19 \quad 3, 8, 13, 14, 18$$

Then substitute each of these into $y = (x + 7) \bmod 26$:

$$19, 11, 11, 0 \quad 19, 11 \quad 7, 0 \quad 10, 11, 20, 21, 25$$

Finally, translate back to letters using (2.1):

$$\text{TLLA TL HA KLUVZ} \quad \diamondsuit$$

Application of Modular Arithmetic to Shift Ciphers

Though we can perform encipherment and decipherment by hand easily in the way illustrated in Example 2.1.5, we can also employ a computer spreadsheet to do it. In many spreadsheet programs, there is a function called something like CODE that accepts as input a character and returns the **ASCII code**[1] for that character. (There is an ASCII code for every character on a keyboard plus others designated for communication between computers. See Table 2.2.)

For instance, in Apple Works or Microsoft Excel,[2] putting the formula =CODE("A") in a cell returns the value 65; putting the formula =CODE(B7) in a cell returns the ASCII code for whatever character is in the spreadsheet cell B7.

There is also a function in Works and Excel called CHAR, which is the **inverse** of CODE: An integer input is interpreted as an ASCII code, and it returns the corresponding character. For instance, =CHAR(90) returns Z; =CHAR(C6) returns the character corresponding to any valid ASCII code that sits in cell C6.

Finally, there is a function in both Works and Excel called MOD that takes two arguments, the first an integer and the second a positive integer. MOD returns the remainder when the first number is divided by the second. For example, =MOD(32,26) returns the value 6; =MOD(K4,2) returns either 0 or 1 depending on whether the integer in cell K4 is even or odd.

We combine these functions to make encipherment and decipherment slick and automatic.

---

[1] American Standard Code for Information Interchange.

[2] Most spreadsheet programs have functions similar to those described here. These specific pieces of software are mentioned only for concreteness in this exposition; this is not an endorsement of either of these products.

char	code	char	code	char	code	char	code	char	code	char	code
space	32	0	48	@	64	P	80	`	96	p	112
!	33	1	49	A	65	Q	81	a	97	q	113
"	34	2	50	B	66	R	82	b	98	r	114
#	35	3	51	C	67	S	83	c	99	s	115
$	36	4	52	D	68	T	84	d	100	t	116
%	37	5	53	E	69	U	85	e	101	u	117
&	38	6	54	F	70	V	86	f	102	v	118
'	39	7	55	G	71	W	87	g	103	w	119
(	40	8	56	H	72	X	88	h	104	x	120
)	41	9	57	I	73	Y	89	i	105	y	121
*	42	:	58	J	74	Z	90	j	106	z	122
+	43	;	59	K	75	[	91	k	107	{	123
,	44	<	60	L	76	\	92	l	108			124
-	45	=	61	M	77	]	93	m	109	}	125
.	46	>	62	N	78	^	94	n	110	~	126
/	47	?	63	O	79	_	95	o	111	del	127

Table 2.2 ASCII codes for printable characters.

Put the characters of a message to be enciphered in a spreadsheet row (for simplicity we often omit the spaces between words). Then calculate the first entry of the second row to be the numerical equivalent ($A \to 0$, $B \to 1$, etc.) of the first message letter by the spreadsheet formula =CODE(A1)-CODE("A"):

A2=CODE(A1)-CODE("A")									
	A	**B**	**C**	**D**	**E**	**F**	**G**	**H**	**I**	**J**
1	S	K	Y	I	S	C	L	E	A	R
2	18									
3										

Use the spreadsheet's Fill Right function to fill this formula into the rest of row 2:

A2=CODE(A1)-CODE("A")									
	A	**B**	**C**	**D**	**E**	**F**	**G**	**H**	**I**	**J**
1	S	K	Y	I	S	C	L	E	A	R
2	18	10	24	8	18	2	11	4	0	17
3										

Next, we want row 3 to be row 2 plus 7, modulo 26, so we put = MOD(A2 + 7, 26) in cell A3 and fill right:

A3=MOD(A2 + 7, 26)									
	A	**B**	**C**	**D**	**E**	**F**	**G**	**H**	**I**	**J**
1	S	K	Y	I	S	C	L	E	A	R
2	18	10	24	8	18	2	11	4	0	17
3	25	17	5	15	25	9	18	11	7	24
4										

Finally, we want row 4 to be the characters corresponding to the numbers in row 3. We first add CODE("A") to each element of row 3 and then find the character corresponding to each of the resulting ASCII codes. So put =CHAR(A3 + CODE("A")) in cell A4 and fill right:

A4=CHAR(A3 + CODE("A"))									
	A	**B**	**C**	**D**	**E**	**F**	**G**	**H**	**I**	**J**
1	S	K	Y	I	S	C	L	E	A	R
2	18	10	24	8	18	2	11	4	0	17
3	25	17	5	15	25	9	18	11	7	24
4	Z	R	F	P	Z	J	S	L	H	Y

Thus row 4 contains the enciphered message. The recipient of this message can likewise use a spreadsheet to reverse the steps of encipherment (by knowing the key 7). Since you, the reader, are the recipient, try it!

One other comment is in order. The steps of encipherment can be combined into one formula by, in effect, substituting the formulas in column A, one into the next:

```
A2 = CODE(A1) - CODE("A")
A3 = MOD(A2 + 7, 26) = MOD (CODE(A1) - CODE("A") + 7,26)
A4 = CHAR(A3 + CODE("A")) = CHAR(MOD(CODE(A1) - CODE("A") +
        7, 26) + CODE("A"))
```

Thus we could do the work of encipherment with just two spreadsheet rows, but at the expense of a more complicated formula. How would this formula be different if the key were 18 instead of 7? A spreadsheet can also be used to break a shift cipher. You are asked in one of the exercises to do this.

Summary

A shift-type cipher is one in which plaintext numerical equivalent x is used to calculate numerical ciphertext y by $y = (x+k)$ MOD 26 for some number k in the range 1 to 25. It is easy to use for sender and receiver. It is also easy to break for an unintended recipient. By knowing about modular arithmetic, we can enlist a computer in the enciphering, deciphering, and (as you will find in the Exercises) breaking of shift ciphers.

EXERCISES

1. The following are ciphertexts produced with the Caesar cipher. Decipher them.

   (a) HOYLV ZDV VLJKWHG DW PDLQ DQG XQLRQ

   (b) SUHVL GHQWD QGFRQ JUHVV UHDFK EXGJH WDJUH HPHQW

2. (a) Encipher your full name using a 10-shift and using a 16-shift.

   (b) Take the 10-shift enciphered name and encipher *it* using the 16 shift. Explain the result.

3. In each of the following, find q and r such that $b = qm + r$, according to the division principle.

   (a) $b = 127,\ m = 7$

   (b) $b = 473,\ m = 26$

   (c) $b = 1024,\ m = 16$

   (d) $b = 3,\ m = 14$

   (e) $b = -43,\ m = 4$

   (f) $b = -123,\ m = 124$

4. For each of the following, find the smallest nonnegative integer x that satisfies the congruence.

   (a) $x \equiv 14 \pmod 3$

   (b) $x \equiv 130 \pmod{26}$

   (c) $x \equiv -1 \pmod 5$

(d) $x \equiv -258 \pmod{16}$

5. Make a table of y-values for each of the following.

   (a) $y = (x + 2)$ MOD 8
   (b) $y = (x + 2)$ MOD 11
   (c) $y = (x + 5)$ MOD 10
   (d) $y = (x - 6)$ MOD 24
   (e) $y = (x - 11)$ MOD 12

6. Make a list of at least five solutions to the following congruences.

   (a) $x - 4 \equiv 5 \pmod{26}$
   (b) $x + 23 \equiv 1 \pmod{4}$

7. The MOD and DIV operations can be incorporated into expressions with the usual arithmetic operations of addition subtraction and multiplication. It is customary to place them in the evaluation hierarchy at the same level as multiplication ($\cdot$). That is, in an expression without parentheses, multiplication, division, and remainder extraction (MOD) are performed first left to right, and after that addition and subtraction left to right. For instance, $5 \cdot 3 - 13$ MOD $3 + 8 \cdot 7$ MOD 9 would evaluate on a first pass to $15 - 1 + 56$ MOD 9, then to $14 + 2$, and then to 16. Evaluate the following.

   (a) 22 MOD $9 + 1$
   (b) 273 MOD $10 - 10$ MOD 273
   (c) 100 DIV 13 DIV 2
   (d) 100 MOD 13 MOD 2
   (e) 26 DIV $8 + 26$ MOD 6
   (f) 58237910023 MOD $100 + 32001973285$ DIV 100

8. Explain why if $a \equiv b \pmod{m}$, then $a \equiv b$ MOD $m \pmod{m}$, $b \equiv a$ MOD $m \pmod{m}$, and a MOD $m = b$ MOD m.

9. Use the formula $y = (x + 7)$ MOD 26 to encipher

   THE FULLNESS OF LIFE IS IN THE HAZARDS OF LIFE[3]

---

[3]Edith Hamilton (1867–1963), U.S. writer and educator, *The Great Age of Greek Literature*.

10. Use a modular arithmetic formula to encipher the message

    EDUCATION IS THE BEST PROVISION FOR OLD AGE[4]

    with an 11-shift.

11. The formula $y = (x + 12)$ MOD 26 was used to encipher a message to obtain

    URKAG OMZFN QWUZP MFXQM EFNQH MSGQ

    Find the formula for decryption and decipher.

12. Use a modular arithmetic formula to decipher the message

    OZWF QGM UGEW LG S XGJC AF LZW JGSV LSCW AL[5]

    which was enciphered with an 18-shift.

13. The following message was enciphered with a shift. Using letter frequency and other facts about English, identify one plaintext-ciphertext letter pair and use it to obtain the key and a decipherment of the message.

    BZCM EWZBP QA QV JMQVO VWB AMMUQVO[6]

14. The message

    ZIFFIQSIOLVFCMM[7]

    was enciphered using a shift cipher. By pure brute force (listing all possible shift decipherments, e.g., by using a spreadsheet or writing a computer program), decipher the message and recover the key.

15. The following message is enciphered using a shift. By using letter frequencies, determine the likeliest values of the shift and use a process of elimination to obtain the plaintext.

---

[4]From Aristotle (384–322 B.C.), Diogenes Laertius, *Lives of Eminent Philosophers*.

[5]Attributed to Yogi Berra (b. 1925).

[6]Alice Cary (1820–1871), "Nobility," in *One Hundred and One Famous Poems*, Roy J. Cook, ed., Contemporary Books, Inc., Chicago, 1958.

[7]Joseph Campbell (1904–1987), *The Power of Myth*.

EGDHE TGXIN XHCDI LXIWD JIBPC NUTPG HPCSS XHIPH ITHPC
SPSKT GHXIN XHCDI LXIWD JIRDB UDGIH PCSWD ETH[8]

2.2 Affine Ciphers; More Modular Arithmetic

Shift ciphers, as you have seen in the previous section, offer little security. The problem is that the letter substitutions are not mixed up enough. The idea of an affine cipher is to use multiplication combined with addition, modulo 26, to create a more "mixed-up" substitution. Generally, an **affine cipher** is one in which plaintext letters are enciphered by the formula

$$y = (kx + b) \text{ MOD } m, \tag{2.2}$$

where m is the number of letters in the alphabet (typically 26), where k and b are chosen (with a few restrictions) from among the integers 0, 1, 2, ..., $m - 1$, where x is the numerical equivalent of a cleartext letter, and where y is the numerical equivalent of the corresponding ciphertext letter.

Before we discuss affine ciphers, we need to establish an algebraic tool that will be quite helpful in working with affine ciphers. In essence, this fact says that, analogous to what we do with ordinary equations, we can multiply both sides of a congruence by congruent numbers and preserve the solution set. Suppose that a, b, c, and d are integers such that $a \equiv b \,(\text{mod}\, m)$ and $c \equiv d \,(\text{mod}\, m)$. Then

$$ac \equiv bd \pmod{m}. \tag{2.3}$$

To see this, note that the first congruence means that $a - b = k_1 m$ for some integer m, and the second that $c - d = k_2 m$ for some integer m. So $a = b + k_1 m$ and $c = d + k_2 m$. Multiplying these equations, we get

$$
\begin{aligned}
ac &= (b + k_1 m)(d + k_2 m) \\
&= bd + (k_1 d + k_2 b)m + k_1 k_2 m^2 \\
&= bd + [k_1 d + k_2 b + k_1 k_2 m]m.
\end{aligned}
$$

Then

$$ac - bd = [k_1 d + k_2 b + k_1 k_2 m]m$$

---

[8]Francis Bacon, "Of Adversity" in *Essays*, 1625.

and therefore
$$ac \equiv bd \pmod{m}.$$

Decimation Ciphers

We first look at a special type of affine cipher where the constant b is zero. A **decimation cipher** (on the Roman alphabet) is one in which the numerical equivalent of the ciphertext y is obtained by the formula

$$y = kx \text{ MOD } 26, \tag{2.4}$$

where k is an integer key agreed upon by the correspondents and x is the numerical equivalent of a plaintext letter. For example, if k is 3, then plaintext A undergoes the transformation $A \rightarrow 0 \rightarrow 3 \cdot 0 = 0 \rightarrow A$, plaintext B undergoes $B \rightarrow 1 \rightarrow 3 \cdot 1 \equiv 3 \rightarrow D$, plaintext C undergoes $C \rightarrow 2 \rightarrow 3 \cdot 2 \text{ MOD } 26 = 6 \rightarrow G$, and so on. Applying this transformation to each letter of the alphabet gives the following table:

plain	A	B	C	D	E	F	G	H	I	J	K	L	M	N	O	P	Q	R	S	T	U	V	W	X	Y	Z
cipher	A	D	G	J	M	P	S	V	Y	B	E	H	K	N	Q	T	W	Z	C	F	I	L	O	R	U	X

$$\tag{2.5}$$

Another way of thinking about the decimation is this: We start with letting A substitute for A. (Is there any problem with this one **collision**—a cleartext letter being encrypted as itself?) Then we skip two letters and let D substitute for B; we skip two more letters and let G substitute for C; we continue in this way wrapping around to the beginning of the alphabet whenever we reach the end. (Do you see any other collisions? Could you explain why it occurs where it does?) This provides a systematic sort of mixing that is easy for correspondents using this key to remember. At the same time, an interceptor of the ciphertext

$$\text{CFQGE KAZEMF ZMAGVMC NMO VYSV} \tag{2.6}$$

would obtain nonsense with a systematic attack treating this as a shift-type ciphertext.

It appears that this approach is marginally better than a shift cipher, but we will see that it is, in some sense, even weaker than any shift cipher! If we try a key of $k = 4$, we get the table

plain	A	B	C	D	E	F	G	H	I	J	K	L	M	N	O	P	Q	R	S	T	U	V	W	X	Y	Z
cipher	A	E	I	M	Q	U	Y	C	G	K	O	S	W	A	E	I	M	Q	U	Y	C	G	K	O	S	W

which is useless (without further knowledge about the underlying plaintext) because there is no way to decipher uniquely a message enciphered this way: A ciphertext A would correspond to A or N, an E to B or O, and so on. If we examine the values of $4x$ MOD 26,

x	0	1	2	3	4	5	6	7	8	9	10	11	12	13	$\cdots$
$4x$ MOD 26	0	4	8	12	16	20	24	2	6	10	14	18	22	0	$\cdots$

we see that 0 appears when $x = 13$. The reason is that $4 = 2 \cdot 2$ and $26 = 2 \cdot 13$: If the integer $4x$ ever contains a factor of 26—which it will when x is 13—then $4x$ is congruent to 0 modulo 26. A similar situation would arise if k were 6. The problem arises because these potential keys k have a factor in common with 26. Thus we cannot allow the values 0, 2, 4, 6, 8, 10, 12, 14, 16, 18, 20, 22, 24, or 13 for k. Moreover, if k is any of the values 1, 3, 5, 7, 9, 11, 15, 17, 19, 21, 23, 25, then kx will take on each value in the range 0 to 25. To see this, we reason that if $kx_1 \equiv kx_2 \pmod{26}$ for two different values x_1 and x_2 of x, then $kx_1 - kx_2 \equiv 0 \pmod{26}$ and consequently $k(x_1 - x_2) \equiv 0 \pmod{26}$. Since k contains no factors of 26, $x_1 - x_2$ would have to be a multiple of 26. That, however, is impossible because the difference between x_1 and x_2 is less than 26, greater than -26, and not 0. We conclude that (2.4) gives a complete list of substitutions precisely when k has no factors other than 1 in common with 26.

We see, then, that there are only 12 decimation ciphers on a 26-letter alphabet, and it would be relatively easy—especially with a spreadsheet—to try all of them on a ciphertext suspected of being produced in this way.

Example 2.2.1 Decipher (2.6) and find the key.

Solution Since this is a decimation cipher, we already know that A "is" A. If we can determine the substitution for one other letter, then we can uncover the key k. After that we will solve

$$kx \equiv y \pmod{26}$$

for x for each choice of y from the ciphertext (2.6).

A letter frequency tally reveals that M occurs four times in the ciphertext; V occurs three times; C, F, G, E, A, and Z each occur twice; and Q, K, N, O, Y, and S each occurs once. Since E is the most commonly occurring letter in English, we make the tentative assumption that ciphertext M corresponds to plaintext E. Since the numerical equivalents of M and E are, respectively, 12 and 4, we substitute them for y and x in (2.2.1) so that we can solve for k:

$$k \cdot 4 \equiv 12 \pmod{26}.$$

One solution is $k = 3$, and the only other one in the range 1 to 25 is $k = 16$. But we can rule out the latter (why?).

The numerical equivalent of (2.6) is

$$2, 5, 16, 6, 4 \quad 10, 0, 25, 4, 12, 5 \quad 25, 12, 0, 6, 21, 12, 2$$
$$13, 12, 14 \quad 21, 24, 18, 21$$

So we must solve successively the congruences

$$
\begin{aligned}
3x &\equiv 2 \pmod{26} \\
3x &\equiv 5 \pmod{26} \\
3x &\equiv 16 \pmod{26} \\
3x &\equiv 6 \pmod{26} \\
&\vdots \\
3x &\equiv 18 \pmod{26} \\
3x &\equiv 21 \pmod{26}
\end{aligned}
\tag{2.7}
$$

for x. (How many of these congruences are there?) If the congruences in (2.7) were ordinary equations, we could multiply both sides by $\frac{1}{3}$ to obtain a succession of solutions. There is no "$\frac{1}{3}$" in integers, but there is, in fact, an integer r in the range 2 to 26 such that $3 \cdot r \equiv 1 \pmod{26}$. A moment's thought reveals that since $3 \cdot 9 = 27$ is one bigger than 26, we have $3 \cdot 9 \equiv 1 \pmod{26}$, so $r = 9$. Then we multiply both sides of the congruences in (2.7) by 9, and we reason by (2.3) that $9 \cdot 3x \equiv x \pmod{26}$. So (2.7) is equivalent to

$$
\begin{aligned}
x &\equiv 9 \cdot 2 \equiv 18 \pmod{26} \\
x &\equiv 9 \cdot 5 \equiv 19 \pmod{26} \\
x &\equiv 9 \cdot 16 \equiv 14 \pmod{26} \\
&\vdots \\
x &\equiv 9 \cdot 21 \equiv 7 \pmod{26}.
\end{aligned}
$$

So the numerical equivalent of the cleartext is

$$18, 19, 14, 2, 10 \quad 12, 0, 17, 10, 4, 19 \quad 17, 4, 0, 2, 7, 4, 18$$
$$13, 4, 22 \quad 7, 8, 6, 7$$

and the message is

STOCK MARKET REACHES NEW HIGH $\diamondsuit$

The idea of a multiplicative inverse, which we used in Example 2.2, is very useful. We take time to deal with it in general.

Modular Multiplication and Its Inverse

A **multiplicative inverse** of an integer a modulo m is an integer b such that $ab \equiv 1 \, (\text{mod} \, m)$. If b is any multiplicative inverse, we define a^{-1} by $a^{-1} = b \, \text{MOD} \, m$. Thus a^{-1} designates a single number in the range 1 to $m - 1$.

Example 2.2.2 Modulo 5, the number 2 has inverses $\ldots, -2, 3, 8, 13, \ldots$ because $\ldots, -2 \cdot 2 \equiv -4 \equiv 1 \, (\text{mod} \, 5), 3 \cdot 2 \equiv 6 \equiv 1 \, (\text{mod} \, 5), \ldots$. All of these inverses are congruent to 3 modulo 5; $\ldots, (-2) \, \text{MOD} \, 5 = 3, 3 \, \text{MOD} \, 5 = 3, 8 \, \text{MOD} \, 5 = 3, \ldots$. Thus $2^{-1} = 3$. $\diamondsuit$

Example 2.2.3 Modulo 6, the number 2 has no multiplicative inverse: 2 times any integer is even, and any even number leaves an even remainder when divided by 6. $\diamondsuit$

In order to characterize when multiplicative inverses exist, we review a couple of familiar but important notions in arithmetic.

A **prime number** is an integer greater than 1 with no divisors other than itself and 1. The list of primes starts off 2, 3, 5, 7, 11, 13, 17, $\ldots$ and—as Euclid (c. 300 BC) knew and we will prove later—it never stops. The remaining integers 4, 6, 8, 9, 10, 12, 14, 15, $\ldots$ are **composite numbers**; each of these can be factored into the product of two or more smaller numbers greater than 1. The following fact is familiar, and it is so important in mathematics that it has its own name.

Theorem 2.2.1 *(fundamental theorem of arithmetic) Each positive integer is either prime or the product of powers of primes. Moreover, in the latter case, if an integer is written as a product of powers of primes, and these factors are written in increasing order of the primes, then no other such factorization is possible.*

In more formal mathematical language, the sentence in the theorem beginning "Moreover" reads, "The factorization is **unique**, up to the order of the factors." We can see, at least in rough terms, why this theorem is true. If a given number is prime then, well, it's prime. Otherwise it is composite so it can be written as the product of two nontrivial factors. If these two are both prime, then the given number is a product of (first) powers of primes. On the other hand, if one or both of these factors is composite, then we apply the same reasoning again to that factor. Since the factors get smaller with each step of this line of reasoning, and since all these factors are positive, the process eventually ends with the smallest factors being prime. Gathering any duplicate prime factors together into powers of those factors, we have a product of powers of primes.

For example, $540 = 5 \cdot 108 = 5 \cdot [6 \cdot 18] = 5 \cdot [(2 \cdot 3) \cdot (2 \cdot 9)] = 5 \cdot [(2 \cdot 3) \cdot (2 \cdot 3 \cdot 3)] = (2 \cdot 2) \cdot (3 \cdot 3 \cdot 3) \cdot 5 = 2^2 \cdot 3^3 \cdot 5$. Moreover, there is no other increasing list of primes $p_1, p_2, \ldots, p_k$ and exponents $e_1, e_2, \ldots, e_k$ such that $540 = p_1^{e_1} p_2^{e_2} \cdots p_k^{e_k}$.

Two numbers are **relatively prime** if their prime factorizations have no factors in common. For example, 540 and 539 are relatively prime because $539 = 7^2 \cdot 11$ has no prime factor in common with $540 = 2^2 \cdot 3^3 \cdot 5$.

With these terms in mind we can now say precisely when numbers have inverses in modular arithmetic.

Theorem 2.2.2 *Let $m \geq 2$ be a positive integer and let a be a number in the range from 1 to $m - 1$. Then a has a multiplicative inverse modulo m if and only if a and m are relatively prime.*

Proof Suppose that a has a multiplicative inverse b. Then

$$ab \equiv 1 \pmod{m}. \tag{2.8}$$

We want to show that a and m are relatively prime. For the sake of a contradiction, suppose that a and m have a common factor c. Then $a = a_1 c$ and $m = m_1 c$ for some numbers a_1 and m_1 in the range from 2 to $m - 1$. Substituting for a in (2.8), we have

$$a_1 c b \equiv 1 \pmod{m}, \tag{2.9}$$

and multiplying (2.9) by m_1, we have

$$a_1 c b m_1 \equiv m_1 \pmod{m}.$$

However,

$$a_1 c b m_1 \equiv (a_1 b)(c m_1) \equiv a_1 b m \equiv 0 \pmod{m},$$

and this contradiction shows that our assumption of a common factor of a and m was incorrect. Therefore, a and m are relatively prime.

Conversely, suppose that a and m are relatively prime. Consider the numbers

$$
\begin{aligned}
a &\cdot 0 \ \text{MOD} \ m, \\
a &\cdot 1 \ \text{MOD} \ m, \\
a &\cdot 2 \ \text{MOD} \ m, \\
a &\cdot 3 \ \text{MOD} \ m, \\
&\ \vdots \\
a &\cdot (m-1) \ \text{MOD} \ m.
\end{aligned}
\tag{2.10}
$$

If there were any duplicates in this list, then $a \cdot i \equiv a \cdot j \,(\text{mod}\, m)$ for some choices of i and j. This says that $a \cdot (i - j) \equiv 0 \,(\text{mod}\, m)$. Since a and m have no common factor, $i - j$ must be a multiple of m. But that is impossible since $0 < |i - j| < m$. Thus there are no duplicates in the list (2.10), and in particular, one of the values must be 1. That is, there exists i such that $ai \equiv 1 \,(\text{mod}\, m)$; a has a multiplicative inverse. $\diamond$

When we are working with a small modulus, a systematic trial-and-error approach will find multiplicative inverses for us. Later in this book when we work with large moduli, we will present the extended **Euclidean algorithm** for calculating inverses. See Section 4.1.

Example 2.2.4 Since 5 is relatively prime to 24, by Theorem 2.2.2, 5 has a multiplicative inverse modulo 24. By trying a few values [$5 \cdot 2 \equiv 10 \,(\text{mod}\, 24)$, $5 \cdot 3 \equiv 15 \,(\text{mod}\, 24)$, $5 \cdot 4 \equiv 20 \,(\text{mod}\, 24)$, $5 \cdot 5 \equiv 25 \equiv 1 \,(\text{mod}\, 24)$], we see that $5^{-1} = 5$. In a similar fashion, we find $7^{-1} \equiv 7 \,(\text{mod}\, 24)$, $11^{-1} \equiv 11 \,(\text{mod}\, 24)$, $13^{-1} \equiv 13 \,(\text{mod}\, 24)$, $17^{-1} \equiv 17 \,(\text{mod}\, 24)$, $19^{-1} \equiv 19 \,(\text{mod}\, 24)$, and $23^{-1} \equiv 23 \,(\text{mod}\, 24)$. Moreover, Theorem 2.2.2 says that 2, 3, 4, 6, 8, 9, 10, 12, 14, 15, 16, 18, 20, 21, and 22 do *not* have multiplicative inverses modulo 24. $\diamond$

Whenever the modulus m is a prime number, every number in the list 1, 2, 3, ..., $m - 1$ has a multiplicative inverse.

Example 2.2.5 Find a table of multiplicative inverses for 1, 2, 3, 4, 5, and 6 modulo 7.

Solution Since 7 is prime, Theorem 2.2.2 guarantees an inverse for each of the numbers 1, ..., 6. Evidently, $1^{-1} = 1$. An inverse y of $x = 2$ will satisfy

$2y = 7k + 1$ for some choice of k; by trial and error we get $k = 1$ and $y = 4$, so $x^{-1} = 2^{-1} = 4$. Similarly, an inverse y of $x = 3$ will satisfy $3y = 7k + 1$ for some y and k; trial and error again gives $k = 2$ and $y = 5$. The complete list of inverses is

x	1	2	3	4	5	6
$x^{-1} \pmod 7$	1	4	5	2	3	6

$\diamondsuit$

Table 2.3 shows multiplicative inverses modulo 26 for all the numbers in the range 1 to 25 that have them. You should check these values by multiplying the two numbers and verifying that the result is 1 modulo 26.

x	1	3	5	7	9	11	15	17	19	21	23	25
$x^{-1} \pmod{26}$	1	9	21	15	3	19	7	23	11	5	17	25

Table 2.3 Inverses modulo 26.

Affine Ciphers

At the beginning of this section, we said that an affine cipher is a composition of a decimation followed by a shift: Given a relatively prime to 26 and b in the range 0 to 25, when we encipher a plaintext numerical equivalent x, the numerical cipher equivalent y given by (2.2) satisfies $y \equiv ax + b \pmod{26}$. Our knowledge of multiplicative inverses now allows us to derive a decipherment formula. First subtract b from both sides of this congruence:

$$y - b \equiv ax \pmod{26}.$$

Since a has an inverse modulo 26, multiply both sides of this congruence by a^{-1}:

$$\begin{aligned} a^{-1}(y - b) &\equiv a^{-1}ax \pmod{26} \\ a^{-1}(y - b) &\equiv x \pmod{26} \\ x &\equiv a^{-1}(y - b) \pmod{26}. \end{aligned}$$

That is,

$$x = (a^{-1}(y - b)) \text{ MOD } 26. \tag{2.11}$$

Example 2.2.6 Suppose we want to set up correspondence where messages are encrypted by the formula $y = (11x + 4)$ MOD 26, where x is the numerical equivalent of a plaintext letter. Then the message

SEND MONEY

has the numerical equivalent

$$18, 4, 13, 3 \quad 12, 14, 13, 4, 24,$$

and to encrypt it we apply the given formula to each of these numbers. We get

$$(11 \cdot 18 + 4) \text{ MOD } 26 \ = \ 202 \text{ MOD } 26 = 20$$
$$(11 \cdot 4 + 4) \text{ MOD } 26 \ = \ 48 \text{ MOD } 26 = 22$$
$$\vdots$$
$$(11 \cdot 24 + 4) \text{ MOD } 26 \ = \ 268 \text{ MOD } 26 = 8,$$

so the numerical equivalents of the ciphertext are

$$20, 22, 17, 11 \quad 6, 2, 17, 22, 8.$$

Then we translate this back into letters:

UWRL GCRWI

Now, suppose that we receive from our correspondent the message EVV UNWRF, and that she is using the same encryption formula. How do we decrypt the message? By Table 2.3, $11^{-1} = 19$, so our decryption formula (2.11) will be

$$x = 19(y - 4) \text{ MOD } 26. \tag{2.12}$$

The numerical equivalents of the received message are

$$4, 21, 21, \quad 20, 13, 22, 17, 5.$$

Substituting these values for y into (2.12), we get

$$0, 11, 11 \quad 18, 15, 4, 13, 19,$$

which becomes ALL SPENT. $\diamondsuit$

Cryptanalysis of an affine cipher involves some wits and a bit of algebra, as we see in the next example.

Example 2.2.7 The ciphertext

SUYMC PTTWC MLCPU FRRUG KCPWI TJQMA O

was obtained by an affine cipher. Recover the plaintext.

Solution We know that the numerical equivalents y of the ciphertext come from a formula

$$y = (ax + b) \text{ MOD } 26, \tag{2.13}$$

where a and b are unknown, and where x takes on the plaintext numerical equivalent values. One approach that would guarantee success is first to solve this for x:

$$x = a^{-1}(y - b) \text{ MOD } 26.$$

Then select values for a and b and start plugging in y-values from the ciphertext. If the resulting x-values are sensible English (we are assuming the plaintext *is* English), then it is almost certain we have the correct choice of a and b. If not, pick a different pair of values for a and b and repeat this process. Continue until a pair of values for a and b gives English plaintext. In the Exercises, you are asked to determine, in the worst case, how many pairs of values for a and b it may be necessary to try.

An alternative is to narrow the search of ab-pairs by using letter frequencies. First, a tally of the letters in the ciphertext gives the following frequencies

Letter	S	U	Y	M	C	P	T	W	L	F	R	G	K	I	J	Q	A	O
Frequency	1	3	4	3	4	3	3	2	1	1	2	1	1	1	1	1	1	1

Since C, U, M, P, and T are the highest-frequency letters in this (admittedly small) ciphertext, it stands to reason that the corresponding plaintext letters are among E, T, N, O, R, I, A and S. So, for example, suppose E and T encipher to C and U, respectively. Then when $x = 4$ in (2.13), we get $y = 2$, which gives the congruence

$$2 \equiv 4a + b \pmod{26}. \tag{2.14}$$

Also, T enciphering as U means that $x = 19$ in (2.13) gives $y = 20$; thus a second congruence,

$$20 \equiv 19a + b \pmod{26}, \tag{2.15}$$

results. We can eliminate the unknown b from (2.14) and (2.15) by subtracting one from the other:

$$\begin{aligned} 20 - 2 &\equiv 19a - 4a + b - b \pmod{26} \\ 18 &\equiv 15a \pmod{26} \\ a &\equiv 15^{-1} \cdot 18 \equiv 7 \cdot 18 \equiv 22 \pmod{26}. \end{aligned}$$

If plaintext	enciphers as	a and b satisfy	Solutions are	Possible key?
ET	CU	$4a + b \equiv 2 \quad 19a + b \equiv 20$	$a \equiv 22 \quad b \equiv 16$	no
ET	CM	$4a + b \equiv 2 \quad 19a + b \equiv 12$	$a \equiv 16 \quad b \equiv 8$	no
ET	CP	$4a + b \equiv 2 \quad 19a + b \equiv 15$	$a \equiv 13 \quad b \equiv 2$	no
ET	CT	$4a + b \equiv 2 \quad 19a + b \equiv 19$	$a \equiv 15 \quad b \equiv 20$	yes
TE	CU	$19a + b \equiv 2 \quad 4a + b \equiv 20$	$a \equiv 4 \quad b \equiv 4$	no
TE	CM	$19a + b \equiv 2 \quad 4a + b \equiv 12$	$a \equiv 8 \quad b \equiv 6$	no
TE	CP	$19a + b \equiv 2 \quad 4a + b \equiv 15$	$a \equiv 13 \quad b \equiv 15$	no
TE	CT	$19a + b \equiv 2 \quad 4a + b \equiv 19$	$a \equiv 11 \quad b \equiv 1$	yes
EN	CU	$4a + b \equiv 2 \quad 13a + b \equiv 20$	$a \equiv 2 \quad b \equiv 20$	no
EN	CM	$4a + b \equiv 2 \quad 13a + b \equiv 12$	$a \equiv 4 \quad b \equiv 12$	no
EN	CP	$4a + b \equiv 2 \quad 13a + b \equiv 15$	$a \equiv 13 \quad b \equiv 2$	no
EN	CT	$4a + b \equiv 2 \quad 13a + b \equiv 19$	$a \equiv 25 \quad b \equiv 6$	yes
NE	CU	$13a + b \equiv 2 \quad 4a + b \equiv 20$	$a \equiv 24 \quad b \equiv 2$	no
NE	CM	$13a + b \equiv 2 \quad 4a + b \equiv 12$	$a \equiv 22 \quad b \equiv 2$	no
NE	CP	$13a + b \equiv 2 \quad 4a + b \equiv 15$	$a \equiv 13 \quad b \equiv 15$	no
NE	CT	$13a + b \equiv 2 \quad 4a + b \equiv 19$	$a \equiv 1 \quad b \equiv 15$	yes
NT	CU	$13a + b \equiv 2 \quad 19a + b \equiv 20$	no unique solution	no
NT	CM	$13a + b \equiv 2 \quad 19a + b \equiv 12$	$a \equiv 4 \quad b \equiv 2$	no
NT	CP	$13a + b \equiv 2 \quad 19a + b \equiv 15$	$a \equiv 0 \quad b \equiv 2$	no
NT	CT	$13a + b \equiv 2 \quad 19a + b \equiv 19$	$a \equiv 5 \quad b \equiv 2$	yes

Table 2.4 Looking for keys to an affine cipher.

Since this value of a is not relatively prime to 26, it could not be part of a valid key pair.

Suppose, then, that E and T encipher as C and M. Then the same reasoning leads to the pair of congruences

$$2 \equiv 4a + b \pmod{26}$$
$$13 \equiv 19a + b \pmod{26}.$$

Subtracting and solving for a gives $a = 16$, which again could not be part of a valid key. Table 2.4 shows the results of these sorts of trials.

Applying the decipherment algorithm using the possible key pairs in the table, we obtain the results shown in Table 2.5. The last line looks promising; continuing the decipherment yields

YOU CANT TEACH AN OLD DOGMA NEW TRICKS.[9]   ◇

---

[9]Dorothy Parker (1893–1967), U.S. author, poet, journalist, and humorist, in *The Algonquin Wits*, ed. Robert Drennan, Citadel Press, New York, 1968.

Key pair	Decipherment formula	"Plaintext"
$a = 15$ $b = 20$	$x = 7y + 16$	MACWERTT...
$a = 11$ $b = 1$	$x = 19y + 7$	LXVBTGEE...
$a = 25$ $b = 6$	$x = 25y + 6$	OMIUERNN...
$a = 1$ $b = 15$	$x = y + 11$	DFJXNAEE...
$a = 5$ $b = 2$	$x = 21y + 10$	YOUCANTT...

Table 2.5 Looking for the plaintext.

Summary

In general, an **affine cipher** is a cipher system in which letter substitutions are made according to the formula

$$y = (ax + b) \text{ MOD } m, \tag{2.16}$$

where m is the number of alphabet letters (typically 26), a is any number in the range 1 to $m - 1$ that is relatively prime to m, and b is any number in the range 0 to $m - 1$. Under these conditions on a and m, by Theorem 2.2.2, a has a multiplicative inverse a^{-1}, and any message encrypted by (2.16) can be decrypted by

$$x = a^{-1}(y - b) \text{ MOD } m, \tag{2.17}$$

where y is the numerical equivalent of the ciphertext. Such ciphers provide more "mixing" of the cipher alphabet than do shift ciphers.

EXERCISES

1. Construct multiplication tables modulo 5, 8, 9, and 11. Contrast the ones for 5 and 11 with those for 8 and 9: Explain why nonzero numbers multiply together to give zero in the tables for 8 and 9 but not in those for 5 and 11.

2. Find the following multiplicative inverses.

   (a) $23^{-1} \pmod{26}$

   (b) $8^{-1} \pmod{13}$

   (c) $2^{-1} \pmod 9$

(d) $59^{-1} \, (\mathrm{mod}\, 60)$

3. Solve the following congruences for x.

    (a) $2x + 1 \equiv 4 \, (\mathrm{mod}\, 5)$

    (b) $9x + 5 \equiv 1 \, (\mathrm{mod}\, 10)$

    (c) $4x - 3 \equiv 5 \, (\mathrm{mod}\, 7)$

    (d) $x + 1 \equiv 4 \, (\mathrm{mod}\, 5)$

    (e) $19x \equiv 3 \, (\mathrm{mod}\, 26)$

    (f) $25x + 2 \equiv 4 \, (\mathrm{mod}\, 26)$

4. Solve the following pairs of congruences for a and b.

    (a) $4a + b \equiv 11 \, (\mathrm{mod}\, 26)$
       $a + b \equiv 6 \, (\mathrm{mod}\, 26)$

    (b) $22a + b \equiv 1 \, (\mathrm{mod}\, 26)$
       $13a + b \equiv 5 \, (\mathrm{mod}\, 26)$

5. Find formulas for x in terms of y in each of the following.

    (a) $y = (23x + 10) \ \mathrm{MOD} \ 26$

    (b) $y = (8x + 5) \ \mathrm{MOD} \ 13$

    (c) $y = (2x + 8) \ \mathrm{MOD} \ 9$

    (d) $y = (59x + 30) \ \mathrm{MOD} \ 60$

6. Find a table of multiplicative inverses for (a) modulus 10, (b) modulus 11, (c) modulus 24.

7. Encipher the following message using the affine function $y = (3x + 1) \ \mathrm{MOD} \ 26$:

IMITATION IS THE SINCEREST FORM OF FLATTERY[10]

8. Knowing that the message

SKIWSVIJSGV SY KGNA SKRGNJIVJ JHIV OVGQZAPWA[11]

---

[10]C. C. Colton (1780–1832), *Lacon, or Many Things in Few Words Addressed to those who Think*, Bliss and White, New York, 1823.

[11]Albert Einstein (1879–1955).

was enciphered with the formula $y = (11x + 8)$ MOD 26, decipher it.

9. Consider the ciphertext

$$\text{QJKES REOGH GXXRE OXEO}^{12}$$

which was enciphered with an affine cipher. Given that plaintext T becomes ciphertext H and plaintext O becomes ciphertext E, find

   (a) The encipherment formula

   (b) The decipherment formula

   (c) The plaintext

10. The ciphertext

$$\text{EUJPE HUNKL NPOJK VNKSJ FKTBO LCHBU PBOMM NPKBK HPBOM}$$
$$\text{BMAHU PNKLN POJKV NKSJF KRJTC JUKPB OMSJE HP}^{13}$$

is the result of an affine encipherment. Use the method of Example 2.2.7 to find the key and decipher it. (*Hint*: The three most frequent letters in the ciphertext correspond to the plaintext letters O, S, and T—not necessarily in that order.)

11. Suppose that a and q are two positive integers satisfying

$$34 \cdot a = 39 \cdot q.$$

   (a) Determine the smallest positive values for a and q.

   (b) Obtain formulas for a and q in terms of a variable x that generates all possible values of a and q as x ranges over the positive integers.

12. Determine the total number of affine ciphers for a

   (a) 26-letter alphabet

   (b) 29-letter alphabet

13. Explain why $(n-1)^{-1} \equiv n - 1 \, (\mathrm{mod}\, n)$ for each positive modulus n.

14. If p is a prime, explain why $a^{-1} \not\equiv a \, (\mathrm{mod}\, p)$ for $2 \leq a \leq p - 2$.

---

[12]Chinese proverb.

[13]Francis Bacon, "Of Adversity," *Essays*, 1625.

15. The mixing property of an affine cipher can be utilized in a **linear congruential pseudorandom number generator** (LCPNG). Choose a modulus m, two coefficients a and b in the range 0 to $m-1$, and a **seed** value x_0 also in the range 0 to $m-1$. Then the sequence of integers x_0, x_1, x_2, x_3, ..., given by

$$x_n = (ax_{n-1} + b) \text{ MOD } m, \quad n = 1, 2, 3, \ldots$$

may satisfy some statistical tests for randomness. Indeed, the "random" number generators built into some computers are of this type.

(a) Compute several values produced by a LCPNG with the following choices of parameters.

(i) $m = 13$, $a = 7$, $b = 0$, $x_0 = 1$

(ii) $m = 13$, $a = 3$, $b = 0$, $x_0 = 1$

(iii) $m = 11$, $a = 6$, $b = 1$, $x_0 = 1$

(iv) $m = 11$, $a = 6$, $b = 6$, $x_0 = 1$

(b) Explain why an LCPNG produces a sequence that eventually repeats a pattern.

(c) Suppose that an LCPNG with modulus $m = 23$ produces the three successive numbers 22, 7, and 5. Determine the coefficients a and b.

16. Write a computer program that takes as input a text string and two numerical coefficients a and b, that converts the string to an array of numerical equivalent values, that applies the affine cipher $y = (ax + b) \text{ MOD } 26$ to the elements of the array, and that outputs the resulting array as a text string.

2.3 Substitution Ciphers

In his short story "The Gold-Bug," Edgar Allen Poe's character Legrand comes into possession of enciphered instructions written on parchment. He suspects that the instructions tell how to get to Captain Kidd's buried treasure, and that the symbols in the instructions are substituted for letters in the Roman alphabet. He quickly breaks the cipher by examining symbol frequencies and then reads the instructions. As this story illustrates, while a letter-for-letter substitution cipher may not offer strong security against being broken, such ciphers are easy to use for both sender and receiver. They are analogous to the cheap locks that sometimes come with luggage: a deterrent to the casual intruder but not to someone with even modest intentions of breaking in.

There are two reasons for examining substitutions here. One is that the methods of mixing the alphabet are interesting and can lead to clever cryptanalyses in some cases. The other is that the general concept of substitution is mathematically important and can be used to design cipher systems that offer greater security than simple substitutions.

Definition 2.3.1 A **monoalphabetic** or **simple substitution** cipher is one in which correspondents agree on a rearrangement (permutation) of the alphabet in which messages will be written. This permutation serves as the key and is referred to as the **cipher alphabet**. The sender enciphers a message by replacing each letter in it with the corresponding letter in the cipher alphabet. The recipient deciphers by replacing each letter in the received message by the corresponding letter in the **plaintext alphabet**, the alphabet in its usual ordering.

Mixed Alphabets with Key Words

A key word or words can provide a way of mixing of the alphabet that is easy for two correspondents to remember.

Example 2.3.1 To obtain a mixed alphabet based on the keywords POE GOLD BUG, we first write the letters of the keywords in their order of appearance, without repetitions: POEGLDBU. Then we simply list after this the rest of the alphabet in its usual order. This gives the following correspondence between cleartext and ciphertext:

```
plain    A B C D E F G H I J K L M N O P Q R S T U V W X Y Z
cipher   P O E G L D B U A C F H I J K M N Q R S T V W X Y Z
```

Then, for instance, the plaintext BURIED TREASURE becomes the ciphertext OTQALG SQLPRTQL; the ciphertext MPQEUILJS deciphers as PARCHMENT. As you can see, this particular key produces collisions: V, W, X, Y, and Z are enciphered as themselves.   ◇

Mixed Alphabets from Columnar Transpositions

Another way of using a keyword to generate a mixed alphabet is first to write the keyword letters in their order of appearance on one line and then the remaining letters of the alphabet on successive lines beneath the first. Then the mixed alphabet is obtained by writing the letters of this array column by column, going left to right. This method is called **keyword columnar transposition substitution**.

Example 2.3.2 Suppose the keyword is GEODESIC. Then we write

```
G E O D S I C
A B F H J K L
M N P Q R T U
V W X Y Z
```

and copy off the cipher alphabet as

```
plain   A B C D E F G H I J K L M N O P Q R S T U V W X Y Z
cipher  G A M V E B N W O F P X D H Q Y S J R Z I K T C L U
```

With this substitution, we can decipher

```
                AIMPDOHRZEJ BIXXEJ
```

as

```
            BUCKMINSTER FULLER   ◇
```

By this example, it appears that the alphabet is more thoroughly mixed with the keyword columnar transposition method than with ordinary keyword mixing. This is true in the sense that with keyword mixing, letters toward the end of the alphabet are more likely to be invariant. The methods do not, however, disguise letter frequency in the underlying plaintext, nor do they disguise the positions of the plaintext letters relative to one another. By knowing a bit of statistical data on the language in which the plaintext was written, we can exploit these deficiencies in the encipherment method and uncover the original message and also the type of encipherment.

Table 2.6 shows letter frequencies in a fairly large sample of English. These are in remarkable agreement with letter frequencies reported, for instance, in [8] and [77]. Tables 2.7 and 2.8 show frequencies of common digraphs and trigraphs in the same sample. Such information provides a strong basis for cryptanalyzing a ciphertext produced by a substitution.

Example 2.3.3 Shown here is a ciphertext.

Letter	Relative frequency (%)	Letter	Relative frequency (%)
A	8.399	N	6.778
B	1.442	O	7.493
C	2.527	P	1.991
D	4.800	Q	0.077
E	12.150	R	6.063
F	2.132	S	6.319
G	2.323	T	8.999
H	6.025	U	2.783
I	6.485	V	0.996
J	0.102	W	2.464
K	0.689	X	0.204
L	4.008	Y	2.157
M	2.566	Z	0.025

Table 2.6 Letter Frequencies in a 7834-letter sample of English.

RSZWORSZCKCSGP SGV RTPCKCSGP RSJ PYOGV RNPZ ND ZWOCH ZCRO CG
ZWO RSZWORSZCKSX QNHXV ND WJYNZWOPCP SGV HOSPNG BTZ ZWO
CGGOH XCDO ND ZWOCH SHZP CP CG ZWO QNHXV ND DNHRP CG ZWO
YHNKOPP ND VCSXOKZCK SGV CZP SHLTROGZ BJ ROZSYWNH

The natural word divisions are evidently preserved, and this will be a big
help. By tallying we find the following letter counts:

Letter	Z	C	O	S	P	N	G	R	H	W	D	V	K
Count	19	18	18	16	14	13	13	11	11	11	7	7	6
Letter	X	Y	J	T	B	Q	L	A	E	F	I	M	U
Count	5	4	3	3	2	2	1	0	0	0	0	0	0

We find the following counts of occurrence as first letters.

Letter	Z	R	C	S	N	Q	B	P	W	H	X	D	Y	V
Count	7	6	6	5	5	2	2	1	1	1	1	1	1	1

On the basis of letter frequency alone, we would conjecture that ciphertext Z corresponds to plaintext E. However, in this text, Z is also the most
frequent initial letter, and since the frequency of E as a first letter in English
words is considerably smaller than that of such letters as T, A, S, and O, it is
more likely that ciphertext Z corresponds to plaintext T. Also, the four occurrences of the trigraph ZWO in the ciphertext suggest that it corresponds to

plaintext THE; this is corroborated by our belief that ciphertext Z is plaintext T.

Digraph	% Frequency	Digraph	% Frequency
TH	3.319	ES	1.213
HE	2.859	TO	1.213
IN	2.081	NT	1.200
ER	1.596	EA	1.059
ED	1.493	OU	1.047
AN	1.430	NG	1.034
ND	1.430	ST	1.034
AR	1.302	AS	0.9957
RE	1.302	RO	0.9957
EN	1.289	AT	0.9829

Table 2.7 Commonest digraphs and their frequencies in the sample used to make Table 2.6. These frequencies are consistent with those reported in [77].

Trigraph	%	Trigraph	%
THE	1.82	EAR	0.26
AND	0.77	HAT	0.24
ING	0.68	OFT	0.22
HER	0.5	WAS	0.21
NTH	0.4	EST	0.21
ENT	0.36	HEN	0.2
THA	0.35	IVE	0.2
INT	0.3	ALL	0.2
ERE	0.29	THI	0.2
DTH	0.28	HIN	0.2

Table 2.8 Commonest trigraphs and their frequencies in the sample used to make Table 2.6. Among the ten commonest trigraphs reported in [77], four appear in this table: THE, AND, THA, and ERE.

The second most common trigraph in English is AND, and since SGV is the second most common three-letter word in the ciphertext, we may tentatively conjecture that plaintext AND becomes ciphertext SGV. With these six letters associated, we have

```
RSZWORSZCKCSGP SGV RTPCKCSGP RSJ PYOGV RNPZ ND ZWOCH ZCRO CG
   ATHE AT   AN  AND       N    A   END  T    THE    T E  N
```

```
ZWO RSZWORSZCKSX QNHXV ND WJYNZWOPCP SGV HOSPNG BTZ ZWO
THE  ATHE AT  A        D    H    T E      AND  EA  N    T THE

CGGOH XCDO ND ZWOCH SHZP CP CG ZWO QNHXV ND DNHRP CG ZWO
 NNE   E      THE   A T      N THE      D            N THE

YHNKOPP ND VCSXOKZCK SGV CZP SHLTROGZ BJ ROZSYWNH
   E        A E T    AND  T A    ENT     ETA H
```

All of the tentative plaintext is consistent with English, so we seem to be on
the right track.

Because the two-letter ciphertext `CG` corresponds to `_N`, cipher `C` must
correspond to a plaintext vowel. Since `A`, `E` and `U` are ruled out (why?), it
is either `I` or `O`. If it is `O`, then ciphertext `ZWOCH` becomes `THEO_`, and there
is no such word. Thus cipher `C` corresponds to plain `I`. The only choice for
`ZWOCH` is now `THEIR`, so cipher `H` corresponds to plain `R`.

Now `P` and `N` are the most frequent remaining cipher letters, and `O` and
`S` are the most frequently occurring plaintext letters, so we conjecture that
these go together. Because cipher `CP` must be `I_`, we tentatively assign cipher
`P` to plain `S` and cipher `N` to plain `O`. Thus our cipher-to-plain key is

```
cipher  Z C O S P N G R H W D V K X Y J T B Q L A E F I M U
plain   T I E A S O _ R H _ D _ _ _ _ _ _ _ _ _ _ _ _ _ _ _
```

and the translation is now

```
RSZWORSZCKCSGP SGV RTPCKCSGP RSJ PYOGV RNPZ ND ZWOCH ZCRO CG
 ATHE ATI IANS AND    SICI NS  A  S END  OST O   THEIR TI E IN

ZWO RSZWORSZCKSX QNHXV ND WJYNZWOPCP SGV HOSPNG BTZ ZWO
THE  ATHE ATI A   OR D O  H   OT ESIS AND REASON    T THE

CGGOH XCDO ND ZWOCH SHZP CP CG ZWO QNHXV ND DNHRP CG ZWO
INNER  I E O  THEIR ARTS IS IN THE  OR D O   OR S IN THE

YHNKOPP ND VCSXOKZCK SGV CZP SHLTROGZ BJ ROZSYWNH
 RO ESS O   IA E TI  AND ITS  AR   ENT    ETA HOR
```

The first word is evidently `MATHEMATICIANS`, so we obtain the cipher-to-
plaintext correspondences `R → M` and `K → C`. We then easily see that the
third word is `MUSICIANS` and the last word is `METAPHOR`. These observations
and others quickly give the remaining correspondences between cipher and
plaintext:

```
cipher   Z C O S P N G R H W D V K X Y J T B Q L A E F I M U
plain    T I E A S O N M R H F D C L P Y U B W G _ _ _ _ _ _
```

Then the message deciphers as[14]

```
RSZWORSZCKCSGP SGV RTPCKCSGP RSJ PYOGV RNPZ ND ZWOCH ZCRO CG
MATHEMATICIANS AND MUSICIANS MAY SPEND MOST OF THEIR TIME IN

ZWO RSZWORSZCKSX QNHXV ND WJYNZWOPCP SGV HOSPNG BTZ ZWO
THE MATHEMATICAL WORLD OF HYPOTHESIS AND REASON BUT THE

CGGOH XCDO ND ZWOCH SHZP CP CG ZWO QNHXV ND DNHRP CG ZWO
INNER LIFE OF THEIR ARTS IS IN THE WORLD OF FORMS IN THE

YHNKOPP ND VCSXOKZCK SGV CZP SHLTROGZ BJ ROZSYWNH
PROCESS OF DIALECTIC AND ITS ARGUMENT BY METAPHOR
```

By sorting on the plaintext alphabet, we obtain

```
plain    A B C D E F G H I J K L M N O P Q R S T U V W X Y Z
cipher   S B K V O D L W C _ _ X R G N Y _ H P Z T I Q _ _ _
```

The cipher alphabet does not appear to be derived from a simple keyword. Let us experiment with possible keyword columnar transpositions. The first keyword letter is S and the next possible letter in a real word is O. This suggests that, if this is the mixing method, we should be able to fill in

```
S O _ _ _ _ _
B _ _ _ _ _ _
K _ _ _ _ _ _
V _ _ _ _
```

by columns, left to right, to obtain the keyword in the top row. We quickly obtain

```
S O C R _ T _
B D _ G H I _
K L _ N P Q _
V W X Y Z _
```

The keyword appears to be SOCRATES, so we are able to finish filling in the table and recover the most likely cipher alphabet:

---

[14]Edward Rothstein, *Emblems of Mind: The Inner Life of Music and Mathematics*, Times Books, New York, 1995.

```
S  O  C  R  A  T  E
B  D  F  G  H  I  J
K  L  M  N  P  Q  U      ◇
V  W  X  Y  Z
```

Not all substitution ciphers are purely alphabetical or numerical. Figure 2.2 shows page 21 of a manual on Masonic ritual prepared around 1827 by Robert B. Folger, a New York physician. It uses a simple substitution to encipher English, though there are a few variant forms to disguise the frequencies of some letters. S. Brent Morris has written a fascinating monograph [55] on the Folger manuscript and its cryptanalysis. This page is reproduced from it. You might wish to decipher the text yourself. Some cribs are "this Great Light of Masonry," "the designs and rules of the Master," "splendid monuments of the ancients," and "the pillar of beauty."

Many derive considerable enjoyment from deciphering cryptograms, which are just ciphertexts obtained by simple substitutions. Many daily newspapers publish amusing statements or quotations in cryptograms. There are interactive cryptogram solvers on the World-wide Web.

Summary

A (monoalphabetic or simple) **substitution cipher** is one in which each occurrence of a symbol in a plaintext is replaced by another specified symbol. The key for a substitution cipher can be represented by a table in which the top row is the plaintext alphabet and the bottom row is the ciphertext alphabet. Methods of generating keys include the use of a keyword and columnar transposition. Cryptanalysis of simple substitutions uses word divisions—if available, letter frequencies, digraph frequencies, trigraph frequencies, and trial and error.

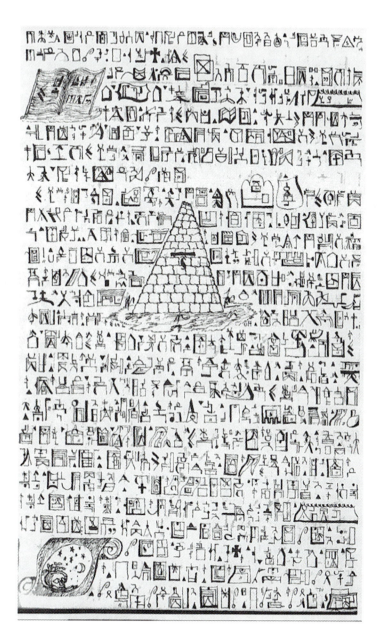

Figure 2.2 Page 21 of the Folger manuscript. (Source: S. Brent Morris, *The Folger Manuscript.*)

EXERCISES

1. The keywords NATURAL SELECTION are to be used to mix the alphabet for a substitution cipher.

   (a) Use this mixed alphabet to encipher[15]

   I HAVE CALLED THIS PRINCIPLE BY WHICH EACH SLIGHT
   VARIATION IF USEFUL IS PRESERVED NATURAL SELECTION

   (b) Use this mixed alphabet to decipher[16]

   WR WCBB FGW UCMTQMM CF N BCPPBR DGKR URPNCB
   PER MPKQSSBR LGK RXCMPRFTR

2. The keywords PRIME MINISTER are to be used to construct a mixed cipher alphabet by columnar transposition.

   (a) Obtain the cipher alphabet.

   (b) Use it to encipher[17]

   ITISM UCHEA SIERT OBECR ITICA LTHAN TOBEC ORREC T

   (c) Use it to decipher

   PFNRK RYRQV RDAPM DGPFN IQKIF MR

3. Decipher the following (word divisions have been preserved).

   (a) SKIUU LBT VUUW B JUDIUS GZ SCQ QZ SKUL BIU OUBO.[18] (*Hint:* Y enciphers as T.)

   (b) BHLOZEJDK QZM UBODRB Z GSJMDKBS DP ODKEBRGDSZKBJEF. JE JM EQB GZME, KDE EQB HJIIF GSBMBKE, EQZE JM EQB UBME HDDS ED EQB PLELSB.[19] (*Hint:* S enciphers as M.)

[15]Charles Darwin (1809–1882), *The Origin of Species by Natural Selection*, Appleton and Co., New York, 1885.

[16]ibid.

[17]Benjamin Disraeli, speech January 24, 1860.

[18]Benjamin Franklin (1706–1790), *Poor Richard's Almanac*, 1733.

[19]Camille Paglia (b. 1947), *Sex, Art, and American Culture*, Vintage Books, New York, 1992.

(c) DX HBPV RLL JRQI VWIXVJXG WG RPPBGXTLU DX PJRLL RLL JRQI
PXERGRVXLU.[20] (*Hint:* L enciphers as L.)

(d) H'M DKQBTD AT K NHEBQIHIE DPM QBKI K JTHJCPEDKVB.[21] (*Hint:*
G enciphers as E.)

(e) RADH AJ CRWCMJ C OANZ CSY JVHCYM VAGH WZHS MLT COH WCAVASP
DLO JLGHVZASP VL ZCIIHS LO ZCVNZ.[22] (*Hint:* F enciphers as
D.)

(f) FJY FVMFJ RA SDGSPA ATKYFJRUC FJSF RA FTDQ, UTF ATKYFJRUC
FJSF RA NUTGU. RO FJYVY GYVY UT AEYSNRUC TV GVRFRUC, FJYVY
GTMDQ BY UT FVMFJ SBTMF SUPFJRUC. FJYVY GTMDQ TUDP BY GJSF
RA.[23] (*Hint:* K enciphers as N.)

(g) MC XGMHZKJ MQ PAYWZSIU, PFWJ PAYWZSQ SMWW VZHI XGMHZKJ.[24]

4. The following is an encipherment using a keyword columnar transposition substitution. Obtain the original plaintext and the keyword.

ZRXE KGREU LJP KUOUJ TULEK LIR RXE ZLSBUEK AERXIBS ZRESB
RJ SBHK GRJSHJUJS L JUF JLSHRJ GRJGUHOUP HJ NHAUEST LJP
PUPHGLSUP SR SBU WERWRK HSHRJ SBLS LNN DUJ LEU GEULSUP
UCXLN[25]

5. The following ciphertext is the result of a monoalphabetic substitution
with natural word divisions ignored:

TNFOS FOZSW PZLOC GQAOZ WAGQR PJZPN ABCZP QDOGR AMTHA
RAXTB AGZJO GMTHA RAVAP ZW[26]

If the word LIBERTY is known to be part of the corresponding plaintext,
recover the rest of the plaintext.

---

[20]Benjamin Franklin, on signing the Declaration of Independence, July 4, 1776.

[21]Ken Kesey (b. 1935), U.S. author: quoted in Tom Wolfe, *The Electric Kool-Aid Acid Test*, Farrar, Strauss and Giroux, New York, 1968.

[22]E. B. White, *Charlottes Web*, Scholastic, New York, 1952.

[23]Susan Sontag (b. 1933), U.S. essayist, *The Benefactor*, Farrar, Strauss, New York, 1963.

[24]Phil Zimmerman, privacy advocate in debates concerning e-mail encryption and author of **Pretty Good Privacy** (PGP).

[25]Abraham Lincoln (1809–1865), dedication address, Gettysburg National Cemetery, November 19, 1863.

[26]Patrick Henry (1736–1799), speech in Virginia Convention, Richmond, March 23, 1775.

6. Table 2.9 shows character frequency data obtained from a 10 000-character sample of English. Assuming the following text is enciphered

Character	Frequency per 10000 characters	Character	Frequency per 10000 characters
Space/Punctuation	2166	C	198
E	952	W	193
T	705	G	182
A	658	Y	169
O	587	F	167
N	531	P	156
I	508	B	113
S	495	V	78
R	475	K	54
H	472	X	16
D	376	J	8
L	314	Q	6
U	218	Z	2
M	201		

Table 2.9　Frequencies of characters in a 10 000-character sample of English.

using a simple substitution, use the table to help determine where the actual word boundaries lie and decipher the text.[27]

```
WNMPTIYWPWNIWPWNMVMPIVMP VVIW UEIQPERALMVOPWNIWPIVMPEUWPTVIYW
UEOPYIAMPIOPIPCVMIWPORVGV OMPWUPWNMPCVMMDOPIEBP OPOW
QQPGVULILQKPRETIA Q IVPWUPAUOWPUTPWNMPXUVQBOP ENIL WIEWO
```

7. The Polybius checkerboard cipher (see Table 1.1) uses a form of substitution in which *pairs* of numerical digits substitute for letters. The first digit is the row in which the letter appears, and the second digit is the column. For example, 42 substitutes for R. Use the Polybius checkerboard to decipher the following quote attributed to one of his contemporaries:[28]

```
11 4323344244 431154243322 342144 1334334411243343
32451323 522443143432
```

----

[27] John H. Conway and Richard K. Guy, *The Book of Numbers*, Springer, New York, 1996.

[28] Sophocles (c.496 B.C.–406 B.C.), *Aletes*.

8. In his book *Gadsby*, author Wright avoids words using that fifth in our list of writing symbols. That is, the letter E never appears in the book. (Note that the first sentence in this exercise has this property!)

   (a) Obtain a copy of *Gadsby* and sample a page to estimate letter frequencies in it. (The author's first name is Ernest.)

   (b) Try writing a paragraph in your next e-mail or letter without using the letter "e."

9. Make a list of all two-letter English words (include common imperatives such as *ah*, *ha*, and *yo*. What percentage start with consonants? with vowels? What percentage have no vowel?

10. How many different monoalphabetic substitution keys are there? Suppose that it is possible for a computer to decipher a message using one of these keys and check if the resulting plaintext is sensible English in one nanosecond (10^{-9} s). In the worst case, roughly how long would it take such a computer to find the original plaintext?

11. (a) Write a computer program that takes as input a 26-letter string constituting the cipher alphabet for a monoalphabetic substitution and a second string constituting the plaintext. The program's output is to be the ciphertext obtained by applying the given substitution to the plaintext. (*Suggestion*: Convert the key string to a numerical array k_0, k_1, ..., k_{25} and the plaintext to a numerical array x_1, x_2, ..., x_n. Then numerical ciphertext y_1, ..., y_n is obtained by
$$y_i = k_{x_i}, \ i = 1, \ldots, \ n.)$$

    (b) Observe, for instance, that if Table 2.10 represents the key for an encryption, then the key for decryption can be obtained by swapping the plain and cipher columns and then sorting the two columns in increasing order of the left values. This is shown in Table 2.11. Incorporate such a sort into the program in part (a) to extend its capability to include deciphering a ciphertext with a given encipherment key string.

12. Write a computer program that takes a ciphertext as input and that produces output consisting of (relative) frequencies of letters in the input. Try it out on ciphertext prepared by someone else using the program in Exercise 11 and attempt a cryptanalysis.

Plain	Cipher	Plain	Cipher
0	16	13	21
1	4	14	13
2	15	15	2
3	0	16	22
4	14	17	20
5	24	18	7
6	5	19	25
7	10	20	19
8	11	21	8
9	1	22	9
10	12	23	6
11	23	24	17
12	3	25	18

Table 2.10 Table for Exercise 11.

Cipher	Plain	Cipher	Plain
0	3	13	14
1	9	14	4
2	15	15	2
3	12	16	0
4	1	17	24
5	6	18	25
6	23	19	20
7	18	20	17
8	21	21	13
9	22	22	16
10	7	23	11
11	8	24	5
12	10	25	19

Table 2.11 Inverse of permutation in Table 2.10.

2.4   Transposition Ciphers

Spartan government officials and military officers of the fourth century B.C.
used a device called a **scytale** (pronounced sit′-a-lee) to encipher and decipher important messages (Figure 1.2). To encipher a message, a sender
would wrap a strip of parchment around a wooden cylinder of an agreed-

upon diameter in a helical fashion, as the figure shows, and write the message parallel to the cylinder's axis. Removing the completed message from the cylinder, the sender effectively jumbled the letters of the message. A receiver would decipher the message when he or she wrapped the parchment around a cylinder of the same diameter as the one the sender used.

The scytale is one example of a **transposition cipher**, one in which plaintext characters are permuted by some means agreed upon by sender and receiver. While, as we will see, simple transposition ciphers do not offer great security, the basic idea can be extended to achieve stronger systems. During World War I, for instance, the French military used a type of double transposition for its field ciphers. In the present, some block ciphers uses a form of transposition as part of their encryption algorithms.

Simple Transpositions

We examine a few instances of simple transposition ciphers and show how cryptanalysis can be done.

Example 2.4.1 The **rail fence cipher** is a simple transposition. For instance, to encipher POETRY IS WHAT IS LOST IN TRANSLATION,[29] we write the message on two lines as

```
P E R I W A I L S I T A S A I N
O T Y S H T S O T N R N L T O
```

in a zig-zag pattern (hence the term *rail fence*) and then write the letters from the first row followed by the letters from the second. The result is the ciphertext

```
PERIWAILSITASAINOTYSHTSOTNRNLTO
```

To decipher MKHSELWYAEATSOL, which was rail-fence enciphered, we divide the ciphertext in half and reverse the steps of encipherment. (When, as in this case, there is an odd number of ciphertext letters, we include the middle letter in the first row):

```
M K H S E L W Y
A E A T S O L
```

This gives a bit of pithy wisdom: MAKE HASTE SLOWLY.[30]   ◇

---

[29]Attributed to Robert Frost (1874–1963) by Louis Untermeyer in a lecture, *Robert Frost: a Backward Look*, 1964.

[30]Suetonius (A.D. 75–150), Roman historian, *Lives of the Caesars*.

The rail fence is one instance of a **columnar transposition**, where the message is written horizontally in a fixed and agreed-upon number of columns and then transcribed letter by letter vertically from the columns, proceeding from left to right.

Example 2.4.2 Suppose sender and receiver have agreed upon a four-column transposition cipher. Then the message THE GOLDEN RULE IS THAT THERE ARE NO GOLDEN RULES[31] is enciphered by first writing

THEG
OLDE
NRUL
EIST
HATT
HERE
AREN
OGOL
DENR
ULES

and then listing the contents of the columns:

TONEHHAODUHLRIAERGELEDUSTREONEGELTTENLRS

Under the agreement between correspondents on four columns for the transposition, a message with length exactly a multiple of 4 can be swiftly deciphered by putting the first quarter of the message in the first column, the second quarter in the second, and so on. Then the original message can be read off row by row. If the length of the message is not exactly a multiple of 4, the receiver makes a small modification. For instance, suppose the message is 62 characters long. Then since $62 = 4 \cdot 15 + 2$, the second two columns of the decipherment tableau will have 15 letters, and the first two will have 16. Thus the receiver writes the first 16 letters of ciphertext in the first column, the next 16 in column 2, the next 15 in column 3 and the final 15 in column 4. $\diamondsuit$

In general, suppose sender and receiver agree on a columnar transposition with c columns. If n is the number of characters in a ciphertext, let $n = qc + r$, where $0 \le r < c$. The receiver will decipher by constructing r columns of

---

[31] George Bernard Shaw (1856–1950), Irish dramatist, critic, and novelist, *Man and Superman, Nine Plays by Bernard Shaw*, Dodd, Mead, and Co., New York 1935.

$q + 1$ characters from the first $r(q + 1)$ ciphertext letters and then $c - r$ columns of q letters from the remaining $(c - r)q$ ciphertext letters.

A ciphertext-only cryptanalysis of a columnar transposition is relatively straightforward. We illustrate by an example.

Example 2.4.3 Suppose we have intercepted the following message and suspect it to have been enciphered by a columnar transposition (What statistical information would suggest this?):

```
TDRLT ILTIE AEIYH VSIPW OAMWE IROTO
ILAII DENOR SSRTN ULSTL MPIHD AAHHD
```

How can we recover the plaintext? An exhaustive search is reasonable. Since there are 60 characters and this is a highly composite number, we might get lucky in trying out numbers of columns that are divisors of 60. If the transposition is two columns, then the tableau will be

```
TI
DL
RA
⋮ ⋮
OH
TH
OD
```

However, the sequence of letters `TIDLRA...` is not English. If there are three columns, then the tableau starts

```
TOS
DAS
RMR
⋮ ⋮ ⋮
```

and again the horizontal sequence `TOSDASRMR...` is not English. You can check that the assumptions of four and five columns lead to the same result. You can also verify that assuming six columns gives

```
TAOISM
DEALSP
RIMARI
LYWITH
THEIND
IVIDUA
```

```
LSRELA
TIONSH
IPTOTH
EWORLD
```

which we easily read as TAOISM DEALS PRIMARILY WITH THE INDIVIDUALS RELATIONSHIP WITH THE WORLD.[32] The worst case in this systematic search would be that we would have to try out the beginnings of 30 tableaus. ◇

Keyword Columnar Transpositions

In a columnar transposition, the order in which the columns of plaintext are transcribed can be determined by a keyword that contains one letter for each column. The column corresponding to the alphabetical first letter of the keyword is the first to be transcribed; the column corresponding to the alphabetic second letter of the keyword is transcribed next; and so on. This procedure can make cryptanalysis incrementally more difficult.

Example 2.4.4 Suppose correspondents have agreed on the keyword BLAKE for a columnar transposition. Then, once the plaintext has been written in five columns, the third column will be the first to be transcribed (because A is the alphabetical first letter in the keyword), followed by the first, fifth, fourth, and second. For instance, if the message is NO BIRD SOARS TOO HIGH IF IT SOARS WITH ITS OWN WINGS,[33] then we encipher it by first writing

```
BLAKE
NOBIR
DSOAR
STOOH
IGHIF
ITSOA
RSWIT
HITSO
WNWIN
GSXQJ
```

---

[32]Benjamin Hoff, *The Te of Piglet*, Dutton, New York, 1992.

[33]William Blake (1757–1827) English poet, engraver, and painter, *The Marriage of Heaven and Hell*, *The Norton Anthology of English Literature*, W. W. Norton & Co., New York, 1979.

(Note that we have added X, Q, and J as filler so that the message length is exactly a multiple of 5. Explain why not doing this would make decipherment difficult, if not impossible.) Then we write

BOOHSWTWXNDSIIRHWGRRHFATONJIAOIOISIQOSTGTSINS

as ciphertext. The recipient, knowing the keyword, would first divide the message length by the length of the keyword and then start filling in the A column with that many letters. Next, he or she would fill in the B column, and so on.   ◇

A cryptanalyst intercepting a message enciphered in this way will not know the keyword or its length, so that person's job is somewhat involved. Nevertheless, it is still possible to break such a cipher.

Example 2.4.5 We have intercepted

OKSAW RNPYG ONEEN EERWI HBEDD IWDFT
YEIDA XORDW TPASZ

and suspect it is a keyword columnar transposition. Since there are 45 characters, the number of columns is either 9 or 5. If we assume five columns, then we write

```
O G W D O
K O I F R
S N H T D
A E B Y W
W E E E T
R N D I P
N E D D A
P E I A S
Y R W X Z
```

and attempt to anagram the columns so that we obtain a sensible beginning in the first row and resulting sensible language in the following rows. The columns can be arranged so that the first row spells such things as WOODG, GODWO, DOWGO, and GOODW. All of these are reasonable beginnings of messages, but only the last one produces meaningful text on the second and following rows:

GOODW
ORKFI

```
NDSTH
EWAYB
ETWEE
NPRID
EANDD
ESPAI
RZYXW
```

which is GOOD WORK FINDS THE WAY BETWEEN PRIDE AND DESPAIR.[34]

The challenge of breaking a keyword transposition is considerable, especially if the number of letters in the cipher (and clear) text is not evenly divisible by the number of letters in the keyword. However, a good guess at—or outright knowledge of—just a bit of the original message may be enough to break such a cipher. The following example illustrates one of the possibilities.

Example 2.4.6 Suppose the message

VNMCY NEAGI WIYLH HKAUR TCLUH EIANR REYEA UANTN NOER

is suspected to have been produced by a keyword columnar transposition and that there is a high likelihood that the original message contained the word MECHANICAL. Recover the original message.

Solution If the number of keyword letters is less than 10, the number of letters in MECHANICAL, then we will see certain digraphs in the ciphertext. For instance, if the keyword length is 9, then ML should appear (why?). Since it does not, we try 8. In this instance, the digraphs MA and EL should appear in the ciphertext. Since they do not, we try a keyword length of 7. If this is correct, then MC, EA, and CL should appear in the ciphertext, and they do! There are seven columns in the encipherment table, five of which have six letters and two of which have seven (why?). One column begins with the first six letters of the ciphertext VNMCYN; we do not yet know whether the next E is included. If we can identify the seven-letter columns, then a process of anagramming the rest should lead quickly to a solution. Because we know that

$$
\begin{array}{ccc}
\vdots & \vdots & \vdots \\
\cdots \quad M & E & C \quad \cdots \\
\cdots \quad C & A & L \quad \cdots \\
\vdots & \vdots & \vdots
\end{array}
$$

---

[34]Wendell Berry, *What are People For?* North Point Press, Berkeley, CA, 1990.

is part of the array, and the MC is part of VNMCYN, we obtain the first parts of three columns:

```
···  V  E  R  ···
···  N  Y  T  ···
···  M  E  C  ···
···  C  A  L  ···
···  Y  O  U  ···
···  N  A  H  ···
     ⋮  ⋮  ⋮
```

Now, looking back at the ciphertext and marking the three columns, we see

$$\overline{\text{VNMCYN}}\text{EAGIWIYLHHKAU}\overline{\text{RTC}}\text{LUHEIANRR}\overline{\text{EYE}}\text{AOANTNNOER}$$

So the second and third beginnings of columns we already have are complete, and one of the first two seven-letter columns is made up of the last seven letters. Thus the message now looks like

```
N     V E R
T     N Y T
N     M E C
N     C A L
O     Y O U
E     N A H
R
```

Since the top row looks like **NEVER**, we tentatively conjecture that the column VNMCYN is complete and that the second column is **EAGIWIY**. This gives

```
N E V E R
T A N Y T
N G M E C
N I C A L
O W Y O U
E I N A H
R Y
```

and the final two groups of letters evidently make the sixth and seventh columns:

```
7 2 1 6 4 3 5
-------------
N E V E R L E
```

```
T A N Y T H I
N G M E C H A
N I C A L K N
O W Y O U A R
E I N A H U R
R Y
```

The plaintext is

NEVER LET ANYTHING MECHANICAL KNOW YOU ARE IN A HURRY[35]

The numbers above the columns indicate the order in which the columns were transcribed to produce the ciphertext, so we have also, in effect, obtained the keyword.   ◇

Permutations and Ciphers

A permutation can serve as the key to a transposition cipher in the following way.

- Correspondents agree on a permutation of n ordered objects, the key.

- The sender enciphers a message by rearranging successive n-letter blocks in the message according to the key permutation. He or she may need to pad the message with extra letters to make its length an even multiple of n.

- The receiver applies the inverse permutation to n-letter blocks to recover the plaintext.

Example 2.4.7 Suppose Maria and Juan agree on the permutation

x	1	2	3	4	5	6	7	8
$p(x)$	5	8	4	2	3	7	1	6

and that Maria wants to encipher

IF YOU ARE MEDIOCRE THEN YOU ARE IN YOUR BEST FORM

Find a ciphertext she would generate.

Solution She might first write

---

[35] Andrew Ross (b. 1956), *Strange Weather: Culture, Science, and Technology in the Age of Limits*, Verso, London, New York, 1991.

IFYOUARE MEDIOCRE THENYOUA REINYOUR BESTFORM

and then encipher by reordering the eight-letter groups according to the key: putting the fifth letter in position 1, the eight in position 2, ..., the sixth in position 8:

UEOFYRIA OEIEDRMC YANHEUTO YRNEIURO FMTESRBO

If she receives the reply

AMIARAMI TABOTYNM OYTSTAED

then she must apply the inverse permutation

x	1	2	3	4	5	6	7	8
$p^{-1}(x)$	7	4	5	3	1	8	6	2

which puts the seventh letter in position 1, the fourth in position 2, the fifth in position 3, and so on. The result is

MARIAIAM NOTATMYB ESTTODAY ◇

Summary

A **transposition cipher** rearranges the characters in a plaintext to produce ciphertext. Standard methods of accomplishing the rearrangement are columnar transposition and keyword columnar transposition. In more mathematical terms, a transposition applies a **permutation** function to the plaintext to produce the ciphertext. Cryptanalysis of columnar transpositions can be initiated by guessing the number of columns or the length of the keyword. Completing a cryptanalysis of a keyword transposition usually involves anagramming. The cryptanalysis is more difficult if some of the columns are incomplete.

EXERCISES

1. Decipher the following message, which was enciphered by the rail fence method: ECIAO EALOE OBATB RULDL NHSOK DNEUY AE.[36]

---

[36]Edna St. Vincent Millay (1892–1950), *Sonnet 22, Harp-Weaver and other Poems*, Harper & Brothers, New York, London, 1923.

2. Suppose a columnar transposition of 9 columns was used to produce the ciphertext WLOWA PELNH NHLEG YSOLD NDWNI TUIEE FHMDR IEBYT CWEOH ARRUE.[37] Decipher the message.

3. Encipher the following quote using a simple columnar transposition with five columns. Pad any partial lines with T: I DO NOT KNOW WHICH MAKES A MAN MORE CONSERVATIVE, TO KNOW NOTHING OF THE PRESENT OR NOTHING OF THE PAST.[38]

4. Encipher COMMON SENSE IS THE BEST DISTRIBUTED COMMODITY IN THE WORLD FOR EVERY MAN IS CONVINCED THAT HE IS WELL SUPPLIED WITH IT[39] using the keyword ALGEBRA.

5. Decipher the following, which was enciphered using a keyword columnar transposition with the keyword GREEK:

   VOESA IVENE MRTNL EANGE WTNIM HTMEE ADLTR NISHO DWOEH[40]

6. The following message was enciphered using a keyword columnar transposition. If it is probable that the plaintext contained the word MATHEMATICS, decipher the message.

   MIDSE WNEIN EAGTS FHTNW RGRWE SEANS HVHTB HAARM YEUEE
   AAUET YUABD BRRTL UTWIE ACETC EOANO RRIHM IEWEW EAWHS
   TTEAJ EKWKT HENX[41]

7. Let p be the permutation given by the table

x	1	2	3	4	5	6	7	8	9	10
$p(x)$	4	6	2	1	8	3	9	10	7	5

   (a) Evaluate the following: $p(5)$, $p(9)$, $p^{-1}(3)$, $p^{-1}(1)$, $p(p(1))$, $p(p(p(8)))$.

   (b) Write the table for $p^{-1}(x)$.

---

[37] James Thurber (1894–1961), cartoon caption, in the New Yorker, June 5, 1937.

[38] John Maynard Keynes (1883–1946), "The End of Laissez-Faire," 1926.

[39] René Déscartes (1596–1650), *Discours de la Méthode*, 1637.

[40] Archimedes (287–212 B.C.), quoted by Pappus of Alexandria in *Synagoge*, Book VIII, c. A.D. 340.

[41] Bertrand Russell (1872–1970), "Mathematics and the Metaphysicians," in J. R. Newman, *The World of Mathematics*, Simon & Schuster, New York, 1956.

(c) Use this permutation to decipher

EHENLVPAER LWHCTIHAID KTATHSICWA FEHHSEHELE
SCACENEDCU[42]

8. Let c be the number of columns for a columnar transposition. If x_1, ..., x_n are the letters of a plaintext, where n is divisible by c and $r = n/c$, then it can be shown that the ciphertext $y_1, y_2, \ldots, y_n$ is given by

$$y_i = x_{((i-1) \text{ MOD } r) \cdot c + ((i-1) \text{ DIV } r) + 1}, \quad i = 1, 2, \ldots, n.$$

Conversely, if ciphertext $y_1, \ldots, y_n$ is obtained with a c-column transposition, then the plaintext is given by

$$x_i = y_{((i-1) \text{ MOD } c) \cdot r + ((i-1) \text{ DIV } c) + 1}, \quad i = 1, 2, \ldots, n.$$

Use these formulas to help in writing a computer program that implements columnar transposition encipherment and decipherment.

2.5 Polyalphabetic Substitutions

Simple substitutions are fairly transparent cipher methods. However, if the cipher alphabet changed periodically throughout a message, then the work of a cryptanalyst would be much harder than for a simple substitution. For instance, suppose that correspondents have agreed to use the substitution given by

```
plain    ABCDEFGHIJKLMNOPQRSTUVWXYZ
cipher   DEFGHIJKLMNOPQRSTUVWXYZABC
```

for the first, third, fifth, etc. letters of a message, and the substitution

```
plain    ABCDEFGHIJKLMNOPQRSTUVWXYZ
cipher   GHIJKLMNOPQRSTUVWXYZABCDEF
```

for the second, fourth, sixth, etc. letters of a message. Then, for instance, the message

---

[42]Maria Montessori (1870–1952), Italian educator, reformer, in *The Speaker's Electronic Reference Collection*, AApex Software, 1994.

ISTHISASGOODASITGETS

enciphers as

LYWNLYDYJURJDYLZJKWY

Notice that the double letters OO are not enciphered as the same characters. This obscuring of letter frequencies is a hallmark of such a method. In this message it turns out that all the I's are spaced an even number of letters apart. A consequence is that each of them is enciphered as L. In fact, the occurrences of the digraph IS are an even number of letters apart. This can provide an entrance for a cryptanalyst.

A legitimate receiver of the enciphered message will reverse the procedure of encipherment by looking up L W L D J R D L J W in the first alphabet to get

$$I\_T\_I\_A\_G\_O\_A\_I\_G\_T\_ \qquad (2.18)$$

and then looking up

Y N Y Y U J Y Z K Y

in the second alphabet to fill in the blanks in (2.18).

The Vigenère Cipher

In Section 1.1, we encountered the Vigenère square and used it to perform an "autokey" method of encipherment using a single-letter priming key. Here we describe a much more secure keyword-based encipherment method that also uses the Vigenère square, which is reproduced for convenience in Table 2.12. With our knowledge of modular arithmetic, we can view this table from a more sophisticated perspective: Since A "is" 0, B "is" 1, C "is" 2, and so on, we can regard the Vigenère square as an addition table modulo 26.

Correspondents agree on a keyword or phrase that can be easily remembered. To encipher a message, one correspondent writes the keyword repeatedly beneath the plaintext, one key letter beneath each plaintext letter. Then for each plain-key pair, she finds the corresponding cipher letter in the Vigenère square where the column headed by the plaintext letter intersects the row labeled by the key letter. For example, a plaintext D with key letter L enciphers as D. (By cutting out an L-shaped piece of paper or cardboard and aligning its vertical and horizontal numbers with the plaintext column and key row, you can make encipherment fairly quick and accurate.)

	A B C D E F G H I J K L M N O P Q R S T U V W X Y Z	(plain)
A	A B C D E F G H I J K L M N O P Q R S T U V W X Y Z	
B	B C D E F G H I J K L M N O P Q R S T U V W X Y Z A	
C	C D E F G H I J K L M N O P Q R S T U V W X Y Z A B	
D	D E F G H I J K L M N O P Q R S T U V W X Y Z A B C	
E	E F G H I J K L M N O P Q R S T U V W X Y Z A B C D	
F	F G H I J K L M N O P Q R S T U V W X Y Z A B C D E	
G	G H I J K L M N O P Q R S T U V W X Y Z A B C D E F	
H	H I J K L M N O P Q R S T U V W X Y Z A B C D E F G	
I	I J K L M N O P Q R S T U V W X Y Z A B C D E F G H	
J	J K L M N O P Q R S T U V W X Y Z A B C D E F G H I	
K	K L M N O P Q R S T U V W X Y Z A B C D E F G H I J	
L	L M N O P Q R S T U V W X Y Z A B C D E F G H I J K	
M	M N O P Q R S T U V W X Y Z A B C D E F G H I J K L	
N	N O P Q R S T U V W X Y Z A B C D E F G H I J K L M	
O	O P Q R S T U V W X Y Z A B C D E F G H I J K L M N	
P	P Q R S T U V W X Y Z A B C D E F G H I J K L M N O	
Q	Q R S T U V W X Y Z A B C D E F G H I J K L M N O P	
R	R S T U V W X Y Z A B C D E F G H I J K L M N O P Q	
S	S T U V W X Y Z A B C D E F G H I J K L M N O P Q R	
T	T U V W X Y Z A B C D E F G H I J K L M N O P Q R S	
U	U V W X Y Z A B C D E F G H I J K L M N O P Q R S T	
V	V W X Y Z A B C D E F G H I J K L M N O P Q R S T U	
W	W X Y Z A B C D E F G H I J K L M N O P Q R S T U V	
X	X Y Z A B C D E F G H I J K L M N O P Q R S T U V W	
Y	Y Z A B C D E F G H I J K L M N O P Q R S T U V W X	
Z	Z A B C D E F G H I J K L M N O P Q R S T U V W X Y	
(key)		

Table 2.12 The Vigenère square. Encipherment of a plaintext letter by a key letter is performed by finding the letter in the table where the column under the plaintext letter and the row beside the key letter intersect. Decipherment of a ciphertext letter with a key letter is performed by locating the cipher letter in the key letter row and looking up the plain letter at the head of that column.

To decipher a received message, the recipient first writes the keyword repeatedly above the ciphertext. For each key-ciphertext letter pair, he finds the row in the Vigenère square labeled with the key letter and then the ciphertext letter in that row. The corresponding plaintext letter appears at the head of the column in which the ciphertext letter sits. (The L-shaped cardboard is handy for this process also.)

Example 2.5.1 Suppose correspondents have agreed on the keyword RHYME and that a sender wants to encipher

```
APRIL SHOWE RSBRI NGMAY FLOWE RS
```

To facilitate encipherment, she writes the keyword repeatedly beneath[43] the plaintext. Then she proceeds to look up the ciphertext letter in the key letter row corresponding to each plaintext letter. Thus A enciphers as R, P enciphers as W, R enciphers as P, and so on. The completed encipherment work is

plain	APRIL	SHOWE	RSBRI	NGMAY	FLOWE	RS
key	RHYME	RHYME	RHYME	RHYME	RHYME	RH
cipher	RWPUP	JOMII	IZZDM	ENKMC	WSMII	IZ

On the other hand, if one of the correspondents receives the ciphertext

```
NOYFH FTYKJ CVUQV JIPUR X
```

then he first writes the key word repeatedly above[44] the ciphertext. He finds the cipher letter in the key letter row and then looks up the plaintext letter at the head of that column: In the R row, cipher N corresponds to plaintext W; in the H row, cipher O corresponds to plaintext H; in the Y row, Y corresponds to A, etc. The complete decipherment work is

key	RHYME	RHYME	RHYME	RHYME	R
cipher	NOYFH	FTYKJ	CVUQR	JIPUR	X
plain	WHATD	OMAYF	LOWER	SBRIN	G ◊

You can see that Vigenère encipherment does not preserve letter frequencies. For instance, if the most frequent letter occurs 25 times in the cleartext and the least frequent occurs 2 times, it is unlikely that there will be this sort of spread in the frequencies of ciphertext letters: The most frequent ciphertext letter is likely to occur fewer than 25 times, and the least frequent is likely to occur more than 2 times. This is part of what makes this method resistant to cryptanalysis. Indeed, the longer and more "random" the keyword, the more even the frequencies of the ciphertext letters.

Example 2.5.2 The bar graphs in Figure 2.3 show the letter distribution of encipherments of an English sentence with keywords of length 3, 4, 5, 6,

---

[43]This practice may vary. The rationale is to provide a helpful mnemonic: Find the *plaintext* letter in the square *first* and then go *down* to the row of the *key* letter.

[44]This is a reminder that decipherment is backward from encipherment, and it also provides a mnemonic: *First* find the *key* letter row, *then* find the *cipher* letter in that row, and *finally* obtain the *plain* letter.

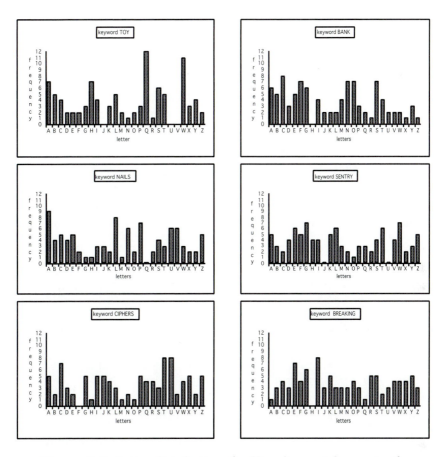

Figure 2.3 Letter distributions for Vigenère encipherments of a 96-letter English plaintext with various-length keywords.

7, and 8. You can see a general flattening of the distribution of letters for longer keywords. ◇

You might think that keyword encipherment would prove to be unbreakable. It is, however, subject to attack if the keyword *length* is known and if the keyword is structured in some way. For instance, the keyword might be an ordinary English word.

Example 2.5.3 Suppose we have intercepted the ciphertext

```
CTMYR DOIBS RESRR RIJYR EBYLD IYMLC CYQXS
RRMLQ FSDXF OWFKT CYJRR IQZSM X
```

and we suspect that it was Vigenère enciphered with a three-letter English word as the key. Then we can discover the message contents and the keyword!

Solution The first, fourth, seventh, tenth, etc. ciphertext letters (call this set 1) are a shift encipherment of the corresponding plaintext letters. So the frequencies of letters in the original message corresponding to these will be preserved. The same is true of the second, fifth, eighth, eleventh, etc. letters (set 2) and of the third, sixth, ninth, twelfth, etc. letters (set 3). Knowing the most frequent letters in English (E, T, N, O, R, I, A, S), we should be able to narrow down the likely plain/cipher correspondences for these three ciphertext letter groups and simply try out the resulting likely keywords.

Table 2.13 shows the frequencies of letters in sets 1, 2, and 3. In set 1,

Set 1 letters	Frequency	Set 2 letters	Frequency	Set 3 letters	Frequency
C	2	T	2	M	2
Y	3	R	4	D	1
O	2	I	4	B	1
S	2	Y	2	E	2
R	3	L	1	R	3
B	1	S	2	J	1
D	2	M	1	L	2
M	1	F	1	Y	1
X	2	X	1	C	2
Q	1	W	1	Q	2
K	1	J	1	S	1
Z	1			F	2

Table 2.13 Letter frequencies for Example 2.5.3.

it is highly likely that ciphertext Y corresponds to a plaintext letter among E, T, N, O, R, I, A, or S. (Because R occurs with the same high frequency, we could just as well work with it. We use Y simply because it occurs first in the ciphertext.) By finding Y in each column of the Vigenère square headed by one of these letters, we find the row corresponding to the keyword letter that would encipher the letter as Y. So plaintext E corresponds to key letter U, plaintext T corresponds to key letter F, and so on. Thus it is likely that the first letter of the keyword is among U, F, L, K, H, Q, Y, and G.

Because R is the first-occurring most frequent letter in set 2, we reason that it is the cipher equivalent of one of E, T, N, O, R, I, A, or S. For this to happen, the second keyword letter must be among N, Y, E, D, A, J, R, or Z. Finally, since R is the most frequent letter in set 3, the third keyword letter is likely to be among these same letters. For readability we arrange these sets of letters in side-by-side columns and systematically look for all three-letter English words we can make by choosing the first letter from the first column, the second from the second, and the third from the third:

$$
\begin{array}{ccc}
U & N & N \\
F & Y & Y \\
L & E & E \\
K & D & D \\
H & A & A \\
Q & J & J \\
Y & R & R \\
G & Z & Z \\
\end{array}
$$

This gives FED, FEN, LEE, LEA, KEN, KEY, HER, GAY, HAY, HEY, LED, HEN, HAD, FAN, FEE, FAD, LAD, LAY, and FEZ. Deciphering the intercepted message with FED gives

```
key      FEDFEDFED...
cipher   CTMYRDOIB...
plain    XPJTN.......
```

which is gibberish. Similarly, FEN, LEE, LEA, and KEN produce nonsense when we decipher with them as keys. With KEY, we obtain

```
KEYKEYKEYKEY....
CTMYRDOIBSRE....
SPOONFEEDING....
```

and the complete plaintext is SPOON FEEDING IN THE LONG RUN TEACHES US NOTHING BUT THE SHAPE OF THE SPOON.[45] You can check that the remaining words do not yield sensible results. ◇

In the preceding example, if we had not known that the keyword was English, then we might have needed to try out *all* of the possible three-letter "words" that could be constructed from the three columns of letters. This would have required checking as many as $8 \cdot 8 \cdot 8 = 512$ keywords, a good deal more than the eight English words we actually used. If we had not known

---

[45]E. M. Forster (1879–1970), quoted in *The Observer*, London, October 7, 1951, quoted in [3].

that the underlying message was English (or any other information about
the distribution of the letters in it), then we would not have been able to
narrow down the choices for keyword letters. This would have necessitated
checking potentially all $26 \cdot 26 \cdot 26 = 17\,576$ possible three-letter keywords. As
you can see, the relatively small bits of knowledge—keyword length, special
structure of the keyword, and structure of the underlying message—have
made cryptanalysis fairly straightforward.

We will eventually learn a couple of methods for estimating the keyword
length from ciphertext. These are the **Friedman**[46] **test** and the **Kasiski**[47]
test. Before we look at these methods, though, we should look at an example
to see how the weaknesses in the Vigenère method, which we exploited in the
last example to crack the cipher, can be overcome. This idea is important in
connection with the notion of **perfect security** in a cipher system, a notion
that was discussed in papers by Claude Shannon[48] in the late 1940s.

Example 2.5.4 Suppose that two correspondents have agreed on a keyword consisting of 30 random letters and that their messages to one another
are never more than 30 characters long. Suppose, moreover, that we know
this and have intercepted the following 24-letter ciphertext, which is an encipherment of English:

$$\texttt{XPQACOPJMFTSSKYEMCUNHDOR}$$

Since we have no knowledge about the keyword (other than it is, in effect, 24
characters long) we might proceed to recover the original message by trying
out all possible keywords that could be formed; there are $26^{24} \approx 9.107 \times 10^{33}$
of them. This is a staggeringly large number, and the task is infeasible even
on the fastest of computers. However, let's assume for the moment that
we have sufficient computer resources to check every one of these possible
keywords. Then, for instance, when we try the keyword

$$\texttt{BLQHVKYCIOPLERYRJHQWJAXT}$$

we obtain the plaintext

$$\texttt{WEATHERHEREHOTANDVERYDRY}$$

---

[46]William Friedman (1891–1969), legendary American military cryptologist.

[47]Friederich W. Kasiski (1805–1881), lieutenant and later major in East Prussian infantry regiment, and author of *Die Geheimschriften und die Dechiffer-kunst*, a book on
secret writing and the art of deciphering.

[48]Claude E. Shannon (1916–2001), engineer at Bell Laboratories regarded as the seminal
writer on modern information theory.

On the other hand, when we try the keyword

$$\text{IBFSJGNJBLGBOSFCYPBFUJKZ}$$

we obtain the plaintext

$$\text{POLITICALUNRESTCONTINUES}$$

Which is the actual message? A knowledge of the correspondents might provide a clue. But there is also a possible keyword that produces the plaintext

$$\text{POLITICALUNRESTNOWWANING}$$

(find it, using the Vigenère square), so if the correspondents are known to be concerned with political matters, the cleartext is not obvious at all. Indeed, as we try out keywords, we will produce *every* sensible English sentence containing 24 letters, along with every sensible 24-letter sentence in any language that uses the Roman alphabet! We will also produce all the nonsense strings of 24 characters as well. Thus, on the basis of this *one* intercepted message and with no knowledge of the keywords length or structure, we cannot break the cipher. ◊

The example illustrates a general fact about the Vigenère method applied appropriately.

> If correspondents have agreed on random keys of some length, and if messages do not exceed this length, then intercepted ciphertext is unbreakable provided a new key is used with each message.

Other Polyalphabetic Ciphers

The Jefferson wheel cypher described in Section 1.1 is another type of polyalphabetic cipher. It uses 36 cipher alphabets, each a rearrangement of the 26 letters of the Roman alphabet. The key information shared by the correspondents would be these cipher alphabets along with the order in which the wheels go on the spindle. The encipherer turned the wheels so that a 36-letter block of plaintext letters lined up, and then he selected another row of aligned letters as the ciphertext. For successive 36-letter blocks, he did the same thing, but the row selected for the ciphertext could vary. There was, then, an element of randomness in the encipherment process. Such a feature is central to the operation of some modern computer-based cryptographic protocols.

The decipherer would align the wheels to show a row of ciphertext letters and then inspect the rows around the wheel to find one that was sensible plaintext. Decipherment, then, relied on the ability of the receiver to recognize plaintext. Cryptanalysis could be performed on a piece of ciphertext by knowing or inferring the period of the alphabet applications and then performing a frequency analysis on the resulting partitions of the ciphertext.

The rotor-type electromechanical cipher machines of the early twentieth century, the most famous example of which is Enigma, carried this idea to an extreme. The changeable nature of electrical connections implemented in the machines' rotors allowed encipherment from millions of alphabets instead of the 36 in Jefferson's design. However, the machine would generate only a fraction of all 26! possible cipher alphabets, and moreover successively generated alphabets were related to one another by the contact arrangements on the rotors. Wiring information about Enigma fell into the hands of the Allies during World War II, and this, along with improper operation of the machines by some of the German code clerks, gave the Allies the ability to read Enigma-enciphered messages.

Rather than have the selection of cipher alphabets made mechanically, some have used so-called **running key** ciphers in which the selection of a cipher alphabet is made according to some agreed-upon stream of characters such as the successive letters in a novel or newspaper. For instance, suppose correspondents agreed to use *Harry Potter and the Prisoner of Azkaban*[49] to generate the running key and to use shifts of the alphabet. Then the cipher alphabets would be those shown in Table 2.14. The ith plaintext letter would be enciphered by finding the column in this array corresponding to the letter and finding the letter in that column at the ith row. Even with running key encipherment, however, the key is ordinary language, and statistics can show up.

Formulas for Polyalphabetic Ciphers

Suppose the keyword for the Vigenère cipher has n letters and that k_0, k_1, k_2, ..., k_{n-1} are the numerical equivalents of these letters. If x_0, x_1, x_2, x_3, ..., is a stream of plaintext letter numerical equivalents and y_0, y_1, y_2, y_3,

---

[49]J. K. Rowling, Scholastic Press, New York, 1999.

```
H  I  J  K  ...  G
A  B  C  D  ...  Z
R  S  T  U  ...  Q
R  S  T  U  ...  Q
Y  Z  A  B  ...  X
P  Q  R  S  ...  O
O  P  Q  R  ...  N
⋮
⋮
```

Table 2.14 Alphabets for a running key cipher.

..., is the ciphertext generated by applying the Vigenère method with this keyword, then

$$y_i = (x_i + k_{i \text{ MOD } n}) \text{ MOD } 26, \quad i = 0, 1, 2, 3, \ldots. \quad (2.19)$$

For a running key cipher, the key letter numerical equivalents k_0, k_1, k_2, k_3, ... are not periodic. If each of these selects a shift of the alphabet, then the plaintext and ciphertext are related by

$$y_i = (x_i + k_i) \text{ MOD } 26, \quad i = 0, 1, 2, 3, \ldots. \quad (2.20)$$

Note the similarity between this formula and that for the keyword Vigenère method. You can use these observations to facilitate writing a computer program that will perform keyword and running-key encryption and decryption. See the Exercises.

Summary

A **polyalphabetic substitution** is a substitution in which the cipher alphabet changes from one plaintext character to the next. One example is the Vigenère cipher: The cipher alphabets are shifts, and the cipher alphabet is selected by a keyword. Any polyalphabetic substitution has the effect of disguising letter frequencies in the underlying plaintext; the longer the keyword (assuming it consists of letters more or less evenly distributed from the alphabet), the more even the letter distribution in the ciphertext. With a knowledge of characteristic letter frequencies in the language of the plaintext and the length of the keyword, a cryptanalysis can be relatively straightforward. However, the general problem of cryptanalysis of a Vigenère-type cipher is very difficult by hand.

EXERCISES

1. Encipher the following plaintexts using the Vigenère method using given keywords.

   (a) LOVE YOUR NEIGHBOR YET PULL NOT DOWN YOUR HEDGE,[50] keyword GEORGE.

   (b) ONE FATHER IS MORE THAN A HUNDRED SCHOOLMASTERS,[51] keyword PRUDENT.

2. Decipher the following ciphertexts using the Vigenère method using the indicated keywords.

   (a) NEKAV MNWJG JBJOA OZXYX RRGRG WRRZN TWIIJ TDEGK JRXBE DVIGI IXETJ RSHJ,[52] keyword BERTRAND.

   (b) MYMRR ODRHF BHRXC SRRTP NZSAA ZKHYK LHLKW GRUXI MIG,[53] keyword TRIANGLE.

3. Determine the eight-letter keywords that will decipher XPBOANYT as the given cleartext.

   (a) ISITOVER

   (b) HEADWEST

   (c) TROUBLES

   (d) HEISFREE

4. Suppose you know the ciphertext EZZXP LEIMH WIYLZ KVBXH KJUE to be a Vigenère encipherment of LIFEI SNOTA DRESS REHEA RSAL.[54] Assuming that

UVUNA RZMHU EPNAL IIIFP LVIYO TGJBU XJM[55]

---

[50] George Herbert (1593–1633), *Jacula Prudentum*, London, 1651.

[51] ibid.

[52] Bertrand Russell (1872–1970), *The Autobiography of Bertrand Russell*, Little Brown, Boston, 1967.

[53] Euclid (c. 300 B.C.), Proclus, *Commentary on the First Book of Euclid's Elements*.

[54] Rose Tremain (b. 1943), quoted in *The Sunday Correspondent*, London, 1989, in [2].

[55] Stendhal (1783–1842), a.k.a. Marie Henri Beyle, *De l'Amour*, 1822.

is enciphered by the same keyword, find the original message.

5. Use the approach of Example 2.5.3 to decipher the following ciphertext, which was Vigenère enciphered with a three-letter English keyword.

```
RLWRV MRLAQ EDUEQ QWGKI LFMFE XZYXA QXGJH FMXKM QWRLA
LKLFE LGWCL SOLMX RLWPI OCVWL SKNIS IMFES JUVAR MFEXZ
CVWUS MJHTC RGRVM RLSZS MREFW XZGRY RLWPI OMYDB SFJCT
                    CAZYX AQ^56
```

6. Shown here are letter distributions for three different ciphertexts, one from a monoalphabetic substitution, one from a polyalphabetic substitution, and one from a transposition.

	A	B	C	D	E	F	G	H	I	J	K	L	M	N	O	P	Q	R	S	T	U	V	W	X	Y	Z
(i)	7	6	9	3	5	6	8	3	4	7	13	10	7	0	1	5	3	6	8	5	4	8	4	8	5	5
(ii)	22	4	12	14	41	10	7	16	29	1	1	6	14	25	21	7	1	15	18	32	0	4	5	0	5	0
(iii)	3	0	3	6	17	1	0	1	5	1	8	6	2	7	0	4	1	5	0	1	4	1	13	1	0	9

Determine which distribution corresponds to which cipher. Explain.

7. Find the decipherment formula corresponding to (2.19) and write a computer program that uses the two formulas to implement the Vigenère cipher.

8. Find the decipherment formula for (2.20) and write a computer program that uses the two inverse formulas to implement the running-key Vigenère cipher.

9. Another possibility for running key encipherment is to use two or more running keys. When the keys are from ordinary language, this tends to obscure key statistics. If k_0, k_1, k_2, ... is one key stream and m_0, m_1, m_2, ... is another, then ciphertext is computed by

$$y_i = (x_i + k_i + m_i) \text{ MOD } 26, \quad i = 1, 2, 3, \ldots.$$

(a) Find a formula for decipherment.

(b) Use this formula to decipher the message

---

[56]Susan Sontag (b. 1933), U.S. essayist, *The Benefactor*, Farrar & Strauss, New York, 1963.

```
XZRLS VSWXN YRCBF IUORK ZOLDR IWBZN SJJVA YXTTL
HDRVB EAKXY CCHEM GZCFS ALUFQ ZCCGL LIIKN DBQGZ
USMXN NQKQH TS⁵⁷
```

which was enciphered with the two running keys, the preamble to the U.S. Constitution and the Gettysburg Address.

(c) Suppose that two keywords $k_0, k_1, \ldots, k_{p-1}$ and $m_0, m_1, \ldots m_{q-1}$ of respective lengths p and q are used to encipher plaintext x_0, $x_1, \ldots$ by the formula

$$y_i = (x_i + k_{i \text{ MOD } p} + m_{i \text{ MOD } q}) \text{ MOD } 26, \qquad i = 1, 2, 3, \ldots.$$

What is the effective length of the keyword with this type of encipherment? Find a formula for decipherment.

2.6   Probability and Expectation

Probability can be defined in rough terms as a quantification of belief in future events. For instance, if you were to toss a coin 100 times and count the number of occurrences of tails, you would expect there to be somewhere close to 50 of them. You quantify this expectation by saying that the probability of getting tails on a *single* coin toss is $\frac{50}{100} = \frac{1}{2}$. Another view is to say that there are two equally likely outcomes, one of which will turn up, so the probability of tails on a single toss is $\frac{1}{2}$.

As another example, consider doing the following with a bag of alphabet soup noodles. Take out 50 A's, 50 B's, and 50 C's, and mix them in a dish. Now conduct the following experiment 75 times: Draw a letter from the dish and then put it back, noting whether it was A, B, or C. Keep a tally for each letter. When you are finished, what do you expect the tallies for A, B, and C to be? On the basis of our knowledge about the equal number of A's, B's, and C's, it is highly plausible that each would be roughly 25; and it is certain that the sum of the tallies will be exactly 75. So the probability of drawing an A on a single trial is about $\frac{25}{75} = \frac{1}{3}$; the same is true for B and C. Another view is simply to say that there are 150 letters in the dish, and

---

⁵⁷Maria Mitchell (1818–1889), U.S. astronomer and educator. From Rosalie Maggio, *The Beacon Book of Quotations by Women*, Beacon Press, Boston, 1992.

50 of them are A's, so the probability of drawing an A on a single trial is $\frac{50}{150} = \frac{1}{3}$. Similarly, the probabilities for B and C are $\frac{1}{3}$.

If the dish instead contained 20 A's, 50 B's, and 80 C's, the same lines of reasoning would lead us to say that the probability of drawing an A on a single trial is $\frac{2}{15}$, of drawing a B is $\frac{1}{3}$, and of drawing a C is $\frac{8}{15}$.

We will formalize these rudimentary notions of probability shortly. But suffice it to say that knowledge of the distribution of possible outcomes of an experiment leads to expectations about the actual outcomes. These expectations can be quantified by probabilities, numbers in the range 0 to 1, which, when they are close to 0, connote low expectation, and when they are close to 1 connote high expectation. Conversely, a knowledge of the probabilities of various outcomes tells us something about the population of possible experimental outcomes.

Counting Permutations and Combinations

In order to work with probabilities of results that are compound in some sense (e.g., rolling *two* or more dice simultaneously, drawing *two* or more letters out of a dish, etc.), we must first examine and practice a few counting techniques.

Example 2.6.1 You are organizing a panel of five people, Andrea, Bill, Carolyn, David, and Emily, and are trying to decide how to arrange them in a row behind the table on the stage. In how many ways can this be done?

Solution You can put Andrea in the leftmost chair and then the remaining four in the others, or you can put Bill in the leftmost chair and the other four in the others, and so on. There are five ways of putting a person in the leftmost chair and seating the remaining people in the other chairs. Thus

$$\begin{pmatrix} \text{Number of ways of} \\ \text{ordering 5 people} \\ \text{in 5 chairs} \end{pmatrix} = \begin{pmatrix} \text{Number of ways} \\ \text{of putting some-} \\ \text{one in the first} \\ \text{chair} \end{pmatrix} \cdot \begin{pmatrix} \text{Number of ways of} \\ \text{ordering 4 people} \\ \text{in 4 chairs} \end{pmatrix}$$

$$= 5 \cdot \begin{pmatrix} \text{Number of ways of} \\ \text{ordering 4 people} \\ \text{in 4 chairs} \end{pmatrix}.$$

Similarly,

$$\begin{pmatrix} \text{Number of ways of} \\ \text{ordering 4 people} \\ \text{in 4 chairs} \end{pmatrix} = 4 \cdot \begin{pmatrix} \text{Number of ways of} \\ \text{ordering 3 people} \\ \text{in 3 chairs} \end{pmatrix}.$$

Continuing this line of reasoning, we see that there are $5 \cdot 4 \cdot 3 \cdot 2 \cdot 1 = 5! = 120$ different orderings of the panelists. $\Diamond$

In general, if an *ordered* array (or **permutation**) of r objects is to be formed by selecting from a collection of n objects (n must be at least r), then there are $n \cdot (n-1) \cdot (n-2) \cdot \cdots \cdot (n-r+2)(n-r+1)$ ways to form the array. Often, the notation $P(n, r)$ is used for the number of permutations of r objects chosen from among n:

$$P(n, r) = n \cdot (n-1) \cdot (n-2) \cdot \cdots \cdot (n-r+2)(n-r+1). \qquad (2.21)$$

While (2.21) is preferable for calculating $P(n, r)$, there is another formula for it that you are asked in the Exercises to prove:

$$P(n, r) = \frac{n!}{(n-r)!}. \qquad (2.22)$$

Example 2.6.2 The letters A, D, F, V, G, and X are written on six cards. In how many ways can a four-letter "word" be formed?

Solution By the general principle, there are $P(6, 4) = 6 \cdot 5 \cdot 4 \cdot 3 = 360$ different such words. $\Diamond$

The concept of an *unordered* selection of objects (or **combination**) is also important.

Example 2.6.3 How many different five-card hands are possible from a standard deck of 52 playing cards?

Solution The key to our problem is to realize that

$$\begin{pmatrix} \text{Number of ways} \\ \text{of ordering 5 cards} \\ \text{selected from 52} \end{pmatrix} = \begin{pmatrix} \text{Number of ways of} \\ \text{selecting 5 cards} \\ \text{from 52} \end{pmatrix} \cdot \begin{pmatrix} \text{Number of ways} \\ \text{of ordering 5 se-} \\ \text{lected cards} \end{pmatrix}.$$

Solving for the left factor on the right-hand side, we have

$$\begin{pmatrix} \text{Number of ways of} \\ \text{selecting 5 cards} \\ \text{from 52} \end{pmatrix} = \frac{\begin{pmatrix} \text{Number of ways of ordering} \\ \text{5 cards selected from 52} \end{pmatrix}}{\begin{pmatrix} \text{Number of ways of ordering} \\ \text{5 selected cards} \end{pmatrix}}.$$

The numerator is $P(52, 5) = 52 \cdot 51 \cdot 51 \cdot 49 \cdot 48$, and the denominator is $P(5,5) = 5 \cdot 4 \cdot 3 \cdot 2 \cdot 1$, so

$$\begin{aligned} \begin{pmatrix} \text{Number of ways of se-} \\ \text{lecting 5 cards from 52} \end{pmatrix} &= \frac{52 \cdot 51 \cdot 50 \cdot 49 \cdot 48}{5 \cdot 4 \cdot 3 \cdot 2 \cdot 1} \\ &= 52 \cdot 51 \cdot 5 \cdot 49 \cdot 4 \\ &= 2\,598\,960. \end{aligned}$$

Note that we have cancelled factors common to the numerator and denominator *before* multiplying out the product. In calculations of this sort, this will always be possible. (Can you explain why?) ◇

The number of combinations of n objects selected r at a time is often denoted $C(n, r)$, or $\binom{n}{r}$ (read "n choose r"). With this notation and the preceding example in mind, we obtain a general formula for $C(n, r)$. We think of two different ways of forming a permutation. On the one hand, we can first select an object from among n objects and immediately put it in its designated position in the ordering; then we select a second and immediately put it in its place; we continue this pattern until we have selected and placed r objects. There are $P(n, r)$ ways to do this, as we already know. On the other hand, we can form a permutation of r objects by first selecting r objects from among the n and then putting the r objects in our ordering. There are $C(n, r)$ ways to select r objects, and for each of these selections there are $P(r, r)$ ways to order them. Thus there are $C(n, r) \cdot P(r, r)$ ways of forming a permutation of r objects from n. So we now know that

$$
\begin{aligned}
P(n, r) &= C(n, r) \cdot P(r, r); \\
C(n, r) &= \frac{P(n, r)}{P(r, r)}.
\end{aligned}
\tag{2.23}
$$

Since we know a formula for $P(n, r)$, we can substitute it into (2.23) to obtain

$$
C(n, r) = \frac{n \cdot (n-1) \cdot (n-2) \cdots (n-r+2) \cdot (n-r+1)}{r \cdot (r-1) \cdot (r-2) \cdots 2 \cdot 1}.
\tag{2.24}
$$

Formula (2.24) is a convenient way to calculate $C(n, r)$, but you may encounter an alternative formula for it in other books:

$$
C(n, r) = \frac{n!}{r!(n-r)!}.
\tag{2.25}
$$

You can easily prove this by using (2.23) and (2.22).

Example 2.6.4 The 22 letters of the Greek alphabet are written on 22 cards and mixed in a box. How many different pairs of letters can we draw? How many different triples?

Solution We are asking for the number of combinations of 22 objects taken two or three at a time. Thus the answer to the first question is

$$
C(22, 2) = \frac{22 \cdot 21}{2 \cdot 1} = 11 \cdot 21 = 231,
$$

and the answer to the second is

$$C(22,\,3) = \frac{22 \cdot 21 \cdot 20}{3 \cdot 2 \cdot 1} = 22 \cdot 7 \cdot 10 = 1540. \quad \diamondsuit$$

We are now ready to return to our exploration of probability.

Probability in General

For an experiment where there are n different equally likely possible outcomes, the **probability** of a result that can occur in r possible ways is $\frac{r}{n}$.

Example 2.6.5 What is the probability of rolling a 2 with a fair six-sided die?

Solution The experiment is rolling the die, so there are six different possible outcomes. The result we seek is rolling a 2, which can occur in 1 way. So the probability of rolling a 2 is $\frac{1}{6}$. $\diamondsuit$

Example 2.6.6 What is the probability of rolling an even number with a die?

Solution The experiment is, again, rolling a die. We obtain an even number if the top face shows a 2, or a 4 or a 6. There are three ways for this result to occur, so the probability of an even number is $\frac{3}{6} = \frac{1}{2}$. $\diamondsuit$

Example 2.6.7 A dish contains 100 alphabet soup noodles: 14 A's, 23 B's, 45 C's, and 18 D's. If one letter is drawn from the dish, what is the probability that it is a C? either an A or a D? not a B?

Solution The experiment is to draw a letter out of the dish; there are 100 possible outcomes of this experiment. Since there are 45 ways of picking a C, the probability of drawing a C is $\frac{45}{100} = 0.45$.

To draw either an A or a D, we pick out one of the 14 A's or one of the 18 D's. There are $14 + 18 = 32$ possible ways to do this, so the probability of drawing A or D is $\frac{32}{100} = 0.32$. Note that this is the same number we would obtain by adding the probability of drawing A, 0.14, to the probability of drawing D, 0.18.

To avoid drawing a B we must draw either an A, a C, or a D. There are $14 + 45 + 18 = 77$ ways to do this, so the probability of not getting a B is

$\frac{77}{100} = 0.77$. Note that this is the same number we would obtain if we first found the probability of drawing a B, 0.23, and then subtracted that from 1. ◇

These examples illustrate some important properties of probabilities:

1. If p is the probability of an experimental result, then $0 \le p \le 1$.

2. If p and q are the probabilities of mutually exclusive results P and Q, then the probability of the result "P or Q" is $p + q$.

3. If p is the probability of a result P, then the probability of the result "not P" is $1 - p$.

Example 2.6.8 There are 26 cards in a box, each with a letter of the Roman alphabet on it. What is the probability of selecting the pair with A and Z on the cards? What is the probability of selecting a pair of letters that are adjacent in the usual ordering?

Solution The experiment is to select a pair of cards from among 26. There are $C(26, 2) = 26 \cdot 25/(2 \cdot 1) = 13 \cdot 25 = 325$ such pairs. For the first question, the result we seek is to select the pair A and Z, and there is just one way to have this pair. Thus the probability of getting the pair A and Z is $\frac{1}{325} = 0.0031$.

To be adjacent, the letters must be AB, BC, CD, ..., XY, YZ. There are 25 such pairs, and each of them has probability $\frac{1}{325} = 0.0031$. Since these results are all mutually exclusive of one another, we add the probabilities to obtain $25 \cdot (0.0031) = 0.075$. ◇

Example 2.6.9 There are 20 alphabet soup A's and 30 B's in a dish. If we select a pair of letters from the dish, what is the probability that both letters are A's? Both are B's? The letters are different?

Solution The experiment is to select a pair of letters from among 50 letters; there are $C(50, 2) = \frac{50 \cdot 49}{2 \cdot 1} = 25 \cdot 49 = 1225$ possible outcomes. The specific result we seek first is that the pair be two A's. Since there are 20 A's from which to choose, there are $C(20, 2) = \frac{20 \cdot 19}{2 \cdot 1} = 10 \cdot 19 = 190$ ways of getting a pair of A's. So the probability of this result is $\frac{190}{1225} = 0.155$.

The reasoning for a pair of B's is the same; there are $C(30, 2) = \frac{30 \cdot 29}{2 \cdot 1} = 15 \cdot 29 = 435$ ways of selecting a pair of B's, so the probability of a pair of

B's is $\frac{435}{1225} = 0.355$. (We would expect this probability to be larger than that for a pair of A's, but are you surprised that it is more than twice the other probability?)

The probability that the selected letters are different is 1 minus the probability that they are the same. Since a pair of A's and a pair of B's are mutually exclusive, the probability that the pair is identical is $0.155 + 0.355 = 0.51$, so the probability they are different is $1 - 0.51 = 0.49$. $\diamond$

Our intuition sometimes fails us in estimating probabilities, and we are surprised at times by the results of our calculations. The following **birthday paradox** is such an example.

Example 2.6.10 If there are 50 people in a room, what is the probability that at least two have the same birthday?

Solution First we observe that the probability of at least two people having the same birthday is 1 minus the probability that at most one person has any given date as a birthday. (We ignore leap years.) Thus if we can find the probability that the birthdays of 50 different people all fall on different days of the year, then we can easily find the probability we want.

Identifying the "experiment" in this case is a bit tricky. It is to "select" birthdays for 50 people. There are 365 choices of a birthday for each of the fifty, so there are 365^{50} ways of selecting birthdays for 50 people. The particular result in which we are interested is that all 50 birthdays be on different dates. The number of ways this can occur is the number of ways of assigning 50 distinct days from among 365 to each of 50 distinct individuals, that is, $P(365, 50)$. So the probability of distinct birthdays for all 50 is

$$\frac{P(365, 50)}{365^{50}} = \frac{365 \cdot 364 \cdot 363 \cdot \cdots \cdot 317 \cdot 316}{365 \cdot 365 \cdot 365 \cdot \cdots \cdot 365 \cdot 365}$$

$$\approx 0.0296.$$

Thus the probability of at least two coincident birthdays is

$$1 - 0.0296 = 0.9704 \approx 97\%;$$

it is highly likely!

In fact, as you can see from Table 2.15 the probability of coincident birthdays grows quickly with size of the crowd. $\diamond$

Another principle of probability is called the **multiplication principle**:

n	p
1	0
2	0.0027
3	0.0082
10	0.117
20	0.411
30	0.706
40	0.891
50	0.97

Table 2.15 Probability p of at least one pair of coincident birthdays in a crowd of n people.

If two (ordered or labeled) experiments are conducted independently of one another (in that the results of one do not influence the results of the other), having respective outcomes with probabilities p and q, then the probability in the compound experiment of the respective outcomes occurring is $p \cdot q$.

Example 2.6.11 Two dice, one red and one blue, are thrown. What is the probability that the red die shows an odd number and the blue die shows a 4?

Solution The dice, we may assume, roll independently of one another. The probability of the red one showing an odd number is $\frac{1}{2}$ and that of the blue showing a 4 is $\frac{1}{6}$, so the probability of the compound outcome is $\frac{1}{2} \cdot \frac{1}{6} = \frac{1}{12}$. $\Diamond$

Example 2.6.12 Two dice, which are not distinguished from one another, are thrown. What is the probability that one die shows an odd number and the other shows a 4?

Solution For the moment, pretend that the dice *are* distinguished: for instance, think of one as red and the other blue. The outcome in which we are interested is that either red is odd and blue is 4 or blue is odd and red is 4. The probabilities of these mutually exclusive events is $\frac{1}{12}$, by the previous example, so the probability of either the first or the second outcome is $\frac{1}{12} + \frac{1}{12} = \frac{1}{6}$. $\Diamond$

Example 2.6.13 There are 20 X's, 15 Y's, and 10 Z's in a dish. Select a letter and put it back. Then mix and select a letter. What is the probability that

1. the first letter is X and the second is Z?

2. the two letters are X and Z?

3. the first letter is Y and the second is also?

4. the two letters are Y?

Solution 1. By replacing the first letter we make the probabilities independent. By the multiplication principle,

$$P(\text{X and then Z}) = P(\text{X}) \cdot P(\text{Z}) = \frac{20}{45} \cdot \frac{10}{45} = \frac{8}{81}.$$

2. We might get X first and then Z, or we might get Z first and then X. These are exclusive of one another, so

$$
\begin{aligned}
P(\text{X and Z}) &= P((\text{X and then Z}) \text{ or } (\text{Z and then X})) \\
&= P(\text{X and then Z}) + P(\text{Z and then X}) \\
&= \frac{8}{81} + \frac{8}{81} = \frac{16}{81}.
\end{aligned}
$$

3. We reason as in 1:

$$P(\text{Y and then Y}) = \frac{15}{45} \cdot \frac{15}{45} = \frac{1}{3} \cdot \frac{1}{3} = \frac{1}{9}.$$

4. The outcome of 2 Y's is the same as the outcome of a Y and then a Y. That is,

$$P(\text{two Ys}) = \frac{1}{9}. \quad \Diamond$$

Example 2.6.14 Think of all the letters of printed English and imagine counting how many A's, B's, C's, ..., Z's there are. Then the probabilities—call them p_0, p_1, ..., p_{25}—of each of these letters would be these counts divided by the total number of letters used in all of printed English. No one has actually done this, but many have estimated p_0, p_1, ..., p_{25} by taking large samples of printed English and doing the same counting and division.

This is how Table 2.6 was produced. How could we use this probability information to determine the probability of selecting two letters at random from printed English and have them be identical? The probability of selecting one letter and having it be an A is p_0. Since the number of letters to choose from is so vast, the probability of selecting a second letter and having it be A is also p_0. Thus, by the multiplication principle, the probability of selecting two A's is $p_0 \cdot p_0 = p_0^2$. The same reasoning shows that the probability of selecting two B's is p_1^2, two C's is p_2^2, and so on. Thus, by property 2 on page 125, the probability that two randomly selected letters in English are identical is[58]

$$p_0^2 + p_1^2 + \cdots + p_{24}^2 + p_{25}^2 = \sum_{i=0}^{25} p_i^2 = 0.065.$$

This probability is different for other natural languages. You are asked in the Exercises to calculate this probability of coincidence for some other languages. This is important in cryptanalysis, as we will see in Section 2.7. ◇

Summary

Probability quantifies expectation: The probability of an outcome from an experiment is the number of ways the outcome can occur divided by the total number of ways the experiment can turn out. For applications, some important consequences of this definition are as follows:

1. A probability is a number in the range 0 to 1; a value near zero indicates the outcome is unlikely, and a value near 1 indicates the outcome is highly likely.

2. The probability that an outcome does not occur is 1 minus the probability that it does occur.

3. If two outcomes are mutually exclusive of one another, then the probability of the outcome "one or the other" is the sum of their respective probabilities.

---

[58]The **summation notation** we use here and in the next section is a helpful shorthand for a sum in which there are many terms, each of which is given by a single formula. If a_i, where $i = 0, 1, 2, \ldots, n$ is a function of i, then $\sum_{i=0}^{n} a_i$ represents the sum of the values of the function a_i at the values of i ranging from 0 to n.

4. If outcomes A and B of two independent experiments have probabilities p and q, then the probability of the compound outcome "A and B" is $p \cdot q$.

EXERCISES

1. Calculate

   (a) $P(6, 3)$ (b) $P(5, 5)$ (c) $P(10, 2)$ (d) $P(26, 4)$ (e) $P(365, 4)$

2. Calculate

   (a) $C(6, 3)$ (b) $C(5, 5)$ (c) $C(10, 2)$ (d) $C(26, 4)$ (e) $C(365, 4)$

3. **Pascal's triangle** provides a way for calculating $C(n, r)$ for small values of n and r. It is the triangular array that begins

   ```
   n
   0                        1
   1                     1     1
   2                  1     2     1
   3               1     3     3     1
   4            1     4     6     4     1
   5         1     5    10    10     5     1
   ```

   Each row in the triangle begins and ends with 1, and the nth row contains $n + 1$ numbers. Successive rows are generated by adding adjacent pairs of numbers on the previous row; for example, the first number on the 6th row is 1, followed by $1 + 5 = 6$, $5 + 10 = 15$, $10 + 10 = 20$, $10 + 5 = 15$, $5 + 1 = 6$, and 1.

   It can be shown in general that if the numbers on row n in the triangle are numbered left to right 0, 1, 2, 3, ..., n, then $C(n, r)$ is the the rth number on the nth row; for example, $C(5, 0) = 1$ and $C(5, 3) = 10$.

   Generate the rows numbered 6, 7, 8, 9, and 10 in Pascal's triangle. Use the triangle to find $C(8, 8)$, $C(9, 4)$, $C(10, 3)$.

4. If the letters K, X, V, P, R, Q, and T are written on seven index cards, how many three-letter "words" can be formed? How many five-letter "words"? In how many ways can three of these cards be selected? In how many ways can five of them be selected?

5. (a) In how many ways can you arrange ten books on a shelf, choosing from among fifteen sitting on the floor?

   (b) In how many ways can you select from among eight people to fill the offices of vice president, secretary, and treasurer in an organization?

6. (a) In how many ways can you choose ten books from among fifteen sitting on the floor?

   (b) In how many ways can you select a committee of four from among eight people?

7. (a) Tennessee auto license plates have three letters followed by three digits. How many different Tennessee plates are possible?

   (b) It used to be that the middle digit of telephone area codes had to be 0 or 1. How many such area codes were possible? If there is no restriction on the choice of the middle digit, how many are there?

   (c) On some Unix-based computer systems, the number of characters in a password must be at least 6. If a password consists of contiguous characters chosen from uppercase, lowercase, and numerical digits, what is the minimum number of different passwords on such a system?

8. You toss a single ordinary fair die. Find the probability that

   (a) the number showing is 6

   (b) the number showing is more than 3

   (c) the number showing is no more than 2

   (d) the number showing is not 4

   (e) the number showing is not 4 or 6

9. You toss two ordinary fair dice. Find the probability that

   (a) the sum of the numbers showing is 2

  (b) the sum of the numbers showing is 3

  (c) the sum of the numbers showing is at most 3

  (d) the sum of the numbers showing is more than 3

  (e) exactly one of the numbers is 6

10. A pot contains 1000 alphabet soup letters, of which there are 257 K's, 321 V's, 105 W's, and 317 Z's. We draw one letter. Find the probability that

   (a) the letter is B

   (b) the letter is W

   (c) the letter is one that comes after H in the alphabet

   (d) the letter is either K or W

   (e) the letter is not Z

   (f) the letter is neither Z nor W

11. A pot contains 1000 alphabet soup letters, of which there are 257 K's, 321 V's, 105 W's, and 317 Z's. We draw two letters. Find the probability that

   (a) both letters are K

   (b) both letters are W

   (c) the first letter is K and the second a Z

   (d) the two letters are K and Z

   (e) neither letter is V

   (f) the letters are identical

12. A pot contains 200 alphabet soup letter A's, 175 B's, 57 C's, and 300 D's.

   (a) If we conduct the experiment of selecting at random a letter out of this pot a thousand times (each time returning the letter to the pot), in how many of these trials would we expect to draw a B? a D?

   (b) If we conduct the experiment of selecting two letters at random (without replacing the first one before drawing the second) a thousand times, in how many of these trials would we expect to draw a pair of A's? B's? C's? D's? In how many of these trials would we expect to draw an identical pair of letters?

13. (a) In English, the probability of three randomly chosen letters being the same is 0.00535 (How is this probability obtained?). If we draw triples of letters a thousand times, about how many of these triples do we expect to be identical?

    (b) Suppose we select three letters from a from an extremely large pool of letters, where the number of A's, B's, ..., Z's are all the same. What is the probability that all three will be identical? If we select a triple of letters ten thousand times, in about how many of these trials would we expect to have all three letters identical?

14. Suppose you have a list of all the students at Rhodes College that have a birthday in May. How many names would you have to select from the list to be at least 50% certain that at least one pair of people you selected shared a birthday? How many would you need if you instead wanted to be at least 90% certain?

15. A sample of 93 letters from a roughly 3000-letter article in the Memphis *Commercial Appeal* on 9/29/98 gave the following letter frequencies:

Letter	A	C	D	E	F	G	H	I	L	M
Count	10	3	7	7	2	5	3	5	2	3

Letter	N	O	P	R	S	T	U	W	Y
Count	7	9	2	8	6	8	2	4	1

    (a) On the basis of this information, what is the probability that a letter chosen at random from the article is N? that it would be either A or Z? that it would be a vowel?

    (b) If you picked a pair of letters at random from the article, what would be the probability that both were G? that one was L and the other T?

16. Find a "typical" text of at least 1000 characters in a foreign language and select a sample of 150 letters. Make a letter frequency table for the sample and use this to estimate the probabilities (a) that a randomly selected letter from the text is E; (b) that a randomly selected letter from the text is a vowel; (c) that a randomly selected pair of letters are both E; (d) that a randomly selected pair of letters are identical vowels.

2.7   The Friedman and Kasiski Tests

In Section 2.5 we were able to cryptanalyze a polyalphabetic cipher under a few assumptions about the keyword and the underlying text. One piece of knowledge we had in that case was the length of the keyword. Usually that information will not be directly available. However, there are two methods of estimating keyword length that we can readily derive and use. These are due to William Friedman[59] and Friederich W. Kasiski.[60]

The Index of Coincidence and the Friedman Test

As we saw in Section 2.3, there is a well-defined distribution of letter probabilities for English. From this distribution, we can calculate the probability that two randomly selected letters are identical. In Example 2.6.14 we found this to be about 0.065. If a shift cipher is applied to an English text, then the distribution is merely shifted. For example, if we apply the Caesar cipher to an English text, then the probability that a letter selected at random is an A is about 0.2% (the probability of cleartext X), the probability of a B is about 2.0% (the probability of cleartext Y), and so on.

However, if we perform a 3-shift on half of the cleartext and a 13-shift on the other half, by using Vigenère encipherment with the two-letter keyword DN, then the probability of selecting an A at random is going to be $\frac{1}{2}(0.2 + 6.7) = 3.45\%$, the probability of selecting a B at random will be about $\frac{1}{2}(2.0 + 7.5) = 4.75\%$, and so on. The distribution of letters is more even than in ordinary English. It is not difficult to see that a longer "random" keyword would even out these probabilities even more. Indeed, for a sequence of increasingly long keywords, all of these probabilities would tend toward $\frac{1}{26} = 0.0385 = 3.85\%$.

One way to test whether a ciphertext is the result of a polyalphabetic cipher is to find the percentage distribution of letters in it. If the frequencies are highly variable, then it is likely the cipher is monoalphabetic, and if the frequencies are more even, then the cipher is likely to be polyalphabetic. We can obtain a single number to measure this for us. The **index of coincidence**, for a ciphertext, denoted I, is the probability that two randomly

---

[59]William F. Friedman (1891–1969) was one of the most eminent pioneers of the twentieth century in applying scientific principles to cryptology.

[60]Friederich W. Kasiski (1805–1881), lieutenant and later major in an East Prussian infantry regiment and author of *Die Geheimschriften und die Dechiffer-kunst*, a book on secret writing and the art of deciphering.

selected letters in it are identical. If this number is close to the probability of selecting identical letters in ordinary English, 0.065, then the cipher is likely to be monoalphabetic. On the other hand, if the index of coincidence is close to the probability of picking two identical letters from a large collection where the letters are evenly distributed, then the cipher is likely to be polyalphabetic. The probability of choosing an identical pair of letters from a pool in which there are equal numbers of the respective letters is easy to calculate: The probability of two A's is $(\frac{1}{26})^2$, of two B's is $(\frac{1}{26})^2$, and so on. So the probability of identical letters is

$$\underbrace{\left(\frac{1}{26}\right)^2 + \left(\frac{1}{26}\right)^2 + \cdots + \left(\frac{1}{26}\right)^2}_{26 \text{ times}} = 26 \cdot \frac{1}{26^2} = \frac{1}{26} = 0.0385.$$

Thus for a polyalphabetic encipherment of English, the index of coincidence will be no less that 0.0385 and no more that about 0.065. We'll first obtain a formula for the index of coincidence and illustrate its use. Then we will derive a way to obtain information about the keyword length from the index.

Let n_0, n_1, n_2, ..., n_{24}, n_{25} be the respective counts of letters A, B, C, ..., Y, Z in the ciphertext, and let $n = n_0 + n_1 \ldots + n_{25}$ be the total number of letters in the text. The experiment is to pick a pair of letters from the text; this can be done in $C(n, 2) = \frac{n(n-1)}{2 \cdot 1}$ ways. The specific result in which we are interested is identical letters. We can choose two A's in $C(n_0, 2) = \frac{n_0(n_0-1)}{2}$ ways, two B's in $C(n_1, 2) = \frac{n_1(n_1-1)}{2}$ ways, and so on. The total number of ways of obtaining identical letters is

$$C(n_0, 2) + C(n_1, 2) + \cdots + C(n_{25}, 2)$$
$$= \frac{1}{2}(n_0(n_0 - 1) + n_1(n_1 - 1) + \cdots + n_{25}(n_{25} - 1)),$$
$$= \frac{1}{2}\sum_{i=0}^{25} n_i(n_i - 1),$$

so the index of coincidence is

$$I = \frac{\frac{1}{2}\sum_{i=0}^{25} n_i(n_i - 1)}{\frac{1}{2}n(n - 1)} = \frac{1}{n(n-1)}\sum_{i=0}^{25} n_i(n_i - 1).$$

Example 2.7.1 Shown here is a ciphertext produced by using the Vigenère method and a keyword[61]:

---

[61] Vaclav Havel, *Disturbing the Peace*, Alfred A. Knopf, New York, 1990.

```
WSPGM HHEHM CMTGP NROVX WISCQ TXHKR
VESQT IMMKW BMTKW CSTVL TGOPZ XGTQM
CXHCX HSMGX WMNIA XPLVY GROWX LILNF
JXTJI RIRVE XRTAX WETUS BITJM CKMCO
TWSGR HIRGK PVDNI HWOHL DAIVX JVNUS
JX
```

Find the index of coincidence.

Solution Shown here are the counts, n_i, of the various letters in the ciphertext.

A	B	C	D	E	F	G	H	I	J	K	L	M
3	2	7	2	4	1	8	9	10	5	5	5	11

N	O	P	Q	R	S	T	U	V	W	X	Y	Z
5	5	5	3	8	8	12	2	8	9	13	1	1

The total number of letters is $n = 152$; also,

$$\sum_{i=0}^{25} n_i(n_i - 1) = 3 \cdot 2 + 2 \cdot 1 + 7 \cdot 6 + \cdots + 13 \cdot 12 + 1 \cdot 0 + 1 \cdot 0 = 1048.$$

Thus the index of coincidence is

$$I = \frac{\sum_{i=0}^{25} n_i(n_i - 1)}{n(n - 1)} = \frac{1048}{152 \cdot 151} = 0.0457. \quad \diamond$$

By taking a different view of the index of coincidence for a text that has been Vigenère enciphered, we can obtain a direct connection with the keyword length.

Suppose that an English text of n letters is Vigenère enciphered with a keyword of length k. We can assume that n is an even multiple of k by ignoring the remainder when n is divided by k. Now arrange the ciphertext letters in k columns, in the order left to right and top to bottom, as shown here:

$$(2.26)$$

Pairs of ciphertext letters can be chosen in one of two ways: from *different* columns, or from *one* column. In how many ways can a pair from different columns be chosen? There are $C(k, 2) = \frac{k(k-1)}{2}$ ways to choose a pair of columns, and there are $\frac{n}{k}$ letters in each column, so there are

$$C(k, 2) \cdot \frac{n}{k} \cdot \frac{n}{k} = \frac{n^2(k-1)}{2k}$$

pairs of letters from different columns. Since the shifts being used to encipher the columns are random, selecting pairs of letters in this fashion will be like choosing them from a collection of letters that is uniformly distributed. The portion of these pairs consisting of identical letters will consequently be about

$$0.0385 \cdot \frac{n^2(k-1)}{2k}. \tag{2.27}$$

In how many ways can a pair of letters be chosen so that both come from *one* column? There are $C(n/k, 2) = \frac{1}{2}(\frac{n}{k})(\frac{n}{k} - 1)$ ways to pick a pair of letters from any single column, and there are k columns, so there are

$$C\left(\frac{n}{k}, 2\right) \cdot k = \frac{1}{2}\left(\frac{n}{k}\right)\left(\frac{n}{k} - 1\right) \cdot k = \frac{n(n-k)}{2k}$$

ways of choosing a pair from one column. The portion of these pairs that are identical should be close to that for ordinary English, so there should be about

$$0.065 \cdot \frac{n(n-k)}{2k} \tag{2.28}$$

identical pairs that arise in this fashion. Thus the total number of ways of getting identical letter pairs is approximately the sum of (2.27) and (2.28). So we can expect the index of coincidence to satisfy

$$I \approx \frac{0.0385 \cdot \frac{n^2(k-1)}{2k} + 0.065\frac{n(n-k)}{2k}}{\frac{n(n-1)}{2}}$$

or, simplifying,

$$I \approx \frac{0.0385 \cdot n(k-1) + 0.065(n-k)}{k(n-1)}. \tag{2.29}$$

(Verify that this formula gives the expected results when $k = 1$ and when $k = n$.) Multiplying both sides of (2.29) by $k(n-1)$, we obtain a linear equation in k that can easily be solved with a bit of algebra. You can check that the final result is

$$k \approx \frac{0.0265n}{(0.065 - I) + n(I - 0.0385)}. \tag{2.30}$$

We have shown that if Vigenère encipherment of an English text is done with a random keyword of length k, then the index of coincidence, text length, and keyword length are related by (2.30). That is, we have an estimate of the keyword length that can be calculated from the text itself.

Example 2.7.2 Consider the ciphertext shown here.

```
IYMEC GOBDO JBSNT VAQLN BIEAO YIOHV XZYZY LEEVI PWOBB OEIVZ
HWUDE AQALL KROCU WSWRY SIUYB MAEIR DEFYY LKODK OGIKP HPRDE
JIPWL LWPHR KYMBM AKNGM RELYD PHRNP ZHBYJ DPMMW BXEYO ZJMYX
NYJDQ WYMEO GPYBC XSXXY HLBEL LEPRD EGWXL EPMNO CMRTG QQOUP
PEDPS LZOJA EYWNM KRFBL PGIMQ AYTSH MRCKT UMVST VDBOE UEEVR
GJGGP IATDR ARABL PGIMQ DBCFW CDFAW UWPPM RGJGN OETGD MCHIM
        EXTBE ENBNI CKYPW NQBLP GIMQO ELICM RCLAC MV
```

Use formula (2.30) to estimate the length of the keyword.

Solution It is necessary to do some counting. We need the frequencies of all the letters and the total number of letters in order to calculate the index of coincidence. Then we can use (2.30) to estimate the keyword length. Table 2.16 gives the letter distributions. There is a total of $n = 337$ letters. Thus

$$
\begin{aligned}
I &= \frac{1}{337 \cdot 336}(13 \cdot 12 + 18 \cdot 17 + 12 \cdot 11 + \cdots + 20 \cdot 19 + 5 \cdot 4 + 6 \cdot 5) \\
&= 0.0428.
\end{aligned}
$$

By (2.30), the keyword length k satisfies

$$k \approx \frac{0.0265 \cdot 337}{(0.065 - 0.0428) + 337(0.0428 - 0.0385)} = 6.20.$$

The closest integer is 6, so on the basis of this information alone, the keyword may be about six letters.

If we felt confident about this keyword length estimate, we could proceed to decipher the message by using the method illustrated in Example 2.5.3. ◇

Letter	Count	Letter	Count
A	13	N	11
B	18	O	17
C	12	P	21
D	15	Q	9
E	26	R	16
F	4	S	7
G	15	T	8
H	9	U	7
I	16	V	8
J	8	W	14
K	9	X	8
L	18	Y	20
M	22	Z	6

Table 2.16 Letter frequencies for Example 2.7.2.

The Kasiski Test

The Kasiski test relies on the occasional coincidental alignment of letter groups in plaintext with the keyword. For example, if the plaintext

THECHILDISFATHEROFTHEMAN[62]

is enciphered with the keyword POETRY, then we obtain ciphertext as follows:

```
plain    THECHILDISFATHEROFTHEMAN
key      POETRYPOETRYPOETRYPOETRY
cipher   IVEVYGARMLMYIVEKFDIVEFRL
```

Notice the repeated ciphertext group IVE appears in this case because the plaintext group THE aligns with the same keyword letters each time it occurs. While a three-letter or longer group may appear more than once in a ciphertext without there being a corresponding repetition in the plaintext, the appearance of a number of such groups indicates more than mere coincidence. By finding the number of letters between such repeated letter groups, we can estimate keyword length. For instance, in our POETRY example, the second occurrence of IVE begins exactly 12 letters after the first, and the third occurs exactly 6 letters after the second. Both of these numbers are multiples of 6, which—*not* coincidentally—is the length of the keyword.

---

[62] William Wordsworth (1770–1850), *My Heart Leaps Up*, in *The Norton Anthology of English Literature*, 4th edition, W. W. Norton & Company, New York, 1979.

The Kasiski test involves finding repeated letter groups in a ciphertext and tabulating the separations between them. The greatest common divisor of these separations, or a divisor of it, stands a good chance of being the keyword length.

Example 2.7.3 The following ciphertext resulted from Vigenère encipherment.

```
WCZOU QNAHY YEDBL WOSHM AUCER CELVE LXSSU
ZLQWB SVYXA RRMJF IAWFN AHBZO UQNAH ULKHG
YLWQI STBHW LJCYV EIYWV YJPFN TQQYY IRNPH
SHZOR WBSVY XARRM JFIAW F
```

Use the Kasiski test to estimate the keyword length.

Solution After some inspection, we find the group NAH repeated three times and the group WBSVYXARRMJFIAWF twice. The second occurrence of NAH begins 48 letters past the beginning of the first, and the third occurrence begins 8 letters after the beginning of the second. Also, the second occurrence of the long repeated group begins 72 letters after the beginning of the first. Since such a long repeated group is very unlikely to occur at random, it is highly likely that the keyword length is a divisor of 72. This is corroborated by the separations for NAH. Since the greatest common divisor of 72, 48, and 8 is 8, a likely keyword length is 8—or possibly 4 or 2. Since a four- or two-letter keyword would offer relatively little security, we reason that the encipherer may have used an eight-letter keyword.   ◇

Summary

The **index of coincidence** I for a ciphertext is the probability that two letters selected at random from it are identical. If the ciphertext is from a monoalphabetic substitution, we expect the index of coincidence to be approximately 0.065; if it is from a polyalphabetic substitution, we expect the index of coincidence to be between this number and 0.0385. With longer keywords, we expect I to be closer to .0385. Formula (2.30) provides an estimate for the length of the keyword from a ciphertext of n characters and index of coincidence I. The **Kasiski test** is another way of estimating the length of the keyword: It obtains possible keyword lengths from the greatest common divisor of the spacing between repeated letter groups in the ciphertext.

EXERCISES

1. In each of the following suppose you have a ciphertext with the given number of letters n and the given index of coincidence I. Assuming that Vigenère encipherment was used in English, estimate the length of the keyword.

   (a) $n = 473$, $I = 0.0422$ (b) $n = 1284$, $I = 0.0518$ (c) $n = 583$, $I = 0.0611$ (d) $n = 20\,849$, $I = 0.0648$

2. Calculate the index of coincidence for the text in Example 2.7.3, and estimate the keyword length. Does it corroborate the estimate obtained from the Kasiski test?

3. Calculate the index of coincidence for the following ciphertext and use it to estimate the keyword length.

   ```
   NGTSA IPNGE PBSFW NCPBN RSAGF ASGEW JSVSF NRCNI WKGPW
   KIGEW PSWWM SYEWN NFUNG EPBSF WNCPB NRSWS PWSWR GMNRS
   USVGH VSBRG MNRSU KCPTS SDNSP BSBMR CNNRS IFHIY INWCF
   SNGMR IKRGP SWMSR CVSCN NCKRS BNCTG GWCPB MRCNN RSUKC
   PNSCK REWCT GENNR SFCVI WRIPA MGFHB MSRCV SNRSX FIVIH
                  SASNG IPRCT IN
   ```

   Use this to estimate the keyword length.

4. Approximately what keyword length will the Friedman test predict if the index of coincidence is 0.03850001? What will it predict if the index of coincidence is 0.06499? Assume that the value of n is large.

5. Find a "typical" text of at least 300 characters in a foreign language you have studied, make a letter frequency table for it, and calculate the probability that a pair of letters selected at random from this sample will be identical.

6. Use the method of Example 2.5.3 to decipher the message in Example 2.7.1. (*Hint*: The keyword length is 5.)

7. It is not hard to see that the derivation of (2.30) can be repeated for any language that uses a 26-letter alphabet.

(a) Show that if the probability of two randomly selected letters being identical is s, then the index of coincidence I for a ciphertext of length n obtained by Vigenère encipherment with a keyword of length k satisfies

$$I \approx \frac{0.0385n(k-I) + s(n-k)}{k(n-1)}.$$

Deduce that

$$k \approx \frac{(s - 0.0385)n}{(s-I) + n(I - 0.0385)}. \qquad (2.31)$$

(b) Use the table of French letter frequencies, obtained from a 1200-letter sample, shown in Table 2.17, to determine an approximate s-value for French.

Letter	Frequency	Letter	Frequency
A	0.0780	N	0.0600
B	0.0053	O	0.0394
C	0.0331	P	0.0260
D	0.0457	Q	0.0027
E	0.2079	R	0.0600
F	0.0161	S	0.0986
G	0.0116	T	0.0717
H	0.0116	U	0.0627
I	0.0538	V	0.0099
J	0.0009	W	0.
K	0.	X	0.0036
L	0.0672	Y	0.0018
M	0.0314	Z	0.0009

Table 2.17 Letter frequences from a sample of French, ignoring diacritical marks.

(c) Suppose a French text of 523 letters has been Vigenère enciphered and has an index of coincidence of 0.0531. Find the likely keyword length.

8. Use the Kasiski test to estimate the length of the keyword used to produce the following ciphertext.

    ANIIX GFXVH XCGZD CWYTU KLZKW HFXSG FARXX GLBRH PTWLI
    IXGFX VHXCG ZDCWY TUKLZ KWCJY OBWHC CCCSF ZDPBO BPTCG

```
FWVXZ LOUJK PRLCE KCCKO CXDRZ YPAPP WQFVV GFANM EFLBV
MYQLL LQPLL NYIJZ MCCXE FWCEW EPMGV RERZY POYCO QYICC
WPVVJ RZCEK HYKNY IJIFY NLZUW PVVJR ZCEKH MJEVH EFWLV
ALQFI VRRGF YVVTL NICZP BWRTI AREUP FPFWQ RWHMJ EZRRR
               ZYIIE MG⁶³
```

2.8 Cryptanalysis of the Vigenère Cipher

The Friedman test for estimating keyword length, even along with the Kasiski test, does not provide a particularly accurate approximation. This is especially true when the ciphertext is small, say 400 characters. Worse, neither method gives any indication of what the keyword is.

There is a wealth of information contained in a Vigenère ciphertext that can be used to sharpen the keyword length estimate and also to obtain the keyword once its length has been established. It is relatively straightforward to use a computer algebra system (CAS) such as Mathematica to tabulate the data in useful forms and perform masses of arithmetic. In what follows, unless it is otherwise stated, calculated results and graphs have been generated in a Mathematica notebook.

The approach taken here was originally communicated to the author by Andrew Simoson who had used the CAS approach in a cryptography course he was teaching. The basic idea here was used as early as 1854 by Charles Babbage⁶⁴ who broke a re-invention of the Vigenère cipher presented to him by John Thwaites, an English dentist. See [76] for more details on Babbage.

We begin with some important observations. When we sort the letter probabilities for printed English in increasing order, plot the points, and connect them with line segments, we obtain the graph shown in Figure 2.4. We'll call this graph the **signature** of English. Now if we take a *sample* of English and apply the same procedure, we will obtain a curve (which we'll

---

⁶³from *Surely You're Joking, Mr. Feynman!*, Richard P. Feynman, as told to Ralph Leighton and edited by Edward Hutchings, Bantam Books, Toronto, 1986.

⁶⁴Charles Babbage (1792 - 1871), brilliant and eccentric Englishman known for such inventions as his mechanical Difference Engines and his design for an Analytical Engine. Though never actually completed, the Analytical Engine is regarded by some as the first programmable computer.

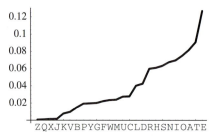

Figure 2.4 The signature of printed English: letter frequencies graphed in ascending order.

call the **signature of the sample**) that increases from left to right as the English signature, but with an important distinction. We expect that one or more letters may not occur at all in our sample, so the left-hand part of this curve is likely to be identically 0. So we expect the sample signature to start out below the English signature. Because the sum of the probabilities for the respective curves must be 1, the sample signature must compensate for the zero value(s) by going above the English signature later. Thus, for a given sample of English, our expectation is that the curves are related as in Figure 2.5.

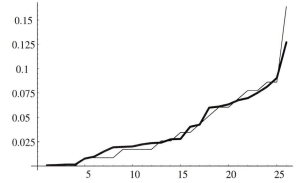

Figure 2.5 The signature of printed English (thick curve) along with that of a sample of English (thin curve).

Observe that *the same sample signature would appear if instead we first enciphered the sample with a monoalphabetic substitution and then plotted the signature of the ciphertext.* We make use of this observation to perform a cryptanalysis on a ciphertext encrypted by the Vigenère method with a keyword of unknown length.

Suppose that the ciphertext

```
ZIHLL WYGSM FAVRE PFBWP ZIHVX FGBVJ JZBRW ZCAFT UMNRO QCRGP
TNBVP BFVDP UBNXX FGBVJ JMJLL UGNOP TIHVW JPRWW JZRAT UBBYE
NYZSC ZCFRZ MCSIL UUYPU VMGED BHVRE FFYMR FHPIH JNUSF UNUIA
PMFMM JFVXJ PZRBA SYFWT PHVWY PNEIL MFLEY JHGIW MCTIY DYBYC
NYZSC ZCFSF SWBLP SYAGP POEVP BMBRZ VLSIP MCAKP WYASF SUPXT
          PHJME IIHXT UQREC FHBXS JHT[65]
```

is enciphered using the Vigenère method using a keyword of unknown length. If the length is 2, then the 1st, 3rd, 5th, etc. letters (which we will call **coset** 1) are all encrypted by a shift corresponding to the first key letter. Similarly, the 2nd, 4th, 6th, etc. letters (which we will refer to as coset 2) are enciphered by a shift corresponding to the second key letter. Here are the letter counts in these two cosets:

Letter	A	B	C	D	E	F	G	H	I	J	K	L	M
Coset 1	2	4	8	2	3	9	6	7	5	7	1	4	5
Coset 2	6	12	3	1	6	10	2	5	7	6	0	5	9

Letter	N	O	P	Q	R	S	T	U	V	W	X	Y	Z
Coset 1	6	2	11	0	7	5	5	6	6	6	6	10	4
Coset 2	3	1	10	2	5	8	4	6	7	5	1	4	8

The letter frequencies are obtained by dividing the numbers in each row by the total number of letters in that coset. Sorting the resulting numbers in ascending order and plotting them, we obtain the signatures of these two cosets, which are shown in Figure 2.6 (a) (the thin curves) along with the signature of English. We see that neither of them is what we would expect from a monoalphabetic substitution on English, so we regard a keyword of length 2 as unlikely.

Supposing the keyword to be of length 3, we divide the ciphertext into 3 cosets (letters 1, 4, 7, ... in the first, letters 2, 5, 8, ... in the second, and letters 3, 6, 9, ... in the third) and plot the signatures of them against that of English. See Figure 2.6 (b) . Again, these signatures are not what we would expect of monoalphabetic substitutions on English. Continuing in this fashion, we generate signatures for the cosets resulting when we assume keyword lengths of 4, 5, 6, and 7. These are shown in Figure 2.6 (c), (d), (e), and (f). The coset signatures for 5 *are* of the form we are seeking, so we tentatively focus on this as the keyword length.

To determine a likely keyword, we first make a general observation. Figure 2.7 shows the letter frequency distribution of English in regular alpha-

---

[65]Luis Buñel (1900 - 1983), Spanish filmmaker, *My Last Sigh*, translated by Abigail Israel, Vintage Books, New York, 1984.

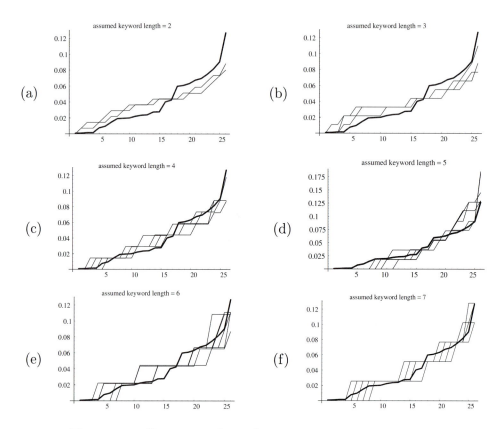

Figure 2.6 Signatures of a ciphertext assuming various length keywords.

betical order. We will call this curve the **scrawl**[66] of English. The letter frequency distribution for a sample of ordinary English (called the **scrawl of the sample**) that is shift enciphered will have roughly the same appearance, except that it will be shifted to the right. To discover the shift amount in such a ciphertext, all we need to do is have the computer draw successive shifts of the sample scrawl until we find the best match.

We apply this reasoning to each of the 5 ciphertext cosets. Coset 1 is a shift encipherment of letters 1, 6, 11, ..., and its scrawl is shown with that of English in Figure 2.8 (a). Sliding the sample scrawl for coset 1 left by one unit, we obtain the graph in Figure 2.8 (b). Notice that the highest peaks

---

[66] A term suggested by Andrew Simoson. The scrawl is reminiscent of bad handwriting, whereas the signature is reminiscent of the flourishes on the signatures of such persons as John Hancock.

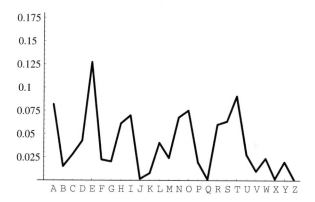

Figure 2.7 The scrawl of English, the graph of letter frequencies in alphabetical order

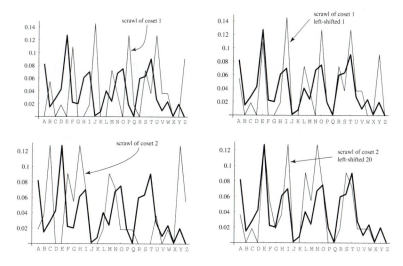

Figure 2.8 Scrawls of cosets 1 and 2 as they come out of the data and shifted to match the scrawl of English.

and the deepest valleys in the two curves tend to coincide fairly well here. If we continue sliding the sample scrawl to the left we find that the two curves do not have such a nice correspondence with the high peaks and low valleys. After trying out all 25 possible shifts, we conclude that the shift of 1 gives the best fit and therefore the first keyword letter is likely to be B.

Figure 2.8 (c) shows the scrawl of coset 2 along with that of English. To align it best with the English scrawl, we find that a left shift of 20 works well, so we conjecture that the second keyword letter is U. We continue in this way (the remaining scrawls, along with the English scrawl in the same scale, are shown in Figure 2.9). You can check the results yourself by pasting together two photocopies of the English scrawl side by side and then sliding a transparent single copy of each coset scrawl over it until you find the best fit. We find the remaining key letters are likely to be N, E, and L. So the keyword

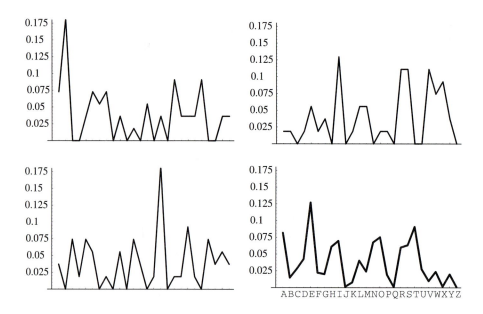

Figure 2.9 The (unshifted) scrawls for cosets 3, 4, and 5 of the ciphertext, along with a same-scale copy of English scrawl for easy photocopying and analysis.

we think might work is BUNEL. We check that Vigenère decipherment with this word gives

```
YOUHA VETOB EGINT OLOSE YOURM EMORY IFONL YINBI TSAND PIECE
STORE ALIZE THATM EMORY ISWHA TMAKE SOURL IVESL IFEWI THOUT
MEMOR YISNO LIFEA TALLJ USTAS ANINT ELLIG ENCEW ITHOU TTHEP
OSSIB ILITY OFEXP RESSI ONISN OTREA LLYAN INTEL LIGEN CEOUR
MEMOR YISOU RCOHE RENCE OURRE ASONO URFEE LINGE VENOU RACTI
ONWIT HOUTI TWEAR ENOTH ING
```

which is sensible English!

To summarize our accomplishment, with only a moderate size piece of ciphertext and a knowledge that it was Vigenère enciphered with a keyword, we have obtained both the plaintext and the keyword. The reader may have though such a feat impossible, and indeed, it would be essentially impossible for one person working alone with only pencil and paper.

Calculating a Keyword

The graphical approach just taken can be quantified. First, we consider the keyword length determination. There is a way to calculate the keyword length that captures the heuristic of the graph inspection method. A likely keyword length l is a number such that the coset signature curves—call them $y = f_j(x)$, $j = 1, 2, \ldots, l$—are on average as low as possible to the left of $x = 13$ and as high as possible to the right of $x = 13$. For each coset signature curve, we can measure this tendency by finding the difference between the area under the curve from $x = 13$ to $x = 26$ and subtracting from that the area under the curve from $x = 1$ to $x = 13$. By taking the average of these differences—call them V_j, $j = 1, 2, \ldots, l$—over all of the l curves, we come up with a measure of how well a family of coset signature curves for a given value of l fits our notion of "overall English-likeness." The averages of the V_j's is

$$A_l = \frac{1}{l} \sum_{j=1}^{l} V_j.$$

A value of l for which A_l is locally as large as possible is a highly likely keyword length. If we compute these averages for various choices of l starting with 1 and working upward, we will encounter a value of l, call it k, such that A_{k+1}, A_{k+2}, ... are smaller than A_k. Then k is highly likely to be the keyword length.

It can be shown that if f_{ij} is the frequency of the ith most frequent letter in coset j, then

$$V_j = \frac{1}{2} \left(\sum_{i=14}^{26} (f_{ij} + f_{i-1,j}) - \sum_{i=2}^{13} (f_{ij} + f_{i-1,j}) \right), \qquad j = 1, 2, \ldots, l.$$

This can be shown by adding up the areas of the trapezoidal regions under the straight line segments constituting the signature curve.

Example 2.8.1 For the ciphertext,

HTIHO RKSLB SZNGM WZJXA BWPON DDMTT SDPOK SFLKC CHIXO TMRUL
RNSUK WFWIO BFITT GFSXN CGXGN REXXI DBIJO TUXYL SFXKR WZKGN
RSMRD WZKRI SELKR SRSUD TAVCO FYWHU HFLKW CDOYH OXPTO HNIRO
GFJUR WFAOL ZMWNE PQPOE JQHGP DQEXO BOISO FQMTA BQAGN RYSXE
SXIMA BFIJI HUSTR SHMYE RMRJC CDVKC HQHHY HTIGU HTSX

several values of V_j, $j = 1, \ldots, l$ and A_l are shown in Table 2.18. The tabulation of the letter frequencies f_{ij} in the various cosets is not presented here, but you can verify that the formulas just given produce the values of V_j shown in the table. You can see that the values of A_l reach a local maximum

l	V_1	V_2	V_3	V_4	V_5	V_6	V_7	V_8	A_l
1	0.326								0.326
2	0.401	0.365							0.383
3	0.427	0.377	0.444						0.416
4	0.573	0.508	0.582	0.475					0.535
5	0.897	0.643	0.806	0.826	0.718				0.778
6	0.585	0.597	0.439	0.682	0.550	0.613			0.578
7	0.686	0.543	0.514	0.685	0.557	0.500	0.559		0.578
8	0.693	0.661	0.758	0.596	0.883	0.633	0.716	0.700	0.705

Table 2.18 Coset signature curve area differences V_j and average A_l of $V_1, \ldots, V_l$ as functions of assumed keyword lengths l. A local maximum value of A_l is attained when $l = 5$.

value at $l = 5$, so this is a likely keyword length. It turns out that if we continue the table past $l = 10$, then there is a second local maximum value of A_l when $l = 10$. Can you explain why this would happen?   ◇

The determination of the letters in the keyword relies on a well-known mathematical fact called the Cauchy-Schwarz inequality. Before we state the theorem, we introduce some terminology that will make our discussion a bit smoother.

A **vector** is an ordered list of numbers; we denote a vector with a boldface letter. For example, $\mathbf{a} = (0.14, 0.06, 0.11)$ is a vector of length 3. The **dot product** of two vectors $\mathbf{a}$ and $\mathbf{b}$ of the same length, denoted $\mathbf{a} \cdot \mathbf{b}$, is the sum of the products of their respective entries: If $\mathbf{a} = (a_1, a_2, \ldots, a_n)$ and $\mathbf{b} = (b_1, b_2, \ldots, b_n)$, then

$$\mathbf{a} \cdot \mathbf{b} = a_1 b_1 + a_2 b_2 + a_3 b_3 + \cdots + a_n b_n.$$

For example, if $\mathbf{a}$ is the vector of length 3 given previously and $\mathbf{b} = (0.078, 0.094, 0.03)$, then $\mathbf{a} \cdot \mathbf{b} = 0.14 \cdot 0.078 + 0.06 \cdot 0.094 + 0.11 \cdot 0.3 = 0.01986$. The **magnitude** of a vector $\mathbf{a}$ is

$$||\mathbf{a}|| = \sqrt{a_1^2 + a_2^2 + \cdots a_n^2}.$$

That is, the magnitude is the square root of the dot product of the vector with itself. For example, if $\mathbf{a}$ is the vector given above, then $||\mathbf{a}|| = \sqrt{0.14^2 + 0.06^2 + 0.11^2} = 0.18788$. Two vectors $\mathbf{a}$ and $\mathbf{b}$ are **parallel** if one is a multiple of the other; that is, $b_i = ca_i$ for $i = 1, 2, 3, \ldots, n$, where c is some constant. We symbolize this by writing $\mathbf{b} = c\mathbf{a}$. For example, if $\mathbf{a} = (1, 3, 2)$ and $\mathbf{b} = (2, 6, 4)$, then $\mathbf{a}$ and $\mathbf{b}$ are parallel; on the other hand, if $\mathbf{a} = (1, 3, 2)$ and $\mathbf{b} = (1, 1, 1)$, then $\mathbf{a}$ and $\mathbf{b}$ are not parallel. There is an important connection among the the dot product of a pair of vectors, the product of their magnitudes, and their parallelness. It is contained in the following theorem.

Theorem 2.8.1 *(Cauchy-Schwarz Inequality) For any two vectors $\mathbf{a}$ and $\mathbf{b}$*

$$\mathbf{a} \cdot \mathbf{b} \le ||\mathbf{a}|| \, ||\mathbf{b}||. \tag{2.32}$$

Moreover, the quantity on the left of the inequality is equal to that on the right if and only if $\mathbf{a}$ is parallel to $\mathbf{b}$.

A proof of this theorem is beyond the scope of the present text.[67] For our purposes here, the important part of this theorem is the last statement. It says that sum on the left of (2.32) is as large as possible when the two vectors $\mathbf{a}$ and $\mathbf{b}$ are parallel. We can infer from this that if the quantity on the left side of (2.32) is *close* to that on the right, then the two vectors are close to being parallel. Also, if we have a fixed vector $\mathbf{b}$ and a collection of other vectors $\mathbf{a}_0, \mathbf{a}_2, \ldots, \mathbf{a}_m$ from which we want to pick one that is "most parallel" to $\mathbf{b}$, we choose i for which $\mathbf{a}_i \cdot \mathbf{b}$ is largest.

Let

$$\begin{aligned}
\mathbf{b} = \ & (0.08167, 0.01492, 0.02782, 0.04253, 0.12702, 0.02228, 0.02015, 0.06094, \\
& 0.06966, 0.00153, 0.00772, 0.04025, 0.02406, 0.06749, 0.07507, 0.01929, \\
& 0.00095, 0.05987, 0.06327, 0.09056, 0.02758, 0.00978, 0.02360, 0.00150, \\
& 0.01974, 0.00074) \tag{2.33}
\end{aligned}$$

---

[67] If you are familiar with two- or three-dimensional vectors and dot products in those contexts, then the identity $\mathbf{a} \cdot \mathbf{b} = ||\mathbf{a}|| \, ||\mathbf{b}|| \cos\theta$, where θ is the angle between the vectors, makes it plausible that the same might hold in n dimensions.

be the letter frequencies in English. Suppose that we have found the keyword length for a Vigenère ciphertext and that

$$\mathbf{a} = (a_1, a_2, a_3, \ldots, a_{26})$$

is one of the sets of coset scrawl values. Because the coset is a shift encipherment of part of an English text, some shift of the values in $\mathbf{a}$ should be close to parallel with $\mathbf{b}$. If we calculate the dot products of all of these shifted copies of $\mathbf{a}$ with $\mathbf{b}$, the largest dot product is likely to correspond to the shift that produced the coset. In other words, we'll get one (likely) key letter. Applying this process to each coset, we can obtain the remaining likely key letters and then check our result by deciphering using the keyword we've found. This numerical procedure quantifies what we did visually with the scrawls.

For instance, to calculate the first keyword letter in our example, we take the vector

$$\mathbf{a} \;=\; (0, 0.05455, 0, 0.01818, 0, 0.1091, 0, 0, 0.01818, 0.1455, 0, 0, 0.07273,$$
$$0.03636, 0, 0.1273, 0.01818, 0, 0.07273, 0.03636, 0.1273,$$
$$0.03636, 0.03636, 0, 0, 0.09091).$$

Then

$$\mathbf{a}_0 \;=\; \mathbf{a}$$
$$\mathbf{a}_1 \;=\; (0.05455, 0, 0.01818, 0, 0.1091, 0, \ldots, 0.03636, 0.03636, \; 0, 0, 0.09091, 0)$$
$$\mathbf{a}_2 \;=\; (0, 0.01818, 0, 0.1091, 0, \ldots, 0.03636, 0.03636, \; 0, 0, 0.09091, 0, 0.05455)$$
$$\mathbf{a}_3 \;=\; (0.01818, 0, 0.1091, 0, \ldots, 0.03636, 0.03636, \; 0, 0, 0.09091, 0, 0.05455, 0)$$
$$\vdots$$
$$\mathbf{a}_{25} \;=\; (0.09091, 0, 0.05455, 0, 0.01818, \ldots 0.03636, 0.03636, 0, 0)$$

and

$$\mathbf{a}_0 \cdot \mathbf{b} \;=\; 0.0249$$
$$\mathbf{a}_1 \cdot \mathbf{b} \;=\; 0.0651$$
$$\mathbf{a}_2 \cdot \mathbf{b} \;=\; 0.0410$$
$$\vdots$$
$$\mathbf{a}_{25} \cdot \mathbf{b} \;=\; 0.0332.$$

Shift	Key letter	$\mathbf{a}_i \cdot \mathbf{b}$				
		$i = 1$	$i = 2$	$i = 3$	$i = 4$	$i = 5$
0	A	0.025	0.035	0.039	0.043	0.041
1	B	0.065	0.038	0.046	0.034	0.044
2	C	0.041	0.038	0.037	0.030	0.039
3	D	0.030	0.034	0.038	0.041	0.030
4	E	0.030	0.035	0.031	0.068	0.040
5	F	0.053	0.043	0.035	0.038	0.040
6	G	0.034	0.036	0.032	0.032	0.029
7	H	0.041	0.039	0.043	0.034	0.045
8	I	0.044	0.038	0.039	0.043	0.040
9	J	0.039	0.040	0.042	0.032	0.036
10	K	0.023	0.034	0.033	0.044	0.030
11	L	0.042	0.036	0.030	0.034	0.065
12	M	0.046	0.036	0.033	0.028	0.039
13	N	0.037	0.038	0.063	0.040	0.030
14	O	0.037	0.044	0.047	0.044	0.030
15	P	0.034	0.034	0.033	0.042	0.050
16	Q	0.045	0.037	0.033	0.035	0.033
17	R	0.043	0.035	0.042	0.049	0.036
18	S	0.042	0.030	0.032	0.042	0.039
19	T	0.027	0.038	0.042	0.042	0.039
20	U	0.037	0.066	0.040	0.036	0.034
21	V	0.042	0.045	0.034	0.036	0.032
22	W	0.038	0.029	0.034	0.029	0.047
23	X	0.035	0.029	0.046	0.037	0.040
24	Y	0.038	0.052	0.039	0.035	0.047
25	Z	0.033	0.039	0.037	0.035	0.025

Table 2.19 Table of dot product values for the coset letter distributions from the ciphertext in this section.

The complete list of values of these dot products is shown in the third column of Table 2.19; the largest value is 0.0651, which corresponds to a key letter B. In the remaining four columns of the same table are shown the dot products resulting when $\mathbf{a}$ is chosen to be the letter frequencies in cosets 2 through 5. In each case the maximum value of the dot product is boxed, and you can read from the second column in the table the corresponding key letter.

Summary

The **signature** of a text is the graph of letter frequencies listed in ascending order. The **scrawl** of a text is the graph of letter frequencies listed in alphabetical order. If a ciphertext is obtained by a simple substitution, then the signature is qualitatively similar to that of English with the difference that the sample signature curve is below that for English at the left end and above it at the right end. For a Vigenère ciphertext, we search for a keyword length by examining coset signatures for various possible keyword lengths. We select the length for which the ensemble of signatures is most like that for monoalphabetic substitutions. We search for keyword letters by shifting the scrawl of each ciphertext coset to match the scrawl of English.

EXERCISES

1. Figure 2.10 shows ciphertext coset signatures for various numbers of cosets. What is the likely keyword length? Explain.

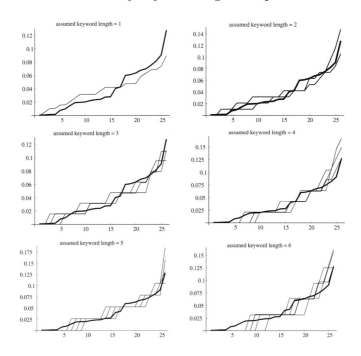

Figure 2.10 Figures for Exercise 1.

2. Find the sample signatures for the following two ciphertexts and compare them with the signature of English.

(a)

```
TSJVI OVGJB AKESP UOJPV EYRDB CZESY NDPHF AQOPJ WHYQD
VZZUC KQSMH WLCSZ ACSJW PUAWA GLUMO VQWYA ANBOG CAKDN
RGOVH ORZBN BZJWP UHDRO JNZUG WYNZI VBZGV WGSJN PHRGE
GHKOF EAUKE RAEWJ GCPUS OHAKS STCSN VSJPS EAJKY IJGON
                VZUNA WFGAQ[68]
```

(b)

```
NLUPB ZPZUV TVYLA OHUJO PSKOV VKYLJ HWABY LKHAD PSSJO
PSKOV VKLXB PWWLK UVDDP AOTHU ZWOFZ PJHST LHUZA VLEWY
LZZPA ZLSMH UKDPA OAOLH UHSFA PJHST PUKAO HALUH ISLZP
AAVIY PUNVY KLYPU AVAOL ZBTVM LEWLY PLUJL PUCVS BUAHY
                PSFHT HZZLK
```

On the basis of your comparison, determine which ciphertext is the monoalphabetic substitution. By looking at signatures for various numbers of cosets, determine the likely keyword length for the other ciphertext.

3. (a) Decipher the monoalphabetic ciphertext in Exercise 2.

   (b) (CAS or other software needed) Determine the keyword for the polyalphabetic ciphertext in Exercise 2 and check the result. [The underlying plaintext in parts (a) and (b) is the same.]

4. By using photocopies of the scrawls in Figure 2.9, verify that the last three letters of the keyword are those indicated in the text.

5. Figure 2.11 shows the coset scrawls from a Vigenère ciphertext encrypted with a four-letter keyword. Determine the keyword.

6. The following ciphertext is the result of a Vigenère encipherment with a four-letter keyword.

```
GPRTS VGNOK BABAR UPPHS KVRBO VGYSB OKMWZ KCVRI OAFGB
GSUBW AKZMB VVMGU NQFYY TIKDP RVYTV ZSKNR LIAJC EUOMP
UGFMP UXVRI DMQZR MZCSB UGXWG NOZNT NBBGC AHSOI ZUXOG
NOXBC OZFUP BUKOI EZRBU KCMCG BIGKK VQKAC NRCBN ZSWAZ
YEUOM PGNOT NCCWS TKBHX OIAJY NAGDC EKCOB JOVGO DTRYD
```

---

[68]Charles Baudelaire (1821–1867), French poet. "The Painter of Modern Life," in *L'Art Romantique*, quoted from [2].

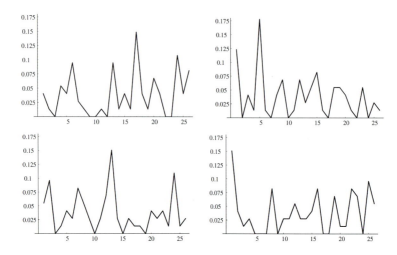

Figure 2.11 Coset scrawls for Exercise 5.

```
PRSKL RIOVG XOACK MBGUD PRUZQ AOYVF UPUNT UQAJB MDASZ
RYDPN ZDPRE CPBAV LQKMT NXOBU KMIHY OAJNS KUOWX RRDPR
SDWGN OARVK ZNZSW A
```

Figure 2.12 shows the scrawls for the four cosets of the ciphertext. Determine the keyword and decipher the ciphertext.

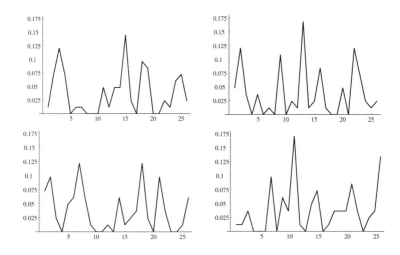

Figure 2.12 Scrawls for the cosets of the ciphertext in Exercise 6.

Shift	Key letter	$\mathbf{a}_i \cdot \mathbf{b}$							
		$i = 1$	$i = 2$	$i = 3$	$i = 4$	$i = 5$	$i = 6$	$i = 7$	$i = 8$
0	A	0.034	0.036	0.033	0.047	0.043	0.069	0.044	0.040
1	B	0.036	0.042	0.045	0.043	0.026	0.040	0.040	0.051
2	C	0.034	0.045	0.033	0.041	0.029	0.035	0.036	0.047
3	D	0.031	0.039	0.030	0.037	0.052	0.034	0.022	0.039
4	E	0.035	0.034	0.046	0.035	0.051	0.036	0.047	0.027
5	F	0.035	0.031	0.052	0.027	0.036	0.037	0.037	0.036
6	G	0.043	0.040	0.037	0.035	0.031	0.036	0.026	0.031
7	H	0.034	0.036	0.028	0.042	0.050	0.029	0.035	0.032
8	I	0.049	0.033	0.044	0.040	0.041	0.025	0.067	0.034
9	J	0.034	0.030	0.047	0.041	0.039	0.036	0.046	0.048
10	K	0.029	0.040	0.041	0.031	0.025	0.042	0.027	0.032
11	L	0.038	0.036	0.028	0.031	0.039	0.053	0.037	0.026
12	M	0.067	0.033	0.039	0.044	0.033	0.041	0.041	0.042
13	N	0.042	0.050	0.031	0.065	0.030	0.037	0.036	0.067
14	O	0.032	0.066	0.038	0.039	0.036	0.042	0.034	0.044
15	P	0.032	0.039	0.035	0.035	0.054	0.054	0.049	0.030
16	Q	0.034	0.023	0.042	0.041	0.034	0.041	0.029	0.033
17	R	0.035	0.037	0.035	0.036	0.017	0.034	0.029	0.043
18	S	0.039	0.044	0.035	0.032	0.044	0.036	0.035	0.031
19	T	0.044	0.035	0.041	0.038	0.071	0.036	0.052	0.037
20	U	0.028	0.034	0.054	0.039	0.043	0.026	0.039	0.039
21	V	0.044	0.042	0.046	0.024	0.027	0.030	0.039	0.031
22	W	0.040	0.026	0.030	0.040	0.042	0.044	0.047	0.031
23	X	0.048	0.031	0.033	0.043	0.039	0.028	0.040	0.046
24	Y	0.037	0.047	0.037	0.041	0.030	0.030	0.039	0.044
25	Z	0.045	0.050	0.038	0.034	0.038	0.049	0.028	0.038

Table 2.20 Data for Exercise 7.

7. The following Vigenère ciphertext has been determined to have a keyword length of 8.

```
MBXLX TPNZG WNLTW EBZII XDBUU GMAHW GJAFF QAENB GBXVM
NWGGB FVDET VRSUG MHMFQ OMUHR MGTSG BGOBB ZMISM HMFOS
HRPAA VZPIG ACIFQ GJEHF WHZRN UXSVB IGIQX EXFAZ CTATA
BPFSN GDACA HFRLS ENEHB RLAVQ ATXBP NJRXC QBGEE NEOMP
EEIAM GNUXO BUQFS BNCWH XRMUT KMGTS MAHWN EAAVB HTANZ
RWYHT PVZUD HLTIF KCOPH UTQFV YSBNM TDCOA WDCFF ZYFLS
BBZSU AWSPR XZJEH DCPFC ZGAEA RMGXR ITPAQ WNUXR TRRHN
```

ETCMO QVCAW[69]

Table 2.20 shows dot products of right-shifts of coset letter frequency vectors and the English letter frequency vector. Use this table to determine the likely keyword that was used to encipher the text and decipher.

2.9   The Hill Cipher; Matrices

In this section we examine a type of **polygraphic** or **block cipher**, one in which blocks of plaintext letters are enciphered as units. The **Hill cipher** is a method of enciphering groups of two or more characters using matrix multiplication. It is exactly analogous to the decimation ciphers we discussed earlier except that the "alphabet" we work with here has $26 \cdot 26 = 676$ "letters." In this sense it amounts to a kind of monoalphabetic substitution, but one where letter frequencies in the plaintext are disguised.

In order to discuss the method, we must first understand matrices and matrix arithmetic.

Matrices

A **matrix** (**matrices** is the plural) is a rectangular array of numbers, such as

$$\begin{bmatrix} 3 & 5 \\ 7 & 1 \end{bmatrix}, \quad \begin{bmatrix} 1 & 0 & 3 \\ 5 & 2 & 8 \end{bmatrix}, \quad \begin{bmatrix} 4 & 1 \\ 1 & 4 \\ 6 & 3 \end{bmatrix}, \quad \begin{bmatrix} 8 & 9 \end{bmatrix}, \quad \begin{bmatrix} 11 \\ 4 \end{bmatrix}.$$

In this book, we will take the entries to be integers. A matrix is said to be of **size** m by n (written $m \times n$) if it has m rows and n columns. The sizes of the preceding matrices are, respectively, 2×2, 2×3, 3×2, 1×2, and 2×1. We write a capital letter such as A or B to represent a matrix.

Multiplication of matrices is an important operation here and elsewhere in this book. Two matrices A and B are **compatible** for multiplication if the number of columns of A is the same as the number of rows in

---

[69]from Thomas Mann, *The Magic Mountain*, Vintage Books Edition, Alfred A. Knopf, Inc., New York, 1969.

B. For example, $A = \begin{bmatrix} 1 & 0 & 3 \\ 2 & 1 & 5 \end{bmatrix}$ and $B = \begin{bmatrix} 8 \\ 9 \\ 10 \end{bmatrix}$ are compatible for mul-

tiplication but $A = \begin{bmatrix} 1 & 2 \\ 3 & 4 \end{bmatrix}$ and $B = \begin{bmatrix} 0 & 5 & 10 & 15 \end{bmatrix}$ are not. You can see that A and B are compatible precisely when their sizes are, respectively, $m \times p$ and $p \times n$.

Whenever $A = \begin{bmatrix} a_1 & a_2 & \cdots & a_p \end{bmatrix}$ is a **row matrix** and $B = \begin{bmatrix} b_1 \\ b_2 \\ \vdots \\ b_p \end{bmatrix}$ is

a **column matrix** , we define their product to be the *number*

$$AB = a_1 b_1 + a_2 b_2 + \cdots a_n b_n.$$

If

$$A = \begin{bmatrix} - & A_1 & - \\ - & A_2 & - \\ & \vdots & \\ - & A_m & - \end{bmatrix},$$

where each row A_i has p entries, and

$$B = \begin{bmatrix} | & | & & | \\ B_1 & B_2 & \cdots & B_n \\ | & | & & | \end{bmatrix},$$

where each column B_j has p entries, then A and B are compatible and we define the **product** of A with B to be the $m \times n$ matrix

$$AB = \begin{bmatrix} A_1 B_1 & A_1 B_2 & \cdots & A_1 B_n \\ A_2 B_1 & A_2 B_2 & \cdots & A_2 B_n \\ \vdots & \vdots & \vdots & \vdots \\ A_m B_1 & A_m B_2 & \cdots & A_m B_n \end{bmatrix}.$$

We will be interested in **square** matrices—those with the same number of rows as columns—and row or column matrices.

If $A = \begin{bmatrix} a & b \\ c & d \end{bmatrix}$ and $B = \begin{bmatrix} e & f \\ g & h \end{bmatrix}$, then you can verify that the product of A with B is the 2×2 matrix

$$AB = \begin{bmatrix} (ae + bg) & (af + bh) \\ (ce + dg) & (cf + dh) \end{bmatrix}.$$

Check also that if $C = \begin{bmatrix} i \\ j \end{bmatrix}$, then

$$AC = \begin{bmatrix} a & b \\ c & d \end{bmatrix} \begin{bmatrix} i \\ j \end{bmatrix} = \begin{bmatrix} ai + bj \\ ci + dj \end{bmatrix},$$

and if $D = \begin{bmatrix} k & l \end{bmatrix}$, then

$$DA = \begin{bmatrix} k & l \end{bmatrix} \begin{bmatrix} a & b \\ c & d \end{bmatrix} = \begin{bmatrix} (ka + lc) & (kb + ld) \end{bmatrix}.$$

Example 2.9.1 Let $A = \begin{bmatrix} 4 & 3 \\ -7 & 1 \end{bmatrix}$, $B = \begin{bmatrix} 2 & 0 \\ 5 & 3 \end{bmatrix}$ and $C = \begin{bmatrix} 10 \\ 20 \end{bmatrix}$. Then

$$AB = \begin{bmatrix} (4 \cdot 2 + 3 \cdot 5) & (4 \cdot 0 + 3 \cdot 3) \\ (-7 \cdot 2 + 1 \cdot 5) & (-7 \cdot 0 + 1 \cdot 3) \end{bmatrix} = \begin{bmatrix} 23 & 9 \\ -9 & 3 \end{bmatrix}$$

and

$$BA = \begin{bmatrix} (2 \cdot 4 + 0 \cdot (-7)) & (2 \cdot 3 + 0 \cdot 1) \\ (5 \cdot 4 + 3 \cdot (-7)) & (5 \cdot 3 + 3 \cdot 1) \end{bmatrix} = \begin{bmatrix} 8 & 6 \\ -1 & 18 \end{bmatrix}.$$

Notice that $AB \neq BA$! Also,

$$AC = \begin{bmatrix} 4 \cdot 10 + 3 \cdot 20 \\ -7 \cdot 10 + 1 \cdot 20 \end{bmatrix} = \begin{bmatrix} 100 \\ -50 \end{bmatrix}. \quad \Diamond$$

Notice in this example that multiplying the two matrices in different orders gave different results. In general, the order in which matrices are multiplied makes a difference in the product. We summarize and emphasize this important fact:

AB may not equal BA: Matrix multiplication is, in general, not commutative.

The **multiplicative identity** matrix is

$$I = \begin{bmatrix} 1 & 0 & 0 & \cdots & 0 \\ 0 & 1 & 0 & \cdots & 0 \\ 0 & 0 & 1 & \cdots & 0 \\ \vdots & \vdots & \vdots & \ddots & \vdots \\ 0 & 0 & 0 & \cdots & 0 \end{bmatrix}.$$

It has the property that $IA = A$ and $AI = A$ for any compatible matrix A. This is the same property that the integer 1 possesses: $1 \cdot a = a \cdot 1 = a$ for any integer a.

For a given matrix A with entries A_{ij} and constant k, we define kA to be the matrix with entries ka_{ij}. For instance, if $k = 5$ and $A = \begin{bmatrix} 9 & 8 \\ 14 & 2 \end{bmatrix}$, then

$$kA = 5 \begin{bmatrix} 9 & 8 \\ 14 & 2 \end{bmatrix} = \begin{bmatrix} 45 & 40 \\ 70 & 10 \end{bmatrix}.$$

You should verify one very important property of this kind of multiplication: $(kA)B = k(AB)$ for any two matrices A and B. This is an exercise.

We can do modular arithmetic with matrices that have integer entries. First, we select a modulus m. Then we say that two integer matrices A with entries a_{ij} and B with entries b_{ij} are **congruent modulo** m if $a_{ij} \equiv b_{ij}$ (mod m), for all choices of i and j. In this case we write

$$A \equiv B \pmod{m}.$$

We also extend the MOD operation to matrices: If A has entries a_{ij}, then

A MOD m is the matrix whose ijth entry is a_{ij} MOD m.

Example 2.9.2 Let $A = \begin{bmatrix} 3 & 8 \\ 11 & 15 \end{bmatrix}$ and $B = \begin{bmatrix} 19 & -8 \\ 43 & -14 \end{bmatrix}$. Then $A \equiv B \pmod{16}$ since $3 \equiv 19 \pmod{16}$, $8 \equiv -8 \pmod{16}$, $11 \equiv 43 \pmod{16}$, and $15 \equiv -1 \pmod{16}$. $\diamondsuit$

Example 2.9.3 Let $A = \begin{bmatrix} 2 & 3 \\ 2 & 1 \end{bmatrix}$ and $B = \begin{bmatrix} 1 & 2 \\ 3 & 2 \end{bmatrix}$, and assume arithmetic is to be done modulo 5. Then

$$AB \equiv \begin{bmatrix} 2 & 3 \\ 2 & 1 \end{bmatrix} \begin{bmatrix} 1 & 2 \\ 3 & 2 \end{bmatrix} \equiv \begin{bmatrix} 11 & 10 \\ 5 & 6 \end{bmatrix} \equiv \begin{bmatrix} 1 & 0 \\ 0 & 1 \end{bmatrix} \pmod{5}$$

and

$$BA \equiv \begin{bmatrix} 1 & 2 \\ 3 & 2 \end{bmatrix} \begin{bmatrix} 2 & 3 \\ 2 & 1 \end{bmatrix} \equiv \begin{bmatrix} 6 & 5 \\ 10 & 11 \end{bmatrix} \equiv \begin{bmatrix} 1 & 0 \\ 0 & 1 \end{bmatrix} \pmod{5}.$$

In each case we get the multiplicative identity matrix. Here A and B are *inverses* modulo 5 in the same sense as 2 and 3 are inverses modulo 5. ◇

Definition 2.9.1 Let m be a given modulus, and let A be a $n \times n$ matrix with integer entries. The matrix is said to be **invertible modulo** m if there is a $n \times n$ matrix B such that $AB = I \,(\text{mod}\, m)$ and $BA = I \,(\text{mod}\, m)$. We call B an **inverse** of A. If there is no such matrix B, we say that A is **not invertible**. If B is any inverse of A moduluo m, then we refer to *the* inverse of A by A^{-1}, where

$$A^{-1} = B \text{ MOD } m.$$

Example 2.9.4 Consider the matrix $A = \begin{bmatrix} 1 & 3 \\ 1 & 3 \end{bmatrix}$, and suppose that arithmetic is modulo 5. Let $B = \begin{bmatrix} a & b \\ c & d \end{bmatrix}$ be an (unknown) inverse. Then we must have

$$\begin{bmatrix} 1 & 3 \\ 1 & 3 \end{bmatrix} \begin{bmatrix} a & b \\ c & d \end{bmatrix} \equiv \begin{bmatrix} 1 & 0 \\ 0 & 1 \end{bmatrix} \quad (\text{mod } 5).$$

That is,

$$\begin{bmatrix} (a + 3c) & (b + 3d) \\ (a + 3c) & (b + 3d) \end{bmatrix} \equiv \begin{bmatrix} 1 & 0 \\ 0 & 1 \end{bmatrix} \quad (\text{mod } 5).$$

Since the corresponding entries of the two matrices must be the same, in particular we have

$$a + 3c \;\equiv\; 1 \quad (\text{mod } 5)$$
$$a + 3c \;\equiv\; 0 \quad (\text{mod } 5).$$

There is no choice of a and c that can satisfy both of these congruences. We conclude from this that there is no inverse matrix B for this particular A; the matrix A is not invertible. ◇

How can we tell if a given matrix has an inverse? The matrix's *determinant* provides the answer.

Definition 2.9.2 The **determinant** of a 2×2 matrix $A = \begin{bmatrix} a & b \\ c & d \end{bmatrix}$ is the number

$$\det(A) = ad - bc.$$

The **determinant of A modulo** m is $\det(A)$ reduced modulo m.

Example 2.9.5 If $A = \begin{bmatrix} 3 & 4 \\ -9 & 8 \end{bmatrix}$, then $\det(A) = 3 \cdot 8 - 4(-9) = 60$, and $\det(A) \equiv 0 \pmod{10}$. $\diamondsuit$

Theorem 2.9.1 *A 2×2 integer matrix $A = \begin{bmatrix} a & b \\ c & d \end{bmatrix}$ is invertible modulo m if and only if $\det(A)$ is relatively prime to m. In this case, the inverse is given by*

$$A^{-1} = \det(A)^{-1} \begin{bmatrix} d & -b \\ -c & a \end{bmatrix} \text{ MOD } m.$$

Proof Suppose that $\det(A)$ is relatively prime to m. Then $\det(A)^{-1}$ is defined modulo m, and we simply check to see whether the two matrices multiplied together yields the 2×2 identity matrix:

$$\left(\det(A)^{-1} \begin{bmatrix} d & -b \\ -c & a \end{bmatrix} \right) \begin{bmatrix} a & b \\ c & d \end{bmatrix}$$

$$= \det(A)^{-1} \left(\begin{bmatrix} d & -b \\ -c & a \end{bmatrix} \begin{bmatrix} a & b \\ c & d \end{bmatrix} \right)$$

$$= \det(A)^{-1} \begin{bmatrix} da - bc & db - bd \\ -ca + ac & -cb + ad \end{bmatrix}$$

$$= (ad - bc)^{-1} \begin{bmatrix} ad - bc & 0 \\ 0 & ad - bc \end{bmatrix}$$

$$= \begin{bmatrix} (ad - bc)^{-1}(ad - bc) & 0 \\ 0 & (ad - bc)^{-1}(ad - bc) \end{bmatrix}$$

$$= \begin{bmatrix} 1 & 0 \\ 0 & 1 \end{bmatrix},$$

and, similarly,

$$A \left(\det(A)^{-1} \begin{bmatrix} d & -b \\ -c & a \end{bmatrix} \right) = \begin{bmatrix} 1 & 0 \\ 0 & 1 \end{bmatrix}.$$

Thus $(\det(A))^{-1} \begin{bmatrix} d & -b \\ -c & a \end{bmatrix}$ is an inverse of A, so by our definition

$$A^{-1} = \det(A)^{-1} \begin{bmatrix} d & -b \\ -c & a \end{bmatrix}.$$

A complete proof of this theorem includes the converse: If A is invertible, then $\det(A)$ is relatively prime to m. However, this part of the proof is a bit technical, and we omit it here. ◇

The first part of the theorem is true in general: An $n \times n$ matrix A is invertible modulo m if and only if $\det(A)$ is relatively prime to m. In cases where the matrix is invertible, the formula for the inverse is more complicated. See the Exercises for the 3×3 case.

Example 2.9.6 Find an inverse of $A = \begin{bmatrix} 1 & 4 \\ 8 & 11 \end{bmatrix}$ modulo 26.

Solution Since $\det(A) = 1 \cdot 11 - 8 \cdot 4 = 11 - 32 = -21 \equiv 5 \pmod{26}$ is relatively prime to 26, by Theorem 2.9.1, the matrix is invertible. By the formula in that theorem,

$$\begin{aligned}
A^{-1} &\equiv 5^{-1} \begin{bmatrix} 11 & -4 \\ -8 & 1 \end{bmatrix} \equiv 21 \begin{bmatrix} 11 & -4 \\ -8 & 1 \end{bmatrix} \\
&\equiv \begin{bmatrix} 21 \cdot 11 & -4 \cdot 21 \\ 21 \cdot (-8) & 21 \cdot 1 \end{bmatrix} \\
&\equiv \begin{bmatrix} 231 & -84 \\ -168 & 21 \end{bmatrix} \\
&\equiv \begin{bmatrix} 23 & 20 \\ 14 & 21 \end{bmatrix} \pmod{26}.
\end{aligned}$$

We can check that this is correct by multiplying by the original matrix:

$$\begin{bmatrix} 1 & 4 \\ 8 & 11 \end{bmatrix} \begin{bmatrix} 23 & 20 \\ 14 & 21 \end{bmatrix} \equiv \begin{bmatrix} 79 & 104 \\ 338 & 391 \end{bmatrix} \equiv \begin{bmatrix} 1 & 0 \\ 0 & 1 \end{bmatrix} \pmod{26}. \quad ◇$$

Example 2.9.7 Solve the system of congruences

$$\begin{aligned}
13x + 4y &\equiv 1 \pmod{26} \\
x + 5y &\equiv 2 \pmod{26}.
\end{aligned} \tag{2.34}$$

Solution We can write the congruences as one single matrix congruence:

$$\begin{bmatrix} 13x + 4y \\ x + 5y \end{bmatrix} \equiv \begin{bmatrix} 1 \\ 2 \end{bmatrix} \pmod{26}. \tag{2.35}$$

Then we recognize the 2×1 matrix on the left as the product of the 2×2 matrix $A = \begin{bmatrix} 13 & 4 \\ 1 & 5 \end{bmatrix}$ with the 2×1 matrix of unknowns $\begin{bmatrix} x \\ y \end{bmatrix}$. So (2.35) can be written as

$$A \begin{bmatrix} x \\ y \end{bmatrix} \equiv \begin{bmatrix} 1 \\ 2 \end{bmatrix} \pmod{26}. \tag{2.36}$$

To solve (2.36), we can multiply both sides of it by A^{-1}:

$$A^{-1}A \begin{bmatrix} x \\ y \end{bmatrix} \equiv A^{-1} \begin{bmatrix} 1 \\ 2 \end{bmatrix} \pmod{26}$$

$$I \begin{bmatrix} x \\ y \end{bmatrix} \equiv A^{-1} \begin{bmatrix} 1 \\ 2 \end{bmatrix} \pmod{26}$$

$$\begin{bmatrix} x \\ y \end{bmatrix} \equiv A^{-1} \begin{bmatrix} 1 \\ 2 \end{bmatrix} \pmod{26}. \tag{2.37}$$

All that remains to do is find A^{-1} from Theorem 2.9.1. Since $\det(A) \equiv 13 \cdot 5 - 4 \cdot 1 \equiv 61 \equiv 9 \pmod{26}$,

$$A^{-1} \equiv 9^{-1} \begin{bmatrix} 5 & -4 \\ -1 & 13 \end{bmatrix} \equiv 3 \begin{bmatrix} 5 & -4 \\ -1 & 13 \end{bmatrix}$$

$$\equiv \begin{bmatrix} 15 & -12 \\ -3 & 39 \end{bmatrix} \equiv \begin{bmatrix} 15 & 14 \\ 23 & 13 \end{bmatrix} \pmod{26}.$$

By (2.37),

$$\begin{bmatrix} x \\ y \end{bmatrix} \equiv \begin{bmatrix} 15 & 14 \\ 23 & 13 \end{bmatrix} \begin{bmatrix} 1 \\ 2 \end{bmatrix} \equiv \begin{bmatrix} 43 \\ 49 \end{bmatrix} \equiv \begin{bmatrix} 17 \\ 23 \end{bmatrix} \pmod{26}.$$

Thus, $x = 17$ and $y = 23$ are solutions, as you can check by substituting back into (2.34). ◇

The Hill Cipher

In 1929, an article appeared in the *American Mathematical Monthly* entitled "Cryptography in an Algebraic Alphabet," written by Lester Hill of Hunter College. The basic idea of the paper was to put the letters of a cleartext into blocks of two, three, four, or however many letters, and to encipher the blocks as other equal-length blocks. In one of his examples, the word MISSISSIPPI, padded with a K on the end to make the number of letters an even multiple of 3, is first blocked into three-letter groups:

MIS SIS SIP PIK

Then the three-letter blocks are enciphered as

BQT SEI AEP YFC

according to the method he describes in the paper. Since there are $26 \cdot 26 \cdot 26 = 26^3 = 17576$ different three-letter blocks possible, each of which can be regarded as a "letter" in a 17576-letter alphabet, Hill's method amounts to a monoalphabetic substitution on this "alphabet."

We are going to use Hill's idea and our knowledge of matrix multiplication to do this same type of substitution using *two-letter* blocks.

The key to our encryption scheme will be a 2×2 matrix A that is invertible modulo 26. If x_1, x_2, x_3, x_4, $\ldots x_{n-1}$, x_n are the numerical equivalents of our n cleartext letters (assume that n is even), we form the matrices $\begin{bmatrix} x_1 \\ x_2 \end{bmatrix}$, $\begin{bmatrix} x_3 \\ x_4 \end{bmatrix}$, $\begin{bmatrix} x_5 \\ x_6 \end{bmatrix}$, $\cdots$, $\begin{bmatrix} x_{n-1} \\ x_n \end{bmatrix}$ and multiply each one by A modulo 26 to obtain $\begin{bmatrix} y_1 \\ y_2 \end{bmatrix} = A \begin{bmatrix} x_1 \\ x_2 \end{bmatrix}$ MOD 26, $\begin{bmatrix} y_3 \\ y_4 \end{bmatrix} = A \begin{bmatrix} x_3 \\ x_4 \end{bmatrix}$ MOD 26,

$\begin{bmatrix} y_5 \\ y_6 \end{bmatrix} = A \begin{bmatrix} x_5 \\ x_6 \end{bmatrix}$ MOD 26, $\cdots$, $\begin{bmatrix} y_{n-1} \\ y_n \end{bmatrix} = A \begin{bmatrix} x_{n-1} \\ x_n \end{bmatrix}$ MOD 26. Then the letters with numerical equivalents y_1, y_2, y_3, y_4, $\ldots$, y_{n-1}, y_n are the ciphertext.

To decipher a message of length n whose numerical equivalents are y_1, y_2, y_3, y_4, $\cdots y_{n-1}$, y_n, we reverse the process. Form $\begin{bmatrix} y_1 \\ y_2 \end{bmatrix}$, $\begin{bmatrix} y_3 \\ y_4 \end{bmatrix}$, $\cdots$, $\begin{bmatrix} y_{n-1} \\ y_n \end{bmatrix}$, and multiply each of these matrices by the inverse of A to obtain $\begin{bmatrix} x_1 \\ x_2 \end{bmatrix} = A^{-1} \begin{bmatrix} y_1 \\ y_2 \end{bmatrix}$ MOD 26, $\begin{bmatrix} x_3 \\ x_4 \end{bmatrix} = A^{-1} \begin{bmatrix} y_3 \\ y_4 \end{bmatrix}$ MOD 26, $\cdots$,

$$\begin{bmatrix} x_{n-1} \\ x_n \end{bmatrix} = A^{-1} \begin{bmatrix} y_{n-1} \\ y_n \end{bmatrix}$$ MOD 26. The numbers $x_1, x_2, x_3, \ldots, x_{n-1}, x_n$ will be the numerical equivalents of the cleartext.

Example 2.9.8 Using the key matrix $A = \begin{bmatrix} 22 & 13 \\ 11 & 5 \end{bmatrix}$, encrypt Hill's example message MISSISSIPPIK.

Solution The numerical equivalents of the message are

$$12, 8, 18, 18, 8, 18, 18, 8, 15, 15, 8, 10.$$

We then calculate

$$A \begin{bmatrix} 12 \\ 8 \end{bmatrix} \equiv \begin{bmatrix} 4 \\ 16 \end{bmatrix} \quad (\text{mod } 26)$$

$$A \begin{bmatrix} 18 \\ 18 \end{bmatrix} \equiv \begin{bmatrix} 6 \\ 2 \end{bmatrix} \quad (\text{mod } 26)$$

$$A \begin{bmatrix} 8 \\ 18 \end{bmatrix} \equiv \begin{bmatrix} 20 \\ 22 \end{bmatrix} \quad (\text{mod } 26)$$

$$A \begin{bmatrix} 18 \\ 8 \end{bmatrix} \equiv \begin{bmatrix} 6 \\ 4 \end{bmatrix} \quad (\text{mod } 26)$$

$$A \begin{bmatrix} 15 \\ 15 \end{bmatrix} \equiv \begin{bmatrix} 5 \\ 6 \end{bmatrix} \quad (\text{mod } 26)$$

$$A \begin{bmatrix} 8 \\ 10 \end{bmatrix} \equiv \begin{bmatrix} 20 \\ 8 \end{bmatrix} \quad (\text{mod } 26)$$

so the numerical equivalents of the ciphertext are

$$4, 16, 6, 2, 20, 22, 6, 4, 5, 6, 20, 8.$$

This corresponds to the letter sequence

EQGCUWGEFGUI

Notice that repeated letters in the cleartext are disguised! ◇

Example 2.9.9 Decipher the message ZGLXTINABCZE, which was enciphered using the key matrix

$$A = \begin{bmatrix} 3 & 7 \\ 9 & 10 \end{bmatrix}.$$

Solution We need A^{-1} to decipher. Since $\det(A) \equiv 30 - 63 \equiv -33 \equiv 19$ (mod 26), we have

$$A^{-1} \equiv 19^{-1} \begin{bmatrix} 10 & -7 \\ -9 & 3 \end{bmatrix} \equiv 11 \begin{bmatrix} 10 & 19 \\ 17 & 3 \end{bmatrix}$$

$$\equiv \begin{bmatrix} 110 & 209 \\ 187 & 33 \end{bmatrix} \equiv \begin{bmatrix} 6 & 1 \\ 5 & 7 \end{bmatrix} \pmod{26}.$$

The numerical equivalent of the ciphertext is

$$25,\ 6,\ 11,\ 23,\ 19,\ 8,\ 13,\ 0,\ 1,\ 2,\ 25,\ 4,$$

so we calculate (modulo 26)

$$\begin{bmatrix} x_1 \\ x_2 \end{bmatrix} \equiv A^{-1} \begin{bmatrix} 25 \\ 6 \end{bmatrix} \equiv \begin{bmatrix} 0 \\ 11 \end{bmatrix}$$

$$\begin{bmatrix} x_3 \\ x_4 \end{bmatrix} \equiv A^{-1} \begin{bmatrix} 11 \\ 23 \end{bmatrix} \equiv \begin{bmatrix} 11 \\ 8 \end{bmatrix}$$

$$\begin{bmatrix} x_5 \\ x_6 \end{bmatrix} \equiv A^{-1} \begin{bmatrix} 19 \\ 8 \end{bmatrix} \equiv \begin{bmatrix} 18 \\ 21 \end{bmatrix}$$

$$\begin{bmatrix} x_7 \\ x_8 \end{bmatrix} \equiv A^{-1} \begin{bmatrix} 13 \\ 0 \end{bmatrix} \equiv \begin{bmatrix} 0 \\ 13 \end{bmatrix}$$

$$\begin{bmatrix} x_9 \\ x_{10} \end{bmatrix} \equiv A^{-1} \begin{bmatrix} 1 \\ 2 \end{bmatrix} \equiv \begin{bmatrix} 8 \\ 19 \end{bmatrix}$$

$$\begin{bmatrix} x_{11} \\ x_{12} \end{bmatrix} \equiv A^{-1} \begin{bmatrix} 25 \\ 4 \end{bmatrix} \equiv \begin{bmatrix} 24 \\ 23 \end{bmatrix}.$$

The numerical equivalent of the cleartext is

$$0,\ 11,\ 11,\ 8,\ 18,\ 21,\ 0,\ 13,\ 8,\ 19,\ 24,\ 23,$$

and the cleartext itself is `ALLISVANITYX`.   ◇

A ciphertext-only cryptanalysis of a Hill cipher is considerable more difficult than for a monoalphabetic substitution. If the underlying plaintext is English, then the characteristic letter frequencies are obscured. For instance, if the plaintext

I THINK 'TASTE' IS A SOCIAL CONCEPT AND NOT AN ARTISTIC
ONE. I'M WILLING TO SHOW GOOD TASTE, IF I CAN, IN SOMEBODY
ELSE'S LIVING ROOM, BUT OUR READING LIFE IS TOO SHORT FOR
A WRITER TO BE IN ANY WAY POLITE. SINCE HIS WORDS ENTER
INTO ANOTHER'S BRAIN IN SILENCE AND INTIMACY, HE SHOULD
BE AS HONEST AND EXPLICIT AS WE ARE WITH OURSELVES.[70]

is enciphered using the key matrix $A = \begin{bmatrix} 4 & 4 \\ 9 & 3 \end{bmatrix}$, then the resulting ciphertext is

```
XZQJY  RYPLL  EIUGM  WWQDH  AIKTN  DYPPW  SDYPA
NHCSW  MNAIU  ZOEYO  VCTHP  HQYUB  OIWMD  GMCSB
FJQAN  NTHMW  QQWZC  VTROS  XNHFT  HFBWM  BHTDA
EXWQK  AZEFG  TOFSW  QFQYU  BHCMJ  QXRPX  ZXJQF
YVTHN  NYWQU  AVGTS  BIEKT  ZFSWC  GFGOS  RSXJT
HQFQX  SDHKX  JZJQX  THTHI  EMHKT  QKPWT  HMNWE
YMWXD  BAEHE  YVMCU  BUZLL  NNGNL  SGTWQ  YPAUQ
KKJYO  HKAEC  ZTRAT  FX
```

(Punctuation and natural word divisions have been removed.) The graphs in Figure 2.13 show that the letter frequencies in the ciphertext (thick curve)

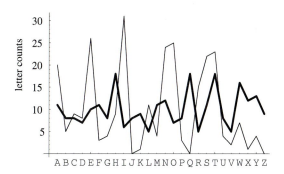

Figure 2.13 The plaintext and ciphertext letter frequencies for a Hill ciphertext.

are much more uniform than in the plaintext (thin curve). So an adversary who had only the ciphertext would not be able to use letter frequency information directly. If that person suspected that a 2×2 Hill matrix was used

---

[70]John Updike (b. 1932) U.S. author and critic, interview in the *New York Times Book Review*, 1977, quoted in [3].

for the encipherment, then she could try out 2×2 matrices on the first couple of letter pairs until the computed plaintext was intelligible in the underlying language. This brute force approach might require the adversary to try out somewhere near $24^4 = 456976$ different matrices before she found one that deciphered correctly.

The story is quite different if the adversary had a ciphertext and even a little bit of the corresponding plaintext. For instance, suppose a ciphertext begins

$$\text{WJMQFMGGANJFWBBJKEJC} \ldots$$

and the adversary finds out that the plaintext corresponding to the first eight letters is STAYHOME. Then she knows that ST enciphers as WJ and AY enciphers as MQ. If A is the presumed Hill matrix used to do the encipherment, then these two pieces of information mean

$$A \begin{bmatrix} 18 \\ 19 \end{bmatrix} \equiv \begin{bmatrix} 22 \\ 9 \end{bmatrix} \pmod{26} \quad \text{and} \quad A \begin{bmatrix} 0 \\ 24 \end{bmatrix} \equiv \begin{bmatrix} 12 \\ 16 \end{bmatrix} \pmod{26}.$$

Because of the way in which matrix multiplication is defined, this means that

$$A \begin{bmatrix} 18 & 0 \\ 19 & 24 \end{bmatrix} \equiv \begin{bmatrix} 22 & 12 \\ 9 & 16 \end{bmatrix} \pmod{26}.$$

If $\begin{bmatrix} 18 & 0 \\ 19 & 24 \end{bmatrix}$ were invertible modulo 26, then the adversary could multiply both sides by its inverse to solve for A. But $\det\left(\begin{bmatrix} 18 & 0 \\ 19 & 24 \end{bmatrix}\right) \equiv 16 \pmod{26}$ is not relatively prime to 26, so the matrix is not invertible. However, there is more plaintext and corresponding ciphertext. Our adversary knows that HO enciphers as FM, which corresponds to

$$A \begin{bmatrix} 7 \\ 14 \end{bmatrix} = \begin{bmatrix} 5 \\ 13 \end{bmatrix}.$$

So A satisfies

$$A \begin{bmatrix} 18 & 7 \\ 19 & 14 \end{bmatrix} = \begin{bmatrix} 22 & 5 \\ 9 & 13 \end{bmatrix}.$$

In this case $\det\left(\begin{bmatrix} 18 & 7 \\ 19 & 14 \end{bmatrix}\right) \equiv 15 \pmod{26}$, which is relatively prime to 26, so the adversary *can* multiply both sides of (2.9) by $\begin{bmatrix} 18 & 7 \\ 19 & 14 \end{bmatrix}^{-1} \equiv$

$\begin{bmatrix} 20 & 3 \\ 23 & 22 \end{bmatrix} \pmod{26}$ to get A:

$$A \begin{bmatrix} 18 & 7 \\ 19 & 14 \end{bmatrix} \begin{bmatrix} 18 & 7 \\ 19 & 14 \end{bmatrix}^{-1} \equiv \begin{bmatrix} 22 & 5 \\ 9 & 13 \end{bmatrix} \begin{bmatrix} 18 & 7 \\ 19 & 14 \end{bmatrix}^{-1} \pmod{26}$$

$$A \equiv \begin{bmatrix} 22 & 5 \\ 9 & 13 \end{bmatrix} \begin{bmatrix} 20 & 3 \\ 23 & 22 \end{bmatrix} \equiv \begin{bmatrix} 9 & 20 \\ 14 & 5 \end{bmatrix} \pmod{26}.$$

She can then calculate A^{-1} and determine the remaining plaintext.

The Hill cipher can be implemented using key matrices with sizes other than 2×2. In the Exercises you have the opportunity to explore what happens with 3×3 key matrices.

An $n \times n$ matrix A can be used as a Hill cipher key provided A has an inverse modulo 26, that is, if there is a $n \times n$ matrix B such that $AB \equiv BA \equiv I \pmod{26}$. However, it is beyond the scope of this book to discuss general methods for finding inverses.

Summary

The **Hill cipher** is a type of **block cipher** in which pairs of plaintext letters are enciphered by a transformation of the form $y \equiv Ax \pmod{26}$, where x is the 2×1 matrix of numerical equivalents of a plaintext letter pair, y is the 2×1 matrix of ciphertext numerical equivalents for a letter pair, and A is an invertible 2×2 matrix, modulo 26. Decipherment is given by $x \equiv A^{-1}y \pmod{26}$. The Hill cipher amounts to a simple substitution on an alphabet of $26^2 = 676$ letters.

EXERCISES

1. Calculate the matrix products modulo the given modulus.

   (a) $\begin{bmatrix} 2 & 2 \\ 3 & 6 \end{bmatrix} \begin{bmatrix} 1 & 4 \\ 5 & 2 \end{bmatrix}$, $m = 7$

   (b) $\begin{bmatrix} 10 & 1 \\ 2 & 5 \end{bmatrix} \begin{bmatrix} 4 & 0 \\ 0 & 4 \end{bmatrix}$, $m = 12$

   (c) $\begin{bmatrix} 1 & 1 \\ 1 & 0 \end{bmatrix} \begin{bmatrix} 1 & 1 \\ 0 & 1 \end{bmatrix}$, $m = 2$

(d) $\begin{bmatrix} 0 & 1 \\ 1 & 0 \end{bmatrix} \begin{bmatrix} 1 \\ 0 \end{bmatrix}, m = 2$

(e) $\begin{bmatrix} 21 & 18 \\ 10 & 20 \end{bmatrix} \begin{bmatrix} 6 & 0 \\ 0 & 8 \end{bmatrix}, m = 26$

(f) $\begin{bmatrix} 5 \\ 10 \end{bmatrix} \begin{bmatrix} 15 & 20 \end{bmatrix}, m = 26$

(g) $\begin{bmatrix} 16 & 30 \end{bmatrix} \begin{bmatrix} 2 & 6 \\ 6 & 2 \end{bmatrix}, m = 17$

2. Calculate kA modulo m for the given values of k, A, and m.

(a) $k = 3$, $A = \begin{bmatrix} 6 & 3 \\ 7 & 2 \end{bmatrix}, m = 9$

(b) $k = 4$, $A = \begin{bmatrix} 4 & 2 \\ 6 & 4 \end{bmatrix}, m = 8$

(c) $k = 13$, $A = \begin{bmatrix} 19 & 4 \\ 10 & 11 \end{bmatrix}, m = 26$

(d) $k = 8$, $A = \begin{bmatrix} 25 \\ 24 \end{bmatrix}, m = 26$

3. Calculate the determinants of the following matrices modulo the given modulus.

(a) $A = \begin{bmatrix} 1 & 0 \\ 1 & 1 \end{bmatrix}, m = 2$

(b) $B = \begin{bmatrix} 4 & 3 \\ 1 & 3 \end{bmatrix}, m = 5$

(c) $C = \begin{bmatrix} 10 & 6 \\ 5 & 3 \end{bmatrix}, m = 11$

(d) $D = \begin{bmatrix} 10 & 11 \\ 7 & 20 \end{bmatrix}, m = 26$

(e) $E = \begin{bmatrix} 2 & 4 \\ 6 & 8 \end{bmatrix}, m = 26$

(f) $F = \begin{bmatrix} 0 & 1 \\ 1 & 0 \end{bmatrix}$, $m = 26$

4. Calculate the inverses of the matrices in Exercise 3 that have inverses.

5. Encipher the message WASHINGTON using the Hill cipher with key matrix $A = \begin{bmatrix} 3 & 7 \\ 9 & 8 \end{bmatrix}$.

6. Decipher the message VPNNNHTPQF, which was enciphered by the Hill method using the key matrix $A = \begin{bmatrix} 3 & 5 \\ 7 & 8 \end{bmatrix}$.

7. (a) Encipher the message MAKE MY DAY using the Hill cipher with key matrix $A = \begin{bmatrix} 5 & 6 \\ 6 & 5 \end{bmatrix}$.

   (b) Decipher KCQJUYXD, which was obtained using the same matrix.

8. The answer to the riddle, "What did one plate say to the other plate?" is

$$UPOTITISGXLD$$

   where the Hill cipher with key matrix

$$A = \begin{bmatrix} 8 & 7 \\ 3 & 3 \end{bmatrix}$$

   was used to encipher. Decipher the answer.

9. Suppose you know that ABLE enciphers as ZXTQ by using the Hill cipher with a matrix A. Determine A.

10. You have intercepted the ciphertext DLHIVDLZHIPNEU, which you know to be produced by a Hill encipherment using a 2×2 key matrix. Moreover, you strongly suspect that the first four characters are an encipherment of DEAR. Determine the key matrix and then use it to decipher the rest of the message.

11. The following ciphertexts are produced either by a monoalphabetic substitution or a Hill cipher. Identify which is which. (There is no need to try cryptanalysis; the quote is not particularly interesting.)

(a)

```
OHKSV DOIKS LIZBC TBKMK RMXYE DXWKE MCLBE GXRPN KBUAZ
RCDAQ PUPPH QVHQI UUNNL XRGZR IMEUO HFUQI TJIKN HWFZE
UUMKX VXJKE AKOCD KBTXV ZOPGI UZBXW PGLVX RBKVU DLDDZ
RFRRM YOBHD LEZCS IKPAH LTECY USZET JTEQI FPOHT MDVPA
VN
```

(b)

```
AOPZI VVRPZ PUALU KLKHZ HALEA MVYHJ VBYZL VUJYF WAVNY
HWOFD PAOLT WOHZP ZVUHS NLIYH PJTLA OVKZP APZDY PAALU
ZVHZA VILHJ JLZZP ISLAV NYHKB HALVY HKCHU JLKBU KLYNY
HKBHA LZABK LUAZH ZDLSS HZAVZ JPLUA PZAZP UVAOL YMPLS
KZ
```

12. Suppose that the Hill cipher with key matrix A is applied to a plaintext and then a keyword columnar transposition is applied to the result. Is this scheme more secure than either a Hill cipher or a transposition by itself? Can you give an example to illustrate your answer?

13. Encipher the telephone number 901-843-3000 using a Hill-type cipher with key matrix $A = \begin{bmatrix} 4 & 3 \\ 3 & 7 \end{bmatrix}$. (*Note*: The modulus here will be 10.)

The **determinant** of a 3×3 matrix

$$A = \begin{bmatrix} a & b & c \\ d & e & f \\ g & h & i \end{bmatrix}$$

is

$$\det(A) = a \det\left(\begin{bmatrix} e & f \\ h & i \end{bmatrix}\right) - b \det\left(\begin{bmatrix} d & f \\ g & i \end{bmatrix}\right) + c \det\left(\begin{bmatrix} d & e \\ g & h \end{bmatrix}\right).$$

A 3×3 matrix A is **invertible modulo** m if there is a 3×3 matrix B such that

$$AB \equiv \begin{bmatrix} 1 & 0 & 0 \\ 0 & 1 & 0 \\ 0 & 0 & 1 \end{bmatrix} \pmod{m}.$$

We write A^{-1} for B MOD m.

It can be verified that if $\det(A)$ is relatively prime to m, then A is invertible. Moreover, its inverse is

$$A^{-1} = \det(A)^{-1} \begin{bmatrix} +a' & -d' & +g' \\ -b' & +e' & -h' \\ +c' & -f' & +i' \end{bmatrix} \text{ MOD } m,$$

where the primed letters symbolize the determinant of the 2×2 submatrix of A obtained by striking out the column and row of A in which the corresponding letter sits. For example,

$$a' = \det\left(\begin{bmatrix} e & f \\ h & i \end{bmatrix}\right) \quad \text{and} \quad b' = \det\left(\begin{bmatrix} d & f \\ g & i \end{bmatrix}\right).$$

14. Calculate the determinants of the following matrices modulo the given modulus. For those with determinant relatively prime to m, find the inverse matrix.

(a) $A = \begin{bmatrix} 1 & 0 & 2 \\ 3 & 3 & 2 \\ 1 & 1 & 1 \end{bmatrix}$, $m = 4$

(b) $A = \begin{bmatrix} 9 & 0 & 0 \\ 0 & 2 & 0 \\ 0 & 0 & 4 \end{bmatrix}$, $m = 13$

(c) $A = \begin{bmatrix} 0 & 0 & 1 \\ 1 & 0 & 0 \\ 0 & 1 & 0 \end{bmatrix}$, $m = 26$

15. An invertible 3×3 matrix can be used as a key for a Hill-type cipher. Blocks of three letters are enciphered by multiplying A by the 3×1 matrix of plaintext numerical equivalents modulo 26; blocks of three letters are deciphered by multiplying A^{-1} by the 3×1 matrix of ciphertext numerical equivalents modulo 26.

(a) Encipher AUTUMN LEAVES by the matrix $A = \begin{bmatrix} 1 & 0 & 2 \\ 3 & 3 & 2 \\ 1 & 1 & 1 \end{bmatrix}$.

(b) The decipherment using the inverse of the matrix in A, of the following, completes a sentence starting with the plaintext of part (a):

OASUDC

Decipher.

16. In Theorem 2.9.1, why do we have the condition that $\det(A)$ be relatively prime to m?

17. How many different matrices $A = \begin{bmatrix} a & b \\ c & d \end{bmatrix}$ are there, modulo 2? How many of these are invertible?

18. How many different matrices $A = \begin{bmatrix} a & b \\ c & d \end{bmatrix}$ are there, modulo 3? How many of these are invertible?

19. Show that $k(AB) = (kA)B$ for any pair of square matrices A and B and number k.

Chapter 3

Symmetric Computer-Based Cryptology

In this chapter, we examine cryptographic algorithms that are used for data or communications based in computers. In this digital age, where the world economy and daily transactions in most businesses rely on computers, security is essential. Some companies, for instance, conduct all of their transactions over the Internet, and this requires methods to encrypt information that customers supply as part of purchases and other transactions. "Hackers"—individuals who, for sport, vandalistic urges, or thievery, attempt to break into computer systems—pose an evolving threat to these sorts of transactions. Consequently, private organizations and government agencies that rely heavily on electronic commerce and transfer of data take measures to thwart hackers' activities by implementing strong cryptographic techniques, most of which have been developed during the past twenty-five years.

To appreciate the techniques and issues involved, it is important to understand the way that computers represent numbers internally. For this reason, in the first section of this chapter, we learn about **binary** representations. Besides binary, we also look at base 26, which provides an efficient way to translate textual data into numerical data.

Modern **symmetric cryptosystems** (i.e., those in which both sender and recipient have the same key) fall roughly into two categories:

- **Stream ciphers**, in which individual symbols (usually bits) are enciphered in a "stream" as they are transmitted

- **Block ciphers**, in which groups or blocks of symbols (bits) of a given length are enciphered to produce blocks of ciphertext that are then transmitted

In this chapter, we examine stream ciphers and how **linear feedback shift registers** can be used to generate a pseudorandom key. Also in this chapter, we examine some simple-minded block ciphers to illustrate the basic principles behind such widely used block ciphers as DES. Sometimes we look at **hash functions**, which are methods for generating digital fingerprints of messages or data. These functions are defined in terms of block ciphers, and they have a wide range of applications in cryptographic protocols.

In all these cases, the methods contrast with the classical paper-and-pen- or mechanically based methods we have discussed in the previous chapter. While we can work with these computer-based methods on paper to understand them, we must remember that their implementations are typically made in computer hardware or software.

3.1   Number Representation

We are accustomed to representing numbers as "words" made from the ten "letters" 0, 1, 2, 3, 4, 5, 6, 7, 8, and 9. The number two thousand eight hundred forty-seven is succinctly represented as 2847; this representation actually means $2000 + 800 + 40 + 7$, or $2 \cdot 1000 + 8 \cdot 100 + 4 \cdot 10 + 7$, or $2 \cdot 10^3 + 8 \cdot 10^2 + 4 \cdot 10^1 + 7 \cdot 10^0$. The number is a sum of multiples of powers of ten, where the multiples are in the range zero to nine. This is the base ten, or **decimal**, representation of the number.

Binary

Among the most important representations of numbers is base 2 or **binary**. Binary representations are important in that they model the electromagnetic "on-off" form in which digital circuits, magnetic and optical storage devices, and certain radio transmitters handle numbers. Translation back and forth between binary and other representations is essential at all phases of user-computer interfaces. Binary is also useful because it provides elegant arithmetic representations of "true-false" logical statements.

Using binary, numbers are represented using only the digits 0 and 1. The number zero is represented as 0 (or 00, 000, ...), and the number one is represented as 1 (or 01, 001, ...). Since two is one times two to the first

Number	Decimal representation	Binary representation	Interpretation of binary representation
zero	0	0	$\boxed{0} \cdot 2^0$
one	1	1	$\boxed{1} \cdot 2^0$
two	2	10	$\boxed{1} \cdot 2^1 + \boxed{0} \cdot 2^0$
three	3	11	$\boxed{1} \cdot 2^1 + \boxed{1} \cdot 2^0$
four	4	100	$\boxed{1} \cdot 2^2 + \boxed{0} \cdot 2^1 + \boxed{0} \cdot 2^0$
five	5	101	$1 \cdot 2^2 + 0 \cdot 2^1 + 1 \cdot 2^0$
six	6	110	$1 \cdot 2^2 + 1 \cdot 2^1 + 0 \cdot 2^0$
seven	7	111	$1 \cdot 2^2 + 1 \cdot 2^1 + 1 \cdot 2^0$
eight	8	1000	$1 \cdot 2^3 + 0 \cdot 2^2 + 0 \cdot 2^1 + 0 \cdot 2^0$
nine	9	1001	$1 \cdot 2^3 + 0 \cdot 2^2 + 0 \cdot 2^1 + 1 \cdot 2^0$
ten	10	1010	$1 \cdot 2^3 + 0 \cdot 2^2 + 1 \cdot 2^1 + 0 \cdot 2^0$
eleven	11	1011	$1 \cdot 2^3 + 0 \cdot 2^2 + 1 \cdot 2^1 + 1 \cdot 2^0$
twelve	12	1100	$1 \cdot 2^3 + 1 \cdot 2^2 + 0 \cdot 2^1 + 0 \cdot 2^0$
thirteen	13	1101	$1 \cdot 2^3 + 1 \cdot 2^2 + 0 \cdot 2^1 + 1 \cdot 2^0$
$\vdots$	$\vdots$	$\vdots$	$\vdots$

Table 3.1 Binary representations of numbers. The boxed coefficients are the digits of some of the numbers' binary representations.

power plus zero times two to the zeroth power, we represent it by 10 (read this as "one-zero, base 2"). Three is one times two, plus one times one, so we write 11 (read this as "one-one, base 2"). Table 3.1 shows several integers and their binary representations.

Example 3.1.1 Find the number with binary representation 101 101.

Solution Following the pattern established in Table 3.1, we see that

$$
\begin{aligned}
101\,101 &= 1 \cdot 2^5 + 0 \cdot 2^4 + 1 \cdot 2^3 + 1 \cdot 2^2 + 0 \cdot 2^1 + 1 \cdot 2^0 \\
&= 32 + 0 + 8 + 4 + 0 + 1 \\
&= 45. \quad \Diamond
\end{aligned}
$$

Conversion from binary to decimal representation is always as simple as determining the "place value" of the digits, as we did in the last example. With a decimal representation of a number in hand, we can also readily find its binary representation. For instance, suppose we want the binary digits for 23. Since 23 is more than $2^4 = 16$ and less than $2^5 = 32$, we know that the binary digits for 23 will be zero in the 32's place, 64's place, and so on. So

$$23 = d_4 \cdot 2^4 + d_3 \cdot 2^3 + d_2 \cdot 2^2 + d_1 \cdot 2^1 + d_0, \tag{3.1}$$

where d_i is either 0 or 1 for $i = 0, 1, 2, 3, 4$. When we divide 23 by 2, we get a quotient of 11 and remainder of 1. By (3.1), this means

$$2 \cdot 11 + 1 = 2 \cdot (d_4 \cdot 2^3 + d_3 \cdot 2^2 + d_2 \cdot 2 + d_1) + d_0,$$

so by comparing right and left sides we see that $d_0 = 1$ and

$$11 = d_4 \cdot 2^3 + d_3 \cdot 2^2 + d_2 \cdot 2 + d_1. \tag{3.2}$$

Dividing 11 by 2, we get a quotient of 5 and a remainder of 1, so by (3.2),

$$2 \cdot 5 + 1 = 2(d_4 \cdot 2^2 + d_3 \cdot 2 + d_2) + d_1.$$

Thus $d_1 = 1$ and

$$5 = d_4 \cdot 2^2 + d_3 \cdot 2 + d_2.$$

Continuing this pattern of extracting quotient and remainder, we obtain $d_2 = 1$, $d_3 = 0$, and $d_4 = 1$. So the binary representation of 23 is

$$d_4 d_3 d_2 d_1 d_0 = 10\,111.$$

The general procedure for finding the binary representation of a number is the same. Let n be a positive integer. The "1's digit" d_0 in its binary representation is the remainder when n is divided by 2:

$$n = 2 \cdot q_0 + d_0.$$

The "2's digit" d_1 is the remainder when q_0 is divided by 2:

$$q_0 = 2q_1 + d_1.$$

The "4's digit" d_2 is the remainder when q_1 is divided by 2:

$$q_1 = 2q_2 + d_2.$$

This pattern continues until we reach

$$q_{k-1} = 2q_k + d_k, \tag{3.3}$$

where k satisfies

$$2^{k-1} < n \leq 2^k, \tag{3.4}$$

or, equivalently, where $q_k = 0$.

Example 3.1.2 Find the binary representation of 683.

Solution By iteratively dividing by 2 to obtain quotient and remainder, we can write

683
$\begin{aligned}
&= 2 \cdot 341 + 1 \\
&= 2(2 \cdot 170 + 1) + 1 \\
&= 2(2 \cdot (2 \cdot 85 + 0) + 1) + 1 \\
&= 2(2 \cdot (2 \cdot (2 \cdot 42 + 1) + 0) + 1) + 1 \\
&= 2(2 \cdot (2 \cdot (2 \cdot (2 \cdot 21 + 0) + 1 + 0) + 1) + 1 \\
&= 2(2 \cdot (2 \cdot (2 \cdot (2 \cdot (2 \cdot 10 + 1) + 0) + 1) + 0) + 1) + 1 \\
&= 2(2 \cdot (2 \cdot (2 \cdot (2 \cdot (2 \cdot (2 \cdot 5 + 0) + 1) + 0) + 1) + 0) + 1) + 1 \\
&= 2(2 \cdot (2 \cdot (2 \cdot (2 \cdot (2 \cdot (2 \cdot (2 \cdot 2 + 1) + 0) + 1) + 0) + 1) + 0) + 1) + 1 \\
&= 2(2 \cdot (2 \cdot (2 \cdot (2 \cdot (2 \cdot (2 \cdot (2 \cdot (2 \cdot \boxed{1} + \boxed{0}) + \boxed{1}) + \boxed{0}) + \boxed{1}) + \boxed{0}) + \boxed{1}) + \boxed{0}) + \boxed{1}) + \boxed{1}
\end{aligned}$

and then read off the binary digits, which are boxed, in order from left to right: $683 = 1\,010\,101\,011$. ◇

An issue naturally arises concerning the amount of "space" a computer needs in order to represent a number. For instance, if someone wants to store 10 000 (ten thousand) numbers on a computer, and each number has as many as 50 digits in its decimal representation, about how many binary digits (**bits**) will be needed? If n is a 50-decimal digit number, then $10^{49} \leq n < 10^{50}$, and the largest such number would be $n = 10^{50} - 1 \approx 10^{50}$. By (3.4), the number k of binary digits satisfies

$$2^{k-1} < 10^{50} \leq 2^k.$$

The natural logarithm function (which we discuss in the next section) is increasing, so we can apply it to the three quantities here and preserve the inequalities:

$$\ln(2^{k-1}) < \ln\left(10^{50}\right) \leq \ln(2^k)$$

Also, using the property that $\ln(a^x) = x\ln(a)$, we have

$$\begin{aligned}
(k-1)\ln 2 &< 50\ln 10 &\leq& \ k\ln 2 \\
k - 1 &< \frac{50\ln 10}{\ln 2} &\leq& \ k \\
k - 1 &< 166.096 &\leq& \ k
\end{aligned}$$

Since k is a whole number, $k = 167$ bits will be needed for each 50-decimal-digit number. To store $10\,000$ such numbers would take—at a minimum—$10\,000 \cdot 167 = 1\,670\,000$ bits, or about 0.209 megabytes.

Example 3.1.3 Determine the number of binary digits needed to represent a number n.

Solution Let b stand for the number of binary digits needed to represent n. Then b is the integer satisfying the inequality

$$2^{b-1} \leq n < 2^b.$$

Taking the natural logarithm of the three quantities, we obtain

$$\begin{aligned} (b-1)\ln 2 &\leq \ln(n) \leq b\ln 2 \\ b-1 &\leq \frac{\ln(n)}{\ln(2)} \leq b. \end{aligned}$$

For instance, if $n = 43216$, then $\ln(43216)/\ln(2) = 10.6739/0.6931 = 15.399$, so the number of binary digits is $b = 16$. ◇

Base Twenty-Six

Another interesting base, especially for cryptography on languages that use the Roman alphabet, is 26. We adopt the following convention: A represents the number zero, B represents one, C represents two, ..., Y represents twenty-four, and Z represents twenty-five. This is merely a reiteration of the convention that the "numerical equivalent" of A is 0, of B is 1, and so on. Then, by mimicking the pattern for base two, we see that the first number with a two-digit representation in base twenty-six is twenty-six itself: BA one (B) twenty-six and zero (A) ones. Then twenty-seven is BB, twenty-eight is BC, and so on. The last two-digit base twenty-six number is ZZ, which is $25 \cdot 26 + 25 = 675$. It is followed by BAA, which is $1 \cdot 26^2 + 0 \cdot 26 + 0 \cdot 1 = 676$. This provides a very natural way to turn text into numbers.

Example 3.1.4 By the convention we've established, the text TREE can be interpreted as the base twenty-six representation of the number

$$19 \cdot 26^3 + 17 \cdot 26^2 + 4 \cdot 26 + 4 = 345\,544. \quad ◇$$

By reversing the process, we can turn numbers represented in the usual base ten into text.

Example 3.1.5 Convert the number $17\,629$ to base twenty-six.

Solution We carry through the same procedure that we used for converting to a binary representation: repeated division by 26 until a quotient of zero is obtained. The sequence of remainders will give the base twenty-six digits.

$$
\begin{aligned}
17\,638 &= 26 \cdot 678 + 10 \\
&= 26 \cdot (26 \cdot 26 + 2) + 10 \\
&= 26 \cdot (26 \cdot (26 \cdot \boxed{1} + \boxed{0}) + \boxed{2}) + \boxed{10}
\end{aligned}
$$

The letter equivalents of the remainders 1, 0, 2, and 10 are BACK. ◇

Arithmetic in bases other than ten is done in the same way as in base ten.

Example 3.1.6 Add the numbers with base twenty-six representations ONE and TWO.

Solution The addition tableau is

$$
\begin{array}{r}
\text{ONE} \\
+\text{TWO} \\
\hline
\boxed{}
\end{array}
$$

We fill in the box by first adding E + O = S (because $4 + 14 = 18$); there is nothing to "carry," so the rightmost digit in the sum is S. Next, N + W = BJ (because $13 + 22 = 35$), so we write J under N and W and "carry" the B. Finally, B + O + T = BI; these are the leftmost digits. The final form of the tableau is

$$
\begin{array}{r}
\text{ONE} \\
+ \ \text{TWO} \\
\hline
\boxed{\text{BIJS}}
\end{array}
$$

You can also check this result by changing every number to its decimal representation:

$$
\begin{aligned}
\text{ONE} &= 14 \cdot 26^2 + 13 \cdot 26 + 4 = 9806 \\
\text{TWO} &= 19 \cdot 26^2 + 22 \cdot 26 + 14 = 13\,430
\end{aligned}
$$

and $9806 + 13\,430 = 23\,236$. Also,

$$
\begin{aligned}
\text{BIJS} &= 1 \cdot 26^3 + 8 \cdot 26^2 + 9 \cdot 26 + 18 \\
&= 23\,236.
\end{aligned}
$$

Here is an instance where ONE plus TWO is definitely *not* THREE! ◇

It is tempting to use these ideas to create a new type of cipher system. Suppose, for simplicity, that cleartext messages will be segmented into five-letter groups, each regarded as a base twenty-six representation of a number in the range from 0 to $26^5 - 1$. Pick a number k in the range 1 to $26^5 - 1$ to use as a key, and encipher a number x represented by a five-letter group by

$$y = (x + k) \ \text{MOD} \ \text{BAAAAA}. \tag{3.5}$$

Decipherment is then simply

$$x = (y - k) \ \text{MOD} \ \text{BAAAAA}.$$

This is a shift cipher, but on an "alphabet" of $26^5 = 11\,881\,376$ letters.

Example 3.1.7 Let $k = $ AGING be the key. Encipher FINDA GOODD OCTOR. Decipher BBWVJ OVNEG TOVTN EHELS AIPVT EYHLD.

Solution To encipher, we just calculate blocks of ciphertext by adding the key to plaintext blocks:

$$
\begin{aligned}
y_1 &\equiv \text{FINDA} + \text{AGING} \equiv \text{FOVQG} \quad (\text{mod BAAAAA}) \\
y_2 &\equiv \text{GOODD} + \text{AGING} \equiv \text{GUWQJ} \quad (\text{mod BAAAAA}) \\
y_3 &\equiv \text{OCTOR} + \text{AGING} \equiv \text{OJCBX} \quad (\text{mod BAAAAA}).
\end{aligned}
$$

Thus the ciphertext is FOVQG GUWQJ OJCBX.

To decipher the given ciphertext, we must subtract the keyword from each block of five letters, borrowing as necessary:

$$
\begin{aligned}
x_1 &\equiv \text{BBWVJ} - \text{AGING} \equiv \text{AVOID} \quad (\text{mod BAAAAA}) \\
x_2 &\equiv \text{OVNEG} - \text{AGING} \equiv \text{OPERA} \quad (\text{mod BAAAAA}) \\
x_3 &\equiv \text{TOVTN} - \text{AGING} \equiv \text{TINGH} \quad (\text{mod BAAAAA}) \\
x_4 &\equiv \text{EHELS} - \text{AGING} \equiv \text{EAVYM} \quad (\text{mod BAAAAA}) \\
x_5 &\equiv \text{AIPVT} - \text{AGING} \equiv \text{ACHIN} \quad (\text{mod BAAAAA}) \\
x_6 &\equiv \text{EYHLD} - \text{AGING} \equiv \text{ERYXX} \quad (\text{mod BAAAAA}).
\end{aligned}
$$

The two pieces of advice given in these texts come from a card the author received on a recent birthday. ◇

Summary

Numbers can be represented in any base; base two (**binary**) and base twenty-six are interesting for cryptology. Assuming that we do arithmetic using decimal representations, conversion from binary to decimal entails repeated multiplication; conversion from decimal to binary entails repeated division. Using base twenty-six, any text can be regarded as a list of numbers and therefore encryption can be regarded in many cases as the application of a numerical valued function.

Exercises

1. Find the decimal representation for each of the following binary-represented numbers.

   (a) 100 001

   (b) 110 000

   (c) 10 101 011

   (d) 111 111 111

2. Find the binary representation for each of the following decimal-represented numbers.

   (a) 64

   (b) 129

   (c) 53

   (d) 279

3. Without actually finding the representation, determine how many binary digits will be needed to represent the following numbers.

   (a) 72 891

   (b) 10 643 522

4. List the binary representations for the sixteen numbers following the number with binary representation 1 001 101.

5. The following is the binary representation of an ASCII-encoded text. Each 8-bit block is the binary representation of one ASCII value. Decode the text.

01010011 01010100 01000001 01011001 01000011 01000001
01001100 01001101

6. Find the decimal representation for each of the following base twenty-six representations.

   (a) BAA

   (b) ZZZ

   (c) DOG

   (d) CAT

   (e) TOWER

7. Find the base twenty-six representation for each of the following decimal-represented numbers.

   (a) 27

   (b) 679

   (c) 35 152

   (d) 44 958

   (e) 220 845 590

8. Without actually finding the representation, determine how many base twenty-six digits will be needed to represent the following numbers.

   (a) 43 719

   (b) 88 991 226

9. List the base twenty-six representation of the fifteen numbers following the number with base twenty-six representation MEMPHIS.

10. Using binary representations, calculate $a + b$ and $a - b$.

    (a) $a = 11\,011$, $b = 10\,101$

    (b) $a = 100\,100$, $b = 1011$

    (c) $a = 111\,011$, $b = 111\,001$

    (d) $a = 1\,111\,111$, $b = 101$

11. Using base twenty-six representations, calculate $a + b$ and $a - b$.

    (a) $a = $BOX, $b = $BAT

    (b) $a = $HORSE, $b = $COW

    (c) $a = $HOQ, $b = $HGD

12. Find a and b such that $a + b =$ YES and $a - b =$ NO.

13. Let $k =$ APPLE.

    (a) Encipher THEWA LLSHA VEARS using the shift cipher defined in (3.5) on blocks of five letters.

    (b) Decipher MEEDI LYFDW JDADL JFIBU.

14. Suppose someone is using the encryption method described at the end of this section and that you know both the plaintext

    $$\text{THERESNOMIDDLEGROUND}$$

    and the corresponding ciphertext

    $$\text{VVZEXVCJABFSFRZUDPAW}$$

    Recover the keyword and use it to decipher

    $$\text{VVZDALAJGHRVZFLRSUYL}$$

15. Find a formula for the number of digits in a base twenty-six representation of a number n. Use it to determine the number of base twenty-six digits in $n = 1234567890$.

3.2 Boolean and Numerical Functions

Boolean Functions

A **Boolean**[1] **function** is a function whose domain consists of ordered lists (or strings) of zeros and ones of a specified length, and whose range consists of strings of zeros and ones of a specified length. In light of our discussion of binary representation of numbers, we can see that any Boolean function can be thought of as assigning numerical values to other numerical values. Thus

---

[1] George Boole (1815–1864), British mathematician, known for laying the ground work of what is now called Boolean algebra in his work *An Investigation of the Laws of Thought on Which Are Founded the Mathematical Theories of Logic and Probabilities*, 1854.

Boolean functions serve as a way to compute generic numerical functions from finite sets of numbers to other finite sets of numbers, where the numbers are represented in binary form. In particular, the operation of an encryption function implemented on a computer is modeled by a Boolean function. Thus our brief discussion here will be germane to our later presentation of block ciphers in this chapter.

Example 3.2.1 The function f given by Table 3.2 is a Boolean function.

$x_1\,x_2\,x_3$	$f(x_1\,x_2\,x_3)$
000	01
001	10
010	11
011	01
100	00
101	10
110	00
111	11

Table 3.2 Table for Example 3.2.1.

For instance,

$$f(011) = 01 \text{ and } f(000) = 01. \quad \diamondsuit$$

Any Boolean function of n variables and any number of output bits can be specified completely by a table with 2^n entries in it. To see this, just think of the n variables as "slots" into which one of two symbols can be inserted. Since there are n such slots for which the the symbols can be selected independently, there are

$$\underbrace{2 \cdot 2 \cdot 2 \cdots \cdots 2}_{n \text{ times}} = 2^n$$

possible n-bit strings. For a large number of variables, however, this could require very large tables. Boolean functions can be given instead by formulas that are much more compact than tables. For instance, $g(x_1\,x_2\,x_3) = (1 + x_1 + x_1 \cdot x_2 + x_2 \cdot x_3)$ MOD 2 is a one-bit Boolean function. Some of its values are

$$g(000) = (1 + 0 + 1 \cdot 0 + 0 \cdot 0) \text{ MOD } 2 = 0$$
$$g(001) = (1 + 0 + 0 \cdot 0 + 0 \cdot 1) \text{ MOD } 2 = 0$$
$$g(100) = (1 + 1 + 0 + 0) \text{ MOD } 2 = 2 \text{ MOD } 2 = 0.$$

You should complete the table of its values.

Not that, in the context of Boolean function, we are explicitly writing the multiplication operation ($\cdot$). The reason is that we do not want to confuse it with the **concatenation** operation, that is, writing 0's and 1's and expressions that represent them side by side.

Somewhat surprisingly, we can take the table of values of any Boolean function and write down a formula for it. Moreover, we can often simplify that formula substantially using modular arithmetic. We illustrate in the following example.

Example 3.2.2 Let $h(x_1 \, x_2 \, x_3)$ be given by Table 3.3. An expression that

$x_1 \, x_2 \, x_3$	$h(x_1 \, x_2 \, x_3)$
000	1
001	0
010	0
011	1
100	1
101	1
110	0
111	1

Table 3.3 Table for Example 3.2.2.

contains the information in the first table entry is

$$(1 + x_1) \cdot (1 + x_2) \cdot (1 + x_3) \text{ MOD } 2; \tag{3.6}$$

if x_1, x_2, and x_3 are all zero, then the value of this expression is 1. Moreover, for any of the other seven possible assignments of values to x_1, x_2, and x_3, at least one factor in (3.6) will be zero, so the entire product will be zero in these instances. In fact, this expression also contains the information in the second, third, and seventh entries of the table. So the next table entry that needs to be incorporated in the formula is the fourth one. The product

$$(1 + x_1) \cdot x_2 \cdot x_3 \text{ MOD } 2 \tag{3.7}$$

is 1 precisely when $x_1 = 0$, $x_2 = 1$, and $x_3 = 1$. Similarly,

$$x_1 \cdot (1 + x_2) \cdot (1 + x_3) \text{ MOD } 2 \tag{3.8}$$

is 1 when $x_1 = 0$, $x_2 = 1$, and $x_3 = 1$;

$$x_1 \cdot (1 + x_2) \cdot x_3 \ \text{MOD} \ 2 \tag{3.9}$$

is 1 when $x_1 = 1$, $x_2 = 0$, and $x_3 = 1$;

$$x_1 \cdot x_2 \cdot x_3 \ \text{MOD} \ 2 \tag{3.10}$$

is 1 when $x_1 = x_2 = x_3 = 1$. Since the expressions in (3.6), (3.7), (3.8), (3.9), and (3.10) are all equal to zero except at one specific choice of the variables, their sum modulo 2 will exactly agree with the table. Indeed you can verify that

$$\begin{aligned}
h(x_1 \, x_2 \, x_3) \ = \ & ((1 + x_1) \cdot (1 + x_2) \cdot (1 + x_3) + (1 + x_1) \cdot x_2 \cdot x_3 \\
& + x_1 \cdot (1 + x_2) \cdot (1 + x_3) + x_1 \cdot (1 + x_2) \cdot x_3 \\
& + x_1 \cdot x_2 \cdot x_3) \ \text{MOD} \ 2.
\end{aligned}$$

Since the distributive, commutative, and associative laws of arithmetic work for modular arithmetic, since even numbers are congruent to zero modulo 2, since odd numbers are congruent to 1 modulo 2, and since -1 is congruent to 1 modulo 2, we can simplify the formula for h as follows:

$$\begin{aligned}
h(x_1 \, x_2 \, x_3) \ \equiv \ & (1 + x_1 + x_2 + x_1 \cdot x_2) \cdot (1 + x_3) + x_2 \cdot x_3 + x_1 \cdot x_2 \cdot x_3 \\
& + x_1 \cdot (1 + x_2 + x_3 + x_2 \cdot x_3) + x_1 \cdot x_3 + x_1 \cdot x_2 \cdot x_3 \\
& + x_1 \cdot x_2 \cdot x_3 \\
\equiv \ & 1 + x_1 + x_2 + x_1 \cdot x_2 + x_3 + x_1 \cdot x_3 + x_2 \cdot x_3 + x_1 \cdot x_2 \cdot x_3 \\
& + x_2 \cdot x_3 + x_1 \cdot x_2 \cdot x_3 + x_1 + x_1 \cdot x_2 + x_1 \cdot x_3 + x_1 \cdot x_2 \cdot x_3 \\
& + x_1 \cdot x_3 + x_1 \cdot x_2 \cdot x_3 + x_1 \cdot x_2 \cdot x_3 \\
\equiv \ & 1 + 2x_1 + x_2 + 2x_1 \cdot x_2 + x_3 + 3x_1 \cdot x_3 \\
& + 2x_2 \cdot x_3 + 5x_1 \cdot x_2 \cdot x_3 \\
\equiv \ & 1 + x_2 + x_3 + x_1 \cdot x_3 + x_1 \cdot x_2 \cdot x_3 \pmod{2}.
\end{aligned}$$

So, in fact,

$$h(x_1 \, x_2 \, x_3) = (1 + x_2 + x_3 + x_1 \cdot x_3 + x_1 \cdot x_2 \cdot x_3) \ \text{MOD} \ 2. \quad \diamondsuit$$

In the preceding example, the function's value was a single number, but even in a case such as Table 3.4, where the function's value is a string of

x	$S(x)$
000	101
001	000
010	110
011	001
100	011
101	111
110	010
111	100

Table 3.4 A 3-bit Boolean function.

numbers, the same procedure can be applied to find a formula for each digit in the value of f. You can verify that the formulas for the left and right digits of the function f in Table 3.4 are y_1 and y_2, respectively:

$$y_1 = (x_2 + x_1 \cdot x_2 + x_3) \text{ MOD } 2$$
$$y_2 = (1 + x_1 + x_3 + x_1 \cdot x_3 + x_2 \cdot x_3) \text{ MOD } 2.$$

We write this as

$$f(x_1\, x_2\, x_3) = ((x_2 + x_1 \cdot x_2 + x_3) \text{ MOD } 2)((1 + x_1 + x_3 + x_1 \cdot x_3 + x_2 \cdot x_3) \text{ MOD } 2).$$

In the context of representing Boolean functions, remember, this notation does *not* mean multiply the two quantities in parentheses; it means write the respective values of these expressions side by side (concatenated).

Numerical Functions

At various times in this book, we will make use of certain types of numerical functions, that is, functions whose domain and range are subsets of the real numbers. These functions arise naturally when we discuss computational complexity as it pertains to public-key cryptosystems. You are probably familiar with many of these, so the discussion here will focus on features of these functions that will be important in the context of cryptology.

Polynomial and Rational Functions

A **polynomial function** is one whose domain is the real numbers and that has the form

$$p(x) = a_0 + a_1 x + a_2 x^2 + \cdots + a_n x^n,$$

where n is a nonnegative integer and a_0, a_1, ..., a_n are given constants. For instance, $p(x) = 3$, $q(x) = 2x + 5$, $r(x) = x^2$, and $s(x) = x^3 - x^2 + 4x + 5$ are polynomial functions.

The graphs of the simplest polynomials, x^n for various choices of n, have qualitatively the same shape, though the larger values of n correspond to functions with faster rates of increase. Figure 3.1 shows the graphs of $y = x^2$ and $y = x^4$ with the vertical scale one eighth that of the horizontal.

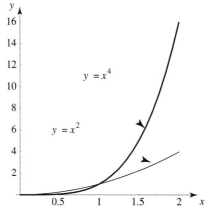

Figure 3.1 The graphs of the polynomial functions $y = x^2$ and $y = x^4$.

A **rational function** is a quotient of two polynomials. For example,

$$f(x) = \frac{x + 2}{x^2 + 5}, \quad g(x) = \frac{2x^3}{x + 1}, \quad \text{and } h(x) = \frac{1}{x^4}$$

are rational functions. The simplest rational functions are those of the form $\frac{1}{x^n}$, for various choices of n. The graphs of some of these functions are shown in Figure 3.2.

Exponential and Logarithmic Functions

An **exponential function** is one of the form $f(x) = a^x$ for some constant a (called the **base**). For instance, the graph of $f(x) = 2^x$ is shown in Figure 3.3.

An important property of exponential functions is that they all "outgrow" every polynomial function for sufficiently large x. Figure 3.4 shows the relationships among $y = x$, $y = x^2$, $y = x^3$ and $y = 2^x$. While $y = 2^x$ doesn't overtake $y = x^3$ until about where x is 10, after that it grows much faster than x^3.

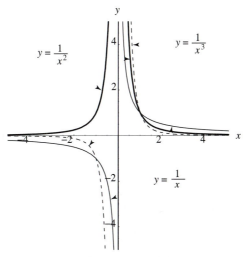

Figure 3.2 The graphs of the rational functions $y = \frac{1}{x}$, $y = \frac{1}{x^2}$, and $y = \frac{1}{x^3}$.

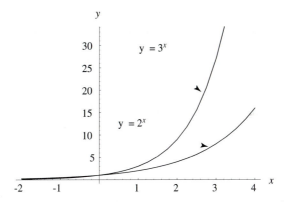

Figure 3.3 The graphs of the exponential functions $f(x) = 2^x$ and $g(x) = 3^x$.

Three other properties of exponential functions are useful for purposes of computation:

- $a^x \cdot a^y = a^{x+y}$ for all real numbers x and y

- $\dfrac{a^x}{a^y} = a^{x-y}$ for all real numbers x and y

- $(a^x)^y = a^{xy}$ for all real numbers x and y

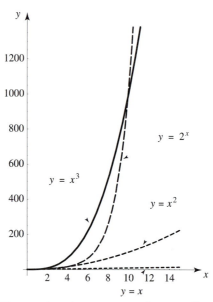

Figure 3.4 The graphs of $y = x$, $y = x^2$, $y = x^3$, and $y = 2^x$. The exponential function 2^x is larger than each of the polynomial functions 1, x, x^2, and x^4 for $x > 10$. Indeed, 2^x eventually "outruns" x^n for any given positive integer n.

You are doubtless familiar with these, and you will have opportunities to apply them in the exercises and elsewhere in this book.

For any positive a not equal to 1, the exponential function $f(x) = a^x$ is one-to-one (every horizontal line intersects the graph at most once), so it has an inverse. The inverse function is called the **logarithm to base** a, and it is denoted $\log_a(x)$. For instance, $\log_2(8) = 3$ because $2^3 = 8$; $\log_2(1/16) = -4$ because $2^{-4} = 1/16$. The graphs of $y = \log_2(x)$ and $y = \log_3(x)$ are shown in Figure 3.5.

There are three important properties of logarithms that are essentially restatements of the three properties of exponential functions just listed :

- $\log_a(x \cdot y) = \log_a(x) + \log_a(y)$ for x, $y > 0$

- $\log_a(\dfrac{x}{y}) = \log_a(x) - \log_a(y)$ for x, $y > 0$

- $\log_a(x^y) = y \log_a(x)$ for $x > 0$ and all y

These properties are also familiar, and you will need them from time to time in this book.

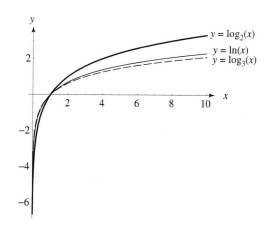

Figure 3.5 Graphs of logarithmic functions.

There is one particular exponential function, called exp, of great importance in mathematics: $\exp(x) = e^x$, where $e = 2.718281828459045\ldots$. Readers who have studied calculus will know many of the properties of this function. However, for our purposes here, you can think of exp just as you would, say, 2^x or 3^x. Indeed, its graph is shaped like those of these functions and lies between the two curves in Figure 3.3. The inverse of exp is the logarithm to base e, and it is denoted $\ln(x)$. The graphs of $y = e^x$ and $y = \ln x$ are shown in Figure 3.6.

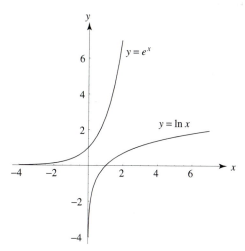

Figure 3.6 The graphs of $y = \ln(x)$ and its inverse $y = e^x$.

All exponential functions can be written in terms of exp by the following **base conversion formula for exponentials**:

$$a^x = e^{a\ln(x)}. \tag{3.11}$$

Moreover, all logarithmic functions can be written in terms of ln by the following formula:

$$\log_a(x) = \frac{\ln(x)}{\ln(a)}. \tag{3.12}$$

The functions exp and ln are programmed into most scientific calculators. In some instances, there is only one key, perhaps labeled ln; to compute exp, you must press an inverse key labeled something like "inv" followed by the ln key. Using these two functions on your calculator along with the base conversion formulas (3.11) and (3.12), you can use your calculator to compute logarithms to any base.

Example 3.2.3 Use (3.11) and (3.12) to calculate $3^{4.31}$ and $\log_2(10)$.

Solution By (3.11),

$$3^{4.31} = e^{3 \cdot \ln(4.31)} = e^{4.38281} = 80.063$$

and

$$\log_2(10) = \frac{\ln(10)}{\ln(2)} = \frac{2.3059}{0.693147} = 3.32193. \quad \Diamond$$

Example 3.2.4 Let x be the number of decimal digits in a number, and let $T(x)$ represent the maximum number of divisions we must do—by naive trial division starting at 2 and working our way up to one less than the number—to determine the primeness of an x-decimal-digit number. Then, in the worst case (that is, if the number is

$$\underbrace{999\ldots9}_{x \text{ digits}}$$

and we actually divide it by every number in the range from 2 to $10^x - 1$ without ever obtaining a zero remainder), we will have to perform $10^x - 2$ divisions. Thus $T(x) = 10^x - 2$. $\quad \Diamond$

Other Special Functions

There are a few other functions arising in cryptology that are appropriate to introduce at this point.

The **greatest integer function** or **floor function**, denoted $\lfloor \ \rfloor$, has domain the real numbers and range the integers; for each real number x, $\lfloor x \rfloor$ is the largest integer less than or equal to x. For instance, $\lfloor 2.34 \rfloor = 2$, $\lfloor 6 \rfloor = 6$, and $\lfloor -3.8 \rfloor = -4$.

Example 3.2.5 If a positive integer a is divided a positive integer m, there is an integer quotient q and a remainder r in the range 0 to $m-1$ such that $a = qm+r$. These are the quotient and remainder that you learned to obtain by long division. The division your calculator does is called **floating point division**, which is analogous to long division in which you place a decimal point in the quotient and obtain digits to the right of it. It is different from the sort of division that produces a whole number quotient and remainder. But there is a connection:

$$q = \left\lfloor \frac{a}{m} \right\rfloor$$

and

$$r = a - qm.$$

For instance, if $a = 155$ and $m = 7$, then $a/m = 155/7 = 22.1429$, so the quotient and remainder are

$$q = \lfloor 22.1429 \rfloor = 22$$
$$r = 155 - 7 \cdot 22 = 1.$$

You will have many opportunities in this text to make use of this property. ◇

Example 3.2.6 Let x be a positive integer, and let $D(x)$ represent the number of digits in the decimal representation of x. Then, for example, $D(854323456) = 9$. It is possible to write down a formula for D as a composition of two other functions:

$$D(x) = \lfloor \log_{10}(x) \rfloor + 1.$$

To get an idea of why this formula should work, consider the number $x = 4379$. Since the largest power of 10 less than or equal to x is $1000 = 10^3$, and since $\log_{10}(x)$ is the exponent to which 10 must be raised to obtain x, we know that $\lfloor \log_{10}(4379) \rfloor = 3$; the number of digits in 4379 is 1 more than

3. The same reasoning applies in general: If n is the number of digits in x, then $\lfloor \log_{10}(x) \rfloor = n - 1$, so $n = \lfloor \log_{10}(x) \rfloor + 1$. $\diamondsuit$

Example 3.2.7 Determine the number of digits in the number $234^{95432678}$.

Solution We can use the formula in the preceding example along with the third property of logarithms and the base conversion formula:

$$
\begin{aligned}
D(234^{95432678}) &= \left\lfloor \log_{10}\left(234^{95432678}\right) \right\rfloor + 1 \\
&= \lfloor 95432678 \log_{10}(234) \rfloor + 1 \\
&= \left\lfloor 95432678 \frac{\ln(234)}{\ln(10)} \right\rfloor + 1 \\
&= \lfloor 95432678 \cdot 2.3692158574101425117 \rfloor + 1 \\
&= \lfloor 226100614.0327160754892757851442888979 \rfloor + 1 \\
&= 226100615.
\end{aligned}
$$

See if you can determine approximately how many pages of paper it would take to write out this number, say in a 10-point font on $8\frac{1}{2} \times 11$ inch sheets of paper with half-inch margins. $\diamondsuit$

As you can see from this example, the logarithm provides a way of working with exceedingly large numbers. In certain areas of cryptography, large numbers are used, and logarithm functions can be for some purposes.

The **prime counting function** $\pi(n)$ is the number of primes less than or equal to n. For example, $\pi(2) = 1$, $\pi(3) = 2$, $\pi(4) = 2$, and so on. Modern cryptosystems such as RSA and ElGamal rely crucially on specially selected large prime numbers; such primes are found in practice by probabilistic methods that depend on an understanding of this function. Part of our understanding of this function is the **prime number theorem**, one version of which states that

$$
\pi(n) \approx \frac{n}{\ln n} \text{ for large values of } n.
$$

We will examine this theorem in Section 4.1.

The **Euler phi function**, denoted $\phi(n)$, is the count of positive integers less than n that are relatively prime to n. For example, $\phi(2) = 1$, $\phi(3) = 2$, $\phi(4) = 2$, $\phi(5) = 4$. This function plays a role in what is often called **Euler's theorem**, a special case of which ensures that the RSA cryptosystem encrypts and decrypts correctly. We will study a special case of Euler's theorem, called **Fermat's little theorem**, in Section 4.3.

The Euler phi function has important and interesting properties. For example, it is not difficult to see that $\phi(p) = p - 1$ if p is prime. Also, $\phi(pq) = (p-1)(q-1)$ if p and q are distinct primes. You are asked in the exercises to show this.

Summary

Boolean functions provide formulaic representations of algorithms that turn strings of 0's and 1's into other strings of 0's and 1's. Since encryption and decryption on computers is done in terms of such strings, Boolean functions provide a concrete way of representing the computer's actions for human understanding. Categories of real-valued functions—such as polynomials and exponentials, and logarithms—will help us to express the computational effort needed to evaluate cryptographic functions. Other special functions, such as floor, prime counting, and Euler phi, arise in the subsequent exposition.

EXERCISES

1. For each of the following Boolean function tables, find a formula for the function:

(a)

$x_1 x_2$	$f(x_1 x_2)$
00	1
01	0
10	0
11	1

(b)

$x_1 x_2$	$g(x_1 x_2)$
00	1
01	1
10	1
11	1

(c)

$x_1 x_2 x_3$	$h(x_1 x_2 x_3)$
000	1
001	0
010	0
011	1
100	1
101	0
110	0
111	1

(d)

$x_1 x_2 x_3$	$k(x_1 x_2 x_3)$
000	0
001	1
010	1
011	1
100	0
101	1
110	1
111	0

2. The **exclusive or** function takes as its argument two binary strings of the same length, $x = x_1 x_2 \ldots x_n$ and $k = k_1 k_2 \ldots k_n$ and returns an n-bit string $y_1 y_2 \ldots y_n$, where

$$y_i = (x_i + k_i) \text{ MOD } 2.$$

It is denoted by $x \oplus k$. Calculate

(a) $10110 \oplus 01011$

(b) $101011 \oplus 101011$

(c) $010010 \oplus 010010$

3. A function f takes a 4-bit string as input and produces a 4-bit output string according to the formula

$$f(x_1 x_2 x_3 x_4) = x_3 x_2 x_4 x_1.$$

Find a formula for f^{-1}.

4. A function E takes input two 2-bit string x and k and produces a 2-bit output string according to the formula

$$E(x_1 x_2, \ k_1 k_2) = x_2 x_1 \oplus k_1 k_2.$$

Find a function D such that

$$D(E(x, k), \ k) = x \text{ and } E(D(x, k), \ k) = x$$

for all choices of x and k.

5. Evaluate exactly if possible; otherwise use a calculator.

(a) $\log_2(16)$	(b) $\log_2(1/32)$	(c) $\log_2(2048)$
(d) $\log_{26}(676)$	(e) $\log_{26}(1)$	(f) $\ln(10)$
(g) $\ln(2)$	(h) $\log_2(41)$	(i) $\log_{10}(101)$
(j) $\lfloor 111/5 \rfloor$	(k) $\lfloor -36/7 \rfloor$	(l) $(2/3)\lfloor 3/2 \rfloor$
(m) $\lfloor \log_{10}(348972) \rfloor$	(n) $\phi(47)/\pi(47)$	(o) $\phi(48)/\pi(48)$

6. Determine the domain and range of each of the following functions and evaluate the functions at the given values.

(a) $f(x) = 2^x$; 6, 7, 8, -1, -4, 3.52, -4.91

(b) $g(x) = 3^x$ MOD 7; 0, 1, 2, 3, 4, 5, 6

(c) $h(x) = \log_{10}(x)$; 1, 10, 100, 1000, 0.01, 0.00001, 3.1415

(d) $k(x, y)$ is the number of positions in the string x in which the symbol is not the same as the corresponding symbol in y; (Y2K, Y2K), (SUMMER, SIMMER), (IDEOLOGICAL, IDEOLOGIQUE), (11011101, 00100010).

(e) $T(x)$ is the telephone number of the person whose name is x; you, the person you call most often.

(f) $S(x) = x - \lfloor x/2 \rfloor$; 0, 0.35, -2.4, 9485.32

7. Evaluate the following functions at the indicated values.

(a) $f(x) = 3 \cdot 2^x - 1$, $x = 0, 1, 3, -4$

(b) $g(x) = x^4 - 4^x$, $x = 0, 1, 2, 3, 4, 5$

8. (a) Knowing that $\ln(5) \approx 1.60944$, calculate $\ln(5^{10000})$.

(b) Knowing that $\log_2(3) \approx 1.58496$, calculate $\log_2(3^{-84371})$.

(c) If $2^x < 10^7$, what is the largest possible integer value of x?

(d) If $3^{13} \leq 4^x$, what is the smallest possible integer value of x?

9. Find the number of decimal digits in $3^{3141592}$.

10. Find formulas for the following functions:

(a) $f(x)$, whose domain is the integers and whose value is $+1$ if x is even and -1 if x is odd

(b) $q(n)$, the number of decimal digits in the square root of n

(c) $w(n)$, the number of n-letter strings that can be formed using a 26-letter alphabet (a letter can be used any number of times)

(d) $v(n)$, the number of four-letter words that can be made with an n-letter alphabet.

11. Use the table of primes on page 370 to prepare a table of $\pi(n)$ for n ranging from 2 to 50.

12. Prepare a table of values of $\phi(n)$ for n ranging from 2 to 50.

13. Show that $\phi(pq) = (p-1)(q-1)$ for any two distinct primes p and q. Use this result to calculate $\phi(9797)$.

3.3   Computational Complexity

The term **computational complexity** is applied to the time or storage requirements for an algorithm to run completely. This function answers one of these questions: "What is the worst case?" "What is the average case?" "What is the best case?" It is often easiest to determine the number of steps the algorithm will require in the worst case as a function of the size of its inputs. Unfortunately, it is not possible in general to find this function exactly; we we must resort to estimating it.

There is a large body of mathematical research literature devoted to computational complexity, and we are not in a position to get deeply into it. But in order to have a clearer sense of where the strengths of some cryptographic methods lie, we need a rudimentary introduction to complexity theory. We begin with some examples.

Example 3.3.1 Consider the problem of adding the integers 1, 2, 3, 4, ..., n, for some positive integer n. One way to approach this is directly: adding the first two numbers, then adding the third to that, and so on: $1 + 2 = 3$, $3 + 3 = 6$, $6 + 4 = 10$, ..., $s_{n-1} + n = s_n$, where s_i is the sum of the first i integers. You can see that the algorithm we have adopted takes exactly $n - 1$ additions. In more formal terms, if $\mu_{\text{slow sum}}(n)$ represents the number of arithmetic operations needed to solve the summing problem with input n, then $\mu_{\text{slow sum}}(n) = n - 1$.[2]

It can be shown, however, that s_n can also be computed by the formula

$$s_n = \frac{n(n+1)}{2}, \qquad n = 1, 2, 3, \ldots. \tag{3.13}$$

You can see this by first observing that

$$s_n = 1 + 2 + 3 + \cdots + n$$

and

$$s_n = n + (n-1) + (n-2) + \cdots + 1$$

so that

$$\begin{aligned} s_n + s_n &= (1+n) + (2 + (n-1)) + (3 + (n-2)) + \cdots + (n+1) \\ 2s_n &= \underbrace{(n+1) + (n+1) + (n+1) + \cdots + (n+1)}_{n \text{ terms}} \end{aligned}$$

---

[2]We use the Greek letter μ as a reminder of μoney. Each step in the algorithm take a certain amount of time, and—by conventional wisdom—time is money.

$$2s_n = n \cdot (n+1)$$
$$s = \frac{n \cdot (n+1)}{2}.$$

Using the algorithm given by formula (3.13), calculating s_n requires one addition, one multiplication, and one division, for a total of three ordinary arithmetic operations. So if $\mu_{\text{clever sum}}(n)$ represents the number of arithmetic operations to sum the integers 1 to n using (3.13), then $\mu_{\text{clever sum}}(n) = 3$. The two algorithms accomplish the same result for each value of n, but the first one does it at much greater computational expense. $\diamond$

The **computational expense function** for an algorithm, denoted in this book as $\mu(n)$, is the maximum number of steps the algorithm to finish running on an input of size n. The term *size* may refer to the number of symbols in the input or the numerical value of the input, or some other reasonable measure of size. It is fairly standard in computer literature to regard the size of an input as the number of bits in it. Also, the term *algorithm* is usually understood in the context of a computational scheme, such as pencil-and-paper base ten computation, or the machine code generated by a C compiler.

In Example 3.3.1 we were able to find a formula for the computational expense function, but generally that is a hopeless task, and we must settle for an estimate.

Example 3.3.2 Consider this problem: Given the numbers 8, 47, 3, 21, 5, 10, 14, determine whether or not a subcollection can be chosen to add up to 44. In this case you can answer the question by a casual inspection, but you can also be systematic so as to obtain an approach that will work even when there are lots of numbers and no obvious answer. The systematic approach is to compute all possible sums that involve these numbers:

$$c_1 \cdot 8 + c_2 \cdot 47 + c_3 \cdot 3 + c_4 \cdot 21 + c_5 \cdot 5 + c_6 \cdot 10 + c_7 \cdot 14 \qquad (3.14)$$

where $c_1, \ldots, c_7$ are either 0 or 1. Seven of these are trivial in that they do not actually involve any addition. You should check that there are $2^6 = 64$ sums involving two or more terms. Along the way, if you find a selection of $c_1, \ldots, c_7$ such that (3.14) is 44, then you can stop and proclaim the answer is "Yes, there is a subcollection of the numbers that sums to 44." On the other hand, if there is no such subcollection, then you will not be sure of it until you have computed *all* 64 of the sums and verified that 44 never

n	$\mu_{\text{slow sum}}(n)$	$\mu_{\text{clever sum}}(n)$	$\mu_{\text{subset sum}}(n)$
2	1	3	1
4	3	3	17
6	5	3	129
8	7	3	769
10	9	3	4097
12	11	3	20481
14	13	3	98305
16	15	3	458753
18	17	3	2097153
20	19	3	9437185

Table 3.5 Comparisons of computational expense functions.

showed up. Thus in the worst case, you have to calculate 2^6 sums to solve this problem. Moreover, the total number of addition operations to compute these sums is $1 \cdot C(7, 2) + 2 \cdot C(7, 3) + \cdots + 6 \cdot C(7, 7)$, which can be shown to equal $7 \cdot 2^6 - 2^7 + 1$.

More generally, if $a_1, a_2, \ldots, a_n$ are given positive integers and t is a "target" positive integer, determining whether a subcollection of the a_is adds up to "hit" the target takes, in the worst case, $\mu_{\text{subset sum}}(n) = n2^{n-1} - 2^n + 1$ additions. Note that the worst-case computational expense of this problem grows much more rapidly with the size n of the input than does the worst-case computational expense of either algorithm in Example 3.3.1. Table 3.5 shows the comparisons. Unlike for the sum problem, there is no known algorithm that solves subset sum problems in general substantially faster than this. $\Diamond$

Example 3.3.3 Consider the following variant of the subset-sum problem: Given $a_1, \ldots, a_n$ and t, determine whether or not there are *two* or fewer numbers among the a_is that sum to t.

The first step is to determine if t itself is in the list; the next thing to try is computing all sums of pairs of numbers. There are

$$C(n, 2) = \frac{n \cdot (n-1)}{2 \cdot 1}$$

such pairs, so at worst, solving the problem in this way will require computing $\mu(x) = \frac{1}{2}(n^2 - n)$ sums. $\Diamond$

We say that a function $\mu(n)$ is **big-oh** of $f(n)$, where f is a nonnegative function, if there are positive constants M and N such that

$$|\mu(n)| \leq M \cdot f(n) \quad \text{for all } n \geq N. \tag{3.15}$$

For a given f, the collection of all functions μ satisfying this relationship is designated by $\mathcal{O}(f(n))$. For any particular μ in $\mathcal{O}(f(n))$, we write $\mu(n) \in \mathcal{O}(f(n))$. We say that an algorithm is **big-oh** of $f(n)$ if its computational expense function μ satisfies $\mu(n) \in \mathcal{O}(f(n))$. We sometimes say that a function in $\mathcal{O}(f(n))$ is of **complexity class** $f(n)$. Another way to think of $\mathcal{O}(f(n))$ is that it is the collection of all functions that never eventually outgrow $f(n)$.

Example 3.3.4 The computational expense function, $\mu(n)$, of Example 3.3.3 satisfies $\mu(n) \in \mathcal{O}(n^2)$.

To see this, first observe that $n^2 - n \leq n^2$ for all $n \geq 1$. Multiplying this inequality by $\frac{1}{2}$ gives $\frac{1}{2}(n^2 - n) \leq \frac{1}{2}n^2$, which says that $\mu(n) \leq \frac{1}{2}n^2$ for all $n \geq 1$. $\diamond$

Example 3.3.5 The computational expense function of the general subset sum problem satisfies $\mu_{\text{subset sum}}(n) \in \mathcal{O}(n2^n)$.

To see this, first observe that $1 \leq 2^n$ for all $n \geq 1$. So $\mu_{\text{subset sum}}(n) = n2^{n-1} - 2^n + 1 \leq n2^{n-1} - 2^n + 2^n = n2^{n-1} = \frac{1}{2}n2^n$ for all $n \geq 1$. Thus the systematic trial-and-error algorithm for solving the subset sum problem is $\mathcal{O}(n2^n)$. $\diamond$

There is a hierarchy of containment among the sets $\mathcal{O}(f(n))$ that is important and not difficult to remember. Any constant function $\mu(n) = c$ is in $\mathcal{O}(1)$, any linear function $\mu(n) = an + b$ (where $a \neq 0$) is in $\mathcal{O}(n)$, and moreover *no* nontrivial linear function is in $\mathcal{O}(1)$. Thus $\mathcal{O}(1)$ is a proper subset of $\mathcal{O}(n)$. Similarly, $\mathcal{O}(n)$ is a proper subset of $\mathcal{O}(n^2)$. In general, if $r < s$, then $\mathcal{O}(n^r)$ is a proper subset of $\mathcal{O}(n^s)$. Any polynomial function $\mu(n)$ of degree r is in $\mathcal{O}(n^s)$ for all $s \geq r$, and it is not in any of the sets $\mathcal{O}(n^s)$ for $s < r$. This is a precise way of saying that any polynomial of degree r eventually outgrows polynomials of degree lower than r.

Another suite of containments that you are asked to verify in the exercises is this: $\mathcal{O}(a^n)$ is a proper subset of $\mathcal{O}(b^n)$ for $a < b$. That is, any exponential function $\mu(n) = b^n$ with base b larger than a eventually outgrows any constant multiple of a^n.

One important identity is this: For any positive number m,

$$\ln(n) \leq mn \quad \text{for all sufficiently large } n. \tag{3.16}$$

It is easiest to see and remember this fact from the graphs of $y = \ln(x)$ and $y = mx$, which are shown together in Figure 3.7. An important consequence

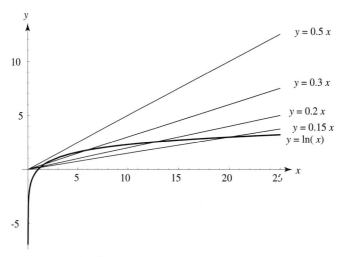

Figure 3.7 The function $y = mx$ eventually outgrows $y = \ln(x)$ for all positive values of m.

of (3.16) is that

$$\mathcal{O}(n^r) \subset \mathcal{O}(a^n)$$

for any $r > 0$ and $a > 1$. This follows because, for the choices of r and a given, we know that $m = \ln(a)/r$ is a positive number, so by (3.16),

$$\ln(n) \leq \left(\frac{\ln(a)}{r}\right) n \quad \text{for all sufficiently large } n.$$

Using properties of logarithms, we can transform the inequality as follows:

$$
\begin{aligned}
r \ln(n) &\leq n \ln(a) \\
\ln(n^r) &\leq \ln(a^n) \\
n^r &\leq a^n, \quad \text{for all sufficiently large } n.
\end{aligned}
$$

The last inequality, by (3.15), says that $\mathcal{O}(n^r) \subset \mathcal{O}(a^n)$.

This gap between the polynomial and exponential complexity classes is much studied in the research literature. Algorithms whose computational expense functions are in, say, $\mathcal{O}(n)$ or $\mathcal{O}(n^2)$ are generally regarded as efficient: The number of steps to complete the algorithm does not grow uncontrollably beyond the size of the input itself. Algorithms whose complexity functions are in $\mathcal{O}(2^n)$ or $\mathcal{O}(n!)$ are regarded as "bad" in that the number of steps to complete the work becomes exceedingly large as the size of the input increases.

A mathematical problem is said to be **computationally infeasible** if for each known algorithm that solves it, the computational expense function is not in $\mathcal{O}(n^r)$ for any $r > 0$. In other words, the computational expense function grows faster, eventually, than any polynomial function. Computationally infeasible problems are "good" from the viewpoint of cryptographers. If they can design an encipherment-decipherment function pair such that an opponent would have to solve a computationally infeasible problem in order to recover plaintext or key information, then the cipher would be unbreakable. This is the basic idea behind public-key cryptography. It has already been illustrated briefly in Exercise 24 of Section 1.1, and it is the subject of Chapter 4.

Summary

Many mathematical problems can be solved in a finite number of steps, perhaps using a systematic trial-and-error approach. For such a solution method, the worst-case number of steps may grow very fast with increasing size of the instance of the problem, so that even a moderate size instance of the problem may not be soluble by this method in a reasonable amount of time. However, for many finite mathematical problems, there are other algorithms for which the number of steps to solve the problem grows only moderately fast with the size of the instance. Complexity theory is concerned with finding the functional relationship between instance size and worst-case (or average, or best case) number of steps to solve the instance using a specific algorithm. If this functional relation is exponential, the algorithm may be regarded as inefficient. If the relation is a polynomial, the algorithm may be regarded as efficient. Problems for which there exists an algorithm with worst-case complexity a polynomial function are called **polynomial-time** problems and are thought of as being feasible. Other problems for which there is no known polynomial-time algorithm may still be feasible in that the computational expense function does not grow immensely faster than polynomials. Computationally infeasible problems are those for which all known solution algorithms have computational expense functions that grow nearly as exponential functions or faster. The big-oh notation $\mathcal{O}(f)$ is used to represent the collection of functions that do not eventually outgrow f. It also serves as a way of talking about computational complexity in that when we refer to an algorithm as being "$\mathcal{O}(f)$" we mean that the computational expense function of the algorithm is in this set. Similarly, a mathematical problem is "in $\mathcal{O}(f)$" if all known algorithms that solve it are in this set. Complexity theory is currently a very active area of research in mathematics and computer science.

EXERCISES

1. Let a_1, a_2, ..., a_n be given positive integers and let t be a given positive integer.

   (a) At most how many comparisons will be needed to determine if t is among the a_i's? At best, how many comparisons are needed?

   (b) At best, how many comparisons will be needed to determine the number of times t appears in the list?

2. Explain why $\mathcal{O}(\log_b(n)) = \mathcal{O}(\ln(n))$ for all $b > 1$.

3. Explain why $\mathcal{O}(a^n)$ is a proper subset of $\mathcal{O}(n^n)$ for all positive values of a.

4. Explain why $\mathcal{O}(n!)$ is a proper subset of $\mathcal{O}(n^n)$. (*Hint:* Use Stirling's[3] formula, $n! \approx \sqrt{2\pi n}e^{-n}n^n$.)

5. Put the following complexity classes in their proper order of containment. If any are equal, indicate that as well. $\mathcal{O}(1.1^n)$, $\mathcal{O}(n^3)$, $\mathcal{O}(3^n)$, $\mathcal{O}(\ln(n))$, $\mathcal{O}(n!)$, $\mathcal{O}(n^3 + n^2)$, $\mathcal{O}(n^{100})$, $\mathcal{O}(n2^n)$, $\mathcal{O}(\log_{10}(n))$, $\mathcal{O}(10^{100})$.

6. Explain why, if $a < b$, any function in $\mathcal{O}(a^n)$ is in $\mathcal{O}(b^n)$. Give an example of a function in $\mathcal{O}(b^n)$ that is not in $\mathcal{O}(a^n)$.

---

[3] James Sterling (1692–1770) was a British mathematician and an associate of Isaac Newton (1642–1727). The approximation formula here was actually developed by Abraham deMoivre (1667–1754).

7. A direct approach to determining whether an integer n bigger than z is prime is **trial division**. It can be described by the following algorithm:

$$\begin{aligned}
\text{Input:} \quad & n \\
\text{Initialize:} \quad & i \leftarrow 2, \ p \leftarrow \text{TRUE} \\
\text{Computation:} \quad & \text{While } i^2 \leq n \text{ and } p = \text{TRUE} \\
& \quad \text{if } n \text{ MOD } i = 0 \\
& \quad\quad \text{then } p \leftarrow \text{ FALSE} \\
& \quad\quad \text{else } i \leftarrow i + 1 \\
\text{Output:} \quad & p
\end{aligned}$$

(a) Implement trial division in your favorite programming environment. Compare how long it takes for it to run to completion on $n = 1234567891$ with how long it takes to run for $n = 12345678929$.

(b) How many multiplications are performed each time the computation part is executed? How many divisions? How many comparisons? Counting each of these operations as a "step" in this algorithm, find the worst-case computational expense function $\mu_{\text{trial division}}(n)$.

(c) Find the smallest value of r such that $\mu_{\text{trial division}}(n) \in \mathcal{O}(n^r)$.

(d) If a number with x digits in its binary representation is used as input to the trial division algorithm, determine the computational expense function $\mu_{\text{binary}}(x)$ in terms of x.

(e) Find a value of a such that $\mu_{\text{binary}}(x) \in \mathcal{O}(a^x)$.

3.4 Stream Ciphers and Feedback Shift Registers

The idea behind the Vigenère encipherment method can be applied to messages written in any alphabet. In particular, the binary alphabet $\{0, 1\}$ is ubiquitous in computer applications, and we therefore examine in this section how the Vigenère method works in binary. In addition, we examine a method of generating keys.

The term **stream cipher** is applied to a cipher in which messages are enciphered symbol by symbol, just before transmission. Simple and polyalphabetic substitutions are examples of stream ciphers. Such ciphers are distinguished from **block ciphers** in which blocks of symbols are enciphered as units. The Hill cipher, for instance, is a block cipher. We will examine block ciphers in Section 3.5.

Binary Vigenère and One-Time Pads

The Vigenère square for the alphabet $\{0, 1\}$ is shown in Table 3.6. It consists

	0	1	plaintext
0	0	1	
1	1	0	
key			

Table 3.6 The Binary Vigenère square.

of all possible shifts of the alphabet. To carry on an enciphered binary correspondence, two parties, Alice and Bob, first agree on a keyword of zeros and ones. Then they encipher plaintext messages in the following way: Locate a plaintext digit in the square's heading and the corresponding key digit in the row labels; the resulting ciphertext digit lies in the column headed by the plaintext and row labeled by the key digit. For instance, if the plaintext is 0, and the key digit is 1, then the ciphertext is 1.

We illustrate with an example.

Example 3.4.1 Let $k = 10110110$ be the key on which Alice and Bob agree, and suppose the plaintext Alice wants to send is

$$x = 10101100\ 10010110\ 00001000.$$

Then she quickly determines the ciphertext by writing the keyword repeatedly beneath the plaintext and then adding plaintext and key bits according to Table 3.6:

$$
\begin{array}{ll}
\text{plain } (x) & 10101100\ \ 10010110\ \ 00001000 \\
\text{key } (k) & 10110110\ \ 10110110\ \ 10110110 \\
\hline
\text{cipher } (y) & 00011010\ \ 00100000\ \ 10111110
\end{array}
$$

Suppose that Bob formulates a reply, enciphers it with this same key, and sends the result

01101000 01101010 01100111 01100111 01100110 01101110

back to Alice. Then Alice can decipher it by writing the keyword repeatedly above the ciphertext and, for each key bit, looking up the ciphertext bit corresponding to it in Table 3.6 and reading off the plaintext bit at the head of that column. Her work would look something like this:

key	00101011	00101011	00101011	00101011	00101011	00101011
cipher	01101000	01101010	01100111	01100111	01100110	01101110
plain	01000011	01000001	01001100	01001100	01001101	01000101

If, for instance, she is expecting the plaintext to be 8-bit representations of ASCII values, then she would find that the blocks represent 67, 65, 76, 76, 77, 69. This yields the plaintext letters CALLME. ◇

There is another way to regard Table 3.6: It is an addition table modulo 2! With this observation, we can write a formula for encipherment. If $k = k_0 k_1 k_2 \ldots k_{m-1}$ is the m-bit keyword and $x = x_0 x_1 x_2 x_3 \ldots$ is a stream of plaintext, then the ciphertext is

$$y_i = (x_i + k_{i \text{ MOD } m}) \text{ MOD } 2, \qquad i = 0, 1, 2, \ldots . \qquad (3.17)$$

Decipherment is a reversal of the enciphering process. Indeed, by (3.17) we know that $y_i \equiv x_i + k_{i \text{ MOD } m} \pmod{2}$, so $x_i \equiv y_i - k_{i \text{ MOD } m} \pmod{2}$. Moreover, since addition and subtraction modulo 2 are the *same*, we actually have

$$x_i = (y_i + k_{i \text{ MOD } m}) \text{ MOD } 2, \qquad i = 1, 2, 3, \ldots . \qquad (3.18)$$

Suppose we have intercepted a reasonably long binary ciphertext that (1) represents an ASCII-encoded English plaintext, and (2) is Vigenère enciphered with a keyword of small known length m but unknown composition. Is it possible to retrieve the original message and the keyword? This is exactly analogous to a cryptanalysis we did in Section 2.5, so the answer is *yes*. The most direct attack would be to write a computer program to generate all the 2^m possible keywords, successively applying them to the ciphertext and decoding the 8-bit groups as ASCII codes. Chances are that only one or a very few of the deciphered and decoded messages will be intelligible. However, if m is fairly large (and the keyword bits are random), then 2^m becomes very large, and it becomes infeasible to generate this many keywords—even with a computer. Moreover, the chances increase for having more than one intelligible deciphered and decoded plaintext. If the keyword is as long as the ciphertext, then—even if it were feasible to generate all the possible keys and try them out—*every* possible intelligible plaintext would be generated and there would be no way to discern the actual message.

This line of reasoning shows that, in order to have a reasonable level of security, a stream of random bits that can be used by sender and receiver simultaneously would be ideal. Such random noise generators have been developed and used in some applications, but they are generally unwieldy to use. The next best solution is for sender and receiver to agree upon an easy way of generating long random-*looking* sequences of 0s and 1s. One such pseudorandom key generator is a **linear-feedback shift register** (LFSR).

Feedback Shift Registers

To motivate the idea of a shift register, we begin with a somewhat silly, but illustrative, example.

Example 3.4.2 In a Memphis neighborhood, four neighbors have established a pattern by which they leave their porch lights on at night:

- Anne does whatever Barbara did the night before.

- Barbara does whatever Cathy did the night before.

- Cathy does whatever Denise did the night before.

- Denise leaves the light on if either Anna or Barbara (but not both) left theirs on the night before; otherwise she leaves it off.

On a particular night, Denise left her porch light on, Cathy had hers off, Barbara had hers off, and Anne had hers off. Determine Anne's pattern of porch lighting on successive nights.

Solution Figure 3.8 shows schematically how the neighbors' porch lighting patterns influence one another. We will think of the boxes as containing lights-on and lights-off information at successive times.

If we represent

$$0 = \text{Lights off}$$
$$1 = \text{Lights on}$$

and

$$D = \text{Denise's porch light status on a given night}$$

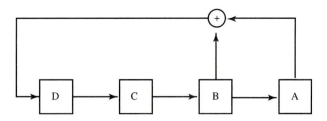

Figure 3.8 Schematic of porch-lighting pattern. The symbol +
indicates addition modulo 2, or exclusive OR.

$$C = \text{Cathy's porch light status on a given night}$$
$$B = \text{Barbara's porch light status on a given night}$$
$$A = \text{Anne's porch light status on a given night}$$

then with A', B', C', and D' representing the light status on the next night, we have

$$A' \leftarrow B$$
$$B' \leftarrow C$$
$$C' \leftarrow D$$
$$D' \leftarrow (B + A) \text{ MOD } 2,$$

where $\leftarrow$ indicates "is replaced by."

The initial configuration of lights is 1 0 0 0, and we calculate light statuses on successive nights as shown in Table 3.7. The pattern in the A column appears "random" through time 14; at time 15 it starts over. $\Diamond$

A **feedback shift register** is an electronic circuit that implements this sort of pattern. Mathematically it is represented by " shift equations" and one "feedback equation." If b_k, ..., b_4, b_3, b_2, b_1 are the bits in the register at given time and b'_k, ..., b'_4, b'_3, b'_2, b'_1 are the bits at the next time, then

$$b'_1 \leftarrow b_2$$
$$b'_2 \leftarrow b_3$$
$$b'_3 \leftarrow b_4$$
$$\vdots$$
$$b'_k \leftarrow (c_k \cdot b_k + c_{k-1} \cdot b_{k-1} + \cdots + c_3 \cdot b_3 + c_2 \cdot b_2 + c_1 \cdot b_1) \text{ MOD } 2,$$

t	D	C	B	A	t	D	C	B	A
0	1	0	0	0	12	0	1	1	1
1	0	1	0	0	13	0	0	1	1
2	0	0	1	0	14	0	0	0	1
3	1	0	0	1	15	1	0	0	0
4	1	1	0	0	16	0	1	0	0
5	0	1	1	0	17	0	0	1	0
6	1	0	1	1	18	1	0	0	1
7	0	1	0	1	19	1	1	0	0
8	1	0	1	0	20	0	1	1	0
9	1	1	0	1	21	1	0	1	1
10	1	1	1	0	22	0	1	0	1
11	1	1	1	1	23	1	0	1	0

Table 3.7 Light statuses of Denise, Cathy, Barbara, and Anne as a function of time t.

where c_1, c_2, c_3, ..., c_{k-1}, c_k are coefficients that are either 0 or 1. The reason that such a shift register is called **linear** is because the bit values at each time are linear functions of the bit values at the previous time; that is, each is a sum of constant multiples of the bit values at the previous time. This is to be distinguished from a **nonlinear-feedback shift register**, which is one where the feedback equations are not linear. For instance, a 4-bit shift register given by

$$b_1' \leftarrow b_2$$
$$b_2' \leftarrow b_3$$
$$b_3' \leftarrow b_4$$
$$b_4' \leftarrow (1 + b_1 + b_2 \cdot b_3 \cdot b_4) \text{ MOD } 2 \tag{3.19}$$

is nonlinear. It is an exercise for you to determine the successive states of this feedback shift register starting with the initial configuration $b_1 = 1$, $b_2 = 0$, $b_3 = 1$, and $b_4 = 1$.

Example 3.4.3 Suppose we have a 4-bit linear shift register with the feedback equations

$$b_1' \leftarrow b_2$$
$$b_2' \leftarrow b_3$$
$$b_3' \leftarrow b_4$$
$$b_4' \leftarrow 1 \cdot b_3 + 0 \cdot b_2 + 1 \cdot b_1$$

and the initial condition $b_4 = 1$, $b_3 = 0$, $b_2 = 1$, and $b_1 = 1$. How long will it take for the shift register pattern in b_1 to begin repeating?

Solution We first calculate

$$
\begin{aligned}
b_1' &\leftarrow b_2 = 1 \\
b_2' &\leftarrow b_3 = 0 \\
b_3' &\leftarrow b_4 = 1 \\
b_4' &\leftarrow b_3 + b_1 = 0 + 1 = 1.
\end{aligned}
$$

Then

$$
\begin{aligned}
b_1' &\leftarrow b_2 = 0 \\
b_2' &\leftarrow b_3 = 1 \\
b_3' &\leftarrow b_4 = 1 \\
b_4' &\leftarrow b_3 + b_1 = 1 + 1 = 0,
\end{aligned}
$$

and so on. It is simpler to represent these bit patterns in tabular form, as shown in Table 3.8. At time 3, you can see that all of the shift register bits

t	b_4	b_3	b_2	b_1
0	1	0	1	1
1	1	1	0	1
2	0	1	1	0
3	1	0	1	1
4	1	1	0	1
5	0	1	1	0

Table 3.8 States of the LFSR in Example 3.4.3.

have returned to their values at time 0, so the pattern of b_1 repeats starting at times 3, 6, 9, ... ◇

Example 3.4.4 For the same shift register as in the previous example, but with the initial condition $b_4 = 1$, $b_3 = 0$, $b_2 = 0$, and $b_1 = 1$, how long will the register run without repeating?

Solution We construct a table of values as before; it is shown in Table 3.9. Since the values of b_4, b_3, b_2, and b_1 at time 6 are the same as they were at time 0, the pattern begins again at times 6, 12, 18, ... ◇

t	b_4	b_3	b_2	b_1
0	1	0	0	1
1	1	1	0	0
2	1	1	1	0
3	1	1	1	1
4	0	1	1	1
5	0	0	1	1
6	1	0	0	1
7	1	1	0	0

Table 3.9 States for the LFSR in Example 3.4.4.

As you can see, the initial pattern of bits in a shift register and the feedback equation determine how long the pattern in b_1 (or any other bit) will run before repeating. There is, for a given number of bits, a bound on the time before a shift register's output begins to repeat: since an n-bit shift register can be in at most 2^n states, any sequence generated by one must begin repeating at or before time $2^n - 1$. It can be shown that for any given n, there are feedback equations and initial conditions that do run $2^n - 1$ time units before repeating.

Example 3.4.5 Suppose Alice and Bob have agreed to use binary Vigenère encipherment with the bit stream b_1 generated by the 5-bit shift register

$$b_5' \leftarrow b_4 + b_2 + b_1$$

started with the initial configuration $b_5 = 1$, $b_4 = 0$, $b_3 = 0$, $b_2 = 0$, and $b_1 = 0$. Alice receives the ciphertext

01001100 00100010 01010001 10011001

Determine what message Alice deciphers, assuming that the 8-bit plaintext blocks represent ASCII values.

Solution You can verify that the stream from b_1 in Alice and Bob's shift register is of period 15, a repetition of the pattern 000010100110111. Then, to decipher, she writes

key	00001010	01101110	00010100	11011100
cipher	01001100	00100010	01010001	10011001
plain	01000110	01001100	01000101	01000101

The 8-bit plaintext blocks represent 70, 76, 69, and 69, which decodes as FLEE. ◇

Cryptanalysis of Shift Register Ciphers

Suppose that Eve has intercepted both a portion of binary plaintext $x = x_1 x_2 \ldots x_n$ and the corresponding ciphertext $y = y_1 y_2 y_3 \ldots y_n$ produced by Vigenère encipherment. Then she can easily recover the portion of the keystream $k = k_1 k_2 k_3 \ldots k_n$ that was used to produce y:

$$k_i = (x_i + y_i) \text{ MOD } 2, \qquad i = 1, \ldots, n.$$

If the keystream is random, then this provides no information about k_{n+1}, k_{n+2}, …. However, if the keystream is only pseudorandom, generated by a linear feedback shift register, then it is possible—indeed easy—for her to reconstruct the shift register, provided there are enough keystream bits recovered. We illustrate with a small example.

Example 3.4.6 Suppose 1000110010 is part of a keystream produced by a 5-bit linear-feedback shift register Eve has obtained by the means outlined previously. She wants to determine the LFSR that produced this piece of the keystream. How can this be done?

Solution Since she knows the number of bits in the register, she can immediately fill in a portion of the table of register states. Assuming the stream comes from bit 1, she puts the given sequence in the column under b_1 (Table 3.10). Also, because bit values shift from higher to lower order, each

t	b_5	b_4	b_3	b_2	b_1
0	1	0	0	0	1
1	1	1	0	0	0
2	0	1	1	0	0
3	0	0	1	1	0
4	1	0	0	1	1
5	0	1	0	0	1
6		0	1	0	0
7			0	1	0
8				0	1
9					0

Table 3.10 Partial table of shift register states for Example 3.4.6.

value shown in the b_1 column, except the first, got there by being shifted down one row and right one column. Exactly the same reasoning allows her to fill in the upper portions of columns b_3, b_4, and b_5. Again, see Table 3.10.

She now also has the initial condition of the shift register, which is the top row of the table.

Eve knows that

$$b_5' \leftarrow c_5 b_5 + c_4 b_4 + c_3 b_3 + c_2 b_2 + c_1 b_1, \qquad (3.20)$$

for $t = 1, 2, \ldots$, where c_1, c_2, c_3, c_4 are unknown. From this and the data in the top six rows of the table, she can construct a system of four congruences (equations) in four unknowns that can readily be solved for the c_is. Figure 3.9 illustrates how she can generate these equations. When $t = 1$,

t	b_5	b_4	b_3	b_2	b_1
0	1	0	0	0	1
1	1	1	0	0	0
2	0	1	1	0	0
3	0	0	1	1	0
4	1	0	0	1	1
5	0	1	0	0	1
6		0	1	0	0
7			0	1	0
8				0	1
9					0

Figure 3.9 Mnemonic for constructing the coefficient equations in Example 3.4.6.

she knows that the current value of the leftmost bit is $b_5' = 1$ and that the bit values at time $t = 0$ are $b_5 = 1$, $b_4 = 0$, $b_3 = 0$, $b_2 = 0$, and $b_1 = 1$. The dependence of b_5' on the values at time $t = 0$ is indicated by the first downward pointing arrow. Substituting these values into (3.20), she gets

$$1 \equiv c_5 \cdot 1 + c_4 \cdot 0 + c_3 \cdot 0 + c_2 \cdot 0 + c_1 \cdot 1.$$

Similarly, when $t = 2$, she has $b_5' = 0$, $b_5 = 1$, $b_4 = 1$, $b_3 = 0$, $b_2 = 0$, $b_1 = 0$, and $b_5' = 0$, so substituting into (3.20) gives

$$0 \equiv c_5 \cdot 1 + c_4 \cdot 1 + c_3 \cdot 0 + c_2 \cdot 0 + c_1 \cdot 0.$$

When $t = 3$, she knows the current value of the leftmost bit is $b_5' = 0$ and that the values of the bits at time $t = 2$ are $b_5 = 0$, $b_4 = 1$, $b_3 = 1$, $b_2 = 0$,

$b_1 = 0$, which gives

$$0 \equiv c_5 \cdot 0 + c_4 \cdot 1 + c_3 \cdot 1 + c_2 \cdot 0 + c_1 \cdot 0.$$

She continues this pattern to obtain two more equations, and combining these with the first two she obtains the system of equations

$$
\begin{array}{rclcccccc}
1 & \equiv & c_5+ & & & & & & c_1 \\
0 & \equiv & c_5 & + & c_4 & & & & \\
0 & \equiv & & & c_4 & + & c_3 & & \\
1 & \equiv & & & & & c_3 & + & c_2 \\
0 & \equiv & c_5 & + & & & & c_2 & + & c_1
\end{array}
$$

By adding the first and fifth congruences, she sees that $c_2 \equiv 1$. Substituting into the fourth congruence, she gets $c_3 \equiv 0$; putting this into the third gives $c_4 \equiv 0$; putting this into the second gives $c_4 \equiv 0$; finally, putting this into the first gives $c_1 \equiv 1$. Thus, Eve can now write down the feedback equation for the shift register:

$$b_5' \leftarrow (0 \cdot b_5 + 1 \cdot b_4 + 1 \cdot b_3 + 0 \cdot b_2 + 1 \cdot b_1) \ \text{MOD} \ 2.$$

If, for instance, she needed to read ciphertext encrypted using the stream from this shift register, she could generate key streams as long as she likes. ◇

Summary

A random or random-looking binary keystream is needed to ensure the integrity of binary Vigenère encryption, the 2-symbol analog of the alphabet-based Vigenère method. Linear-feedback shift registers with appropriate initial values can be used to generate random-looking but periodic keystreams, but they are susceptible to a known-plaintext attack with very little data.

EXERCISES

1. Encode the message TALK by representing the ASCII values for the letters in 7-bit binary blocks and use binary Vigenère to encipher the resulting bits using the key 1010011.

2. The following is a binary Vigenère encipherment of a plaintext using the key 11100010100010. Decipher and decode the message, regarding each 7-bit block as an ASCII value:

0100010 1100111 0111101 1101110 0100010 1110110 0111110
1100001 0111010

3. Complete the table of outputs for the following linear-feedback shift registers, with the given initial condition.

(a) $b_5 \leftarrow b_4 + b_1$, 10101

(b) $b_4 \leftarrow b_3 + b_2 + b_1$, 1000

(c) $b_6 \leftarrow b_4 + b_2$, 100000

(d) $b_6 \leftarrow b_4 + b_2$, 111000

4. Find the 4-bit linear-feedback shift registers that produce the following output streams.

(a) 10100010

(b) 11101001

5. Encipher the message NEED WATER by encoding the ASCII values for the letters in 8-bit binary blocks and use binary Vigenère to encipher the resulting bits using the key generated by the shift register in Exercise 3 (a).

6. Find the 5-bit linear-feedback shift registers that produce the following output streams.

(a) 1000111110

b) 1000110111

7. Suppose that the bit sequence 0000010111 was generated by a linear-feedback shift register. Could that register have 3 bits? 4? 5? Explain.

8. What is the maximal period of a 10-bit shift register? Suppose you were going to try out all possible two-term feedback equations for this 10-bit register to try to find one of maximal period. Potentially how many would you have to try? Is it certain that any of them would produce a maximal-period output?

9. Find the states of the nonlinear-feedback shift register given in (3.19) until it begins to repeat earlier states. What is its period?

3.5 Block Ciphers

A **block cipher** is a symmetric encryption method in which blocks of plaintext of a fixed length are turned into blocks of ciphertext of the same length. The Hill cipher is an example: Plaintext is enciphered in blocks of two letters to produce two-letter ciphertext blocks. A desirable feature of a block cipher is that each symbol in a block of ciphertext depend on all of the symbols of the corresponding plaintext block and on all the symbols in the key. For instance, a Vigenère cipher with a five-letter keyword would *not* be a true block cipher because it does not have this sort of distributed dependence: cipher letter number 3 would be independent of letters 1, 2, 4, and 5 in both plaintext and key. It might more properly be termed a *stream cipher*.

In modern usage, the symbol alphabet is usually $\{0, 1\}$. The design of block ciphers has been an active area of cryptographic research over the years. Its general objective is to scramble the plaintext bits in such a way so that[4]

- Each bit of ciphertext should depend on all bits of the key and on all bits of the plaintext.

- There should be no evident statistical relationship between plaintext and ciphertext.

- Altering any single plaintext or key bit should alter each ciphertext bit with probability $\frac{1}{2}$.

- Altering a ciphertext bit should result in an unpredictable change to the recovered plaintext.

In practice it is very difficult to attain all of these criteria.

It is beyond the scope of this text to describe in detail how such standard block ciphers as DES, FEAL (Fast Data Encipherment Algorithm), and IDEA (International Data Encryption Algorithm) work, but it is possible at least to illustrate the pattern by which these ciphers operate. The block cipher defined in the following example is very loosely modeled after these sorts of algorithms.

Example 3.5.1 Let $S(x)$ be a function defined by the following table:

---

[4]See Menezes, van Oorschot, and Vanstone [52], page 256.

$x_1x_2x_3$	$S(x_1x_2x_3)$
000	11
001	01
010	00
011	10
100	01
101	00
110	11
111	10

Such a function is sometimes referred to in the literature as an **s-box**. For a given 4-bit block of plaintext $x_1x_2x_3x_4$ and 3-bit key $k_1k_2k_3$, let

$$t_1t_2 = S(x_3x_4x_3 \oplus k_1k_2k_3)$$
$$u_1u_2 = x_1x_2 \oplus t_1t_2$$
$$E(x_1x_2x_3x_4, k_1k_2k_3) = x_3x_4u_1u_2,$$

where $\oplus$ represents **exclusive or** (see Exercise 2 in Section 3.2). For example, if $x = 1100$ and $k = 011$, then

$$t_1t_2 = S(000 \oplus 011) = S(011) = 10$$
$$u_1u_2 = 11 \oplus 10 = 01$$
$$E(1100, 011) = 0001.$$

You can verify that the encipherment function E can be inverted as follows. Given a ciphertext $y_1y_2y_3y_4$ computed with E and key $k_1k_2k_3$, compute

$$t_1t_2 = S(y_1y_2y_1 \oplus k_1k_2k_3)$$
$$u_1u_2 = y_3y_4 \oplus t_1t_2$$
$$D(y_1y_2y_3y_4, k_1k_2k_3) = u_1u_2y_1y_2.$$

Try calculating $D(0001, 011)$.

Now, we agree to compute ciphertext by applying E to the plaintext three times. Each of these applications of E is called a **round**. Thus the ciphertext $y = y_1y_2y_3y_4$ from plaintext $x = x_1x_2x_3x_4$ and key $k = k_1k_2k_3$ is given by

$$y = F_k(x) = E(E(E(x, k), k), k).$$

For instance, if $x = 1100$ and $k = 011$, as above, then the ciphertext is

$$y = E(E(E(1100, 011), 011), 011)$$

$$= E(E(0001, 011), 011)$$
$$= E(0101, 011)$$
$$= 0100,$$

as you can verify by evaluating E at the appropriate values.

If a plaintext is SPEAK FREELY, then its binary ASCII representation is, with the 8-bit values subdivided into 4-bit blocks,

0101 0011 0101 0000 0100 0101 0100 0001 0100 1011 0100 0110
0101 0010 0100 0101 0100 0101 0100 1100 0101 1001

We encipher each block with three rounds of E and a chosen key. You can verify (by hand this would be very tedious; a computer algebra system or program in some appropriate language would be useful) that, with the key $k = 101$, the ciphertext is

0101 1100 0101 0000 1010 0101 1010 1001 1010 0010 1010 0100
0101 1000 1010 0101 1010 0101 1010 0011 0101 0110

To decipher a binary message in 4-bit blocks enciphered by this method, we apply three rounds of the decryption function D with the key to each 4-bit block. That is, $F_k^{-1}(y) = D(D(D(y, k), k), k)$. ◇

All block ciphers can be represented, either for application or cryptanalysis, as Boolean functions (see Section 3.2).

Example 3.5.2 The encipherment function in Example 3.5.1 can be represented by a formula. First, use the method of Example 3.2.2 to obtain formulas for the digits of the function S:

$$S(x_1 \, x_2 \, x_3) = ((1+x_1+x_2+x_3+x_1 \cdot x_3) \text{ MOD } 2)((1+x_2+x_1 \cdot x_2+x_1 \cdot x_3) \text{ MOD } 2).$$

Here, each set of parentheses encloses a formula for one bit. Then use these in the formulas used to define the encipherment function E:

$$
\begin{aligned}
t_1 \, t_2 = \; & ((1 + k_1 + k_2 + k_3 + k_1 \cdot k_3 + k_1 \cdot x_3 + k_3 \cdot x_3 + x_3^2 + x_4) \text{ MOD } 2) \\
& ((1 + k_2 + k_1 \cdot k_2 + k_1 \cdot k_3 + k_1 \cdot x_3 + k_2 \cdot x_3 + k_3 \cdot x_3 + x_3^2 + x_4 \\
& + k_1 \cdot x_4 + x_3 \cdot x_4) \text{ MOD } 2),
\end{aligned}
$$

$$
\begin{aligned}
u_1 \, u_2 = \; & (x_1 \, x_2) \oplus (t_1 \, t_2) \\
= \; & ((1 + k_1 + k_2 + k_3 + k_1 \, k_3 + x_1 + k_1 \, x_3 + k_3 \, x_3 + x_3^2 + x_4) \text{ MOD } 2) \\
& ((1 + k_2 + k_1 \cdot k_2 + k_1 \cdot k_3 + x_2 + k_1 \cdot x_3 + k_2 \cdot x_3 \\
& + k_3 \cdot x_3 + x_3^2 + x_4 + k_1 \cdot x_4 + x_3 \cdot x_4) \text{ MOD } 2),
\end{aligned}
$$

and

$$E(x_1\, x_2\, x_3\, x_4, k_1\, k_2\, k_3)$$
$$= (x_3)(x_4)(u_1)(u_2)$$
$$= (x_3)(x_4)((1 + k_1 + k_2 + k_3 + k_1 \cdot k_3 + x_1 + k_1 \cdot x_3 + k_3 \cdot x_3$$
$$+x_3^2 + x_4) \ \text{MOD} \ 2)((1 + k_2 + k_1 \cdot k_2 + k_1 \cdot k_3 + x_2 + k_1 \cdot x_3$$
$$+k_2 \cdot x_3 + k_3 \cdot x_3 + x_3^2 + x_4 + k_1 \cdot x_4 + x_3 \cdot x_4) \ \text{MOD} \ 2).$$

You can also verify that decipherment is given by the formula

$$D(y_1\, y_2\, y_3\, y_4, k_1 k_2 k_3)$$
$$= ((1 + k_1 + k_2 + k_3 + k_1 \cdot k_3 + k_1 \cdot y_1 + k_3 \cdot y_1 + y_1^2 + y_2 + y_3) \ \text{MOD} \ 2)$$
$$((1 + k_2 + k_1 \cdot k_2 + k_1 \cdot k_3 + k_1 \cdot y_1 + k_2 \cdot y_1 + k_3 \cdot y_1 + y_1^2 + y_2$$
$$+k_1 \cdot y_2 + y_1 \cdot y_2 + y_4) \ \text{MOD} \ 2)(y_1)(y_2). \quad \diamond$$

Feistel Networks

The overall design of many currently used block ciphers follows a pattern suggested by Claude Shannon in [73]. Alternation of substitutions and transpositions of appropriate forms applied to a block of plaintext can have the effect of obscuring statistical relationships between the plaintext and ciphertext and between the key and ciphertext. One means of accomplishing these goals, which Shannon called *diffusion* and *confusion*, is by employing what we will call here a **Feistel[5] function**.

We begin by looking at a simple example of such a function, and then we look at the idea in greater generality. For a 3-bit k and 2-bit x, let $f_k(x)$ be the Boolean function given by

$$f_{k_1 k_2 k_3}(x_1\, x_2) = ((1 + k_1 \cdot x_1^2 + k_2 \cdot x_1 \cdot x_2) \ \text{MOD} \ 2)((k_1^2 \cdot x_1 \cdot x_2 + k_3 \cdot x_2^2) \ \text{MOD} \ 2),$$

where the parentheses surround the respective bit values and all arithmetic is done modulo 2. Then, for instance,

$$f_{011}(1\,0) = (1 + 0 \cdot 1^2 + 1 \cdot 1 \cdot 0)(0 \cdot 1 \cdot 0 + 1 \cdot 0^2) = 10.$$

Now define $F_{k_1 k_2 k_3}(x_1 x_2 x_3 x_4)$ by

$$F_{k_1\, k_2\, k_3}(x_1\, x_2\, x_3\, x_4) = (x_3\, x_4) \,\|\, (x_1\, x_2 \oplus f_{k_1\, k_2\, k_3}(x_3\, x_4)),$$

---

[5] Horst Feistel headed the team at IBM that developed Lucifer, the precursor to DES.

where $\|$ denotes concatenation of the two string. For example,

$$
\begin{aligned}
F_{011}(1110) &= (1\,0)\,\|\,(1\,1 \oplus f_{011}(1\,0)) \\
&= (1\,0)\,\|\,(1\,1 \oplus 1\,0) \\
&= (1\,0)\,\|\,(0\,1) \\
&= 1\,0\,0\,1.
\end{aligned}
$$

The function $F_k(x)$ is invertible. To find its inverse we need to solve

$$
y_1\,y_2\,y_3\,y_4 = (x_3\,x_4)\,\|\,(x_1\,x_2 \oplus f_k(x_3\,x_4))
$$

for $x_1\,x_2\,x_3\,x_4$ in terms of $y_1\,y_2\,y_3\,y_4$. The first two bits on each side of the equation must be equal, so

$$
x_3 = y_1 \text{ and } x_4 = y_2.
$$

Consequently $x_3\,x_4 = y_1\,y_2$.

The second two bits on each side of (3.5) must also be equal, so

$$
y_3\,y_4 = x_1\,x_2 \oplus f_k(y_1\,y_2).
$$

When we XOR both sides with $f_k(y_1\,y_2)$, this part cancels from the right-hand side, so

$$
x_1\,x_2 = y_3\,y_4 \oplus f_k(y_1\,y_2).
$$

Thus the inverse of F_k is

$$
F_k^{-1}(y_1\,y_2\,y_3\,y_4) = (y_3\,y_4 \oplus f_k(y_1\,y_2))\,\|\,y_1\,y_2.
$$

Notice that finding the inverse of F_k did not rely on the specific form of f_k. Because, for each choice of $k = k_1\,k_2\,k_3$, F_k is invertible, it can serve as an encipherment function with key k.

In general, if $f_k(x)$ is a function of an n-bit string and a m-bit string k that produces an n-bit value, define $F_k(x)$ to be the function of $2n$-bit x and m-bit k given by

$$
F_k(x) = R(x)\,\|\,(L(x) \oplus f_k(R(x))),
$$

where $L(x)$ denotes the left n bits of x and $R(x)$ the right n bits of x. We call $F_k(x)$ a **Feistel function**. For each choice of k, it is invertible, and (you should verify) its inverse is

$$
F_k^{-1}(y) = (R(y) \oplus f_k(L(y)))\,\|\,L(y).
$$

The general design criterion in block ciphers that use this model is to choose $f_k(x)$ so that when $F_k(x)$ is applied over and over with a succession of different key values k (perhaps derived from one main key), it will be exceedingly difficult to recover the key even if the cryptanalyst knows a considerable amount of ciphertext and the corresponding plaintext. You can think of a well-designed Feistel function as analogous to efficient bread kneading in which the ingredients (flour, oil, water, yeast, etc.) are well mixed. Indeed, in his paper [73], Shannon makes this sort of analogy. The difference is that it is impossible to un-knead bread dough, whereas it is possible to reverse the application of $F_k(x)$, with knowledge of the key k.

Modes of Block Cipher Operation

A block cipher F_k is said to be used in **electronic codebook** (ECB) **mode** if ciphertext blocks $y_1\, y_2\, \ldots\, y_n$ are computed from plaintext blocks $x_1\, x_2\, \ldots\, x_n$ by

$$y_i = F_k(x_i), \; i = 1, \ldots, n.$$

Figure 3.10 shows this in diagram form. In effect, each plaintext block is

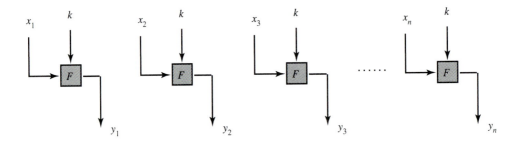

Figure 3.10 A block cipher F operating in ECB mode.

enciphered by looking up the block to substitute for it in a "codebook" specified by F_k. In Example 3.5.1 the block cipher was applied in ECB mode. ECB mode is the most straightforward mode of operation, but it is vulnerable to the same sort of attack as simple substitutions: Frequencies of cipher blocks may be evident. Even if the encipherment were done in 32-bit or 64-bit blocks, frequency analysis might still be used to break the cipher.

To circumvent that problem, designers of digital block ciphers have resorted to a trick used in the sixteenth century: a form of Vigenère autokey encipherment! If $F_k(x)$ is a function that enciphers a block x with key k, then F_k is said to be used in **cipher block chaining (CBC) mode** if ciphertext blocks y_1, y_2, ..., y_n are computed from plaintext blocks x_1, x_2, ..., x_n by

$$
\begin{aligned}
y_1 &= F_k(x_1) \\
y_i &= F_k(y_{i-1} \oplus x_i), \qquad i = 2, 3, \ldots, n.
\end{aligned}
$$

This is shown schematically in Figure 3.11.

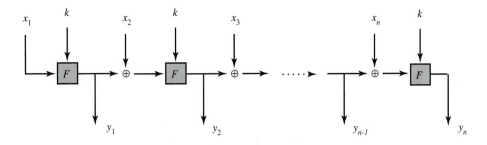

Figure 3.11 A block cipher F in CBC mode, with initial vector the first plaintext block.

For example, the simple-minded block cipher at Example 3.5.1, used in CBC mode with key $k = 101$ to encipher 0101 0011 0101 0000, would give the following results:

$$
\begin{aligned}
y_1 &= F_{101}(0101) \\
&= E(E(E(0101, 101), 101), 101) \\
&= 0101 \\
y_2 &= F_{101}(y_1 \oplus 0011) \\
&= E(E(E(y_1 \oplus 0011, 101), 101), 101) \\
&= E(E(E(0101 \oplus 0011, 101), 101), 101) \\
&= E(E(E(0110, 101), 101), 101) \\
&= 0100 \\
y_3 &= F_{101}(y_2 \oplus 0101) \\
&= E(E(E(y_2 \oplus 0101, 101), 101), 101) \\
&= E(E(E(0100 \oplus 0101, 101), 101), 101) \\
&= E(E(E(0001, 101), 101), 101)
\end{aligned}
$$

$$
\begin{aligned}
&= 1001 \\
y_4 &= F_{101}(y_3 \oplus 0000) \\
&= E(E(E(y_3 \oplus 0000, 101), 101), 101) \\
&= E(E(E(1001 \oplus 0000, 101), 101), 101) \\
&= E(E(E(1001, 101), 101), 101) \\
&= 0110.
\end{aligned}
$$

From (3.21) and (3.21) we can readily obtain the CBC mode decryption scheme. Evidently, $x_1 = F_k^{-1}(y_1)$. Also, by the second equation, $y_{i-1} \oplus x_i = F_k^{-1}(y_i)$. When we XOR both sides of this with y_{i-1}, we obtain $x_i = F_k^{-1}(y_i) \oplus y_{i-1}$. Thus CBC decryption is

$$
\begin{aligned}
x_1 &= F_k^{-1}(y_1) \\
x_i &= F_k^{-1}(y_i) \oplus y_{i-1}, \ i = 2, \ldots, n.
\end{aligned}
$$

In other situations CBC mode is initiated by using an **initial value**, an arbitrary priming key agreed upon by sender and receiver that is used as the first block of ciphertext. This is analogous to the priming key used in Vigenère autokey (see Section 1.1).

A n-bit block cipher F can be "wired up" with a shift register to make a new with a different block length m. This is referred to as using F in **cipher feedback (CFB) mode**. In particular, if the new block length is 1, then the result is a stream cipher (that is, plaintext is enciphered bit by bit).

A shift register is a function of the form

$$
S(a_1\, a_2\, \ldots\, a_n, \, b_1\, b_2\, \ldots\, b_m) = a_{m+1}\, a_{m+2} \ldots a_n\, b_1 \ldots b_m,
$$

where $a_1 \ldots a_n$ and $b_1 \ldots b_m$ are bit strings and $m < n$. Notice that the input to S is two strings and its output is a single string with the first m bits of the first string "forgotten" and the second input string appended to provide a new "remembered" string. For example,

$$
S(10101101, \, 1111) = 11011111.
$$

We can think of S schematically, as shown in Figure 3.12.

With $L_m(y)$ representing the leftmost m bits of a string y, we can now specify cipher feedback mode in general. Figure 3.13 summarizes: We see that plaintext blocks x_1, x_2, $\ldots$, each with m bits, initial n-bit block I and key k are turned into m-bit ciphertext blocks y_1, y_2, $\ldots$. The gray box

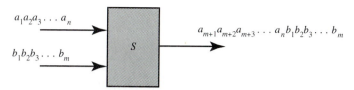

Figure 3.12 Schematic of a shift register. S shifts the bit string $a_1 a_2 \ldots a_n$ left by m bits ("forgetting" bits $a_1 a_2 \ldots a_m$) and appends the bit string $b_1 b_2 \ldots b_m$ to make a new n-bit string $a_{m+1} a_{m+2} \ldots a_n b_1 b_2 \ldots b_m$.

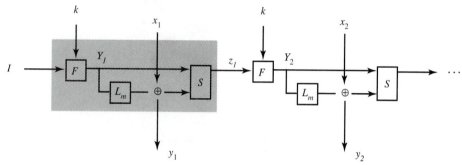

Figure 3.13 An n-bit block cipher F in CFB mode becomes an m-bit $(m < n)$ block cipher.

encompasses one m-bit encipherment, which takes three inputs and produces two outputs. The encipherment steps can then be written as

$$
\begin{aligned}
z_0 &= I \\
y_i &= x_i \oplus L_m(F_k(z_{i-1})) \\
z_i &= S(F_k(z_{i-1}), y_i), \quad i = 1, 2, 3, \ldots.
\end{aligned} \tag{3.21}
$$

It is an exercise for you to determine formulas and a diagram for CFB decryption.

Example 3.5.3 Suppose that F_k is the 4-bit block cipher of Example 3.5.1 and that it is to be run in CFB mode as a 2-bit cipher on the three plaintext blocks $x_1 = 10$, $x_2 = 11$, $x_3 = 00$ with key $k = 101$ and initialization $I = 1011$. Determine the ciphertext.

Solution We use (3.21). First, note that $z_0 = I = 1011$ and $m = 2$. Then

$$
\begin{aligned}
y_1 &= x_1 \oplus L_2(F_k(z_0)) \\
&= 10 \oplus L_2(F_{101}(1011)) = 10 \oplus L_2(0010)
\end{aligned}
$$

$$= \quad 10 \oplus 00 = 10$$

and

$$
\begin{aligned}
z_1 &= S(F_k(z_0), y_1) \\
&= S(0010, 10) = 1010.
\end{aligned}
$$

The next step is

$$
\begin{aligned}
y_2 &= x_2 \oplus L_2(F_k(z_1)) \\
&= 11 \oplus L_2(F_{101}(1010)) \\
&= 11 \oplus L_2(0001) \\
&= 11 \oplus 00 = 11
\end{aligned}
$$

and

$$
\begin{aligned}
z_2 &= S(F_k(z_1), y_2) \\
&= S(0001, 11) = 0111,
\end{aligned}
$$

and finally

$$
\begin{aligned}
y_3 &= x_3 \oplus L_2(F_k(z_2)) \\
&= 00 \oplus L_2(F_{101}(0111)) \\
&= 00 \oplus L_2(0111) \\
&= 00 \oplus 01 = 01.
\end{aligned}
$$

It is not necessary to compute z_3. Why? Thus the plaintext 10, 11, 00 becomes the ciphertext 10, 11, 01 when F is run in CFB mode with key $k = 101$. ◇

Commonly Used Block Ciphers

It is possible to sketch the operation of the Data Encryption Standard with the toy block cipher of Example 3.5.1 in mind. In Chapter 5 we will discuss DES in greater detail. DES takes as input a 64-bit plaintext $x = x_1 x_2 x_3 \ldots x_{64}$ and a 56-bit key $k = k_1 k_2 k_3 \ldots k_{56}$, and it produces a 64-bit ciphertext $y = y_1 y_2 y_3 \ldots y_{64}$. First, it applies a transposition that merely rearranges the bits in x to give a new 64-bit block, which we designate x'. Then it divides x' into a left half L of 32 bits and a right half R of 32 bits (note the parallel with the example) and performs 16 rounds of the following procedure:

$$
\begin{aligned}
T &\leftarrow L \\
L &\leftarrow R \\
R &\leftarrow T \oplus f(R, K).
\end{aligned}
\tag{3.22}
$$

Here, as elsewhere in this book, the symbol $\leftarrow$ indicates that the variable on the left takes the value of the expression on the right. The variable T is temporary storage for the value of L, which is destroyed with the operation $L \leftarrow R$. In the third line of (3.22), f is a function defined in terms of eight s-boxes, each of which maps a 6-bit input into a 4-bit output (analogous to the function S in Example 3.5.1). The **round key** K is different for each round and is derived from the 56-bit key k in a way specified in the standard. (In our toy example, we used the same key in each round.) When the 16 rounds are completed, the resulting 32-bit left and right halves are arranged as (L, R) and the inverse of the transposition at the beginning is applied to this 64-bit combined string to produce the 64-bit ciphertext. A schematic diagram of DES is given in Figure 5.1 on page 325, where it is discussed in more detail than here.

You might expect that decryption is just as arcane, but, in fact, the same algorithm works for decryption! The only difference is that the round keys are used in reverse order. That is, if K was the key for round 1 of encryption, then it will be the key for round 16 in decryption; if K was the key for round 2 of encryption, then it will be the key for round 15; and so on. This is explained in more detail in Section 5.1, but the basic reason is the form of Feistel decipherment.

Another widely used block cipher is the **International Data Encryption Algorithm (IDEA)**, which was designed by two researchers, James Massey and Xuejia Lai, in Switzerland in 1990. IDEA takes 64-bit plaintext blocks as input and produces 64-bit output blocks. A 128-bit key is used to generate subkeys that are used in each of eight rounds of an encryption function. IDEA's decryption algorithm is the same as its encryption algorithm. CAST-128, developed by **C**arlisle **A**dams and **S**tafford **T**avares at NORTEL, is another widely used block cipher, again built on the Feistel function model.

The new Advanced Encryption Standard, Rijndael, selected by NIST in fall 2000, is a block cipher. The block length can be 128, 192, or 256 bits, and the key length can independently be set to any of these values as well. Like the other block ciphers mentioned here, it uses s-boxes and several rounds using subkeys derived from the main key. Unlike DES and CAST, for instance, Rijndael is not based on the Feistel structure.

Summary

A **block cipher** is an encryption method (function) that takes as input a fixed number of plaintext symbols and that, for each choice of key, produces output consisting of a fixed number of ciphertext symbols. In applications, the function incorporates **confusion** and **diffusion**, features that make ciphertext-only, known-plaintext, and chosen-plaintext cryptanalyses difficult. In other words, a genuinely useful block cipher obscures statistical properties of plaintext and key. The definitions of block ciphers are often arcane, as the examples in this section show, but they do adhere to some design principles, such as the Feistel function model, which allows the decryption function to be specified readily from encryption. Modes of block cipher operation, such as CBC, and CFB, can strengthen the encryption; CFB can also be used to turn a block cipher into a random number generator or a feedback shift register.

EXERCISES

1. Use the block cipher $F_k(x)$ in Example 3.5.1 to encipher the plaintext AH by using the 8-bit binary ASCII representation of the letters, subdividing into 4-bit blocks, and using the key $k = 001$.

2. Verify that if an encryption function $E(x, k)$, with corresponding decryption function $D(y, k)$ is used in CBC mode according to

$$
\begin{aligned}
c_0 &= \text{initial value} \\
c_i &= E(m_i, c_{i-1}), \quad i = 1, 2, 3, \ldots
\end{aligned}
$$

then decryption is accomplished by

$$
\begin{aligned}
c_0 &= \text{initial value} \\
m_i &= c_{i-1} \oplus D(c_i, k), \quad i = 1, 2, 3, \ldots.
\end{aligned}
$$

3. A block cipher can be used in CBC mode with an initial vector I, as shown in Figure 3.14.

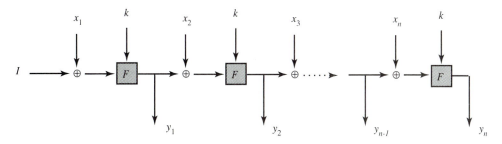

Figure 3.14 Figure for Exercise 3.

  (a) Find the formulas for encryption.

  (b) Find the formulas for decryption.

4. (a) Find formulas for CFB mode decryption, and draw a flow diagram that represents it.

  (b) Verify that it works by decrypting the ciphertext produced in Example 3.5.3.

5. Let $f_{k_1 \, k_2}(x_1 \, x_2) = ((k_1 \, k_2 \, x_1 + k_1 \, x_2^2) \ \text{MOD} \ 2)((k_1 \, x_1^2 \, x_2 + k_2^2 \, x_1 \, x_2) \ \text{MOD} \ 2)$, and let $F_{k_1 \, k_2}(x_1 \, x_2 \, x_3 \, x_4)$ be the corresponding Feistel function. Write an explicit formula for $F_k^{-1}(x)$.

6. Write a computer program in your favorite programming environment that implements CBC mode and CFB mode for the toy cipher of Example 3.5.1. Test it by reproducing the results given in the text.

3.6   Hash Functions

In general, a **hash**[6] **function** is an efficiently evaluated function that takes an input string (usually binary) of arbitrary length and produces an output string of some fixed length, called a **hash value** or **message digest**. This

---

[6]According to the dictionary, the word *hash* used as a verb can mean "to chop into pieces; to mince" or "to make a mess of; to mangle." Both of these capture some of what hash functions are supposed to do: Chop up the input data and make a "mess" of it so that the original data would be difficult or impossible to deduce from the mangled remains.

value provides a way of checking whether the message has been manipulated or corrupted in transit or storage. It is a sort of "digital fingerprint." Moreover, the message digest can be encrypted using either conventional or public-key (which is the subject of the next chapter) cryptography to produce a **digital signature**, which is used to help the recipient feel confident that the received message is not forged.

The desiderata of a hash function H are these:

- It should be **one-way**: For a given hash value v it should be infeasible for an opponent to find a message x such that $H(x) = v$.

- It should at least be **weakly collision resistant**: Given a hash value v and the message x from which it was computed, it should be computationally infeasible for an opponent to find another message y different from x such that $H(y) = v$.

- It might be **strongly collision resistant**: It is computationally infeasible for an opponent to find a pair of distinct messages x and y such that $H(x) = H(y)$.

Sender, recipient, and opponent all know the hash function. A recipient of a hashed message can check for manipulation by "hashing" the message (that is, applying the hash function to the received message) and comparing the result with the hash value that was prepended to the received message. If the two hash values agree, the probability is high that there was no manipulation; if the two disagree, it is certain that some manipulation or corruption in the data took place. Thus hash functions generate a sort of error detecting code.

Example 3.6.1 Grace and Alan are concerned that their e-mails may be intercepted and modified in transit. They agree to compute a hash value $H(x)$ of an e-mail message x as follows. Group the letters (ignoring spaces and punctuation) into five-letter blocks and pad if necessary at the end to make the message length exactly a multiple of 5. Then, treating the letters as representing numbers in the range 0 to 25, they sum letters 1, 6, 11 ... modulo 26 to obtain the first hash letter y_1, sum letters 2, 7, 12, ... modulo 26 to obtain a second hash letter y_2, and so on. The five letters representing these five sums are the value of this hash function: $H(x) = y_1\, y_2\, y_3\, y_4\, y_5$. The hash value will be sent first in a preliminary message, and then the message itself will be sent.

For example, suppose Grace wants to send

$$x = \text{ITISM UCHEA SIERT OAPOL OGIZE THANI TISTO GETPE RMISS IONXX}^7$$

in this scheme to Alan then she computes the hash letters by

$$y_1 \equiv \text{I} + \text{U} + \text{S} + \text{O} + \text{O} + \text{T} + \text{T} + \text{G} + \text{R} + \text{I} \equiv \text{N} \pmod{\text{BA}}$$
$$y_2 \equiv \text{T} + \text{C} + \text{I} + \text{A} + \text{G} + \text{H} + \text{I} + \text{E} + \text{M} + \text{O} \equiv \text{C} \pmod{\text{BA}}$$
$$y_3 \equiv \text{I} + \text{H} + \text{E} + \text{P} + \text{I} + \text{A} + \text{S} + \text{T} + \text{I} + \text{N} \equiv \text{W} \pmod{\text{BA}}$$
$$y_4 \equiv \text{S} + \text{E} + \text{R} + \text{O} + \text{Z} + \text{N} + \text{T} + \text{P} + \text{S} + \text{X} \equiv \text{K} \pmod{\text{BA}}$$
$$y_5 \equiv \text{M} + \text{A} + \text{I} + \text{L} + \text{E} + \text{I} + \text{O} + \text{E} + \text{S} + \text{X} \equiv \text{J} \pmod{\text{BA}}.$$

She first sends NCWKJ and then she sends the plaintext unencrypted.

On the other end, after receiving a hash value and a message, Alan sums the message letters in the same way to produce a hash word. He compares this with the one that preceded the message. If the two are the same, he regards the message as likely to be the one Grace sent. If they are different, he is certain that either the message was altered, or the hash value was altered, or both. In this case, he rejects the received message.

Why does agreement between Alan's computed and received hash words make it likely that the message was unaltered? Suppose, for instance, that Evelyn, an opponent, knows the hashing algorithm, has learned the hash value Grace sent, and would like to alter or replace the message to Alan. If, for example, she changed the letters EASI to HARD in the message, then she would change the message, but Alan would (you should verify) compute the hash word MXWNJ and compare it with NCWKJ to see that something was amiss. If Evelyn picked an intelligible English sentence at random, what would be the probability that it hashed to NCWKJ? An easier question is, if Evelyn picked a random string of letters, what would be the probability that it hashed to NCWKJ? Assuming that the strings that do hash to NCWKJ are in some sense uniformly distributed throughout all strings, then this probability is $\frac{1}{26^5} = \frac{1}{11881376} \approx 8.4 \times 10^{-8}$ (why?). The subcollection of these strings hashing to NCWKJ that are also intelligible English sentences is only a tiny proportion, so the probability of Evelyn choosing an English text at random that hashes to NCWKJ is small indeed. Of course, knowing the details of the hashing algorithm, Evelyn might be able to improve her odds significantly. ◇

---

[7]Grace Murray Hopper (1906–1992), admiral in the U.S. navy and inventor of the COBOL programming language, in a 1987 speech.

Example 3.6.2 Consider the following procedure applied to strings of bits whose length is a multiple of 8: Divide the string into 8-bit blocks; let f denote the operation of reversing bits in adjacent pairs in a single 8-bit block. That is,

$$f(x_1x_2x_3x_4x_5x_6x_7x_8) = x_2x_1x_4x_3x_6x_5x_8x_7.$$

We apply f in CBC mode to a plaintext m and keep the last 8 bits of ciphertext generated as the hash value. In other words, if m_1, m_2, m_3, ..., m_k are the 8-bit blocks of a message m, then we calculate

$$
\begin{aligned}
c_1 &= f(m_1) \\
c_2 &= f(c_1 \oplus m_2) \\
c_3 &= f(c_2 \oplus m_3) \\
&\;\vdots \\
c_k &= f(c_{k-1} \oplus m_k)
\end{aligned}
$$

and set

$$h(m) = c_k.$$

For example, if $m = 10110101\ 11010001\ 00101101$, then $k = 3$ and we have

$$
\begin{aligned}
c_1 &= f(10110101) = 01111010 \\
c_2 &= f(01111010 \oplus 11010001) = f(10101011) = 01010111 \\
c_3 &= f(01010111 \oplus 00101101) = f(01111010) = 10110101
\end{aligned}
$$

so

$$h(10110101\ 11010001\ 00101101) = 10110101. \quad \diamondsuit$$

In the foregoing example, there are $2^{24} = 16777216$ different possible plaintexts but only $2^8 = 512$ different hash values. Thus, if we computed the hash value for all the possible different messages, we would find hash values occurring many times. By pure guesswork, however, it might take a while to find another, but an examination of f reveals a genuine weakness. Just apply f to the hash value, use that result as the last 8-bit block of a message, and make the preceding blocks all zeros. Also, you can construct two different messages very easily that hash to the same value. This is an exercise.

Hash functions are selected so that their values will be essentially uniformly distributed for the population of expected messages. If there are M possible messages, and z is a k-bit hash value, then there are about $M/2^k$ messages that hash to z, so the probability of an adversary guessing a message that hashes to z is about

$$\frac{M/2^k}{M} = \frac{1}{2^k}.$$

So with a secure hash function that produces, say, a 160-bit hash value—as does the federal **Secure Hash Standard**[8]—the probability of random guesswork leading to a message for a given hash value is

$$\frac{1}{2^{160}} = \frac{1}{1461501637330902918203684832716283019655932542976}$$
$$= 6.84228 \, 10^{-49}.$$

Presumably, very sophisticated guessing might raise this number a few orders of magnitude, but the probability will still be infinitesimal.

The MD4 hash function—so named because it was the fourth in a series of **m**essage **d**igest algorithms (or **m**anipulation **d**etection algorithms)—was proposed by Rivest in 1990. Later it was strengthened, and the new version was called MD5. MD5 first **pads** (that is, appends bits to) the plaintext so that its length is congruent to 448 modulo 512. Then the length of the original message, represented as a 64-bit number, is appended to produce an input whose length is $448 + 64 \equiv 512 \equiv 0 \, (\mathrm{mod} \, 512)$. This is shown schematically in Figure 3.15. The full details of the MD5 algorithm are more complex then we can present here, but we can represent it in schematic form. Figure 3.16 shows how one 512-bit block x of padded plaintext is processed. A 128-bit **chaining variable**, denoted by v in the figure, keeps track of the hash value. It contains the output from the processing of the previous 512-bit block of plaintext. The bits of x are subdivided into 128-bit subblocks and processed in four "rounds" that depend on the four 32-bit subblocks of v through a complex regime of nonlinear functions, which are represented by the rectangular boxes in the diagram. The 32-bit subblocks of v are then added modulo 2^{32} (denoted by ⊞) to the respective subblocks of the fourth round, and the result, y, is a new value of the chaining variable that will

---

[8]This standard was proposed by the National Institute of Standards and Technology (NIST), published in the Federal Register on January 31, 1992 and adopted as a standard in 1993.

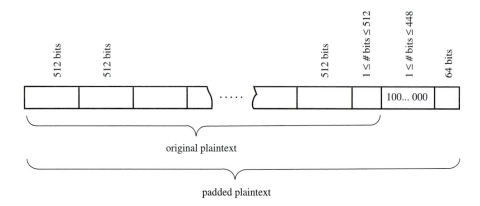

Figure 3.15 For MD5, the original plaintext is padded with enough bits so that the overall message length is a multiple of 512.

be used to process the next block of plaintext. To process the very first plaintext block, the blocks of the chaining variable are always set to the values

$$01100111010001010010001100000001$$

$$11101111110011011010101110001001$$

$$10011000101110101101110011111110$$

$$00010000001100100101010001110110.$$

The last value computed for the chaining variable is the hash value. We can summarize this in a formula: If $F(v, x)$ represents the portion of Figure 3.16 in the gray box, v_0 represents the initial value of the chaining variable just given, and x_1, x_2, ..., x_m are the 512-bit blocks of padded plaintext, then the MD5 algorithm is

$$
\begin{aligned}
v &\leftarrow v_0 \\
v &\leftarrow F(v, x_i), \ i = 1, 2, \ldots, m \\
\mathrm{MD5}(x) &= v.
\end{aligned}
$$

A detailed description of the "round" functions can be found in [71], [80], and [83].

The Secure Hash Algorithm (SHA), the function used to implement the SHS, is based on the same methods. It also works with 512-bit message

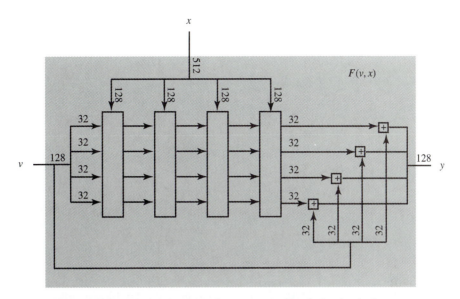

Figure 3.16 A schematic of one "round" of the hash function MD5. The numbers on the lines indicate the number of bits in that portion of the processing.

blocks, but the output of its mixing function is 160 bits. Consequently, its output is a 160-bit hash value, and nominally it is 2^{32} times more secure than MD5. However, it is slower, and the fact that the hash value length is not a power of 2 may be an inconvenience in some applications. A detailed description of SHA is beyond the scope of this text, but there is considerable information about SHA in [80].

Keyed Hash Functions, MACs

In our general discussion of hash functions, the manipulation detection will be successful only when the hash value is transmitted *before* the message itself. If, for instance, the hash value is appended to the message, then Evelyn can intercept the message-hash pair from Grace, discard the hash value, modify the message, generate a new hash value from the altered message, and send this new pair on to Alan. The received message will hash to the received hash value, so Alan will be oblivious to Evelyn's modifications. Worse yet, Evelyn can simply initiate communication with Alan and masquerade as Grace. For instance, she could create a message such as "Alan, meet me at *Chez Phillipe* on Tuesday at 7:00. Grace," hash it, and send the pair on to unwitting Alan.

To provide the convenience of a single transmission and the assurance that the message is not forged or altered, Alan and Grace can generate a hash value that depends on a secret *key* shared only by them. The reason this will work is that if Evelyn were to forge a message to Alan, then she would have to know the key shared by Grace and Alan in order to generate a hash value that he would find to correspond with the message and key. Similarly, Evelyn's attempts at modifying messages would be thwarted as well. Explaining this is one of the exercises.

A short fixed-length keyed hash value such as we have described here is called a **message authentication code** (**MAC**). It might well be called a **signature** since, as long as the correspondents keep the key secret and the hashing algorithm is reasonably effective, the chances are low that an intermediary will be able to forge or modify messages.

Any block cipher can be used to generate MACs. If $F_k(x)$ is a block cipher and two correspondents share a key k and initialization value I, then one party can obtain a MAC from a message m with blocks m_1, m_2, m_3, ..., m_n by computing

$$
\begin{aligned}
c_1 &= I \\
c_i &= c_{i-1} \oplus F_k(m_i), \quad i = L, 3, \ldots, n
\end{aligned}
$$

and setting

$$h_k(m) = c_n.$$

Example 3.6.3 Let $E(x, k)$ be the encipherment function in Example 3.5.1, and let $F_k(x) = E(E(E(x, k), k), k)$. Suppose that two correspondents have set up a keyed hash function as described here, so that a binary message in 4-bit blocks hashes to 4-bits. If the initial value is $I = 0101$ and $k = 110$, then, for instance, the message $m = 1101\ 0010\ 1001\ 0110$ is hashed as follows:

$$
\begin{aligned}
c_0 &= I = 0101 \\
c_1 &= c_0 \oplus F_k(m_1) = 0101 \oplus f(1101, 110) = 1010 \\
c_2 &= c_1 \oplus F_k(m_2) = 1010 \oplus f(0010, 110) = 1011 \\
c_3 &= c_2 \oplus F_k(m_3) = 1011 \oplus f(1001, 110) = 1011 \\
c_4 &= c_3 \oplus F_k(m_4) = 1011 \oplus f(0110, 110) = 0101
\end{aligned}
$$

and

$$h_k(m) = h_{010}(1101\ 0010\ 1001\ 0110) = c_4 = 0101. \quad \diamond$$

Another approach to generating MACs is to use an unkeyed hash function such as MD5 or SHA, which will typically run much faster than an encryption algorithm on a computer, to generate a message digest and then "sign" the digest by applying a block cipher to it.

Summary

Hash functions take arbitrary-length input and generate a fixed-length output that serves as a "fingerprint" of the input. This value is called a hash value or a message digest. Hash functions are designed so that different inputs are unlikely to hash to the same value, thus providing a level of certainty that the input was not corrupted or altered in transit or storage. Sophisticated hash functions such as MD5 and the Secure Hash Algorithm are used as part of generating digital signatures. Hash functions can be based on block ciphers and therefore may have key values associated with them.

EXERCISES

1. Use the hashing algorithm in Example 3.6.1 to find the hash value for the message

   IF IT'S A GOOD IDEA, GO AHEAD AND DO IT.

2. Determine which of the following message hash-value pairs shows that there has been a manipulation or corruption of the message or hash.

   (a) $x =$ MAKEH AYWHI LETHE SUNSH INESX
   hash: QYAJD

   (b) $x =$ MAKEH AYWHI LETHE MOONS HINES
   hash: QYAJD

   (c) $x =$ TODAY ISTHE FIRST DAYOF THERE STOFY OURLI FEXXX
   hash: NMRRH

   (d) $x =$ THERE STOFY OURLI FEXXX
   hash: NMRRH

3. Find two sensible five-letter English words such that the 10-letter message consisting of them hashes to DSCWR. (*Hint*: Try words starting with H and W.)

(a) Determine how many 10-letter strings hash to XBVTK by the hash function described in Example 3.6.1. What fraction of *all* 10-letter strings is this?

(b) Determine how many 15-letter strings hash to XBVTK. What fraction of all 15-letter strings is this?

(c) In general, determine how many $5n$-letter strings hash to XBVTK. What fraction of all $5n$-letter strings is this?

4. For the hash function described in Example 3.6.2, construct two different 24-bit plaintexts that hash to the same value.

5. Suppose that a hash function H is defined as follows: Let m be a message with blocks m_1, m_2, ..., m_k be a binary message with 8-bit blocks m_i, $i = 1, \ldots, k$. Let f be the function defined in Example 3.6.2; let

$$
\begin{aligned}
c_1 &= f(m_1) \\
c_i &= c_{i-1} \oplus f(m_i), \quad i = 2, \ldots, k
\end{aligned}
$$

and let

$$H(m) = c_k.$$

Determine the hash value for the message

$$m = 10100110\ 00101101\ 10111000.$$

6. Explain why a keyed hash function will prevent Evelyn from modifying communications between Grace and Alan.

7. Write a computer program that implements the text-based hash function of Example 3.6.1.

Chapter 4

Public-Key Cryptography

The notion of **public-key cryptography** is very new. It dates from the late 1960s, when a British cryptographer, James H. Ellis, published an article in an internal journal at The Government Communications Headquarters[1] (GCHQ) entitled "Non Secret Encryption." His work was not made public until much later, after the mid-1970s, when academic researchers such as Rivest, Adelman, Shamir, Hellman, Diffie, and Merkle discovered and published what they called "public-key cryptography." In essence, public-key cryptography entrusts mathematics itself with keys to a cryptosystem. An individual wishing to receive encrypted communication from others would no longer have to trust those others with her keys. Instead, she entrusts certain presumably intrinsically difficult mathematical problems to keep the decryption key in her possession alone.

One of the first public-key systems was proposed by Ralph Merkle and Marty Hellman, a faculty-graduate student pair at Stanford University. Their method, often called the **knapsack**, is elegant and startlingly simple, and we present it here as an example to introduce the concept.

To understand such methods as **RSA** encryption, we must study some **number theory**; consequently, there are sections here devoted to this area of mathematics. Besides providing a beautiful application of mathematics and a strong cryptographic tool, RSA and related ideas also provide the basis for **key exchange**, **digital signatures**, and **message authentication**.

Finally, in this chapter we discuss **user identification** schemes that are also based on public-key cryptological concepts.

---

[1]The United Kingdom's foremost codebreaking organization. See [4], page xvii, for more information.

4.1 Primes, Factorization, and the Euclidean Algorithm

The purpose of this section is to discuss facts of arithmetic that play an important role in public-key cryptology. It is no exaggeration to say that these ideas are fundamental to understanding and using a wide array of modern cryptosystems.

The prime numbers appear to be irregularly distributed among the integers, and yet there are striking regularities that permit us to find large prime numbers quickly. Factoring large numbers, however, seems to be a computationally infeasible problem to solve, in general. For this reason, cryptosystems that rely directly on this difficulty are often thought to be secure. Generating keys for public-key cryptosystems such as RSA requires computing modular inverses of integers, and the extended Euclidean algorithm provides an efficient means of doing this.

Prime Numbers

The prime numbers are the basic building blocks of arithmetic, and they are of profound importance in cryptology. Understanding fundamental facts about these numbers will help you to see where the strengths and weaknesses of some modern cryptosystems lie. To begin, you should look at the table of primes on page 370, which contains a list of all the prime numbers less than 10 860. You can generate part of this table yourself simply by trial division (see Exercise 7 in Section 3.3). For instance, if you are testing 1241 to see if it is prime, it is easy to check for small factors such as 2, 3, 5, and 7. None of these divides 1241. The largest possible proper divisor would be no more than $\sqrt{1241} = 35.2278\ldots$, so at worst we will have to check primes up through 31. We check that 11 and 13 do not divide 1241, but we find $17 \cdot 73 = 1241$, so 1241 is not prime.

In general, if we want to determine whether a positive integer n is prime and we do not have a complete list of primes up to $\lfloor \sqrt{n} \rfloor$, we try dividing n by 2, and then all of the odd numbers from 3 up to $\lfloor \sqrt{n} \rfloor$. If along the way we encounter a zero remainder, then n is composite and we can stop; if we do not, then n is prime. We can shorten the work: If n is not divisible by 2, then there is no point in checking to see if it is divisible by 4, 6, 8, $\ldots$; if n is not divisible by 3, there is no point in checking divisibility by 6, 9, 12, $\ldots$.

There is a method, known as the **sieve of Erathosthenes,**[2] that can be helpful in locating all of the primes in a range of integers. We illustrate its use to find all of the primes in the range from 1 to 100. Write all these numbers in a rectangular array as shown in Figure 4.1. Any multiple of 2 is not prime, so strike out all the numbers below 2 in the second column and all of columns 4, 6, 8, and 10. Next strike out all multiples of 3; notice that these all lie on parallel diagonal lines on the grid. The next number not crossed out is 5, which is the next prime; cross out all multiples of 5 not already crossed out. The next number not crossed out is 7, so it is the next prime, as we already know. Marking through all multiples of 7, which lie on lines of "slope" -2 passing through 7, 14, and 21, we have now struck out all numbers in the table that are not prime! Why is this? Any nonprime still left must contain at least two prime factors neither of which can be 7 or smaller. That is, any composite number left in the array must have at

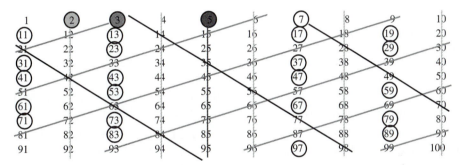

Figure 4.1 The sieve of Eratosthenes used to find the primes in the range 1 to 100.

least two prime factors, both of which are 11 or more. In other words, the smallest composite number left after this process is $11 \cdot 11 = 121$, which is bigger than 100. Indeed, if we extended the list of numbers to 121 and continued each line into the enlarged array, then the primes up to 121 would be found as well. It is an exercise for you to do this.

It seems intuitive that if we test successive integers greater than the largest prime in our table, 10 860, then we will eventually turn up another prime. Indeed, it seems that, given any positive integer, we should be able to find a *prime* integer larger than it. For instance, if you start at 4 trillion

---

[2]Erathosthenes (c. 230 B.C.), a native of Cyrene, longtime citizen of Athens, and chief librarian at Alexandria. Besides being known as a mathematician, he was also recognized as an astronomer, athlete, geographer, historian, philosopher, and poet.

(a composite number) and check 4 trillion and 1, 4 trillion and 3, ..., you would expect to encounter a prime eventually. However, notice in the table of primes that there are long stretches where there are no primes. For instance, if you started searching for primes at 1328, you would find that $1\,329, 1\,330, 1\,331, \ldots, 1\,358, 1\,359$, and $1\,360$ are all composite; this is a list of 33 consecutive composite numbers! Indeed, it can be proven that there are *arbitrarily long* lists of consecutive composite numbers. This fact and the general "thinning" we see in the primes in larger ranges of integers makes it plausible that we might eventually run out of primes. However, we have the following theorem, which was proved by Euclid (c. 300 B.C.).

Theorem 4.1.1 *There are infinitely many prime numbers.*

Proof The proof method we use is *contradiction*. We suppose that the statement we want to prove is actually false, and from this supposition deduce something that is contrary to a theorem that is already known.

Suppose that there are finitely many primes $p_1 = 2$, $p_2 = 3$, $p_3 = 5$, ..., p_n. Then $p_n + 1$, $p_n + 2$, $p_n + 3$, ..., are all composite. Now consider the number

$$N = p_1 \cdot p_2 \cdot p_3 \cdots \cdot p_n + 1.$$

It is larger than p_n, and it is not divisible by p_1, p_2, p_3, ..., p_{n-1}, or p_n because the remainder in each case is 1. Thus N has no proper prime divisors, so by the fundamental theorem of arithmetic, it must be prime. But this contradicts our assumption that all integers larger that p_n are composite. This means that our assumption of finitely many primes was false: There must be infinitely many primes. $\diamondsuit$

There is no known formula, in terms of elementary functions,[3] for the nth prime. This is part of what makes prime numbers so interesting and useful to cryptographers. Also, there is no known formula in terms of elementary functions that gives the next prime following a given one. For instance, we know that $224\,737$ is prime, but we do not have an easy way to calculate the next prime after this one other than to do trial division on $224\,739$, $224\,741$, etc. The graph in Figure 4.2 shows the lengths of the gap between successive primes, and these certainly appear to be rather erratic.

Another view of the prime distribution data, however, shows some striking *regularity*. Let $\pi(n)$ stand for the number of primes less than or equal to n. For example, $\pi(29) = 10$. Then the *proportion* of the numbers 1, 2, 3,

---

[3]Polynomials, exponentials, logarithms, trigonometric functions, etc.

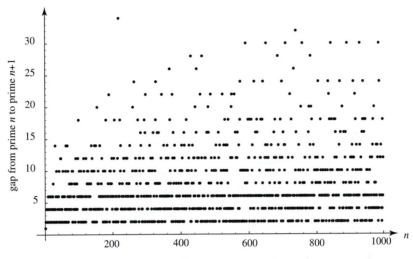

Figure 4.2 Gaps between successive primes.

4, ..., n that are prime is $\pi(n)/n$. Figure 4.3 shows $\pi(n)/n$ as a function of n. These points, especially for larger values of n, seem to lie along a curve.

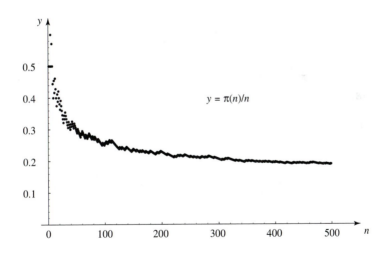

Figure 4.3 The density of primes as a function of n, $y = \pi(n)/n$.

Indeed the curve resembles the graphs of such functions as $\frac{1}{n}$, $\frac{1}{n^2}$, $\frac{1}{\sqrt{n}}$, and $\frac{1}{\ln n}$. Figure 4.4 shows the graph of $\pi(n)/n$ superimposed on that of $1/\ln n$. Great mathematicians of the late eighteenth and early nineteenth centuries,

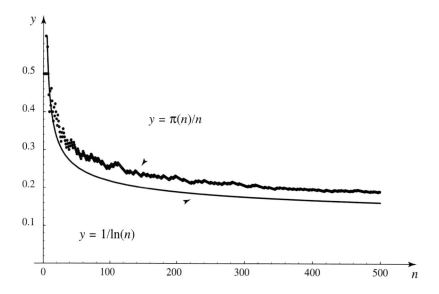

Figure 4.4 Graphs of $y = \pi(n)/n$ and $y = 1/\ln n$ superimposed.

such as Gauss and Legendre, noticed this and conjectured that

$$\frac{\pi(n)}{n} \approx \frac{1}{\ln n}$$

for large values of n or, equivalently,

$$\pi(n) \approx \frac{n}{\ln n}.$$

Later, the following theorem was proved.

Theorem 4.1.2 (Prime Number Theorem) *The ratio $\frac{\pi(n)}{n/\ln(n)}$ is arbitrarily close to 1 for all sufficiently large[4] values of n.*

The theorem says that if we wish to find a value n_0 of n such that

$$\frac{\pi(n)}{n/\ln(n)} - 1 < 0.000001 \quad \text{for} \quad n = n_0,\ n = n_0 + 1,\ n = n_0 + 2,\ \dots,$$

then—in principle—our wish can come true.

---

[4]If you have studied calculus, then you will recognize that this statement can be expressed as $\displaystyle\lim_{n \to \infty} \frac{\pi(n)}{n/\ln(n)} = 1$.

From the prime number theorem it follows that

$$\frac{\pi(n)}{n} \approx \frac{1}{\ln n}, \quad \text{for large values of } n. \tag{4.1}$$

The approximation in (4.1) can be interpreted in terms of probabilities. It says that if we choose a large value of n and a number at random from among $1, 2, \ldots, n$, the probability that it is prime is approximately $\frac{1}{\ln n}$. The graph suggests that $\frac{1}{\ln n}$ is an *underestimate* of the probability.

Suppose we wish to find a prime number with ten decimal digits. Then, since we are accustomed to ignoring leading zeros, this means that we are looking for a number in the range 1000000000 to 9999999999 that is prime. If we assume that the distribution of primes across the range 1 to 9999999999 is roughly uniform, then about 90% of the primes in this range will be between 1000000000 and 9999999999. So the probability that a randomly selected 10-digit number is prime is—by the prime number theorem—the product $0.9 \cdot \frac{1}{\ln(9999999999)} = 0.9 \cdot 0.0434 = 0.0391$. Thus, the probability of failing to get a prime with one choice is $1 - 0.0391 \approx 0.961$.

How many random 10-digit numbers would we have to choose in order to be reasonably confident of finding at least one that is prime? This question can be answered by extending our line of reasoning. We want to find a number k such that the probability at least one of k random choices from the range 1000000000 to 9999999999 is prime. By one of the properties of probability, this is

$$1 - \text{prob}\begin{pmatrix} k \text{ successive composite} \\ \text{10-digit numbers} \end{pmatrix}.$$

Let's assume for the moment that each time we pick a number, we "put it back" before selecting the next one. We already know that the probability of a 10-digit number being composite is about 0.961. By the multiplication principle,

$$\text{prob}\begin{pmatrix} k \text{ successive composite} \\ \text{10-digit numbers} \end{pmatrix}$$

$$= \text{prob}\begin{pmatrix} \text{composite} \\ \text{number on} \\ \text{1st choice} \end{pmatrix} \cdot \text{prob}\begin{pmatrix} \text{composite} \\ \text{number on} \\ \text{2nd choice} \end{pmatrix} \cdots \cdots \text{prob}\begin{pmatrix} \text{composite} \\ \text{number on} \\ k\text{th choice} \end{pmatrix}$$

$$= \underbrace{0.961 \cdot 0.961 \cdots \cdots 0.961}_{k \text{ factors}}$$

$$= 0.961^k.$$

Thus the probability of getting at least one prime by choosing k 10-digit numbers is about

$$1 - 0.961^k.$$

Table 4.1 shows several values of this expression for various k. You can see

k	p_k	k	p_k
1	0.0391	21	0.567
2	0.0766	22	0.584
3	0.113	23	0.600
4	0.147	24	0.616
5	0.181	25	0.631
6	0.213	26	0.645
7	0.244	27	0.659
8	0.273	28	0.673
9	0.302	29	0.685
10	0.329	30	0.698
11	0.355	31	0.709
12	0.380	32	0.721
13	0.404	33	0.732
14	0.428	34	0.742
15	0.450	35	0.752
16	0.472	36	0.762
17	0.492	37	0.771
18	0.512	38	0.780
19	0.531	39	0.789
20	0.550	40	0.797

Table 4.1 Probabilities that among k 10-digit numbers, at least one is prime.

that even with $k = 40$, the probability is only about 80%. In order to raise the probability to, say, 95%, we must take k to be about 76.

Factoring

The fundamental theorem of arithmetic tells us that every positive integer can be written as a product of powers of primes in essentially one way. (Remember that we regard a prime number as a trivial product of one prime to the first power.) However, it does not tell us what the prime factors or exponents are. A direct and sure-fire approach to finding the prime factors of a number is **trial division**: Simply divide successive primes into the number to see whether the division leaves a zero remainder. When a prime divides the number, then apply trial division to the quotient of the number by the prime. If, at any stage of this process, we divide a number by all of the primes up to the square root of that number and none of these divides it, then that number is prime. Any other prime factors already found, along with the last one, constitute the prime factorization.

Example 4.1.1 Find the prime factorization of $n = 6647$.

Solution At a glance we see that n is not divisible by 2, 3, or 5. Since $\sqrt{n} = 81.529\ldots$, we only need to check at most among the 20 remaining primes up to 79 to find divisors. So we check that n is not divisible by 7, 11, and 13. Then $6647 = 391 \cdot 17$, so 17 is a prime divisor. We find the divisors of 391 by starting with 17. In this case we find $391 = 17 \cdot 23$. Since we recognize 23 as prime, we have our factorization:

$$6647 = 17^2 \cdot 23. \quad \Diamond$$

Fermat's factoring method can sometimes be used to find any large factors of a number fairly quickly. It relies on the algebraic fact that the difference of two squares factors as the product of the sum and the difference of the two squared numbers: $b^2 - a^2 = (b+a)(b-a)$. If n is a number to be factored, let b be the smallest integer such that $b^2 \geq n$. Then compute $q = b^2 - n$. If q is a perfect square, then $q = a^2$ for some integer a and $n = b^2 - a^2 = (b+a)(b-a)$, a factorization. If q is not a perfect square, then replace b^2 with $b^2 + 2b + 1$, the next larger perfect square, and recompute $q = b^2 - n$. If this is a perfect square, then n is factored; if not, then repeat the process. This cannot go on indefinitely since

$$n = b^2 - q = (b + \sqrt{q})(b - \sqrt{q})$$

and if $b + \sqrt{q} > n/2$, then there is no hope of finding an integer value of b such that $b^2 - n$ is a perfect square.

Example 4.1.2 Let $n = 43947$. Then $\sqrt{n} \approx 209.64$, so let $b = 210$ be the starting value of b. We have

b	$q = b^2 - n$	$\sqrt{q}$	$b + \sqrt{q}$
210	153	12.37	222.37
211	574	23.96	234.96
212	997	31.58	243.58
213	1422	37.71	250.71
214	1849	43	257

When $b = 214$, we see that $q = 43^2$ is a perfect square, so n factors as $n = (214 + 43) \cdot (214 - 43) = 257 \cdot 171$. Then either Fermat's method or trial division can be applied to the respective factors to produce a prime factorization. Better yet, just observe that the two factors appear in the table of primes, so the job is complete!   ◊

Example 4.1.3 Let $n = 97$. Then start with $b = 10$:

b	$b^2 - n = q$	$b + \sqrt{q}$
10	$100 - 97 = 3$	11.73
11	$121 - 97 = 24$	15.90
12		18.86
13	$\vdots$	21.4
14		
$\vdots$		
24	479	45.89
25	528	47.98
26	579	50.06

We see that since $50.06 > 97/2$, all possible values of $a = \sqrt{q}$ have been tried and there are no whole numbers among them. Thus this shows that 97 is prime, which, of course, we already knew. This also illustrates that, the behavior of Fermat's method at its worst: Sixteen steps were needed to verify the primeness of 97. By comparison, even if we used trial division by each number in the range 2, 3, 4, 5, 6, 7, 8, $9 = \lfloor \sqrt{97} \rfloor$, we would use only 8 steps.   ◊

There are many clever methods for factoring large numbers such as Pollard's $p - 1$ method, the elliptic curve method, and the number field sieve method; see, for instance, [40] and [10]. It is beyond the scope of this text to discuss any of these. However, it is worth pointing out that the expected computational expense of factoring n, for the Number Field Sieve is in $\mathcal{O}(e^{c\ln(n)^{1/3}\ln(\ln(n))^{2/3}})$ for some constant c. We compare $e^{\ln(n)^{1/3}\ln(\ln(n))^{2/3}}$ with $\sqrt{n}$, which is the function representing the complexity class of trial division, by graphing the two functions together. This is shown in Figure 4.5. As you can see, the square root function grows much faster than the other, so for very large n, the number field sieve, can be expected to take much less time than trial division. However, the number field sieve is not a polynomial-time algorithm. For instance, Figure 4.6 compares $e^{\ln(n)^{1/3}\ln(\ln(n))^{2/3}}$ and $\ln(n)^2$, which would be the representative function for a factoring algorithm whose expense function was in $\mathcal{O}(x^2)$, where x is the number of digits in the number. The general problem of factoring is thought to be intrinsically hard,

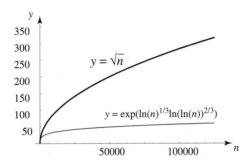

Figure 4.5 Comparing the computational expense of trial division (upper curve) with the number field sieve (lower curve).

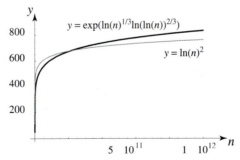

Figure 4.6 Comparing the computational expense of the number field sieve (dark curve) with that of a putative polynomial time algorithm (light curve).

in the category of non-polynomial-time problems, which was described in Section 3.3.

The Euclidean Algorithm

In Section 2.2, we learned that a positive integer a has a multiplicative inverse modulo m precisely when a and m are relatively prime; that, is when their greatest common divisor is 1. We write $\gcd(a, m) = 1$. Determining whether two given numbers are relatively prime is fairly easy when the numbers are small or when the numbers are factored into their prime factors. Also, finding a multiplicative inverse is straightforward when the modulus is small: Trial and error quickly turns up the inverse. However, for cryptographic purposes, we often need to determine whether two *large* numbers are relatively prime and what the multiplicative inverse of one is modulo the other. Factoring the numbers would tell if they are relatively prime, but that process, using any known method, would take a very long time for numbers with, say, 75 digits in their decimal representations. Moreover, once we obtained the factorizations, there would remain the problem of determining the multiplicative inverse of one.

Consider the problem of finding the greatest common divisor of 285 and 54 435. The smaller number could actually *be* the greatest common divisor, and indeed we find, upon dividing it into the larger one, that the quotient is 191 and the remainder is 0. Thus $\gcd(54\,435, 285) = 285$.

The same question is not quite so easily addressed for 1512 and 5628. When we divide the larger by the smaller, the remainder is not zero:

$$5628 = 3 \cdot 1512 + 1092. \tag{4.2}$$

If we write this as

$$1092 = 5628 - 3 \cdot 1512,$$

we see that the greatest common divisor d of 5628 and 1512 is a divisor of 1092. Moreover, by (4.2), any divisor of 1512 and 1092 is no bigger than d (if there were some other larger common divisor of 1512 and 1092, then it would be a divisor of 5628, contradicting our identification of d as the *greatest* common divisor of 5628 and 1512). In short, $\gcd(5628, 1512) = \gcd(1512, 1092)$.

We have reduced the question of finding $\gcd(5628, 1512)$ to that of finding the gcd of two smaller numbers. We can now divide 1092 into 1512 and repeat the reasoning to reduce again the size of the numbers involved:

$$1512 = 1 \cdot 1092 + 420.$$

By reasoning as earlier, $\gcd(1512, 1092) = \gcd(1092, 420)$. Now

$$1092 = 2 \cdot 420 + 252$$

so $\gcd(1092, 420) = \gcd(420, 252)$. Next,

$$420 = 1 \cdot 252 + 168$$

so $\gcd(420, 252) = \gcd(252, 168)$. Next,

$$252 = 1 \cdot 168 + 84,$$

so $\gcd(420, 252) = \gcd(252, 168)$. Then

$$168 = 2 \cdot 84,$$

so $\gcd(168, 84) = 84$. Because all of the gcd's are equal, we now know that

$$\gcd(5628, 1512) = 84.$$

The reasoning here is not tied to the particular numbers used in the example. Indeed, both of the examples illustrate the only two possible outcomes in each step. This process is known as the **Euclidean algorithm**, and it can be succinctly described in this way: If $a = qb + r$, where q and r are the quotient and remainder given by the division algorithm, then

$$\gcd(a, b) = \begin{cases} b, & \text{if } r = 0 \\ \gcd(b, r), & \text{if } r \neq 0. \end{cases}$$

This is an example of a **recursive formula**, one that defines a function's value at one point in terms of its value at another point. Using MOD notation, we can write the Euclidean algorithm very compactly:

$$\gcd(a, b) = \begin{cases} b, & \text{if } a \text{ MOD } b = 0 \\ \gcd(b, a \text{ MOD } b), & \text{if } a \text{ MOD } b \neq 0. \end{cases} \tag{4.3}$$

The reason that this algorithm always works to find the greatest common divisor of two positive integers is that the value of (4.3) is either one of the two numbers, in which case the algorithm halts, or else the value of (4.3) is the gcd of a smaller pair of positive numbers. At successive steps, the same reasoning applies: Either the gcd is one of the two numbers or the value is the gcd of a still smaller pair of positive integers. The process cannot continue indefinitely because there are only finitely many positive integer pairs (x, y) with $1 \leq x \leq a$ and $1 \leq y \leq b$. Indeed, in Figure 4.7 you can see the ordered pairs generated by the Euclidean algorithm in our example and that they all lie in the gray trapezoidal region shown. We can also use our

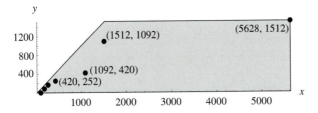

Figure 4.7 The steps in applying the gcd algorithm to the pair
of numbers $(5628, 1512)$.

work here to write the gcd in a useful form in terms of the original numbers.
Writing the results of our divisions as

$$5628 - 3 \cdot 1512 \quad = \quad 1092 \tag{4.4}$$
$$1512 \quad = \quad 1 \cdot 1092 + 420 \tag{4.5}$$
$$0 \quad = \quad -1092 \; + 2 \cdot 420 + 252 \tag{4.6}$$
$$0 \quad = \qquad\qquad -420 \quad + 1 \cdot 252 + 168 \tag{4.7}$$
$$0 \quad = \qquad\qquad\qquad\qquad -252 + 1 \cdot 168 + 84 \tag{4.8}$$

we see that we can eliminate all of the remainders except 84 from these
equations. Adding $(-1) \times (4.7)$ to (4.8) eliminates 168:

$$0 = 420 - 2 \cdot 252 + 84. \tag{4.9}$$

Then adding $2 \times (4.6)$ to (4.9) eliminates 252 to yield

$$0 = -2 \cdot 1092 + 5 \cdot 420 + 84. \tag{4.10}$$

Then $(-5) \times (4.5)$ added to (4.10) gives

$$(-5) \cdot 1512 = -7 \cdot 1092 + 84. \tag{4.11}$$

Finally adding $7 \times (4.4)$ to (4.11) gives

$$7 \cdot 5628 - 26 \cdot 1512 = 84. \tag{4.12}$$

These additional steps constitute what is sometimes called the **extended
Euclidean algorithm**, which results in a representation of the gcd as a
linear combination of the two original numbers. The backward elimination
we performed here can be done with any pair of positive integers, so we have
an outline of the proof of the following theorem.

Theorem 4.1.3 *For any two positive integers a and b there exists integers s and t such that*

$$as + bt = \gcd(a, b).$$

The situation in which we are particularly interested is when $\gcd(a, b) = 1$. In this case we know from Chapter 2 that b has a multiplicative inverse modulo a. The theorem tells us what the inverse *is*!

Corollary 4.1.1 *If a and b are relatively prime (that is, $\gcd(a, b) = 1$), then b has an inverse modulo a. Moreover, $b^{-1} \equiv t \,(\mathrm{mod}\,a)$, where s and t are any integer solutions to*

$$as + bt = 1.$$

The proof is an exercise.

Example 4.1.4 Find $\gcd(629, 357)$, and find s and t such that $629s + 357t = \gcd(629, 357)$.

Solution We apply the Euclidean algorithm:

$$
\begin{aligned}
629 &= 1 \cdot 357 + 272 \\
357 &= 1 \cdot 272 + 85 \\
272 &= 3 \cdot 85 + 17 \\
85 &= 5 \cdot 17 + 0.
\end{aligned}
$$

By the earlier discussion, the greatest common divisor is 17. Writing the first three equations as

$$629 - 1 \cdot 357 = 272 \tag{4.13}$$
$$357 = 1 \cdot 272 + 85 \tag{4.14}$$
$$0 = -272 + 3 \cdot 85 + 17, \tag{4.15}$$

we can do the backward elimination procedure: $(-3) \times (4.14)$ added to (4.15) gives

$$(-3)(357) = -4 \cdot 272 = 17. \tag{4.16}$$

Then adding $4 \times (4.13)$ to (4.16) gives

$$4 \cdot 629 - 7 \cdot 357 = 17,$$

which shows that $s = 4$ and $t = -7$ are solutions to the linear equation.   ◇

Example 4.1.5 Find $63^{-1} \pmod{97}$.

Solution Following the Euclidean algorithm, we find

$$
\begin{aligned}
97 &= 1 \cdot 63 + 34 \\
63 &= 1 \cdot 34 + 29 \\
34 &= 1 \cdot 29 + 5 \\
29 &= 5 \cdot 5 + 4 \\
5 &= 1 \cdot 4 + 1,
\end{aligned}
$$

which shows that $\gcd(97, 63) = 1$. Thus there is an inverse of 63 modulo 97. Writing the equations in reverse order as

$$
\begin{aligned}
1 &= -1 \cdot 4 + 5 \\
0 &= -4 - 5 \cdot 5 + 29 \\
0 &= -5 - 1 \cdot 29 + 34 \\
0 &= -29 - 1 \cdot 34 + 63 \\
0 &= -34 - 1 \cdot 63 + 97,
\end{aligned}
$$

we can summarize the backward elimination with the following tableau:

$$
\begin{array}{rcl}
1 &=& -1 \cdot 4 + 5 \\
(-1) \times (0 &=& -4 - 5 \cdot 5 + 29) \\
\hline
1 &=& 6 \cdot 5 - 29 \\
(6) \times (0 &=& -5 - 1 \cdot 29 + 34) \\
\hline
1 &=& -7 \cdot 29 + 6 \cdot 34 \\
(-7) \times (0 &=& -29 - 1 \cdot 34 + 63) \\
\hline
1 &=& 13 \cdot 34 - 7 \cdot 63 \\
13 \times (0 &=& -34 - 1 \cdot 63 + 97) \\
\hline
1 &=& -20 \cdot 63 + 13 \cdot 97
\end{array}
$$

At each step, the equation beneath a horizontal line is the sum of the indicated multiple of the equation above the line and the equation with 1 on the left side above that one. Thus

$$
63^{-1} \equiv -20 \equiv 77 \pmod{97}. \quad ◇
$$

Surprisingly, the extended Euclidean algorithm takes relatively few steps—that is, divisions—even when the numbers are large.

Example 4.1.6 With $a = 428\,391\,862$ and $b = 9973$, we obtain

$$
\begin{aligned}
a &= 42\,955 \cdot b + 1647 \\
b &= 6 \cdot 1647 + 91 \\
1647 &= 18 \cdot 91 + 9 \\
91 &= 10 \cdot 9 + 1,
\end{aligned}
$$

or

$$
\begin{aligned}
1 &= -10 \cdot 9 \; + \; 91 \\
0 &= -9 \qquad - \; 18 \cdot 91 \; + \; 1647 \\
0 &= \qquad\qquad - \; 91 \qquad - \; 6 \cdot 1647 \; + \; b \\
0 &= \qquad\qquad\qquad\qquad - \; 1647 \qquad - \; 42955b + a.
\end{aligned}
$$

Backward eliminating, we obtain

$$
\begin{array}{rcl}
1 &=& -10 \cdot 9 + 91 \\
(-10) \times (0 &=& -9 - 18 \cdot 91 + 1647) \\
\hline
1 &=& 181 \cdot 91 - 10 \cdot 1647 \\
181 \times (0 &=& -91 - 6 \cdot 1647 + b) \\
\hline
1 &=& -1096 \cdot 1647 + 181b \\
-1096 \times (0 &=& -1647 - 42955b + a) \\
\hline
1 &=& 47078861 \cdot b - 1096a
\end{array}
$$

So

$$
9973^{-1} \equiv 47\,078\,861 \;(\mathrm{mod}\;428\,391\,862).
$$

(*Note*: If you attempt to check this result by multiplying 9973 by 47 078 861 on a hand-held calculator, chances are that the product will have more digits than the calculator will display. The calculator will then convert the product to a floating point *approximation* to the product, and this will spoil any attempt at finding an integer quotient and remainder.) $\diamondsuit$

Summary

The apparent inherent computational infeasibility of factoring integers will serve as a source of security in certain cryptographic algorithms and protocols. Statistical information such as that provided in the prime number theorem is helpful in certain prime searching algorithms. While the greatest common divisor of two integers can easily be found from the prime factorization of both numbers, the Euclidean algorithm is a computationally efficient method for finding the gcd of two integers without factoring them. This algorithm will be essential in the setup phase of certain public-key cryptographic methods.

EXERCISES

1. Use the sieve of Eratosthenes to find all of the primes from 100 to 200.

2. Use the prime table or a computer algebra system to find a list of 31 consecutive composite numbers.

3. Let n be an integer greater than 2. Explain why $n! + 2$, $n! + 3$, $n! + 4$, ..., $n! + (n - 1)$, $n! + n$ are all composite numbers. Use this idea to obtain a list of ten consecutive composite integers.

4. A pair of prime numbers is called a **twin prime** pair if the numbers differ by 2. Find all of the twin prime pairs in the table of primes. Based on your findings, state which of the following you think is true: (1) There are infinitely many twin prime pairs. (2) There are finitely many twin prime pairs.[5]

5. Pick two primes from the table of primes and multiply them together. Then give the product to a friend and challenge him or her to find the prime factors.

6. Obtain factorizations of the following integers into products of powers of primes. (*Hint*: There are no prime factors larger than 50.)

   (a) 2310

   (b) 6517

   (c) 961

   (d) 371293

7. Complete the table of prime factorizations shown in Table 4.2.

---

[5]It is not known which of these statements is true. Experts in number theory believe that (1) is true.

n	$n!$	factorization
2	2	2
3	6	$2 \cdot 3$
4	24	$2^3 \cdot 3$
5		
6		
7		
8		
9		
10		
11		
12		
13	6 227 020 800	$2^{10} \cdot 3^5 \cdot 5^2 \cdot 7 \cdot 11 \cdot 13$

Table 4.2 Table for Exercise 7.

8. (a) At most how many primes will you have to divide into 10 001 to determine whether 10 001 is prime? *Is* 10 001 prime?

   (b) At most how many primes will you have to divide into 100, 000, 001 to determine whether it is prime?

9. Three ordinary dice make a perfect random number generator for numbers in the range 0 to $6^3 - 1 = 215$. Number the faces of each die 0, 1, 2, 3, 4, and 5. Throw the dice and read the three digits d_0, d_1, and d_2 showing, in any order you like. Calculate $r = 36d_2 + 6d_1 + d_0$ as the random number. Use this procedure to obtain 7 numbers and use the table of primes to see how many of the numbers are prime. Repeat this experiment five more times, and in each case note whether any primes turn up. Determine the fraction of the trials in which at least one prime turns up.

10. Use whatever means you have at hand to find the two prime factors of 23 981 204 798 221. (*Hint*: Look for large prime factors.)

11. Use the Euclidean algorithm to find the greatest common divisor of the following pairs of integers. Also find s and t such that $as + bt = \gcd(a, b)$.

    (a) $a = 2175$ and $b = 555$

    (b) $a = 667$ and $b = 437$

    (c) $a = 77897$ and $b = 3721$

    (d) $a = 3001$ and $b = 541$

12. Find the inverse modulo the given modulus.

    (a) $17^{-1} \pmod{60}$

    (b) $25^{-1} \pmod{89}$

    (c) $3^{-1} \pmod{131}$

    (d) $131^{-1} \pmod{3}$

    (e) $1006^{-1} \pmod{7233631}$

13. Solve the congruences for x.

    (a) $8x \equiv 3 \pmod{19}$

    (b) $5x \equiv 41 \pmod{54}$

    (c) $2x + 1 \equiv 0 \pmod{97}$

14. Solve for x in terms of y.

    (a) $12x \equiv y \pmod{13}$

    (b) $2x + 3y \equiv 1 \pmod{81}$

    (c) $32x + y \equiv 0 \pmod{17}$

15. **Wilson's theorem** says that a positive integer n is prime if and only if
$$(n-1)! \equiv -1 \pmod{n}.$$

    (a) Verify this theorem for values of n ranging from 2 to 20.

    (b) Prove half of this theorem: If n is prime, then $(n-1)! \equiv -1$ (mod n). [*Hint*: Recall that for a prime modulus n, the multiplicative inverse of any number a in the range 2 to $n-2$ is distinct from a. Thus $(n-1)!$ contains the factor a and a^{-1} for each $2 \le a \le n-2$.]

    (c) Prove the other half of the theorem, stated in this form: If n is composite, then $(n-1)! \not\equiv -1 \pmod{n}$. [*Hint*: Consider three cases; (i) $n = 4$, (ii) n factors into distinct factors, (iii) n is the square of a prime.]

(d) It appears that this theorem provides a nice primality test. However, consider testing $n = 179\,424\,673$ for primality. In the worst case, how many multiplications and divisions will be needed to calculate $(n-1)! \bmod n$? If a computer can perform one multiplication and division per nanosecond (10^{-9} second), how long would it take to determine primality using Wilson's theorem?

16. A **Sophie Germain**[6] **prime** is a prime number p such that $2p+1$ is also prime. For example, 2, 3, and 5 are such primes, but 7 is not. Find the first ten Sophie Germain primes. It is an open question whether there are infinitely many of these primes. Sophie Germain primes are of significance in elliptic curve cryptography.

17. A **Mersenne**[7] **prime** is a prime number of the form $2^n - 1$.

    (a) Find the first four Mersenne primes.

    (b) Explain why $2^n - 1$ cannot be prime whenever n is even.

    (c) Explain why $2^n - 1$ cannot be prime whenever n is composite.

18. Write a computer program that uses trial division to factor integers. Time its running on primes with 1, 2, 3, 4, ..., 9 digits in their decimal representations.

19. Write a computer program that implements the extended Euclidean algorithm. Extend its functionality by implementing the extended Euclidean algorithm.

---

[6]Sophie Germain (1776–1831), a French mathematician known as the Hypatia of the nineteenth century, worked extensively in number theory and proved a special case of Fermat's "last" theorem.

[7]Marin Mersenne (1588–1648), a Minimite friar, conjectured that $2^n - 1$ is prime when n is one of the numbers 2, 3, 5, 7, 13, 17, 19, 31, 67, 127, or 257 and composite for all other values of n. Edouard Lucas showed that $2^{67} - 1$ is composite, and later $2^{257} - 1$ was shown to be composite. It has been shown since then that $2^{61} - 1$, $2^{89} - 1$, and 2^{107} are prime. In 1998, there were 34 known Mersenne primes. At any given time, the largest prime yet found is often a Mersenne prime. The Great Internet Mersenne Prime Search (GIMPS) harnesses the capacity of thousands of personal computers through the Internet to search for Mersenne primes. The current goal, for which there is a $100,000 award, is to find a ten-million-decimal-digit Mersenne prime. You may participate in GIMPS by following instructions given at http://www.mersenne.org.

4.2   The Merkle-Hellman Knapsack

The Idea of Public-Key Cryptography

Suppose that you want to correspond by e-mail with someone else, and you want the messages to be encrypted. For purposes of illustration, suppose the encryption method is Vigenère with a three-letter keyword. Thought of as a base 26 number, this keyword is in the range 0 to $26^2 = 676$; represented in binary, this number is in the range 0 to 1010100100. Since the network of computers and ethernet and fiber optical cable between you and your correspondent is an insecure channel, you do not want to exchange your key by way of e-mail. It would be much more secure—though slower and more cumbersome, particularly if you wanted to change keys with some frequency—to send the keys by ordinary mail.

There are, it turns out, ways of exchanging keys represented in binary form securely over public channels. Experts in algorithm and complexity theory believe that certain mathematical problems will, in general, require inordinate amounts of time to solve. **Public-key** cryptosystems are designed so that breaking one of them is essentially equivalent to solving one of these hard mathematical problems. Even solution methods programmed efficiently on very fast computers may take weeks, months, centuries, or the expected life of the universe to run to completion. These problems usually are, in principle, solvable by trial and error. For instance, factoring a number into its prime factors is just a matter of dividing every prime from 2 up to the square root of the number into the number and seeing if it leaves a zero remainder (of course, finding all those primes is a nontrivial task itself). The expected amount of time to produce a complete factorization of an integer with x decimal digits into a product of primes by trial division grows exponentially with x. Somewhat surprisingly, other known factorization algorithms, while they may work more quickly for special categories of integers, all have instances in which they work as slowly as trial division.

Public-key cryptosystems are so named because part of the key to the system is made public—say by being placed on a person's Web page—for the use of anyone wishing to send that person encrypted messages. From that public-key, an interceptor could, in principle, decipher an encrypted message or determine the secret part of the key that the receiver will use to decrypt. In practical terms, however, both of these cryptanalytic approaches are intractable because decipherment or secret key recovery are some of these thought-to-be-difficult mathematical problems.

One of those mathematical problems thought to be intrinsically time-consuming to solve is the **subset-sum problem** (SSP or **knapsack**[8] **problem**) which we'll describe in a moment. In the 1970s, two Stanford University computer scientists, Ralph Merkle and Martin Hellman, used it to produce what is now considered the first public-key cryptosystem. The method is conceptually transparent and straightforward to use. However, it turns out to have some pitfalls that ultimately make it unattractive for practical implementations.

The Subset-Sum Problem

Consider this problem: Given the numbers 1, 4, 7, 12, and 19, determine whether 42 can be written as a sum of some combination of these numbers. If it can, find a combination of numbers that does the job.

One way to proceed is to generate all possible sums from these numbers:

$$
\begin{aligned}
1 + 4 &= 5 \\
1 + 7 &= 8 \\
1 + 12 &= 13 \\
1 + 19 &= 20 \\
4 + 7 &= 11 \\
4 + 12 &= 16 \\
4 + 19 &= 23 \\
7 + 12 &= 19 \\
7 + 19 &= 26 \\
1 + 4 + 7 &= 12 \\
1 + 4 + 12 &= 17 \\
1 + 4 + 19 &= 24 \\
&\ \vdots \\
1 + 4 + 7 + 12 + 19 &= 43
\end{aligned}
$$

and check to see whether 42 is in the list. You should make this determination yourself.

---

[8] The reason for this moniker is that with a (physical) knapsack of a given volume and a collection of items of various sizes with which to fill it, we will in general have to carry out a trial-and-error approach to fill it in the most efficient manner.

Generally, the process is straightforward, and you can be systematic about it as the column of sums here suggests. For each sum, we either include one of the numbers or we don't: There are these two choices. Since there are five numbers from which to choose, there are at most $2^5 = 32$ numbers generated by computing all these sums. Thus the worst case is that we might have to compute 32 sums and make 32 comparisons.

Now, suppose we have a list of 100 such numbers a_1, a_2, a_3, ..., a_{100} and we want to determine whether a given number t can be written as a sum of a subcollection of these. The same systematic approach that we used previously will certainly work, in principle. We would calculate

$$a_1 + a_2$$
$$a_1 + a_3$$
$$\vdots$$
$$a_{99} + a_{100}$$
$$a_1 + a_2 + a_3$$
$$a_1 + a_2 + a_4$$
$$\vdots$$
$$a_{98} + a_{99} + a_{100}$$
$$\vdots$$
$$a_1 + a_2 + a_3 + \cdots + a_{100}$$

all the while checking to see if one of the sums turned out to be t. However, the worst case is much, much worse than in the case of five numbers. Each a_i is either included in a sum or it is not: two choices. There are 100 numbers from which to choose, so there are at most

$$2^{100} = 1267650600228229401496703205376 \approx 1.3 \times 10^{30}$$

different numbers generated from these sums. This is a huge number, even by the standards of modern computers. In fact, if a computer can do one comparison in a billionth of a second (10^{-9} sec), then in the worst case (having to check nearly all values) it will take roughly 4×10^{13} *years* for it to carry out the comparisons. This estimate does not even include the time it takes for the computer to add the various combinations of the numbers.

We have just seen two instances of the

Subset-Sum Problem (**SSP**, or **knapsack problem**) : Given numbers a_1, a_2, ..., a_n and a "target" value t, determine if there is a subcollection of the a_i whose sum is t. SSP can be stated in somewhat more formal terms: Determine if there is a selection of numbers x_1, x_2, ..., x_n, where each x_i is either 0 or 1, such that

$$x_1 a_1 + x_2 a_2 + \cdots + x_n a_n = t.$$

Example 4.2.1 If the given values are $a_1 = 3$, $a_2 = 5$, $a_3 = 11$, $a_4 = 23$, $a_5 = 51$, and $t = 67$, then the solution to SSP is $x_1 = 0$, $x_2 = 1$, $x_3 = 1$, $x_4 = 0$, and $x_5 = 1$ as you can verify. ◇

We have already seen a way to solve the SSP, but that method—at least in the worst case—can take an unreasonable amount of time even for a moderate value of n such as 100. You might think that there is a shortcut method to solving SSP, and in fact there are methods that can improve on trial and error substantially, but there are no known polynomial-time algorithms for solving SSP.

It turns out that solving SSP can be made very efficient if the a_i's have a special structure. Moreover, with this special structure, for any given target value t there is either no solution or exactly one solution. A finite sequence of numbers is a **superincreasing sequence** if each number in the sequence is greater than the sum of those preceding it. You can verify that 3, 5, 11, 23, 51 is superincreasing but 1, 4, 7, 12, 19 is not.

In the next example we illustrate the ease with which SSP can be solved when the sequence is superincreasing.

Example 4.2.2 Take the sequence of a_i's to be 13, 18, 35, 72, 155, 301, 595; you can verify that this sequence is superincreasing. Let $t = 1003$. Since

$$13 + 18 + 35 + 72 + 155 + 301 + 595 = 1189$$

is greater than 1003, we have not ruled out a collection that adds up to 1003. Moreover, since

$$13 + 18 + 35 + 72 + 155 + 301 = 594$$

is less than the target value 1003, we know that 595 must be in the sum. Thus $x_7 = 1$. Now we repeat this reasoning for $1003 - 595 = 408$. Since

$$13 + 18 + 35 + 72 + 155 = 293$$

is less than 408, it must be that 301 is in the sum: $x_6 = 1$. We do this again for $408 - 301 = 107$. Since

$$13 + 18 + 35 + 72 = 138$$

is larger than 107, it must be that 155 is *not* in the sum: $x_5 = 0$. Continuing in this fashion, we find that $x_4 = 1$, $x_3 = 1$, $x_2 = 0$, and $x_1 = 0$. Putting these in forward order, we have the solution

$$x_1\, x_2\, x_3\, x_4\, x_5\, x_6\, x_7 = 0011011$$

for this instance of SSP.

It is tempting to try this method on an arbitrary increasing sequence. Indeed, if there is a solution to SSP for such an ordinary increasing sequence, this method will find it. However, if the sequence is not superincreasing, the solution may not be unique.

Example 4.2.3 Take the sequence 1, 2, 3, 4, 5, 6, 7 and let $t = 20$. Then the method we outlined in the previous example finds the solution

$$0100111$$

You can verify, however, that

$$0011011$$

is also a solution.

The Merkle-Hellman Cryptosystem

You can begin to see why SSP might be of interest to cryptographers if you think of t as a ciphertext and x_1, x_2, ..., x_n as the enciphered message. However, there are a couple of difficulties with trying to do this directly. If we implemented a cipher system with a random sequence of numbers as the key, then the intended recipient of a ciphertext would have to decipher the message using an algorithm that might take longer than her lifetime to finish; in other words, the intended recipient would have to do just as much work to decipher as an interceptor would have to do in a cryptanalysis (we assume that a cryptanalyst would know the values of a_1, ..., a_n). There is also the nonuniqueness problem that we encountered with the non-superincreasing sequence. Of course, if we used a superincreasing sequence, then decipherment would be quick and the results completely unambiguous, but then so would the work of a cryptanalyst.

The insight of Merkle and Hellmen was that a superincreasing sequence could be *disguised* by a special transformation to look like an arbitrary sequence. The disguised sequence can be published for all the world to see by a person who wishes to receive enciphered messages. Receiving an enciphered message, the recipient first applies the inverse of the transformation and then decodes using the superincreasing property.

Suppose that Alice is going to set things up so that she can receive enciphered messages from others. She first chooses a superincreasing sequence $a_1, \ldots, a_n$, with sum s. Then she chooses a prime p bigger than s and a number w in the range 2 to $p-1$. Then w has a multiplicative inverse v; she calculates v by the Euclidean algorithm. She disguises the superincreasing sequence by calculating a new sequence $b_1, b_2, \ldots, b_n$ by

$$b_i = wa_i \text{ MOD } p, \qquad i = 1, 2, \ldots, n$$

and publicizes it. She keeps the a_i's, p, and w secret.

Now suppose Bob wants to send Alice an enciphered binary message $x_1 x_2 x_3 \ldots x_n$ of n bits. He looks up her public sequence of b_i's and calculates the ciphertext

$$y = (x_1 b_1 + x_2 b_2 + \cdots + x_n b_n) \text{ MOD } p$$

and sends it to Alice.

Receiving y, Alice first calculates $Y = vy \text{ MOD } p$. Now

$$\begin{aligned}
Y &\equiv vy \\
&\equiv v(x_1 b_1 + x_2 b_2 + \cdots + x_n b_n) \\
&\equiv x_1(vb_1) + x_2(vb_2) + \cdots + x_n(vb_n) \\
&\equiv x_1 a_1 + x_2 a_2 + \cdots + x_n a_n \pmod{p},
\end{aligned}$$

and because the a_i's are superincreasing, she can apply the efficient algorithm we outlined previously to recover the x_i's from Y.

Example 4.2.4 Alice has selected the superincreasing sequence

$$47, 52, 112, 216, 436, 868, 1732, 3470, 6937, 13876$$

along with the modulus $p = 27749$ (which is the next prime after the sum $s = 27746$ of the knapsack values) and the multiplier $w = 113$. She calculates the public knapsack values by

$$113 \cdot 47 \text{ MOD } 27749 = 5311$$
$$113 \cdot 52 \text{ MOD } 27749 = 5876$$
$$\vdots$$
$$113 \cdot 13876 \text{ MOD } 27749 = 14044.$$

The complete list of values that she publishes is

$$5311, 5876, 12656, 24408, 21519, 14837, 1473, 3624, 6909, 14044.$$

Since she expects to receive enciphered messages, she also computes $v = w^{-1} \text{ MOD } p$ for use later in decryption. You can verify that $v = 7367$.

Now, suppose that Bob wants to encipher the binary message

$$0110110101$$

and send it to her. He looks up the published knapsack values, calculates the ciphertext

$$y = (0 \cdot 5311 + 1 \cdot 5876 + \cdots + 0 \cdot 6909 + 1 \cdot 14044) \text{ MOD } 27749 = 72556,$$

and sends this number to Alice.

Upon receiving 72556, Alice first calculates

$$vy = 7367 \cdot 72556 \text{ MOD } 27749 = 18814.$$

Then she performs the efficient decoding of this number with her superincreasing sequence:

$$
\begin{aligned}
\left.\begin{array}{r} 27746 - 13876 = 13870; \\ 13870 < 18814 \end{array}\right\} & \quad \text{implies} \quad x_7 = 1 \\[2ex]
\left.\begin{array}{r} 13870 - 6937 = 6933; \\ 18814 - 13876 = 4938; \\ 6933 > 4938 \end{array}\right\} & \quad \text{implies} \quad x_6 = 0 \\[2ex]
\left.\begin{array}{r} 6933 - 3470 = 3463; \\ 3463 < 4938 \end{array}\right\} & \quad \text{implies} \quad x_5 = 1
\end{aligned}
$$

$$\vdots$$

and finds that the decoded message is the one that Bob enciphered.

Where does any security in this system lie? Eve, the cryptanalyst, will know the public key of b_i's. If she intercepts a ciphertext y, in principle, all she needs to do is solve the subset-sum problem. That is, she must solve the equation

$$y = x_1 b_1 + x_2 b_2 + \cdots + x_n b_n \qquad (4.17)$$

for the x_i's. This is solvable by systematic trial and error, but as we observed earlier, Eve can expect whatever method she uses to take an unreasonably long time for fairly large n. The sequence of b_i's will almost certainly not be superincreasing itself, so there may be more than one solution to this equation. So even if Eve finds all the solutions of (4.17), she must still try to determine which is the actual plaintext. Eve might also try to find the multiplier w by systematically choosing values for w, multiplying them by the b_i's, and checking to see if the products form a superincreasing sequence. On average this would require $p/2$ lists of numbers, but if p is large, then this is not feasible.

In [71], Bruce Schneier says, "Real knapsacks should contain at least 250 items." Moreover, each number (item) in the knapsack—he says—should have on the order of 200 bits in its binary representation. This means that each number in the knapsack should be on the order of 10^{60}. To provide a sense of scale, shown here is a superincreasing knapsack, with 100 numbers in it, the largest of which is on the order of 10^{38}.

100000000, 100000018, 200000020, 400000056, 800000113, 1600000225, 3200000443, 6400000878, 12800001759, 25600003533, 51200007062, 102400014126, 204800028251, 409600056496, 819200112984, 1638400225985, 3276800451959, 6553600903910, 13107201807838, 26214403615672, 52428807231331, 104857614462662, 209715228925329, 419430457850656, 838860915701322, 1677721831402638, 3355443662805268, 6710887325610536, 13421774651221080, 26843549302442161, 53687098604884319, 107374197209768651, 214748394419537297, 429496788839074594, 858993577678149178, 1717987155356298355, 3435974310712596711, 6871948621425193425, 13743897242850386848, 27487794485700773704, 54975588971401547403, 109951177942803094811, 219902355885606189614, 439804711771212379242, 879609423542424758472, 1759218847084849516946, 3518437694169699033887, 7036875388339398067778, 14073750776678796135554, 28147501553357592271115, 56295003106715184542219, 112590006213430369084451, 225180012426860738168889, 450360024853721476337776, 900720049707442952675564, 1801440099414885905351117, 3602880198829771810702235, 7205760397659543621404483, 14411520795319087242808955, 28823041590638174485617925, 57646083181276348971235837, 115292166362552697942471680, 230584332725105395884943353, 461168665450210791769886701, 922337330900421583539773403, 1844674466180084316707954681 2, 3689349323601686334159093636, 7378698647203372668318187271, 14757397294406745336636374536, 29514794588813490673272749601, 59029589177626981346545498121, 118059178355253962693090996254, 236118356710507925386181992513, 472236713421015850772363985014, 944473426842031701544727970030, 1888946853684063403089455940057, 3777893707368126806178911880129, 7555787414736253612357823760256, 15111574829472507224715647520514, 30223149658945014449431295041014, 60446299317890028898625900820 32, 120892597863578005779772518016 4073, 241785197271560115595450360328142, 483570394543120231190900720656285, 967140789086240462381801441312557, 1934281578172480924763602882625120, 3868563156344961849527205765250238, 7737126312689923699054411530500484, 15474252625379847398108823061000960, 30948505250759694796217646122001914, 61897010501519389592435292244003844, 123794021003038779184870584488007690, 247588042006077558369741168976015378, 495176084012155116739482337952030756, 990352168024310233478964675904061501, 1980704336048620466957929351808123002, 3961408672097240933915858703616246004, 7922817344194481867831717407232492003, 15845634688388963735663434814464984016, 31691269376777927471326869628929968036, 63382538753555854942653739257859936077

The sum of this knapsack is 6338253875355585494265373925785993**6077**,
and a suitable prime for the modulus is

$$p = 6338253875355585494265373925785993**6127**,$$

which is the next prime after the sum of the knapsack numbers.

It turns out that the method Merkle and Hellman used to disguise the superincreasing sequence has an "Achilles heel" that makes it possible to determine the superincreasing sequence from the public-key. In [72], Adi Shamir presented a polynomial time algorithm for breaking the Merkele-Hellman cryptostystem. Attempts at improving the knapsack method have met with similar cryptanalyses. Even so, the method is easy to understand and forms a conceptual basis for understanding other public-key methods which have not been broken.

Summary

The Merkle-Hellman knapsack is one of the first examples of a public-key cryptosystem: Encryption of a message to Alice is performed with a key that is publicly available, and decryption is done by Alice using a key known only to her and not readily calculated from the public-key by an opponent. The security of the Merkle-Hellman knapsack rests on the presumed inherent time-consuming nature of solving the subset sum problem.

EXERCISES

1. Determine which of the following sequences is superincreasing:

   (a) 12, 13, 27, 55, 111, 219, 450

   (b) 4, 15, 18, 36, 72, 145

   (c) 17, 18, 39, 69, 180, 331

   (d) 1, 3, 9, 27, 81, 243, 729, 2187, 6561, 19683

2. Encode the following binary sequences using the superincreasing sequence 43, 44, 90, 200, 591, 1024, 2001, 4021:

   (a) 10101010   (b) 11110000   (c) 10100111

3. For the superincreasing sequence

$$4, 8, 15, 29, 61, 125, 247, 500$$

   determine whether each given value of t can be written as a sum of a subset of the sequence. For each value of t for which there is a solution, write down the sequence. $x_1, x_2, \ldots, x_n$ of zeros and ones encoded in the number.

   (a) $t = 310$ (b) $t = 489$ (c) $t = 127$ (d) $t = 527$ (e) $t = 989$

4. Use the superincreasing sequence of Exercise 2 along with the prime $p = 8017$ and the multiplier $w = 91$ to generate the public-key sequence for Merkle-Hellman.

5. Use the superincreasing sequence of Exercise 3 along with the prime $p = 1009$ and the multiplier $w = 5$ to generate the public-key sequence for Merkle-Hellman.

6. Suppose Bob has published the Merkle-Hellman public-key sequence 96, 91, 81, 61, 21, 42, 84, 67. and you want to send him the binary message 11011001. Encipher the message.

7. You are using the superincreasing knapsack of Exercise 2 and have received the ciphertext 18233 from someone who used the public-key sequence of Exercise 4. Decipher it.

8. You are using the superincreasing knapsack of Exercise 3 and have received the ciphertext 1607 from someone who used the public-key sequence of Exercise 5. Decipher it.

9. Suppose Bob has chosen the superincreasing sequence 16, 32, 64, 128, 256, 512, 1024, 2048, modulus $p = 4091$ and multiplier $w = 6$. He has published the corresponding public-key, and Veronica sends him the enciphered message 6277. What message will Bob decipher?

10. Assuming that t is a number in the range 0 to s, where s is the sum of the n numbers in a superincreasing knapsack, find a formula in terms of n for the largest number of subtractions in the decoding algorithm.

11. If a knapsack contains n numbers and a message has more than n binary digits, the message is usually padded with extra bits to bring

its length up to an even multiple of n. Then the n-bit blocks are enciphered and sent in sequence.

Suppose a public-key consists of the sequence 1664, 1824, 3856, 7760, and you want to encipher the message STAY COOL. First, encode the letters as 8-bit binary strings by taking the binary representations of their ASCII values (see Table 4.3). Then subdivide the resulting string

Letter	ASCII value	Binary	Letter	ASCII value	Binary
A	65	01000001	N	78	01001110
B	66	01000010	O	79	01001111
C	67	01000011	P	80	01010000
D	68	01000100	Q	81	01010001
E	69	01000101	R	82	01010010
F	70	01000110	S	83	01010011
G	71	01000111	T	84	01010100
H	72	01001000	U	85	01010101
I	73	01001001	V	86	01010110
J	74	01001010	W	87	01010111
K	75	01001011	X	88	01011000
L	76	01001100	Y	89	01011001
M	77	01001101	Z	90	01011010

Table 4.3   8-bit binary representations for ASCII values of A through Z.

of binary data into 4-bit blocks and encipher them using the knapsack.

12. Show that for the sequence 1, 2, 3, ..., n, and t chosen in the range 1 to $n(n+1)/2$, SSP has a solution. Show that if $t = n - 1$, then there are $\lfloor n/2 \rfloor$ solutions to SSP.

13. Show that if r is any integer greater than or equal to 2, then r, r^2, r^3, r^4, ..., r^n is a superincreasing sequence. Such a sequence is called a **geometric**.

4.3   Fermat's Little Theorem

It is astonishing how old discoveries in mathematics are used in modern applications. In the 1970s, three mathematicians who were devising digital signature and public-key cryptosystems realized that a theorem from number theory proved by Pierre de Fermat[9] provided the (figurative and literal) key to their work. The purpose of this section is to learn about this theorem so that we can give a complete description of the public-key cryptosystem of Rivest, Shamir, and Adelman.

Exponentiation

A number of public-key cryptosystems involve exponentiation modulo a given modulus. If $a \equiv b \,(\mathrm{mod}\, m)$, then by (2.3), $a \cdot a \equiv b \cdot b \,(\mathrm{mod}\, m)$, or simply $a^2 \equiv b^2 \,(\mathrm{mod}\, m)$. In general, if $a \equiv b \,(\mathrm{mod}\, m)$, then

$$a^e \equiv b^e \quad (\mathrm{mod}\ m) \tag{4.18}$$

for any positive integer exponent e. That is, we can exponentiate both sides of a congruence.

Also, since exponentiation denotes repeated multiplication, we have

$$
\begin{aligned}
a^{e+d} &\equiv \underbrace{a \cdots \cdots a}_{e+d \text{ times}} \equiv \underbrace{a \cdots \cdots a}_{e \text{ times}} \cdot \underbrace{a \cdots \cdots a}_{d \text{ times}} \\
&\equiv a^e \cdot a^d \quad (\mathrm{mod}\ m),
\end{aligned}
\tag{4.19}
$$

$$
\begin{aligned}
(ab)^e &\equiv \underbrace{(ab) \cdot (ab) \cdots \cdots (ab)}_{e \text{ times}} \\
&\equiv \underbrace{(a \cdot a \cdots \cdots a)}_{e \text{ times}} \cdot \underbrace{(b \cdot b \cdots \cdots b)}_{e \text{ times}} \\
&\equiv a^e \cdot b^e \quad (\mathrm{mod}\ m),
\end{aligned}
\tag{4.20}
$$

and

$$
\begin{aligned}
(a^d)^e &\equiv \underbrace{a^d \cdot a^d \cdots \cdots a^d}_{e \text{ times}} \\
&\equiv \underbrace{a \cdot a \cdots \cdots a}_{e \cdot d \text{ times}} \\
&\equiv a^{de} \quad (\mathrm{mod}\ m).
\end{aligned}
\tag{4.21}
$$

---

[9]Pierre de Fermat (1601–1665), French mathematician whose contributions to number theory include his "last theorem," the conjecture that the equation $a^n + b^n = c^n$ has no integer solutions a, b, c for any integer values of n except 2. This conjecture was at last, in 1996, proved by Princeton mathematician Andrew Wiles.

To summarize, we have the exponent rules

$$a^{e+d} \equiv a^e \cdot a^d \pmod{m} \tag{4.22}$$

$$(ab)^e \equiv a^e \cdot b^e \pmod{m} \tag{4.23}$$

$$(a^d)^e \equiv a^{de} \pmod{m}. \tag{4.24}$$

Example 4.3.1 Find the remainder when 2^{13} is divided by 33; that is, find 2^{13} MOD 33.

Solution We could calculate $2^{13} = 8192$ and then find the remainder when we divide by 33: $8192 = 248 \cdot 33 + 8$. But there is an easier way based on (4.18) and (4.24). We know that $2^2 \equiv 4 \pmod{33}$, $2^4 \equiv (2^2)^2 \equiv 4^2 \equiv 16 \pmod{33}$, and $2^8 \equiv (2^4)^2 \equiv 16^2 \equiv 256 \equiv 25$, so by (4.22) and (2.3),

$$
\begin{aligned}
2^{13} = 2^{8+4+1} &\equiv 2^8 \cdot 2^4 \cdot 2^1 \\
&\equiv 25 \cdot 16 \cdot 2 \\
&\equiv 25 \cdot 32 \\
&\equiv (-8) \cdot (-1) \equiv 8 \pmod{33}. \quad \Diamond
\end{aligned}
$$

We have used "repeated squaring" of the base to obtain large powers quickly, and we have in effect used the binary representation of the desired exponent to calculate the required values.

Example 4.3.2 What is $3^{72} \pmod{143}$?

Solution Since $3^2 \equiv 9 \pmod{143}$, we square both sides to get $3^4 \equiv 81 \pmod{143}$. Squaring again, we have $3^8 \equiv 81^2 \equiv 6561 \equiv 126 \pmod{143}$. Squaring three more times, we have

$$
\begin{aligned}
3^{16} &\equiv 126^2 \equiv 3 \pmod{143} \\
3^{32} &\equiv 9 \pmod{143} \\
3^{64} &\equiv 81 \pmod{143}.
\end{aligned}
$$

So $3^{72} \equiv 3^{64+8} \equiv 3^{64} \cdot 3^8 \equiv 81 \cdot 126 \equiv 10\,206 \equiv 53 \pmod{143}$. Observe that if you calculate $3^{72} \approx 2.25284 \times 10^{34}$ on a calculator, the "floating point" approximation spoils the result. $\Diamond$

The repeated squaring approach can be combined with a knowledge of factorization to make the work even quicker.

Example 4.3.3 Calculate $6^{43} \pmod{13}$.

Solution Since $6 = 2 \cdot 3$, we find 2^{43} MOD 13, and 3^{43} MOD 13 and then multiply. We have

$$
\begin{aligned}
2^2 &\equiv 4 \\
2^4 &\equiv 4^2 \equiv 16 \equiv 3 \\
2^8 &\equiv 3^2 \equiv 9 \\
2^{16} &\equiv 9^2 \equiv 81 \equiv 3 \\
2^{32} &\equiv 3^2 \equiv 9 \pmod{13}
\end{aligned}
$$

so $2^{43} \equiv 2^{32} \cdot 2^8 \cdot 2^2 \cdot 2^1 \equiv 1 \cdot 9 \cdot 4 \cdot 2 \equiv 36 \cdot 2 \equiv 3 \pmod{13}$. Similarly,

$$
\begin{aligned}
3^2 &\equiv 9 \\
3^4 &\equiv 3 \\
3^8 &\equiv 9 \\
3^{16} &\equiv 3 \\
3^{32} &\equiv 9, \pmod{13}
\end{aligned}
$$

so $3^{43} \equiv 3^{32} \cdot 3^8 \cdot 3^2 \cdot 3^1 = 3 \cdot 9 \cdot 9 \cdot 9 \equiv 2187 \equiv 3 \pmod{13}$. Then, by (4.23), $6^{43} \equiv 2^{43} \cdot 3^{43} \equiv 11 \cdot 3 \equiv 7 \pmod{13}$. $\diamondsuit$

Fermat's Little Theorem

Having seen how to calculate powers of integers modulo a given modulus, let us turn our attention to the special situation where the exponent and modulus are the same. That is, we look at values of a^m MOD m for $a = 0$, 1, 2, 3, ..., $m - 1$, where m is chosen to have various values. Table 4.4 shows the results. Notice that when m is 2, 3, 5, 7, and 11, the a-column and the a^m-column are identical. That is, it appears that when m is *prime*, $a^m \equiv a \pmod{m}$. This pattern continues, and the general statement and proof of its truth is due to Pierre de Fermat.

Theorem 4.3.1 *(Fermat's Little Theorem) Let p be a prime number.*

1. *If a is relatively prime to p, then $a^{p-1} \equiv 1 \pmod{p}$.*

2. *$a^p \equiv a \pmod{p}$ for any integer a.*

m	2	3	4	5	6	7	8	9	10	11	12
a	a^m	a^m	a^m	a^m	a^m	a^m	a^m	a^m	a^m	a^m	a^m
0	0	0	0	0	0	0	0	0	0	0	0
1	1	1	1	1	1	1	1	1	1	1	1
2		2	0	2	4	2	0	8	4	2	4
3			1	3	3	3	1	0	9	3	9
4				4	4	4	0	1	6	4	4
5					1	5	1	8	5	5	1
6						6	0	0	6	6	0
7							1	1	9	7	1
8								8	4	8	4
9									1	9	9
10										10	4
11											1

Table 4.4 Powers a^m MOD m, for m through 12.

Proof It is sufficient to know that the theorem is true for $a = 0$, 1, 2, 3, ..., $p-2$, $p-1$, because any integer is congruent, modulo p, to one of these. We have no difficulty seeing that if $a = 0$, then the identity holds. So select a value of a in the range 1, 2, ..., $p-1$, and consider the numbers

$$
\begin{aligned}
a &\cdot 1 \;\text{MOD}\; p \\
a &\cdot 2 \;\text{MOD}\; p \\
a &\cdot 3 \;\text{MOD}\; p \\
&\;\;\vdots \\
a &\cdot (p-1) \;\text{MOD}\; p.
\end{aligned}
\tag{4.25}
$$

Since p is prime, it is relatively prime to a, so by Theorem 2.2.2, the numbers in (4.25) are distinct from one another and in the range 1, 2, 3, ..., $p-1$. In other words, multiplying 1, 2, ..., $(p-1)$ by a has rearranged the numbers. So when we multiply the numbers in (4.25) modulo p we get the same result as multiplying $1 \cdot 2 \cdot 3 \cdot \cdots \cdot (p-1)$ modulo p:

$$
(a \cdot 1)(a \cdot 2)(a \cdot 3)\cdots(a(p-1)) \equiv 1 \cdot 2 \cdot 3 \cdot \cdots \cdot (p-1) \pmod{p}.
$$

Gathering all of the as on the left side, we obtain

$$
\underbrace{(a \cdot a \cdot a \cdots a)}_{p-1 \text{ times}} \cdot 1 \cdot 2 \cdots \cdot (p-1) \equiv 1 \cdot 2 \cdot 3 \cdots (p-1) \pmod{p},
$$

which is equivalent to

$$a^{p-1}(1 \cdot 2 \cdots (p-1)) \equiv 1 \cdot 2 \cdot 3 \cdots (p-1) \pmod{p}. \qquad (4.26)$$

Since each of $1, 2, 3, \cdots \cdot (p-1)$ is relatively prime to p, we can multiply both sides of (4.26) by the multiplicative inverse of $1 \cdot 2 \cdots \cdot (p-1)$ and obtain

$$a^{p-1} \equiv 1 \pmod{p}. \qquad (4.27)$$

This proves part (1).

For part (2), observe first that if a is relatively prime to p, then we can multiply both sides of (4.24) by a to obtain

$$\begin{aligned} a \cdot a^{p-1} &\equiv a \pmod{p} \\ a^p &\equiv a \pmod{p}. \end{aligned}$$

On the other hand, if a is not relatively prime to p, then, because p is prime, $a = kp$ for some integer k. Then

$$a^p \equiv (kp)^p \equiv k^p p^p \equiv k^p 0^p \equiv 0 \equiv kp \equiv a \pmod{p}. \quad \Diamond$$

Example 4.3.4 By Fermat's little theorem, $86^{97} \equiv 86 \pmod{97}$, and $43^{58} \equiv 1 \pmod{59}$. $\Diamond$

Example 4.3.5 What is the remainder when 3^{1000} is divided by 17?

Solution Observe that the modulus 17 is prime. By Fermat's little theorem, $3^{16} \equiv 1 \pmod{17}$. Since

$$1000 = 62 \cdot 16 + 8,$$

we can quickly reduce the exponent:

$$\begin{aligned} 3^{1000} &\equiv 3^{16 \cdot 62 + 8} \equiv (3^{16})^{62} \cdot 3^8 \\ &\equiv 1^{62} \cdot 3^8 \equiv 3^8 \pmod{17}. \end{aligned}$$

By repeated squaring, we get $3^2 \equiv 9$, $3^4 \equiv 9^2 \equiv 81 \equiv 13$, and $3^8 \equiv 13^2 \equiv 169 \equiv 170 - 1 \equiv -1 \equiv 16$. Thus $3^{1000} \equiv 16 \pmod{17}$. $\Diamond$

One restatement of Theorem 4.3.1 is

$$a^e \text{ MOD } p = a^{e \text{ MOD } (p-1)} \text{ MOD } p, \qquad \text{if } a \text{ MOD } p \neq 0, \qquad (4.28)$$

so exponents can be reduced modulo $p - 1$.

There is a theorem that follows from Fermat's little theorem and is of critical importance in designing public key cryptosystems and digital signature schemes. It is a special case of what is often called Euler's theorem.

Theorem 4.3.2 *Let p and q be distinct primes.*

(1) If a is relatively prime to pq, then

$$a^{k(p-1)(q-1)} \equiv 1 \pmod{pq},$$

where k is any integer.

(2) For any integer a,

$$a^{k(p-1)(q-1)+1} \equiv a \pmod{pq},$$

where k is any positive integer.

Proof A proof of part (1) is fairly straightforward, but the issues in part (2) are subtle. In (2) we are concerned about what happens when a has p or q as a factor.

(1) If a is relatively prime to pq, then a is relatively prime to p and to q. So by Fermat's theorem,

$$\left(a^{k(q-1)}\right)^{(p-1)} \equiv 1 \pmod{p}$$

and

$$\left(a^{k(p-1)}\right)^{q-1} \equiv 1 \pmod{q}.$$

These congruences mean that $a^{k(p-1)(q-1)} = 1 + rp$ for some integer r, and $a^{k(p-1)(q-1)} = 1 + sq$ for some integer s. Thus

$$\begin{aligned}
1 + rp &= 1 + sq \\
rp &= sq.
\end{aligned}$$

Since p and q are distinct primes, this equality means that s is divisible by p: $s = s_1 \cdot p$ for some integer s_1. Thus

$$\begin{aligned}
a^{k(p-1)(q-1)} &= 1 + sq \\
&= 1 + s_1 pq,
\end{aligned}$$

and this means precisely that

$$a^{k(p-1)(q-1)} \equiv 1 \pmod{pq}.$$

It is an exercise for you to explain why this reasoning applies even if k is a negative integer.

(2) If a is relatively prime to pq, then, by part (1), $a^{k(p-1)(q-1)} \equiv 1$ (mod pq). Multiplying both sides of this congruence by a yields the desired identity. Otherwise a has a factor in common with pq, and without any loss of generality, we can take it to be p. Thus $a = u \cdot p^v$, where u is relatively prime to p and v is a positive integer. By (1), $u^{k(p-1)(q-1)+1} \equiv u$ (mod pq). Since p and q are distinct, by Fermat's little theorem,

$$p^{vk(p-1)(q-1)} \equiv (p^{vk(p-1)})^{q-1} \equiv 1 \quad (\text{mod } q).$$

So

$$p^{vk(p-1)(q-1)} - 1 = bq$$

for some integer b, and thus

$$p^{vk(p-1)(q-1)+1} - p = b\,pq.$$

That is,

$$p^{vk(p-1)(q-1)+1} \equiv p \quad (\text{mod } pq).$$

Therefore,

$$
\begin{aligned}
a^{k(p-1)(q-1)+1} &\equiv (up^v)^{k(p-1)(q-1)+1} \\
&\equiv u^{k(p-1)(q-1)+1} \cdot (p^{k(p-1)(q-1)+1})^v \\
&\equiv u \cdot p^v \\
&\equiv a \quad (\text{mod } pq). \quad \diamondsuit
\end{aligned}
$$

Example 4.3.6 With $p = 7$ and $q = 11$, we can, for instance, immediately calculate $62^{60} \equiv 62^{6 \cdot 10} \equiv 62^{(7-1)(11-1)} \equiv 1 \,(\text{mod } 77)$. Also, if we want, for instance, to calculate $5^{371} \,(\text{mod } 77)$, we first note that $371 = 6 \cdot 60 + 11$ to see that

$$5^{371} \equiv (5^{60})^6 \cdot 5^{11} \equiv 1 \cdot 5^{11} \equiv 5^{11} \quad (\text{mod } 77).$$

Then $5^2 \equiv 25$, $5^4 \equiv 25^2 = 625 \equiv 9$, $5^8 \equiv 9^2 = 81 \equiv 4$, and so

$$
\begin{aligned}
5^{11} &\equiv 5^8 \cdot 5^2 \cdot 5^1 \equiv 4 \cdot 25 \cdot 5 \\
&\equiv 100 \cdot 5 \equiv 23 \cdot 5 \\
&\equiv 115 \equiv 38 \quad (\text{mod } 77). \quad \diamondsuit
\end{aligned}
$$

k	$1 + 24k$	factorization of $1 + 24k$
0	1	1
1	25	5^2
2	49	7^2
3	73	73
4	97	97
5	121	11^2
6	145	$5 \cdot 29$
7	169	13^2
$\vdots$		

Table 4.5 Factorizations of numbers in the sequence $1 + k(p - 1)(q - 1)$, $k = 1, 2, 3, \ldots$, where $p = 5$ and $q = 7$.

Theorem 4.3.2 draws our attention to the sequence $1 + k(p - 1)(q - 1)$, for $k = 1, 2, 3, 4, \ldots$. For instance, Table 4.5 shows some of these numbers when $p = 5$ and $q = 7$ along with their factorizations. The composite ones are of particular interest. For instance, if we compute $y = x^5$ MOD 35 and then compute y^{29} MOD 35, we get back x: By Theorem 4.3.2,

$$y^{29} \equiv (x^5)^{29} = x^{5 \cdot 29} = x^{145} \equiv x.$$

In general, whenever two positive integers d and e satisfy

$$d \cdot e = 1 + k(p - 1)(q - 1) \tag{4.29}$$

for some positive integer k, then the functions

$$E(x) = x^e \text{ MOD } pq, \ 1 \le x \le pq - 1$$

and

$$D(x) = x^d \text{ MOD } pq, \ 1 \le x \le pq - 1$$

are inverses. To see this, note that

$$
\begin{aligned}
E(D(x)) &= E(x^d \text{ MOD } pq) \\
&= (x^d \text{ MOD } pq)^e \text{ MOD } pq \\
&= (x^d)^e \text{ MOD } pq \\
&= x^{de} \text{ MOD } pq \\
&= x^{1+k(p-1)(q-1)} \text{ MOD } pq \\
&= x^1,
\end{aligned}
$$

for any $1 \leq x \leq pq - 1$. Similarly, $D(E(x)) = x$ for $1 \leq x \leq pq - 1$. This means that E and D can be used as an encryption and decryption pair. We will explore this phenomenon in the next section.

Note Theorem 4.3.1 does *not* claim that if $a^p \equiv a \pmod{p}$ for $a = 0$, 1, 2, 3, ..., $p - 1$, then p is prime. The evidence in Table 4.4, however, suggests that the converse of the theorem may be true. Indeed, if you extend the table you will find that when m takes on the composite values 14, 15, 16, 18, 20, 21, 22, 24, ..., the a-column and the $a^m \pmod{m}$-column are not the same. Try this out using a computer algebra system or a computer program. The evidence mounts for the converse of Fermat's little theorem to be true. It is therefore astounding that, if we continued long enough, we would find that $a^{561} \equiv a \pmod{561}$ for $a = 0$, 1, 2, 3, ..., 560 even though 561 is composite! This counterexample shows that, in fact, *the converse of Fermat's little theorem is false.*

The first **Carmichael**[10] **number** is 561 , a composite integer m such that $a^m \equiv a \pmod{m}$ for $a = 0$, 1, 2, ..., $m - 1$. It turns out that there are other Carmichael numbers, such as 1105, 1729, 2465, 2821, 6601, 8911 and 10 585. Many others have been found, and this has led to the conjecture that there are infinitely many Carmichael numbers. This was an open question until 1992, when Alford, Granville, and Pomerance [1] published a report in the *Notices of the American Mathematical Society* in which they showed that there are infinitely many Carmichael numbers.

Carmichael numbers have been used to develop fast and efficient probabilistic prime search algorithms that are used in modern public-key cryptosystems.

Summary

Exponentiation modulo a given modulus m can be performed very efficiently by repeated squaring and reduction modulo m followed by a few multiplications. In more formal terms, if $e = b_n b_{n-1} \ldots b_2 b_1 b_0$ is the binary representation of an exponent e, then a^e MOD m can be computed as

$$\left(a^{b_n \cdot 2^n} \text{ MOD } m\right) \cdot \left(a^{b_{n-i} 2^{n-1}} \text{ MOD } m\right) \cdot \cdots$$
$$\cdots \cdot \left(a^{b_1 \cdot 2} \text{ MOD } m\right) \cdot \left(a^{b_0} \text{ MOD } m\right) \text{ MOD } m.$$

---

[10]R. D. Carmichael conducted an intensive study of such numbers and presented results related to the concept in [12].

Fermat's little theorem says that if the modulus is a prime p, then

$$a^e \text{ MOD } p = a^{e \text{ MOD } (p-1)} \text{ MOD } p,$$

whenever $a \not\equiv 0 \pmod{p}$. The theorem following it says that if the modulus is the product pq of two distinct primes, then

$$a^e \text{ MOD } pq = a^{e \text{ MOD } (p-1)(q-1)} \text{ MOD } pq$$

whenever $a \not\equiv 0 \pmod{p}$ and $a \not\equiv 0 \pmod{q}$, and that if $e \equiv 1 \pmod{(p-1)(q-1)}$, then $a^e \equiv a \pmod{pq}$ for any integers a. The importance of this last part is that it assures that RSA, which is the encryption algorithm discussed in Section 4.4, is invertible.

EXERCISES

For some of these exercises, you may find it convenient to refer to the table of primes on page 370.

1. Use the repeated squaring method to calculate each of the following.

    (a) 3^7 MOD 12
    (b) 16^{10} MOD 230
    (c) 5^{14} MOD 26
    (d) 4^{22} MOD 11
    (e) 3^{65} MOD 71

2. Use Fermat's little theorem to calculate the remainder when the given number x is divided by the given divisor m.

    (a) $x = 99^{101}$, $m = 101$
    (b) $x = 94^{66}$, $m = 67$
    (c) $x = 14^{7540}$, $m = 7541$
    (d) $x = 4\,968\,732^{7540}$, $m = 7541$
    (e) $x = 65^{144}$, $m = 73$
    (f) $x = 27^{323}$, $m = 107$

3. Show that $2^{56} + 3^{56}$ is divisible by 17.

4. (a) Show that if $a \equiv b \bmod m$, then $ka \equiv kb \pmod{km}$ for any nonzero integer k.

   (b) Use exercise (a) to calculate the remainder when $5 \cdot 14^{23}$ is divided by 115. (*Hint*: Factor 115.)

5. Fermat's little theorem is a special case of a theorem due to Euler: Let n be a positive integer, and let a be relatively prime to n. Then $a^{\phi(n)} \equiv 1 \pmod{n}$, where $\phi(n)$ is the Euler phi function discussed in Section 1.2. A proof of this theorem can be made in much the same way as that for Fermat's theorem. Let $r_1, r_2, \ldots, r_{\phi(n)}$ be the numbers in the range $1, \ldots, n-1$ that are relatively prime to n. Argue that

$$a^{\phi(n)} r_1 \cdot r_2 \ldots \cdot r_{\phi(n)} \equiv r_1 \ldots \cdot r_{\phi(n)} \pmod{n}$$

   and then prove the result by cancelling $r_1, \ldots, r_{\phi(n)}$ from both sides of the congruence.

6. Using Exercise 5, prove the following analog to (4.28):

   If $\gcd(a, n) = 1$, then $a^e \equiv a^{e \text{ MOD } \phi(n)} \pmod{n}$.

7. Verify that

$$E(x) = x^e \text{ MOD } 15$$
$$D(x) = x^d \text{ MOD } 15$$

   are inverses for the following pairs of e and d:

   (a) $e = 3$, $d = 3$
   (b) $e = 5$, $d = 5$
   (c) $e = 3$, $d = 11$
   (d) $e = 7$, $d = 7$

8. Find all pairs of positive integers e and d such that $E(x) = x^e$ MOD 35 and $D(x) = x^d$ MOD 35 are inverses and $1 \le e \le 23$, $1 \le d \le 23$.

9. Explain why, in the proof of part (1) of Theorem 4.3.2, the reasoning applies when k is a negative number. Explain why, in the proof of part (2), the reasoning may not work if k is negative.

10. Fermat's little theorem provides an alternative way to compute the multiplicative inverse of a number modulo a prime p.

   (a) Show that $a^{-1} \equiv a^{p-2} \pmod{p}$ for $1 \le a \le p-1$.

   (b) Explain why this method requires at most $2 \cdot \lfloor \log_2(p-2) \rfloor - 1$ multiplications modulo p, if we use the repeated squaring algorithm for exponentiation.

11. Find factorizations of the Carmichael numbers given in the note on page 283.

4.4   The RSA Public-Key Cryptosystem

In 1978, the journal *Communications of the Association for Computing Machinery* (ACM) published a paper entitled "A Method for Obtaining Digital Signatures and Public Key Cryptosystems." The authors, Ronald Rivest, Adi Shamir, and Leonard Adelman, described a cipher system in which senders encipher messages using a method and a key that are publicly distributed. In contrast to earlier secret-key (or symmetric) cipher systems, knowledge of this key does not readily reveal the decipherment key.

Regarding a message as a number x in the range 1 to $m-1$, a sender enciphers x by calculating $y = x^e$ MOD m, where m and e are chosen in a special way. The recipient of y deciphers it by calculating $x = y^d$ MOD m where d is an inverse of e modulo a number that depends on the prime factorization of m. The modulus m and exponent e are published, and the receiver keeps d a secret. The number e is called the **public key** or **encryption key**, and d is the **private key** or **decryption key**. In actual implementations, p and q are large numbers, on the order of 100 decimal digits. Then m has on the order of 200 decimal digits.

In order to establish a two-way communication, two correspondents Alice and Bob select their own moduli m_A and m_B, and their own exponents e_A, d_A, e_B, and d_B. When Bob wants to send a message x to Alice, he looks up Alice's public exponent e_A and modulus m_A and uses these to calculate $y = x^{e_A}$ MOD m_A. When Alice receives y, she calculates y^{d_A} MOD m_A, which reduces to x. If she wishes to reply, with message u, she looks up

Bob's public key e_B and modulus m_B, calculates $w = u^{e_B} \pmod{m_B}$, and sends w to Bob. Then Bob deciphers w by calculating w^{d_B} MOD m_B, which reduces to u.

Why does such a method offer security? We cannot fully answer this question until we have examined why the method itself works.

Why RSA Works

To prepare for receiving encrypted messages, Alice selects two prime numbers p and q and calculates

$$
\begin{aligned}
m &= pq \\
n &= (p-1)(q-1).
\end{aligned}
$$

Next, she selects another number e that is relatively prime to n. She then uses the extended Euclidean algorithm to find d such that $e \cdot d \equiv 1 \pmod{n}$. Finally, Alice broadcasts e and m.

Now, suppose that Bob has a message to send to Alice. Regarding it, or a block of letters in it, as a number x in the range 0 to $m - 1$, he calculates the corresponding ciphertext as

$$
y = x^e \text{ MOD } m.
$$

Bob sends y to Alice. Upon receiving y, Alice calculates

$$
y^d \text{ MOD } m.
$$

Now by the definition of y, this gives

$$
\begin{aligned}
y^d &\equiv (x^e \text{ MOD } m)^d \\
&\equiv (x^e)^d \\
&\equiv x^{ed} \pmod{m}.
\end{aligned}
$$

Also, since $d \equiv e^{-1} \pmod{n}$, by the definition of multiplicative inverse modulo n we know that $d \cdot e = 1 + kn = 1 + k(p-1)(q-1)$ for some integer k. So by Theorem 4.3.2,

$$
y^d \equiv x^{ed} \equiv x^{1+k(p-1)(q-1)} \equiv x \pmod{m}. \tag{4.30}
$$

That is, Alice recovers the original message.

In order to receive any enciphered replies from Alice, Bob must make preparations analogous to those that Alice carried out. He chooses his own large primes, calculates his own private decipherment exponent, and publishes his own public modulus and encipherment exponent.

Example 4.4.1 Suppose Alice chooses $p = 17$ and $q = 43$. Then her modulus is $m = pq = 731$ and $n = (p-1)(q-1) = 16 \cdot 42 = 672$. Bob will be able to encipher messages or blocks of messages with numerical equivalents in the range 0 to 730. Alice chooses a public key $e = 29$, which is relatively prime to $672 = 2^5 \cdot 3 \cdot 7$. Then she finds the inverse d of e modulo 672 by the extended Euclidean algorithm:

$$
\begin{aligned}
672 &= 23 \cdot 29 + 5 \\
29 &= 5 \cdot 5 + 4 \\
5 &= 1 \cdot 4 + 1,
\end{aligned}
$$

so, by back substituting, she finds

$$
\begin{aligned}
1 &= 5 - 1 \cdot 4 \\
&= 5 - 1 \cdot (29 - 5 \cdot 5) = 6 \cdot 5 - 1 \cdot 29 \\
&= 6 \cdot (672 - 23 \cdot 29) - 1 \cdot 29 \\
&= 6 \cdot 672 - 139 \cdot 29.
\end{aligned}
$$

Thus $d \equiv -139 \equiv 533 \pmod{672}$.

Alice broadcasts the modulus $m = 731$ and the exponent $e = 29$, and she retains the private information d, p, and q. She also publicizes the way in which textual information is to be turned into numerical equivalents. In this case she specifies that two-letter blocks are interpreted as base twenty-six representations. So, if x_1 and x_0 are the numerical equivalents of the letters, then the numerical equivalent of the block will be

$$x = 26 \cdot x_1 + x_0.$$

This will be a number in the range from 0 to 675 (why?), which is within the limits of Alice's modulus 731.

For example, if Bob wants to send her the message HI, for which the numerical equivalents are 7 and 8, he first calculates

$$x = 26 \cdot 7 + 8 = 190.$$

Then he enciphers this by calculating

$$
\begin{aligned}
y \equiv x^{29} &\equiv 190^{29} \\
&\equiv 190^{16} \cdot 190^8 \cdot 190^4 \cdot 190 \\
&\equiv 52 \cdot 169 \cdot 13 \cdot 190 \\
&\equiv 16 \cdot 13 \cdot 190 \\
&\equiv 208 \cdot 190 \\
&\equiv 46 \quad (\mathrm{mod}\ 731).
\end{aligned}
$$

When Alice receives 46, she deciphers it by first calculating y^{533} MOD 731:

$$
\begin{aligned}
y^{533} &\equiv 46^{533} \\
&\equiv 46^{512} \cdot 46^{16} \cdot 46^4 \cdot 46 \\
&\equiv 154 \cdot 324 \cdot 81 \cdot 46 \\
&\equiv 190 \quad (\mathrm{mod}\ 731).
\end{aligned}
$$

The she obtains the numerical equivalents of the message letters by dividing 26 into 190:

$$190 = 7 \cdot 26 + 8.$$

The quotient 7 and remainder 8 are the message's numerical equivalents. $\diamondsuit$

In the previous example, a message of length more than two characters would be subdivided into blocks of two letters and enciphered block by block. The same idea can be applied where the block length is any number of letters.

Example 4.4.2 Suppose Alice has the same public modulus and exponent as in Example 4.4.1, and she has received the ciphertext

$$290\ 369\ 203\ 405\ 033\ 511\ 584\ 612\ 213.$$

Assuming that letter digraphs were translated into digits according to the method described in that example, determine the message she deciphers.

Solution Alice first calculates

$$
\begin{aligned}
290^{533} &\equiv 290 \quad (\mathrm{mod}\ 731) \\
369^{533} &\equiv 513 \quad (\mathrm{mod}\ 731) \\
203^{533} &\equiv 186 \quad (\mathrm{mod}\ 731) \\
405^{533} &\equiv 046 \quad (\mathrm{mod}\ 731)
\end{aligned}
$$

$$33^{533} \equiv 628 \pmod{731}$$
$$511^{533} \equiv 443 \pmod{731}$$
$$584^{533} \equiv 126 \pmod{731}$$
$$612^{533} \equiv 017 \pmod{731}$$
$$213^{533} \equiv 127 \pmod{731}.$$

Since

$$290 = 11 \cdot 26 + 4 = \texttt{LE}$$
$$513 = 19 \cdot 26 + 19 = \texttt{TT}$$
$$186 = 7 \cdot 26 + 4 = \texttt{HE}$$
$$046 = 1 \cdot 26 + 20 = \texttt{BU}$$
$$628 = 24 \cdot 26 + 4 = \texttt{YE}$$
$$443 = 17 \cdot 26 + 1 = \texttt{RB}$$
$$126 = 4 \cdot 26 + 22 = \texttt{EW}$$
$$017 = 0 \cdot 26 + 17 = \texttt{AR}$$
$$127 = 4 \cdot 26 + 23 = \texttt{EX}$$

the plaintext is

$$\texttt{LETTHEBUYERBEWAREX}$$

The X is padding to make the number of letters even. $\Diamond$

Why RSA Seems to Be Secure

To illustrate why RSA is regarded as a secure cryptosystem, we turn first to an attempt at cryptanalysis. The following example shows an obvious attack on the system.

Example 4.4.3 Suppose Alice has published the modulus $m = 459\,659$ and exponent $s = 5$ and has indicated that if x_3, x_2, x_1, x_0 are numerical equivalents of a block of four plaintext letters, then the sender calculates

$$x = x_3 \cdot 26^3 + x_2 \cdot 26^2 + x_1 \cdot 26 + x_0 \qquad (4.31)$$

and produces the ciphertext $y = x^e$ MOD m. Suppose Eve has intercepted the ciphertext

$$y = 223\,376$$

and would like to find the original plaintext. How can this be done?

Solution If Eve knew the prime numbers p and q such that $pq = 459\,659$, then she could calculate $n = (p-1)(q-1)$ and, using the Euclidean algorithm, could find

$$d \equiv 5^{-1} \pmod{n}.$$

Then the numerical equivalent of the plaintext would be

$$223\,376^d \pmod{459\,659},$$

and she could obtain the letters of the plaintext by converting this number to base 26, in effect reversing the procedure in (4.31).

So the direct attack is to factor $459\,659$. Taking a trial-and-error approach, Eve will need to test prime numbers in the range from 2 to $\lfloor\sqrt{459\,659}\rfloor = \lfloor 677.9815\ldots\rfloor = 677$. By examining a table of primes, she sees that there are 123 primes in this range, so the worst case is that she would have to perform 123 divisions. She can rule out 2 and 677 as prime factors (why?). Dividing by 3, 5, 7, 11, 13, 17, ..., she gets nonzero remainders. Continuing in this systematic fashion, she finds, eventually, that $459\,659$ is evenly divisible by 673: $459\,659 = 673 \cdot 683$. Now she easily obtains

$$n = (p - 1)(q - 1) = 672 \cdot 682 = 458\,304,$$

and by the extended Euclidean algorithm,

$$d \equiv 5^{-1} \equiv 91661 \pmod{n}.$$

Thus the numerical equivalent of the plaintext should be

$$223\,376^{91661} \equiv 126\,037 \pmod{459659}.$$

Now successive divisions by 26 give her the base twenty-six representation:

$$
\begin{aligned}
126\,037 &= 4847 \cdot 26 + 15 \\
&= (186 \cdot 26 + 11) \cdot 26 + 15 \\
&= ((7 \cdot 26 + 4) \cdot 26 + 11) \cdot 26 + 15 \\
&= 7 \cdot 26^3 + 4 \cdot 26^2 + 11 \cdot 26 + 15,
\end{aligned}
$$

so the plaintext letters have numerical equivalents 7, 4, 11, 15: HELP. $\diamondsuit$

In the foregoing example, Eve had to perform 120 divisions by prime numbers to determine the prime factorization of a number with six digits in its decimal representation. No other steps involving arithmetic were necessary because she already had a list of primes up to the square root of the number she wanted to factor. Indeed, since the table of primes goes up to 9973, she could take this approach to factoring any product of primes in the range from 6 up to $9973^2 = 99\,460\,729$. For a number on the order of $99\,460\,729$, Eve would, in the worst case, have to perform about 1229 divisions. While doing this by hand would be tedious, a simple program in any computer language could do the job in much less than 1 second.

Now, suppose Eve wants to factor a number n with 100 digits in its decimal representation. Then $n \approx 10^{100}$, and she would need to do trial division by prime numbers in the range from 2 to roughly $\sqrt{n} \approx \sqrt{10^{100}} = 10^{50}$. By the prime number theorem there are approximately

$$\frac{10^{50}}{\ln(10^{50})} = \frac{10^{50}}{50\ln 10} = \frac{10^{50}}{115.1} \approx 8.686 \times 10^{47} \approx 10 \times 10^{47} = 10^{48}$$

prime numbers in this range, so in the worst case Eve might have to perform about 10^{48} divisions by prime numbers. Worse yet, this presupposes that she has already generated a list of these 10^{48} prime numbers. To get an idea of the magnitude of this computational problem, consider the fact that it takes about 160 bits or, equivalently, 20 bytes to represent a 48-decimal-digit number. So just to *store* the list of the first 10^{48} primes would take roughly $20 \times 10^{48} = 2 \times 10^{49}$ bytes. Presently, many personal computers are manufactured with disk drives that have storage capacities of about 10 gigabytes—$10 \times 10^9 = 10^{11}$ bytes. So it would take $2 \times 10^{49}/10^{11} = 2 \times 10^{38}$ such disk drives just to store the list!

There are no known algorithms for factoring numbers n whose computational expense function $\mu(n)$ satisfies $\mu(n) \in \mathcal{O}(n^r)$ for a positive number r. Thus, if Alice and Bob want to use the RSA encipherment method and feel reasonably sure that an adversary cannot practically do what Eve did in our little example, they need to select p and q both to be large primes so that their product is, say, on the order of 10^{200}. This means that to implement RSA for real cryptographic applications Bob and Alice need to *find* prime numbers whose decimal representations have on the order of 100 digits. Prime searching is an interesting and challenging task itself. There are probabilistic methods for this problem, but they are beyond the scope of these materials. For an interesting discussion, see [10].

Even with well-chosen primes and exponents, implementations of RSA can be subverted when information leaks out. For example, if, in addition to knowing $m = pq$, Eve also knows $n = (p-1)(q-1)$, then she can solve for the primes p and q. It is an exercise for you to show how to do this. Also, knowing $(p-1)(q-1)$ and the encipherment exponent e, she can recover the secret decryption exponent d.

If Eve knows the decryption exponent d, along with the modulus m and encryption exponent e, then it is possible—by probabilistic means— for Eve to factor m. There is a discussion of this method in [45]. To see how disaster might befall Alice in this case, suppose that she is using the same modulus all the time and frequently changing the exponent pair. If somehow one of the exponent pairs gets into Eve's hands, then Eve can factor m and easily compute $n = (p-1)(q-1)$. Subsequently, when Alice changes the encryption exponent, Eve merely has to use the value of $(p-1)(q-1)$ she has already found, along with the extended Euclidean algorithm, to compute Alice's new decryption exponent. Thus it appears that if any part of the key information is compromised, then Alice should not reuse the modulus or the exponent.

Even if none of the key information leaks out, subtle misuse of a perfectly solid implementation of RSA can clear the way for Eve. In the exercises, you will investigate the common modulus protocol failure.

Summary

The RSA cryptosystem is a public key method in which Alice sets herself up to receive enciphered messages from others by selecting two large primes p and q and an encryption exponent e that is relatively prime to $n = (p-1)(q-1)$. The setup is completed when she publishes $m = pq$ and e and computes and retains $d = e^{-1} \pmod{n}$. Bob enciphers numerical plaintext x in the range 0 to $m-1$ by $y = x^e$ MOD m; Alice decrypts by computing y^d MOD m. That this computation decrypts correctly is assured by Theorem 4.3.2. To receive encrypted messages himself, Bob must perform the same setup as Alice. Cryptanalysis is believed to be essentially equivalent to factoring m. Since the factors of m are large and the computational expense function for all factoring algorithms is believed to grow very rapidly with the size of m, the method is thought to be very secure.

EXERCISES

1. Encode the following four-letter words in numerical form by the formula $x = x_4 \cdot 26^3 + x_3 \cdot 26^2 + x_2 \cdot 26 + x_1$, where x_4, x_3, x_2, and x are the numerical equivalents of the letters, left to right.

(a) STAY   (b) WALK   (c) CALM

2. Decode the following numbers as four-letter words, assuming the words were encoded as in Exercise 1.

(a) 336 945   (b) 294 963   (c) 093 734

3. Suppose you have intercepted the number $5\,874\,053\,238$, which you suspect to be an encoding of plaintext by the formula $x = x_n \cdot 26^{n-1} + x_{n-1} \cdot 26^{n-2} + x_{n-3} \cdot 26^{n-3} + \ldots x_3 \cdot 26^2 + x_2 \cdot 26 + x_1$. The number n of characters is unknown. Determine the smallest possible number of characters and use this as a starting point to decoding the message.

4. Alice has published the modulus $m = 22\,987$ and exponent $s = 7$. Use a three-letter base twenty-six encoding and RSA to encipher the following messages to her:

(a) LIE   (b) MAD   (c) SUN

5. Alice has chosen primes $p = 113$, $q = 157$, and exponent $e = 113$. Determine her public modulus and private exponent for RSA. If she receives the following messages, determine the plaintext that she obtains.

(a) 13 667   (b) 11 220

6. Use the modulus of Exercise 4 to encipher the following message in block mode. Use three-letter blocks, and write the resulting numbers as five-decimal-digit numbers.

TAKE A HIKE

7. Use the modulus of Exercise 5 to decipher the following message, which was enciphered in block mode with encryption exponent $s = 12707$. Assume that each block of five decimal digits represents a block of three letters.

13681 16451 02046 03519 15362 06610

8. The following message is an encipherment by RSA of a five-letter message using modulus $m = 11\,885\,807$ and exponent $s = 6\,395\,437$:

$$y = 8\,468\,422$$

Perform a cryptanalysis to break this cipher and obtain the message.

9. Suppose that Eve know Bob's public RSA modulus $m = pq$ and also has come by $n = (p-1)(q-1)$. Then it is possible for her to obtain p and q by the following means.

   (a) Show that $p + q = m - n + 1$.

   (b) By using the fact that $q = m/p$, show that p satisfies the quadratic equation $p^2 + (n - m - 1)p + m = 0$.

   (c) Deduce that p and q are

   $$p = \frac{(m - n + 1) + \sqrt{(m - n + 1)^2 - 4m}}{2}$$
   $$q = \frac{(m - n + 1) - \sqrt{(m - n + 1)^2 - 4m}}{2}.$$

   (d) If $pq = 5\,336\,063$ and $(p-1)(q-1) = 5\,331\,408$, find the prime factors p and q.

10. One instance in which an implementation of RSA may be subverted is when there a **common modulus protocol failure**. Suppose that Anna and Zena have the same RSA modulus m and different public encryption exponents e_a and e_z, which are relatively prime. If Matt sends a message x (that is relatively prime to m) to both Anna and Zena encrypted with their respective exponents and Evelyn intercepts both of these ciphertexts, then she can obtain the plaintext without knowing a factorization of m or either decryption exponent!

    (a) By using Theorem 4.1.3 and the fact that

    $$x^{se_a + te_z} \equiv (x^{e_a})^s \cdot (x^{e_z})^t \pmod{m}$$

    for any choice of s and t, show how this can be done.

    (b) If $m = 4171$, $e_a = 47$, and $e_z = 101$, find the numerical plaintext from which the ciphertexts 2467 and 2664 were computed.

4.5   Key Agreement

All current implementations of public-key cryptosystems are much slower than symmetric systems.[11] For instance, in current implementations RSA is roughly a thousand times slower than DES. So public-key methods will produce considerable bottlenecks if a great deal of plaintext is to be enciphered and transmitted quickly. Instead, public-key methods are often used to perform **key exchange** or **key agreement** protocols. A simple instance might be this: Suppose that Alice and Bob both have published their public RSA keys and that the two have never previously communicated. Alice can initiate contact by sending Bob a short message saying, "Hey, Bob. Let's correspond using DES as our symmetric cryptosystem. Let's use this key: $101010 \ldots 1010$." She enciphers this message using Bob's RSA key. Someone intercepting the encrypted message might know that it was enciphered with Bob's RSA key, but if RSA is secure, that person will not be able to obtain the secret DES key that now only Alice and Bob possess. Of course, Bob could object to the key Alice chose, claiming (rightly in this case) that it might be too easily guessed by an adversary. He might counter with his own choice of key. Alice, in turn, might object that his suggested key was too hard to remember. There could be considerable disagreement about which key actually to use.

There are various solutions to this problem.

- **Key predistribution** A trusted authority (TA; for instance, a dedicated computer on a network) generates a key for each of the $C(n, 2)$ pairs of users on an n-person network. Then the TA distributes a set of keys to each user: Alice, for instance, receives separate keys for communicating with Bob, Carol, David, Esmerelda, ... Whenever she wants encrypted communication with one of these people, she must look up that person's key. Similarly, any recipient of a message from Alice who wants to send an encrypted reply must look up their assigned key for Alice. With this scheme, there is no argument between parties about what key will be used, but the difficulty is in keeping a large amount of key information secret.

- **Kerberos**[12] Each network user shares a secret DES key with the TA. Whenever Alice wishes to send encrypted communication to Bob, she

---

[11]It has not been proven that every public-key cryptosystem must be significantly slower than symmetric systems. This is an open question.

[12]This key distribution protocol was developed at the Massachusetts Institute of Tech-

first requests, by DES encrypted communication with the TA, a **session key**. The TA generates a session key, sends it DES encrypted (using the key it shares with Alice) to Alice, and sends it DES encrypted to Bob (using the key it shares with Bob). Then both Alice and Bob possess a key and can communicate with it during their session. If there are n users on the network, then there are only n keys to predistribute, so this method requires a much smaller amount of information be kept secret than key predistribution.

- **Diffie-Hellman Key Agreement** Two parties wishing to communicate with a symmetric cryptosystem agree on a secret key by a public exchange of numbers. The only function a TA serves in this scheme is to generate and make public a large prime number p, which is used as a modulus for calculations, and a number s in the range 2 to $p - 2$, which is exponentiated modulo p in the protocol. The security of this protocol, which we will describe in this section, relies on the hardness of the **discrete logarithm problem**, that is, solving the congruence $s^x \equiv t \pmod{p}$ for x when s and t are given.

The Discrete Logarithm Problem

It is easy to calculate

$$345^{67} \text{ MOD } 4389 = 4251$$

by repeated squaring and reducing. On the other hand, if someone has calculated

$$345^x \equiv 3039 \pmod{4389}$$

for some unspecified value of x, we might have little choice other than trial and error to determine the value of x that person used. In the worst case, we would have to calculate $4389 - 3 = 4386$ (explain why it is not necessary to check the values $x = 0$, $x = 1$, and $x = 4388$) values of 345^x to find x.

If b, c, and m are given integers, then solving the congruence

$$b^x \equiv c \pmod{m} \tag{4.32}$$

nology and named for a multiheaded dog in Greek mythology that stood guard at the gates of Hades. Presumably the dog kept the unwelcome out, so by analogy the protocol keeps the unwelcome out of a computer system. The analogy could be carried a step further: many legitimate users of computer systems have doubtless found attempts at using the machinery hellish.

for x is called the **discrete logarithm**[13] **problem** (DLP). While there are algorithms that solve DLP whose computational expense functions are in $\mathcal{O}(e^{f(x)})$, where $f(x)$ grows slower than x, there is no known algorithms for it whose expense function is in $\mathcal{O}(x^r)$ for any r. Thus it is thought that DLP is intrinsically time consuming to solve. If m is large (e.g., with on the order of 200 digits in its decimal representation), then trying out all of the possible values of a will take an unreasonable amount of computational resources.

Example 4.5.1 Let $m = 19$, $b = 2$ and $c = 14$. We are then looking for a choice of x such that

$$2^x \equiv 14 \pmod{19}.$$

We proceed by systematic trial and error, calculating values of 2^x modulo 19 until we either find an x that works or we exhaust all the possibilities and find that there is no solution. Table 4.6 shows a complete set of values, and we see that $x = 7$ is the only solution. $\Diamond$

x	2^x MOD 19	x	2^x MOD 19
1	2	10	17
2	4	11	15
3	8	12	11
4	16	13	3
5	13	14	6
6	7	15	12
7	14	16	5
8	9	17	10
9	18	18	1

Table 4.6 Solving an instance of the DLP.

Example 4.5.2 If $m = 252097800623$, $b = 43$ and $c = 35087486750$, then approaching the problem as in the previous example is potentially much more involved; it could require calculating approximately 2.5×10^{12} values of 43^x to see if c ever turned up. Even if each exponentiation took, say, a billionth (10^{-9}) of a second on a computer, it could take almost an hour just for that part of the process. It is not hard to find and do exponentiation

---

[13]Recall that the logarithm to base b of a number x, denoted $\log_b(x)$, is the exponent to which b must be raised to obtain x. For example, $\log_2(64)$ is 6 because $2^6 = 64$; $\log_{10}(3)$ is approximately 0.477121, as you can check with a hand-held calculator. The algorithms for calculating this type of logarithm are generally very fast, even for extremely large numbers. The adjective *discrete* is used to distinguish from this sort of "continuous" logarithm.

with numbers much larger than this choice of m. In those cases, the job of finding x grows by a factor of 10 with each additional digit of m. $\diamondsuit$

When m is prime, it is always possible to choose b so that b, b^2, b^3, ..., b^{p-1} (all modulo p) run through the values 1, 2, 3, ..., $p-1$ in some order. Such a b is called a **generator** or a **primitive root of unity**. For instance, in Example 4.5.1, 2 is a generator, as you can see by looking at the table. You can also check that 4 and 5 are not generators. It turns out that for each prime p there is at least one generator. Indeed, the following theorem is true.

Theorem 4.5.1 *(Primitive Root Theorem) For each prime p there are exactly $\phi(p-1)$ generators. (Here ϕ is the Euler ϕ function.)*

A proof of this theorem can be found in books on number theory. See, for instance, [74]. An implication of the theorem is that if we are attempting to solve the DLP (4.32) when n is prime and we know that b is a generator, then we are guaranteed that there is a solution x. The bad news is that the theorem does not tell us how to determine whether a given number b is a generator other than by checking that b, b^2, b^3, ..., b^{p-1} are all distinct modulo m.

The Diffie-Hellman Key Agreement Protocol

Let p be a (large) prime number, and let s be a number in the range 2 to $p-2$. It is preferable, though not essential, that s be a generator. We will refer to p as the **public prime** and s as the **public base** because these will be public information, generated perhaps by a trusted authority. Alice and Bob want to establish a common key k, which we think of as numerical, for some symmetric cryptosystem that they wish to use. They do this over an insecure channel by the following **Diffie-Hellman key agreement protocol**.

- Alice chooses a number a at random in the range 2 to $p-2$ and calculates $\alpha = s^a$ MOD p; she sends α to Bob.

- Bob chooses a number b at random in the range 2 to $p-2$ and calculates $\beta = s^b$ MOD p; he sends β to Alice.

- Alice calculates $k = \beta^a$ MOD $p = (s^b)^a$ MOD $p = s^{ab}$ MOD p; Bob calculates α^b MOD p, which is the same thing: α^b MOD $p = (s^a)^b$ MOD $p = s^{ab}$ MOD p. Thus they both possess the same key $k = s^{ab}$ MOD p.

Example 4.5.3 Suppose that the public prime is $p = 197$ and that the public base is $s = 31$. Alice chooses $a = 101$ and then calculates

$$\alpha = 31^{101} \text{ MOD } 197 = 153$$

and sends this to Bob. Bob chooses $b = 85$ and calculates

$$\beta = 31^{85} \text{ MOD } 197 = 11$$

and then sends this to Alice.

Alice calculates

$$\beta^{101} \text{ MOD } 197 = 11^{101} \text{ MOD } 197 = 48$$

and Bob calculates

$$\alpha^{85} \text{ MOD } 197 = 153^{85} \text{ MOD } 197 = 48.$$

Thus they have agreed on the key $k = 48$. $\Diamond$

Why is the Diffie-Hellman key agreement protocol secure? An opponent, Eve, will know s and p, and she will see α and β. The obvious way for her to discover k is to solve the congruences

$$s^a \equiv \alpha \pmod{p} \tag{4.33}$$
$$s^b \equiv \beta \pmod{p} \tag{4.34}$$

for a and b. If she had some way of solving DLP in a time-efficient manner, then she could easily do this. However, there is no such generally applicable algorithm known, so she is prevented from solving the congruences in this manner. This is *not* to say that there isn't an efficient way for Eve to obtain the key. No one has proven mathematically that she *has* to find it by solving (4.33) and (4.34). It is conceivable that she can, by some other means,

Find s^{ab} MOD p from s^a and s^b in a time-efficient manner.   (4.35)

The statement in (4.35) is called the **Diffie-Hellman problem**, and it remains an open question whether it can be solved. It is also an open question whether a solution to (4.35) implies the existence of a time-efficient solution to the discrete logarithm problem. If the answer to this first question is no, then the answer to the second one is also no. Moreover, experts in this area believe that the answer is, indeed, no.

Example 4.5.4 Suppose the prime $p = 509$ and base $s = 37$ are published. Alice and Bob want to use the Diffie-Hellman key agreement protocol to establish a 9-bit keyword for binary Viegenère encipherment. Alice selects a number at random: $a = 73$. Bob also selects a number at random: $b = 23$. What is the key that they agree on?

Solution We find the number $k = s^{ab}$ MOD p and then convert it to binary:

$$k \equiv 37^{73 \cdot 23} \equiv 37^{1679} \pmod{509}.$$

Since $1679 = 3 \cdot 508 + 155$, we can use Fermat's little theorem to reduce the exponent before starting the square-and-reduce process of exponentiation:

$$
\begin{aligned}
k &\equiv 37^{3 \cdot 508 + 155} \equiv (37^3)^{508} \cdot 37^{155} \\
&\equiv 1 \cdot 37^{155} \pmod{509}.
\end{aligned}
$$

By squaring and reducing, we find $k = 258$. In binary representation, this number is 100000010. $\Diamond$

The ElGamal Cryptosystem

The Diffie-Hellman key agreement protocol can be varied slightly to produce a public-key encipherment scheme. Such a method was first published in a 1985 paper [19], by Taher ElGamal. We describe it here because of its elegance and to illustrate how cryptographic primitives can be adapted and applied.

Setup

- There is a public prime p and base s, where s is in the range 2 to $p-2$. (It is desirable but not essential that s be a generator.) Message blocks must be numbers in the range 2 to $p - 1$.

- Alice has generated a random number a in the range 2 to $p - 2$, which she uses as a private key; she calculates and publishes $\alpha = s^a \pmod{p}$ as a public key.

- Bob has generated a random number b in the range 2 to $p - 2$, which he uses as a private key; he calculates and publishes $\beta = s^b \pmod{p}$ as a public key.

Encryption and Decryption

- To send message x, a number in the range 2 to $p-1$, to Alice, Bob generates a random number k in the range 2 to $p-2$ (sometimes called a "session key"), looks up Alice's α, and calculates $t = s^k$ MOD p and $y = \alpha^k x$ MOD p. He sends t and y to Alice. (Now the message is wearing a "mask"; Bob is sending the masked x along with a "clue" t that can be used to take off the mask. However, the clue can be used only by someone who knows a, and that person is Alice.)

- Receiving t and y, Alice calculates $(t^a)^{-1}$ MOD p. Since

$$t^a \equiv (s^k)^a \equiv s^{ak} \pmod{p},$$

she can then multiply y by $(t^a)^{-1}$ to obtain x:

$$y \cdot (t^a)^{-1} \equiv (x s^{ak}) \cdot (s^{ak})^{-1} \equiv x \pmod{p};$$

that is, the plaintext is $y \cdot t^{-a}$ MOD p.

Note Because the modulus is prime, $(t^a)^{-1} \equiv t^{-a} \equiv t^{p-1-a} \pmod{p}$, and thus the Euclidean algorithm for finding $(t^a)^{-1}$ can be avoided. You are asked in the exercises to explain this.

Example 4.5.5 A public prime of $p = 11881379$ (the next prime after 26^5) and base $s = 23$ are available for use in the ElGamal scheme. Alice has published an α value of 1308503. Bob wants to ask Alice out for lunch, so the message he will send is LUNCH. What must he do to encipher it?

Solution Bob first picks a number at random, $k = 123$. He also converts his message from its base 26 representation to base 10:

$$x = \text{LUNCH} = 5387103.$$

He calculates

$$t = s^k \text{ MOD } 11881379 = 23^{123} \text{ MOD } 11881379 = 1777907$$
$$y = x \cdot \alpha^k \text{ MOD } 11881379 = 5387103 \cdot 1308503^{123} \text{ MOD } 11881379 = 4944577$$

and then sends $(1777907, 4944577)$ to Alice. $\diamondsuit$

Example 4.5.6 With the same public information as in Example 4.5.5, Alice receives the message $(5387871, 7127763)$ from Charles. How does she decipher it?

Solution Alice will need to use her secret key $a = 55$ (you can check that 23^{55} MOD 11881379 is the α value given in the previous example). She calculates

$$t^a \ \text{MOD} \ 11881379 = 5387871^{55} \ \text{MOD} \ 11881379 = 11398977.$$

By the note following the general description of the ElGamal method,

$$t^{-a} \equiv t^{p-1-a} \equiv 1777907^{11881323} \equiv 3552158 \pmod{11881379}.$$

Thus Alice calculates the numerical plaintext to be

$$y \cdot t^{-a} \equiv 7127763 \cdot 3552158 \equiv 6866650 \pmod{11881379}.$$

Converting this number to base 26, she obtains the message PARTY. She decides in favor of the more exciting prospect of an evening partying with Charles and takes a rain check on Bob's offer. $\Diamond$

With the particular implementation of the ElGamal method used in the previous two examples, a message longer than five letters could be divided into five-letter blocks and the encipherment applied to each piece. Of course, Bob (or Charles) would have to generate a random k for each block and compute a different value of t with each block. Thus the ciphertext would be roughly twice as long as the plaintext.

Again, let us ask, "Where is the security in this scheme?" If Eve is eavesdropping, then she will know t and y as well as p, s, and α. A direct way for her to attack is to get k by solving $t \equiv s^k \pmod{p}$. Then she can easily compute α^k and finally solve $y \equiv \alpha^k x \pmod{p}$ for x by multiplying both sides by $(\alpha^k)^{-1} \equiv \alpha^{p-1-k} \pmod{p}$. But the first step in this process is to solve the DLP, which is likely to be intractable.

Summary

The key distribution of classical cryptography can be solved by a variety of methods. Public-key cryptography is one way to do this. The Diffie-Hellman key exchange algorithm is a public-key method by which the correspondents agree upon a key that both have a hand in determining. Its security relies on the computational infeasibility of the discrete logarithm problem: in order for an opponent, Eve, to determine the key from listening in on the key exchange protocol, it seems that she must have a time-efficient algorithm to solve the DLP. The ElGamal encryption method is based on the

Diffie-Hellman key exchange protocol: Messages encrypted using a symmetric cryptosystem are sent and received along with the key, in effect encrypted through the Diffie-Hellman protocol.

EXERCISES

1. (a) Complete the modulo 11 exponentiation table in Table 4.7.

x	2^x	3^x	4^x	5^x	6^x	7^x	8^x	9^x	10^x
1	2			5	6				
2	4	9	5	3	3	5	9	4	1
3					7				
4					9				
5					10				
6					5				
7					8				
8					4				
9					2				
10					1				

Table 4.7 Table for Exercise 1.

(b) Use the table to find all solutions to the following congruences. (i) $6^x \equiv 4 \,(\text{mod}\, 11)$, (ii) $4^x \equiv 9 \,(\text{mod}\, 11)$, (iii) $9^x \equiv 8 \,(\text{mod}\, 11)$

(c) Which numbers are generators?

2. Find a solution x for each of the following congruences. (*Note*: There may be more than one solution in the range 1 to modulus-minus-one.)

(a) $5^x \equiv 2 \,(\text{mod}\, 17)$

(b) $10^x \equiv 4 \,(\text{mod}\, 12)$

(c) $2^x \equiv 1024 \,(\text{mod}\, 3027)$

(d) $23^x \equiv 25 \,(\text{mod}\, 26)$

3. Suppose that the published Diffie-Hellman prime and base are, respectively, $p = 37$ and $s = 6$. If Alice sends Bob the number $\alpha = 36$ and Bob sends $\beta = 31$ to Alice, find the key on which they have agreed.

What makes the recovery of this key so easy? [*Hint*: Look at a table of values of 6^x (mod 37).] From Bob and Alice's viewpoint what would be a better choice of s ?

4. Suppose the prime $p = 251$ and base $s = 53$ are published. Alice and Bob want to use the Diffie-Hellman key agreement protocol to establish an 8-bit keyword for binary Vigenère encipherment. Alice selects a number at random: $a = 63$. Bob also selects a number at random: $b = 55$. What is the key that they agree on?

5. Alice and Bob are using the Diffie-Hellman key agreement protocol to agree on a key for a shift cipher. Suppose that the public prime and base are $p = 23$ and $s = 5$, and that Bob's private key is $b = 6$. If he receives the message

21, KLSQSOSCW,

how will he decipher the message?

6. In each of the following, Bob is to use the ElGamal method to encrypt the given plaintext s for Alice using the parameters p and s, the public key α, and the session key k. Calculate his numerical ciphertext (t, y) in each case.

   (a) $p = 59$, $s = 5$, $x = 28$, $k = 6$, $x = 20$
   (b) $p = 97$, $s = 8$, $x = 33$, $k = 3$, $x = 55$

7. In each of the following, Alice has received the given key-ciphertext pair (t, y). Using the given prime p and the given private key a, calculate her plaintext.

   (a) $p = 59$, $a = 13$, $(t, y) = (9, 34)$
   (b) $p = 97$, $a = 10$, $(t, y) = (8, 66)$

8. The ElGamal system is set up with prime $p = 1009$ and base $s = 109$; Alice's public key is $\alpha = 61$, and Bob's public key is $\beta = 6$.

   (a) Suppose Bob wants to encrypt the plaintext $x = 98$ with session key $k = 25$. Determine the key-ciphertext pair he sends to Alice.
   (b) Suppose Alice wants to encrypt the plaintext $x = 723$ with session key $k = 158$. Determine the key-ciphertext pair she sends to Bob.

9. The ElGamal system is set up as in Exercise 8.

   (a) Verify that Alice's private key is $a = 37$ and that Bob's private key is 61.

   (b) Alice has received the key-ciphertext pair $(t, y) = (10, 675)$ from Bob. Calculate her plaintext.

   (c) Bob has received the key-ciphertext pair $(t, y) = (269, 245)$ from Alice. Calculate his plaintext.

10. (Computer needed) Angela and Bruce are using the ElGamal cryptosystem, agreeing that three-letter blocks of text will represent numbers in the range 0 to $26^3 = 17576$. These will be converted from base twenty-six to base ten for encryption, and from base ten to base twenty-six after decryption. Suppose that the public prime is $p = 17579$, the public base is $s = 987$, Angela's public key is $\alpha = 1582$, and Bruce's public key is $\beta = 11051$.

   (a) Bruce wants to send the message YOU RPL ACE to Angela, and he has selected the three random values 641, 32, and 1187 to do the job. Calculate the ciphertext he sends to her.

   (b) Angela receives the following ciphertext from Caleb:

   $$(16973, 6731), \ (2167, 8293), \ (148, 10303).$$

   If her private key is $a = 1125$ (verify that this agrees with her public key), decipher the message and represent it in base twenty-six to read it.

11. If p is prime, explain why $t^{-a} \equiv t^{p-1-a} \pmod{p}$ for any nonzero t.

12. Explain why it would be unwise to choose $s = p - 1$ for the Diffie-Hellman protocol.

13. Write a computer program that implements ElGamal encryption and decryption.

4.6   Digital Signatures

For many applications, it is important for the recipient of a message to have a way of verifying that it came from the person or entity from which the message content implies the message came. We already encountered this issue in our discussion of hash functions and MACs. For instance, if Zeke receives an e-mail that closes "Sincerely, Audrey," he might not be sure that the sender really was Audrey. One way to accomplish this verification is with a **digital** or **electronic signature**. Unlike an ink-on-paper signature, where forgery is possible by careful copying off one document onto another, a digital signature is knit up with the message itself so as to make forgery almost impossible. According to R. L. Rivest in [67], "The notion of digital signature may prove to be one of the most fundamental and useful inventions of modern cryptography." Indeed, in the summer of 2000, the U.S. federal government approved legislation that gives electronic signatures generated by the Digital Signature Standard the same legal standing as pen-on-paper signatures.

The idea is straightforward and can be illustrated with any public-key method. We use RSA. Let m be an RSA modulus, $E(x) = x$ MOD m, represent the RSA encryption of a plaintext x, and $D(y) \equiv y^d$ MOD m the RSA decryption of a ciphertext y. Then, as we know,

$$D(E(x)) = x \text{ for all } 0 \le x \le m - 1,$$

and

$$E(D(x)) = x \text{ for all } 0 \le x \le m - 1.$$

The latter property provides an elegant way for someone to generate a "signature" of a message that depends on the message contents and is directly tied to the individual sending the message.

Example 4.6.1 Suppose Audrey has RSA modulus[14] $m = 5429515137199$ and encryption exponent $s = 23$. She wants to send Zeke the message YOURECUTE and affix a signature by which Zeke can confirm that it is Audrey who sent the message and not one of his buddies playing a trick.

The message is nine letters long, so it can be regarded as a number in the range 0 to $26^9 - 1 = 5429503678975$, which, conveniently, just fits inside

---

[14]Bear in mind, however, that, large as 5429515137199 may look, it is a "small" number for computer factorization and can be factored by a general-purpose computer algebra system in essentially no time. A genuinely uncrackable versions would use a value of m with 150 to 200 digits in its decimal representation.

the range 0 to m. First she converts the plaintext to decimal:

$$x = \text{YOURECUTE} = 5130677068274$$

and then she uses her *decryption* exponent $d = 4485247785295$ to calculate a signature[15]:

$$\sigma \equiv x^d \equiv 5130677068274^{4485247785295} \equiv 4320048260981 \pmod{5429515137199}.$$

Then she sends the pair (x, σ) to Zeke. At this point she is less concerned about someone else reading the message than about Zeke thinking it's a joke, so she doesn't encrypt the message itself. Receiving the pair, Zeke translates the message into readable plaintext. Doubtful about the origin of the message but hopeful that this might be the real thing, he looks up Audrey's modulus and public exponent e and calculates

$$\sigma^e \equiv 4320048260981^{23} \equiv 5130677068274 \pmod{5429515137199}.$$

Since this is exactly the numerical equivalent of the plaintext, Zeke accepts this message-signature pair as being from Audrey and begins drafting a reply. $\Diamond$

What rationale would Zeke have for believing that this message came from Audrey? Suppose that Norbert—his friend who is prone to practical jokes—was the author of this missive. Then, in order for him to produce the signature that Zeke received, Norbert would have to have obtained Audrey's secret RSA key. As we already know, the general problem of breaking RSA seems to be as difficult as factoring, and that problem is believed to be inordinately time consuming. Thus Zeke regards it as highly unlikely that Norbert—or anyone else—has factored m to obtain Audrey's secret RSA exponent; it is highly likely from his perspective that the message came from Audrey.

Moreover, Zeke has assurance that Norbert didn't intercept a message from Audrey to Zeke that said YOUREUGLY and change it. If Norbert wanted to do this, he would have to change the signature so that when Zeke computed σ^s he would get the corresponding message. Thus the scheme stands in the way of tampering.

This example illustrates an implementation of a digital signature scheme in which Audrey uses RSA to calculate a number that recipients can use to verify that a message came from her and was unmodified. We summarize it here.

---

[15] We use the lowercase Greek letter σ (**sig**ma) to symbolize the **sig**nature.

- **Setup** Audrey establishes an RSA modulus m, private decryption exponent d, and public encryption exponent e.

- **Signing** To generate a digital signature σ for message block x, Audrey calculates

$$\sigma = x^d \ \text{MOD} \ m$$

  and sends the message-signature pair (x, σ) to Zeke.

- **Signature verification** Zeke receives a potentially modified message-signature pair $(\tilde{x}, \tilde{\sigma})$, the message purporting to be from Audrey. He looks up Audrey's public modulus m and exponent e and calculates

$$y = \tilde{\sigma}^e \ \text{MOD} \ m.$$

  If $\tilde{x} = y$, he accepts the identity of the sender as being Audrey and has considerable assurance that the message has not been altered; if $\tilde{x} \neq y$, he is certain that something is wrong with the pair: an altered message or an altered signature.

You can see that this process is analogous to Audrey signing a postcard with a pen and then Zeke later examining the signature to see if it looks like Audrey's. Generally, though, a hand signature gives no assurance that the message itself has not been altered in transit. For instance, if Audrey sent Zeke a postcard and wrote in pencil, Norbert could erase and replace portions of message. The digital signature scheme we have described prevents this from happening with electronic "postcards" such as e-mail messages.

More typically, paper correspondence is enclosed in envelopes. The same is true of electronic correspondence that may be confidential in nature. The "envelope" is encryption. So it is more likely that Audrey would first sign her message and then encrypt it before sending it to Zeke. If Zeke has an RSA modulus and exponent, then she can use that for encryption. We illustrate, using the same message as in Example 4.6.1.

Example 4.6.2 Suppose that Zeke has RSA modulus $m_Z = 5429561739803$, encryption exponent $e_Z = 11$, and decryption exponent $d_Z = 3455175652602$. Assume too that Zeke's public listing of this information also requires encryption of plaintext and signature in two separate blocks. Then, after signing her message to him, Audrey encrypts the plaintext to obtain

$$y \equiv x^{e_Z} \equiv 5130677068274^{11} \equiv 3460878482863 \pmod{m_Z},$$

and she encrypts the signature to obtain[16]

$$\tau \equiv \sigma^{ez} \equiv 4320048260981^{11} \equiv 1367233132093 \pmod{m_Z}.$$

(Why would it be unwise for her not to encrypt the signature?) She sends the pair (y, τ) to Zeke.

Receiving this "envelope"containing an encrypted message and signature pair $(\tilde{y}, \tilde{\tau})$, Zeke proceeds to decrypt and then verify the signature. If he receives exactly the pair that Audrey sent, he then calculates (using his own private decryption exponent)

$$\tilde{y}^{dz} \equiv 3460878482863^{2467980490691} \equiv 5130677068274 \equiv \texttt{YOURECUTE} \pmod{m_Z}$$

and

$$\tilde{\sigma} \equiv \tilde{\tau}^{dz} \equiv 1367233132093^{2467980490691} \equiv 4320048260981 \pmod{m_Z}.$$

Then, using Audrey's public exponent and modulus, he calculates

$$\tilde{\sigma}^e \equiv 4320048260981^{23} \equiv 5130677068274 \equiv \texttt{YOURECUTE} \pmod{m}.$$

Since this last number is the same as what he decrypted as the plaintext, he accepts the message as the one Audrey actually sent. $\Diamond$

A disadvantage to this or similar schemes is that the signature is as long as the message. There is, however, an effective way of reducing the length of a signature: *Hash* the message to a small **message digest** of relatively few bits and then sign the digest. This is a standard technique in signature schemes.

Example 4.6.3 Suppose that Audrey has set up an RSA modulus of $m = 713$ and a public exponent $e = 7$. Her private decryption exponent is $t = 283$. She wants to affix a digital signature to the message TALK FAST by calculating an 8-bit message digest using the hash function h defined in Example 3.6.2 in Section 3.6 and then signing the digest by raising it to her private exponent modulo m. She does this by first writing the plaintext in 8-bit binary representations of the ASCII codes:

$$x \quad = \quad \begin{array}{l} \texttt{01010100 01000001 01001100 01001011} \\ \texttt{01000110 01000001 01010011 01010100} \end{array}$$

---

[16]The letter τ (*tau*) follows σ in the Greek alphabet.

and then hashing. You can verify that the message digest is

$$h(x) = 00100010.$$

In decimal representation,[17] $h(x) = 34$; Audrey then signs this by calculating

$$\sigma \equiv h(x)^d \equiv 34^{283} \equiv 613 \pmod{713}.$$

The binary representation of the signature is $\sigma = 1001100101$. She then sends the pair

$$(x, \sigma) = (01010100\ 01000001\ 01001100\ 01001011$$
$$01000110\ 01000001\ 01010011\ 01010100, 1001100101)$$

to Zeke.

Upon receiving the message-signature pair unmodified, Zeke hashes m to obtain 00100010. He also looks up Audrey's public RSA modulus and exponent and calculates

$$\sigma^e \equiv 1001100101^7 \equiv 613^7 \equiv 34 \pmod{m}.$$

Since 34 in binary is 0010010, he sees that this agrees with the hash value and is confident[18] with probability about

$$1 - \frac{1}{2^8} = 1 - 0.00390625 = 0.996094$$

that the message was unmodified in transit and that it is really from Audrey.

Now, suppose that the very first bit of the message was changed from 0 to 1 during the transmission; let $\tilde{x}$ be this altered message. Then Zeke would hash $\tilde{x}$ as

$$h(\tilde{x}) = 10100010,$$

which is *not* the same σ^e MOD m. He knows for sure that something has changed and should not accept the message as authentic. $\diamondsuit$

---

[17]Of course, in actual implementations, the calculations are done entirely by computer, so there would be no conversion to decimal for calculating the signature.

[18]He is assuming two things: (1) The hash function is one-way and (2) Audrey's decryption exponent t cannot be easily obtained by an adversary. In this particular example, neither of these is true. But with a good hash function and large modulus m, both will be true.

Summary of an RSA-Based Signature Scheme

- **Setup** To sign (unencrypted) messages, Audrey establishes an RSA modulus m and public exponent e; she keeps the private exponent d. She also agrees on a hash function $h(x)$ with potential correspondents; the hash function must produce a binary string short enough so that its maximum numerical value is less than m.

- **Signing** For a message x, typically regarded as blocks of binary strings, Audrey calculates $h(x)$ and then produces a signature by calculating

$$\sigma = h(x)^d \text{ MOD } m;$$

  she sends the pair (x, σ) to Zeke.

- **Encryption (optional)** Before sending, Audrey encrypts the message signature pair using Zeke's public RSA exponent.

- **Decryption (if message-signature pair is encrypted)** Zeke uses his private RSA decryption exponent to obtain a message-signature pair $(\tilde{x}, \tilde{\sigma})$.

- **Verification** Receiving a message-signature pair $(\tilde{x}, \tilde{\sigma})$, Zeke hashes $\tilde{x}$ by computing

$$u = h(\tilde{x}),$$

  and he uses Audrey's public RSA exponent e to calculate

$$v = \tilde{\sigma}^e \text{ MOD } m.$$

If $u = v$, there is a high probability that the message is the one Audrey sent; if $u \neq v$, the message is unacceptable.

EXERCISES

1. Suppose Alice's RSA modulus is $m_A = 91$, her encryption exponent is $e_A = 7$, and her decryption exponent is $d_A = 31$.

   (a) Alice wants to sign the message $x = 21$. Calculate her signature.

(b) Bob receives the message-signature pair $(\tilde{x}, \tilde{\sigma}) = (54, 89)$. Does he regard the pair as likely to be authentic, or does he know that the pair has been altered?

2. Suppose that Alice's RSA parameters are those given in Exercise 1 and that Bob's RSA modulus is $m_B = 187$.

(a) If Bob's public exponent is $e_B = 13$ and Alice wants to encrypt the message-signature pair $(x, \sigma) = (70, 21)$, calculate her encrypted pair.

(b) If Bob's private exponent is $d_B = 37$ and he receives the enciphered message-signature pair $(11, 69)$, what are the original plaintext and signature? Is this a valid message-signature pair?

3. You have received the following message and signature pairs that purport to be from a person whose RSA modulus is 2573 and whose public exponent is 59. Which message-signature pair is valid?

(a) $\tilde{x} = 423$, $\tilde{y} = 2123$

(b) $\tilde{x} = 1111$, $\tilde{y} = 1555$

4. Audrey's RSA modulus is $m = 11292367$, her public exponent is $e = 94321$, and her private exponent is $d = 6327241$. Calculate a digital signature for the message $x = 08041115$.

5. You have hashed a message x, which you want to send with a signature based on the hash value 00101110. If your modulus is 1271 and your private exponent is 19, calculate the signature.

6. You have received a message $\tilde{x}$ and the signature 463. If the message hashes to 11110000 and it purports to come from a person whose RSA modulus is 1271 and whose public exponent is 23, do you accept the message and signature as valid?

7. In Example 4.6.3, find a pair of bits that, when changed, produces a hash value identical with that for the message. Can you find several ways of doing this? (*Suggestion*: Look at the first bit in 8-bit blocks.)

4.7   Zero-Knowledge Identification Protocols

Identification in General

When you open a bank account, the application you fill out may ask for information that is not readily obtained or deduced, such as your mother's maiden name. The bank keeps this on record so that when someone calls concerning the account, the service representative will first ask for that information. If the person calling is unable to give it or answers incorrectly, the representative will refuse to do anything; if the person calling does answer correctly, the representative continues with whatever transactions bank customers are allowed to do by phone. The bank has increased (perhaps marginally) the probability that the caller really is you, the owner of the account. This is a (weak) form of **identification**.

Now suppose that you call the bank and provide the requisite information so you can make a transaction. Some nefarious person overhears your conversation and jots down your account number and the private information. Then that person can call the bank, provide the requisite identification information, and obtain information about your account—or worse.

This scheme could be strengthened against such an attack. When you open the account, instead of asking for just one piece of information that only you would know, the bank could request, say, the maiden names of your mother, maternal grandmother, and paternal grandmother. Then, when a call comes to the bank about the account, the service representative can pick the next of the three pieces of information to request. If someone overhears the conversation and later tries to gain access to your account, the information requested will be different. There is no way—in the absence of other information—for someone to deduce one of the names from the others. In statistical terms, the names are independent.

There are, of course, other cues to the bank's service representative that provide "identification": A man's voice calling about an account whose owner is a woman, or a request to close out the account and send a check to a third party might suggest that the caller was unauthorized.

Consider another analogous identification problem. Suppose that Kathryn has gone to the campus computer center and established an account. She agrees on a username and chooses a password, which the person in the center puts into the computer. Later, when Kathryn dials up the campus system using a modem to connect through her Internet service provider (ISP), she gets a window in which she types her username and password. She does this and logs in. Every keystroke she typed in this login was transmitted through the ISP's computer and potentially through many other machines on the Internet before reaching the intended destination. Snively, a ne'er-do-well on one of these machines, could eavesdrop on her login sequence and pick up the username and password. Then Snively could later log in as Kathryn, and either obtain private information or do mischief. One solution to this weakness in the password protocol would be to do what we described for the bank: Kathryn would provide (or be provided with) a list of passwords that could be used seriatim each time she logged in. Assuming these passwords were not obviously related to one another (e.g., successive numbers), Snively's work would be much more difficult. Of course, this scheme makes it much harder for Kathryn to use the system: She must keep up with the list of passwords and keep track of which one she used last. This could be particularly cumbersome if she logs in regularly. Some companies issue a credit-card size computer just for this purpose to their employees who travel and must log in frequently from remote sites.

The Fiat-Shamir Zero-Knowledge Protocol

Is there, however, a better way to solve the sort of identification problem we have described here? It turns out that there are ways for Kathryn to identify herself in this environment so that

- Kathryn will keep up with just one password, which is linked to her username, and

- Kathryn will be able to convince the host computer that she possesses that password without ever transmitting it or providing information that will allow a third party to deduce it.

Such a method is called a **zero-knowledge (identification) protocols (ZKIP)**. We choose one, the **Fiat-Shamir identification protocol**, which is readily described and illustrative of the basic workings of other ZKIP's. For a nonmathematical introduction, you might find [65] interesting.

Setup

- A trusted authority—call it Tom—selects two large prime numbers p and q, calculates $n = pq$, publishes n, and keeps the primes secret.

- Kathryn, a user of the center, selects a number s in the range 1 to $n - 1$ that is relatively prime to n, calculates $v = s^2$ MOD n, registers

v as her username with Tom, keeps her password s secret, and carries both s and v with her.

- Tom and Kathryn agree on a maximum number of rounds m of the identification protocol that will be carried out at login.

One Round of the Protocol[19]

- At a remote site from which Kathryn wishes to log in, she first generates a number r at random in the range 1 to $n-1$ (sometimes called her **commitment**) and she calculates $w = r^2$ MOD n (sometimes called the **witness**). She sends w to Tom.

- On receiving w, Tom selects a bit e, either 0 or 1, at random (a "coin toss" sometimes called the **challenge**) and sends e to Kathryn.

- On receiving e, Kathryn calculates $y = r \cdot s^e$ MOD n. (If $e = 0$ then $y = r$; if $e = 1$, then $y = r \cdot s$ MOD n; y is called the **response**.) She sends y to Tom.

- Receiving y, Tom calculates

$$z = y^2 \text{ MOD } n$$

and

$$z' = w \cdot v^e \text{ MOD } n.$$

If $z \neq z'$, he refuses the login; if $z = z'$, he accepts that round of the protocol. In the latter case, if fewer than m rounds have been carried out, Kathryn starts a new round by picking another number at random; if m rounds have been successful, Kathryn's identification is complete and she is logged in.

Here is an example to illustrate the process.

Example 4.7.1 Suppose that $p = 37$ and $q = 101$; then $n = 37 \cdot 101 = 3737$. If Kathryn selects $s = 113$ (which is relatively prime to n. Why?), then her username is $v = s^2$ MOD $3737 = 113^2$ MOD $3737 = 1558$. Tom and Kathryn agree on $m = 8$ rounds of the protocol. This completes the setup.

---

[19]For the purpose of explication, we have said, "Kathryn does this" and "Tom does that." In real implementations, steps such as generating random numbers are automated in hardware or software. Kathryn keeps the password on her client computer, and it carries out the protocol for her.

Now Kathryn wants to log in. She chooses a number at random: $r = 3284$. Then her witness is $w = 3284^2$ MOD $3737 = 3411$. She sends her username 1558 and her witness 3411 to Tom. He receives these values and flips a coin to determine the challenge $e = 1$. He sends 1 to Kathryn, and then she calculates $y \equiv 3284 \cdot 113^1 \equiv 1129 \,(\mathrm{mod}\, 3737)$. She sends this back to Tom. He then verifies

$$
\begin{aligned}
z &= y^2 \text{ MOD } 3737 = 1129^2 \text{ MOD } 3737 = 324 \\
z' &= w \cdot v^e \text{ MOD } 3737 = 3411 \cdot 1558 \text{ MOD } 3737 = 324.
\end{aligned}
$$

Because these two are the same, he accepts the first round of the protocol.

The following table shows these numbers along with values generated in the protocol in seven more rounds (the random values were generated in a Mathematica notebook). All values are computed modulo 3737.

Round	r commitment	$w = r^2$ witness	e challenge	$y = r \cdot s^e$ response	$z = y^2$ comparison 1	$z' = w \cdot v^e$ comparison 2
1	3284	3411	1	1129	324	324
2	2404	1814	1	2588	1040	1040
3	2849	37	1	555	1591	1591
4	116	2245	1	1897	3615	3615
5	2147	1888	1	3443	485	485
6	1667	2298	0	1667	2298	2298
7	2370	189	1	2483	2976	2976
8	1743	3605	0	1743	3605	3605

Since z agrees with z' in each case, Tom estimates that the probability this person is *not* Kathryn is $(1/2)^8 \approx 0.0039$; that is, from Tom's perspective, the probability that it *is* Kathryn is $1 - .0039 = 0.9961$. $\diamond$

What is going on the protocol? Perhaps it is easiest to look at things from the perspective of someone trying to log in as Kathryn. Suppose Snively knows Kathryn's username, v, which is public knowledge, and also knows the protocol. But he doesn't actually know her password s. In principle he could calculate a square root of v—by systematic trial and error, if nothing else. However, this could take an unreasonable amount of time for the sorts of values of p and q that would be used in practice: roughly 100 decimal digits each. It could take as many as $\frac{1}{2} \times 10^{200}$ trial squarings to complete this process. Moreover, there are no known polynomial-time algorithms for the square root modulo pq problem. Snively is up against the computationally hard problem of finding square roots modulo n.

Since there is an element of chance in the protocol, and since Snively might be the gambling sort, he could try getting in this way: On a particular round of the protocol, Snively feels that Tom will get 1 in the coin flip. So he picks a random r—as Kathryn would—and then he cheats by making a fake w-valve that will allow him to fool Tom on this round: $w = v^{-1}r^2$ MOD n. When the $e = 1$ coin flip comes, he sends $y = r$ to Tom, and Tom checks that

$$z \equiv y^2 \equiv r^2 \pmod{n}$$

and

$$z' \equiv w \cdot v^e \equiv (v^{-1} \cdot r^2) \cdot v^1 \equiv r^2 \pmod{n}.$$

Since z and z' agree on this round, Tom is satisfied and continues to the next round of the protocol. On the next round, perhaps Snively feels that the coin flip will be 0. This is easier for him: He generates a random r and sends $w \equiv r^2 \pmod{n}$ to Tom. When the expected $e = 0$ challenge comes back, he sends $y \equiv r$ to Tom, who calculates

$$z \equiv y^2 \equiv r^2 \pmod{n}$$

and

$$z' \equiv w \cdot v^e \equiv r^2 \cdot v^0 \equiv r^2 \pmod{n}.$$

Once again, $z = z'$, so Tom is satisfied and continues to the next round of the protocol. So if Snively can guess correctly before each of the m rounds of the protocol what the challenge bit will be, he can in this fashion cheat his way into Kathryn's account. But what are the chances of Snively being able to do this? Assuming that each guess is independent of the others, his chances of correctly guessing the outcome of each coin toss in advance are

$$\underbrace{\frac{1}{2} \cdot \frac{1}{2} \cdot \frac{1}{2} \cdot \cdots \cdot \frac{1}{2}}_{m \text{ times}} = \left(\frac{1}{2}\right)^m.$$

If the number of rounds is, say, $m = 10$, then this probability is $1/2^{10} = 1/1024 \approx 0.000976563$, a very small number. With $m = 20$ rounds, the probability becomes extremely small. In short, Snively would have to be very, very, very lucky to break in this way if the number of protocol rounds was about 20.

If, at any round of the protocol, Snively guessed wrong, then Tom will ask him a question he cannot answer. For example, if Snively thought Tom would flip a 1 but he in fact flipped 0, then to continue the protocol, Snively will have to send the response $y = r$ to Tom's unexpected challenge. So Tom will calculate

$$z \equiv y^2 \equiv r^2 \pmod{n}.$$

But Snively has already sent a fake witness, and this shows up when Tom calculates

$$z' \equiv w \cdot v^e \equiv v^{-1} \cdot r^2 \cdot v^0 \equiv v^{-1} \cdot r^2 \not\equiv r^2 \pmod{n}.$$

The protocol immediately stops, and Snively is refused admission. You should check the steps in the alternative possibility where Snively guesses Tom will flip a 0 but instead flips a 1.

In summary, if Tom gets the least suggestion of cheating in the protocol, he "raises the drawbridge." The probability of an interloper being lucky enough to fake 20 rounds of the protocol in the way we've described is vanishingly small. If 20 rounds of the protocol are completed without incident, the probability is overwhelming that the person logging in really possesses the password s. Assuming Kathryn lets no one else have the password and that it remains only on the computer at her fingertips—the one carrying out the protocol for her—she proves her identity to Tom without ever transmitting the password through the network.

Now suppose that Snively listens in on the protocol between Kathryn and Tom. Can he infer from it the value of s? At each round, Snively will only see w, e, and y. In round 1 of Example 4.7.1, because $e = 1$, Snively will know that

$$r \cdot s \equiv 1129 \pmod{3737} \tag{4.36}$$
$$r^2 \equiv 3411 \pmod{3737}. \tag{4.37}$$

In principle, he could calculate the square root of 3411 modulo 3737 by trial and error, substitute the value of r he obtained into (4.36), and solve for s. Indeed, with this small a value of n, that would be no problem at all. But in real implementations of the protocol, n will be much bigger, and the general square root problem becomes intractable. The same facts will hold for each round of the protocol in which Tom's coin toss produces a 1. In the rounds where the toss gives 0, there is no information at all transmitted about s. From this, you can see that the effectiveness of the protocol relies heavily on the purported intractability of the square root problem modulo pq.

Summary

A ZKIP is a method by which Kathryn can convince Tom that she possesses a password over a public channel without an adversary gaining any information about the password from listening to the protocol. The Fiat-Shamir ZKIP is one particular type of method. Its security relies in a fundamental way on the belief that the square root modulo pq problem is computationally infeasible.

EXERCISES

1. Make a table of squares modulo 39. Use it to find all solutions to the following congruences.

   (a) $x^2 \equiv 1 \pmod{39}$ (b) $x^2 \equiv 4 \pmod{39}$ (c) $x^2 \equiv 12 \pmod{39}$

2. Make a table of squares modulo 32. Use it to find all solutions to the following congruences.

   (a) $x^2 \equiv 0 \pmod{32}$ (b) $x^2 \equiv 17 \pmod{32}$ (c) $x^2 \equiv 2 \pmod{32}$

3. Make a table of squares modulo 31. Use it to find all solutions to the following congruences.

   (a) $x^2 \equiv 1 \pmod{31}$ (b) $x^2 \equiv 2 \pmod{31}$ (c) $x^2 \equiv 8 \pmod{31}$

4. Let n be a positive integer. Show that $x^2 \equiv (n - x)^2 \pmod{n}$ for any integer x.

5. Table 4.8 shows a transcript of several rounds of the Fiat-Shamir protocol. The modulus is $n = 7439$, and Kathryn's username is $v = 5330$. Fill in the missing numbers (at least where it is easy) and determine if the person attempting to be authenticated is likely to be Kathryn.

6. Suppose Teddy, a trusted authority, has chosen primes so that $n = 8473$ for the Fiat-Shamir protocol. Further, suppose that Karla has the username $v = 8224$. Eva wants desperately to log in under Karla's name. Not only does she know Karla's username, she also has somehow

Round	r commit-ment	$w = r^2$ wit-ness	e chal-lenge	$y = r \cdot s^e$ re-sponse	$z = y^2$ compa-rison 1	$z' = w \cdot v^e$ compa-rison 2
1		676	1	2938		
2		1557	0	519		
3		2945	1	5935	560	560
4		6832	1	4414		655
5		6345	1	34	1156	1156
6			0	6263		6761
7		172	1	7310	1763	
8		7176	0	4309		

Table 4.8 Table for Exercise 5.

learned that the "random" challenge bits Teddy will use in the protocol are generated by the 5-bit linear feedback shift register

$$
\begin{aligned}
b_1' &\leftarrow b_2 \\
b_2' &\leftarrow b_3 \\
b_3' &\leftarrow b_4 \\
b_4' &\leftarrow b_5 \\
b_5' &\leftarrow b_3 + b_2 + b_1
\end{aligned}
$$

with initial configuration $b_5 = 1$, $b_4 = 0$, $b_3 = 1$, $b_2 = 1$, $b_1 = 0$. If Eve's random number generator produces the 10 random values 6924, 161, 7784, 5765, 2025, 2610, 1322, 2118, 1505, and 7, find values of w and y for 10 rounds of the protocol that will fool Teddy into letting Eve log in as Karla.

7. Explain why the password s in the Fiat-Shamir setup must be relatively prime to n.

Chapter 5

Case Studies and Issues

In this chapter we look at some of the current applications of cryptology in the contemporary world. While it is now officially to be replaced by the Advanced Encryption Standard, the Data Encryption Standard has been so pervasive in industry and commerce that it bears an examination. It will take some time for AES to replace DES in commercial, industrial, and government applications, so an understanding of DES is not without value.

Private entities have invented cryptographic software that can be used by individuals to encrypt e-mail and files saved on computer disks and also generate digital signatures. A notable example is Phil Zimmerman's Pretty Good Privacy, which uses DSS and SHA for digital signatures, Diffie-Hellman key exchange, and IDEA (International Data Encryption Algorithm) for encryption.

Beyond the technical issues of implementation and proper use of cryptography by individuals, industry, and government, there are larger ethical, political, and legal issues. The debates in these arenas are ongoing. In designing law and public policy, an important question is this: What is the right balance between individuals' and legitimate businesses' needs to ensure confidentiality in their electronic communications and the federal government's need to monitor electronic communications for purposes of law enforcement and national security? Another question is this: How can nations around the world cooperate in establishing cryptographic standards that will strike the same sort of balance between the needs of law-abiding citizens and companies and the needs of national governments to enforce laws effectively and provide necessary national security? We can only scratch the surfaces of these and other issues here, but doing this will provide information for those interested in further inquiry.

5.1 Case Study I: DES

History and General Discussion of DES

In 1971, Horst Feistel filed a patent for a digital encryption algorithm called Lucifer, and it was assigned to IBM, Feistel's employer. The algorithm was sold to Lloyds of London for use in automatic teller machines, and it underwent further development internally at IBM. A basic component of Lucifer was what are now called **Feistel networks** or **Feistel ciphers** which we encountered in Section 3.5.

Prior to the 1970s, nonmilitary cryptography was ad hoc: Organizations and individuals developed or selected cryptographic methods suited to their own particular purposes. In 1972, the National Bureau of Standards (NBS, now NIST), which is under the Department of Commerce, issued a request for proposals for a nonmilitary cryptographic standard meeting the following requirements:

- It would have high security.

- It would be completely specified and easy to understand.

- Its security would reside in the key.

- It would be available to everyone requiring strong cryptographic algorithms.

- It would be adaptable to diverse applications.

- The algorithm would be economically implementable in electronic devices.

- The algorithm would be efficient.

- The algorithm would be validatable.

- The algorithm would be exportable.

NBS received no viable proposals, but it tried again in 1974. This time, IBM proposed its Lucifer cryptosystem. NBS forwarded it to NSA, and NSA suggested modifications. With these modifications, NBS subsequently published the resulting cipher system as a standard in the Federal Register in 1977. The standard was adopted by organizations such as the American National Standards Institute (ANSI), the American Bankers Association, and the Department of Treasury for encryption of sensitive but nonclassified communications. Initially, the standard called solely for the implementation of DES in hardware, but later standards were written for software implementations.

From the beginning, controversies have surrounded the adoption of this standard. For instance, some people suggest that NSA built a back door into DES, which would allow the agency to obtain the contents of secure civilian communications without having to obtain the key. In particular, part of the algorithm involves eight arcane nonlinear, table-lookup s-boxes substitutions. There are no publicized design criteria for these, and no substantial ones have been discovered by the academic cryptographic community after years of research. Intensive scrutiny of these has led to no breakthrough that would allow rapid recovery of key information. The original Lucifer algorithm called for a 128-bit key, enormously larger than the 56-bit key ultimately used in DES. Some felt that this reduction in key size made it feasible for NSA to mount brute force known-plaintext attacks on DES to recover keys. Public announcements of such attacks, however, came only in 1998. Others suggest that NSA did not realize the extent to which NBS was going to promulgate the method and that it had released a stronger cryptographic algorithm into the public domain than it intended.

The introduction of a cryptographic standard for non-military use had political overtones as well, according to Baker and Hurst, [4]. Antimilitary and antigovernment sentiment in the United States brought about by the Vietnam debacle, they claim, fueled the efforts of researchers in the civilian community to find strong cryptographic methods subjected to public scrutiny that did not have the specter of an eavesdropping federal government. Out of this milieu came the early public key cryptographic algorithms such as knapsacks, Diffie-Hellman, and RSA.

Because there were not only political issues (in the country at large as well as within the federal bureaucracy, between the Departments of Commerce and Defense) but also technical ones (how long would it take for the cryptosystem to be effectively broken?), the adoption of the standard came with an agreement to undertake a recertification every five years. Though there were expectations that DES would be replaced by something else within five to ten years, it was recertified in 1982. In the 1987 recertification process, NSA proposed a Commercial COMSEC[1] Endorsement, which would

---

[1]Communications Security.

replace DES with a more advanced tamper-proof VLSI[2] chip. However, this proposal did not make it into use.

Again in 1992, DES was recertified, but by 1997–1998, NIST had begun making serious efforts to identify a replacement. Part of the reason was that in 1998 a group funded by the Electronic Frontier Foundation broke DES in a matter of hours. Events such as this made it clear that for very high security communications, DES would not continue to be adequate.

In spite of the successful cracking of DES by massive brute force attacks, it will be several years before its widespread use declines significantly. DES is an entrenched technology and still useful for many purposes.

Technical Details of DES

DES encryption takes as input a 64-bit block of plaintext along with a 56-bit key, which must be kept secret by the two communicating parties. Its output is a 64-bit block of ciphertext. Decryption takes a 64-bit input block of ciphertext along with a 56-bit key and produces a 64-bit output of plaintext.

The encryption process takes place in 16 rounds in which a round function, defined in terms of the s-boxes mentioned earlier, is applied over and over with various subkeys of the 56-bit input key, which are generated according to a well-defined scheme. The diagram in Figure 5.1 shows the procedure in schematic form. An initial permutation, designated as T, is applied to the 64 bits of plaintext, and then those bits are split into two 32-bit halves designated L (left) and R (right). At the same time, the first subkey K_1, a 48-bit string, is generated, and then it is used as input along with R to the round function f to produce a 32-bit output. The output from the round function is then XOr-ed with the left half of the plaintext. Finally, the old left half of the plaintext is replaced by the old right half, and the output of the XOr replaces the old value of R. This completes one round of DES. The same procedure is applied 15 more times, the only difference being that different subkeys K_2, K_3, ..., K_{15} generated by the subkey schedule are used as input to the round function f. Notice that when $F_{K_{16}}$ is applied, the right and left halves of the pre-output are not switched. The last step of encryption is to reassemble the L and R output by the last round of f_K into a 64-bit string and apply the *inverse* of the initial permutation T.

DES has the feature that the decryption of a ciphertext y produced with a key whose corresponding subkeys are K_1, ..., K_{16} is achieved by applying

---

[2]Very Large Scale Integration.

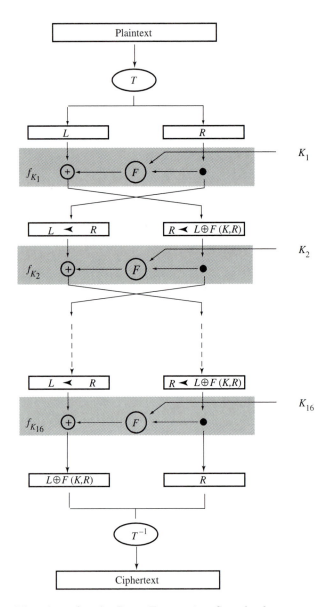

Figure 5.1 Flowchart for the Data Encryption Standard encryption.

exactly the same algorithm that was used to encrypt, except that the subkeys are used in reverse order: K_{16}, ..., K_1.

To see this, we introduce a bit of notation. First let $L(x)$ denote the left half of a bit string x (assuming x has an even number of bits), let $R(x)$ denote the right half, and let $C(x)$ be given by

$$C(x) = R(x)\|L(x).$$

In other words, $C(x)$ changes the right and left halves of x.

For a 48-bit string k and a 64-bit plaintext, let $f_k(x)$ be given by

$$f_k(x) = (L(x) \oplus F(k,\ R(x)))\|R(x). \tag{5.1}$$

Then $f_{K_1}(x)$, $f_{K_2}(x)$, ..., $f_{K_{16}}(x)$ are represented by the gray boxes in Figure 5.1. You are asked in the Exercises to verify that $f_{K_i}(x)$ is invertible for each $i = 1$, ..., 16 and that $f_{K_i}^{-1} = f_{K_i}(x)$, for $i = 1$, ..., 16. Also, you are asked to verify that $C^{-1}(x) = C(x)$.

We are now ready to write a formula for DES. The first step is to calculate $T(x)$. Then the result of this computation is fed into f_{K_1} and after that the result is few into C. So the computation up to this point can be represented $C \circ f_{K_1} \circ T(x)$. Next the result is fed into f_{K_2} and the output of this computation goes into C; the computation to this point is now $C \circ f_{K_2} \circ C \circ f_{K_1} \circ T(x)$. Continuing in this fashion, you can see that following through the flowchart to the end amounts to computing the function

$$T^{-1} \circ f_{K_{16}} \circ C \circ f_{K_{15}} \circ \cdots \circ f_{K_3} \circ C \circ f_{K_2} \circ C \circ f_{K_1} \circ T(x).$$

Thus, if K is the 56-bit key from which the subkeys K_1, K_2, ..., K_{16} are derived, then

$$\text{DES}_K(x) = T^{-1} \circ f_{K_{16}} \circ C \circ f_{K_{15}} \circ \cdots \circ f_{K_3} \circ C \circ f_{K_2} \circ C \circ f_{K_1} \circ T(x).$$

Because you have shown that f_{K_i} and C are all self-inverses, and because the inverse of a composition is the composition of the respective inverses in *reverse* order, we can immediately see that

$$\text{DES}_K^{-1}(x) = T^{-1} \circ f_{K_1} \circ C \circ f_{K_2} \circ \cdots \circ f_{K_3} \circ C \circ f_{K_{15}} \circ C \circ f_{K_{16}} \circ T(x).$$

This means that the same algorithm works to decipher and encipher, except that the subkeys are used in reverse order.

We have not given here the explicit details of how to generate the subkeys or how to compute the round function. These details are available in various sources, such as [71] and [80], as well as in Federal Information Processing Standard (FIPS) Publication 46 (January 15, 1977), which is available at the NIST Web site. This encryption algorithm exhibits what Feistel referred to as the **avalanche effect**: If two plaintexts that differ in only one bit are encrypted with the same key, then after only two or three rounds, the "pre-ciphertexts" L concatenated with R resulting from the respective plaintexts can be expected to differ from one another in roughly half of their bits; and if a plaintext is enciphered with two keys that differ from one another in only one bit, then the number of bits in which the pre-ciphertexts differ from one another rises quickly to around 32.

For example, in [80] and [43], the authors illustrate that if DES is presented with plaintexts

$x_1 = 00000000\ 00000000\ 00000000\ 00000000\ 00000000\ 00000000\ 00000000\ 00000000$

and

$x_2 = 10000000\ 00000000\ 00000000\ 00000000\ 00000000\ 00000000\ 00000000\ 00000000$

and the key

$k = 0000001\ 1001011\ 0100100\ 1100010\ 0011100\ 0011000\ 0011100\ 0110010,$

then DES produces ciphertexts that differ from one another in 34 positions. Another example from [80] and [43] indicates that if the plaintext

$x = 01101000\ 10000101\ 00101111\ 01111010\ 00010011\ 01110110\ 11101011\ 10100100$

is enciphered with two keys

$k_1 = 1110010\ 1111011\ 1101111\ 0011000\ 0011101\ 0000100\ 0110001\ 1101110$

and

$k_2 = 0110010\ 1111011\ 1101111\ 0011000\ 0011101\ 0000100\ 0110001\ 1101110$

that differ in only one bit, then the two resulting ciphertexts

$y_1 = 11001000\ 01101011\ 10010000\ 10010001\ 10101011\ 01110001\ 01100101\ 10000001$

and

$y_2 = 00100011\ 11100010\ 11101011\ 00100100\ 00110101\ 10110010\ 01011100\ 00010001$

differ from one another in about half of their bits.

Another interesting and important feature of DES is that multiple encryptions with it are generally more secure than a single one. To understand this claim a bit better, first recall that if $s_k(x)$ represents a monoalphabetic substitution applied to plaintext x with key k, then for any two keys k_1 and k_2, the function $s_{k_2}(s_{k_1}(x))$ is also a monoalphabetic substitution. Thus there is a third key k_3 such that

$$s_{k_2}(s_{k_1}(x)) = s_{k_3}(x).$$

So if a cryptanalyst is trying to recover key information, she needs to look only for the single key k_3. Effort spent on double encipherment with a monoalphabetic substitution would be wasted. For DES the story is different: If k_1 and k_2 are 56-bit keys, then there is generally *no* other key k_3 such that

$$\text{DES}_{k_2}(\text{DES}_{k_1}(x)) = \text{DES}_{k_3}(x)$$

for all 64-bit plaintexts x. This is not obvious; a proof of this remarkable property was published in 1992 in a paper entitled "Proof that DES is not a Group" (see [11]). This means that a cryptanalyst who possesses ciphertext y from a double DES encryption along with the corresponding plaintext x would have to compute $\text{DES}_{k_2}(\text{DES}_{k_1}(x))$ for various choices of k_1 and k_2 until y turned up. Not only would this take, in the worst case, about 2^{112} evaluations of DES, but there are likely to be many different key pairs k_1 and k_2 such that $\text{DES}_{k_2}(\text{DES}_{k_1}(x)) = y$ for a given pair x and y of 64-bit blocks. Indeed, the cryptanalyst would need a massive amount of ciphertext and corresponding plaintext in order to narrow down the likely choices of key values.

It turns out that there is an attack called the **meet-in-the-middle attack**, which, while space intensive, can be used against any double encipherment with a block cipher. It was first described by Diffie and Hellman in [16]. The method can be applied at roughly twice the computational expense of a brute force known-plaintext cryptanalysis on a single application of the block cipher. See [80] for a description.

Three encryptions with different keys thwarts the meet-in-the-middle attack, and because there are no other analogous attacks known, triple encryption with DES has become popular. To use triple DES, the users must share three 56-bit keys k_1, k_2, k_3 and compute ciphertext by

$$y = \text{DES}_{k_3}(\text{DES}_{k_2}(\text{DES}_{k_1}(x))).$$

Thus the effective key length is 168 bits.

Simplified DES (SDES)

A simplified and representative model for DES was published by Edward Schaefer in *Cryptologia* in 1996 [70], and we present the complete details of this cipher system here to illustrate some of the principles of the full-blown DES. The simplified version has s-boxes, a round function, permutations, but only two rounds. It takes as input an 8-bit plaintext and a 10-bit key and produces an 8-bit ciphertext. Both rounds use an 8-bit subkey.

The subkey generation is accomplished by the following two functions:

$$K_1(k_1 k_2 k_3 k_4 k_5 k_6 k_7 k_8 k_9 k_{10}) = k_1 k_7 k_9 k_4 k_8 k_3 k_{10} k_6$$
$$K_2(k_1 k_2 k_3 k_4 k_5 k_6 k_7 k_8 k_9 k_{10}) = k_8 k_3 k_6 k_5 k_{10} k_2 k_9 k_1.$$

These subkeys depend *linearly* on the key in the sense that each function can be represented by multiplying the input key by a 10×8 matrix, modulo 2. The author of the paper actually describes these functions as compositions of other functions that involve permutation and choosing, but the representation here expresses the key scheduling succinctly.

The encryption process is built up out of a number of basic functions. Two of them are the **initial permutation**

$$\text{IP}(x_1 x_2 x_3 x_4 x_5 x_6 x_7 x_8) = x_2 x_6 x_3 x_1 x_4 x_8 x_5 x_7$$

and the **expansion permutation**

$$\text{EP}(x_1 x_2 x_3 x_4) = x_4 x_1 x_2 x_3 x_2 x_3 x_4 x_1.$$

Two **s-boxes** $s_0(x_1 x_2 x_3 x_4)$ and $s_1(x_1 x_2 x_3 x_4)$ are defined by the tables

s_0		x_2	0	0	1	1
		x_3	0	1	0	1
x_1	x_4					
0	0		01	00	11	10
0	1		11	10	01	00
1	0		00	10	01	11
1	1		11	01	11	10

s_1		x_2	0	0	1	1
		x_3	0	1	0	1
x_1	x_4					
0	0		00	01	10	11
0	1		10	00	01	11
1	0		11	00	01	00
1	1		10	01	00	11

For example, $s_0(1010) = 10$ and $s_1(1010) = 00$.

For any string x of an even number of bits, let $L(x)$ represent the left half of the bit string, and let $R(x)$ represent the right half. Let P_4 be the permutation that acts on 4 bits according to the formula

$$P_4(x_1 x_2 x_3 x_4) = x_2 x_4 x_3 x_1.$$

Define F, which acts on a 4-bit plaintext x and an 8-bit key k, by

$$F(k, x) = P_4(s_0(L(k \oplus \mathrm{EP}(x))) \parallel s_1(R(k \oplus \mathrm{EP}(x)))).$$

The round function for SDES, $f_k(x)$, which is defined in terms of these building blocks, takes an 8-bit (sub)key k and an 8-bit plaintext x and is computed by the formula

$$f_k(x) = (L(x) \oplus F(R(x),\, k)) \parallel R(x).$$

Notice that this is, except for the exchange of right and left halves, a Feistel function of the sort we discussed in Section 1.2. Now the two rounds that constitute SDES encryption of an 8-bit plaintext x with a 10-bit key k to produce ciphertext y are

$$t \leftarrow \mathrm{IP}(x) \tag{5.2}$$
$$t \leftarrow f_{K_1(k)}(t) \quad \text{(round 1)} \tag{5.3}$$
$$t \leftarrow R(t) \parallel L(t) \quad \text{(switch right and left halves)} \tag{5.4}$$
$$t \leftarrow f_{K_2(k)}(t) \quad \text{(round 2)} \tag{5.5}$$
$$y \leftarrow \mathrm{IP}^{-1}(t). \tag{5.6}$$

Here t is a temporary variable in which to store intermediate values in the computation. We can summarize the functional relationship between between the key-plaintext pair $(k,\, x)$ and the ciphertext by writing

$$y = \mathrm{SDES}_k(x).$$

Example 5.1.1 Suppose that $x = 10110101$ and $k = 1000000001$. Then the subkeys are

$$K_1(k) = 01011111$$
$$K_2(k) = 11111100.$$

Also, the rounds of the encryption are

$$t \leftarrow \mathrm{IP}(x) = 00110001$$
$$t \leftarrow f_{K_1(k)}(t) = f_{01011111}(00110001) = 10100001$$
$$t \leftarrow R(t) \parallel L(t) = 00011010$$
$$t \leftarrow f_{K_2(k)}(t) = f_{11111100}(00011010) = 11001010$$
$$y \leftarrow \mathrm{IP}^{-1}(t) = 01011100.$$

That is, $\text{SDES}_{1000000001}(10110101) = 01011100$. It is an exercise for you to carry through the steps in computing

$$f_{01011111}(00110001) \quad \text{and} \quad f_{11111100}(00011010). \quad \diamondsuit$$

Summary

DES has been the most widely used block cipher for nearly a quarter century. Its design principles are based in the 1949 work of Shannon [73] on cryptography. He defined two important elements, confusion and diffusion, by which statistical correlations between ciphertext and plaintext and between ciphertext and key would be obscured. These elements were successfully incorporated into DES by means of the sorts of Feistel functions discussed in this section. Simplified DES, a toy version of DES, illustrates these principles in action.

Exercises

1. Explain why high-security cryptographic algorithms should be implemented in hardware (that is, wired into circuits) rather than in software.

2. Show that the functions f_{K_i}, $i = 1$, ..., 16 in the specification of DES are all self-inverses. Show that the function $C(x)$ that exchanges right and left halves of a bit string x is its own inverse.

3. There are $(2^{64})!$ different permutations of the 2^{64} 64-bit strings of 0's and 1's.

    (a) Determine an approximate value for this number represented in scientific notation. (*Hint*: Use Stirling's formula, given in Exercise 4 in Section 3.3.)

    (b) Suppose you have selected 2^{56} of these permutations at random. If you choose two permutations p and q from among these, then $p \circ q$ is a new permutation that may or may not be one of those selected. What is the probability that $p \circ q$ is in the selected set?

    (c) If we regard the collection $\{\text{DES}_k \mid k \text{ is a 56-bit key}\}$ as a "random" selection of permutations, what does (b) say about the likelihood that, given k_1 and k_2, we can find a k_3 such that $\text{DES}_{k_2} \circ \text{DES}_{k_1} = \text{DES}_{k_3}$?

4. Find the matrices that represent the subkey generating functions K_1 and K_2 for SDES.

5. Find a formula for the inverse of of the initial permutation IP in SDES.

6. Carry through the steps in computing

$$f_{01011111}(00110001) \text{ and } f_{11111100}(00011010)$$

in Example 5.1.1.

7. Write a program that implements SDES.

   (a) Check it by verifying that it yields

   $$\text{SDES}_{1000000000}(10000000) = 00000110$$

   and

   $$\text{SDES}_{0100000000}(10000000) = 10110110.$$

   (b) Suppose that a 10-bit SDES key k was used to encipher two 8-bit blocks to yield the following:

   $$\text{SDES}_k(10101010) = 01100100$$
   $$\text{SDES}_k(01010101) = 11101000.$$

   Use your implementation of SDES to make a brute force known-plaintext attack to recover the key. Time the running of your program.

5.2 Case Study II: PGP

In order to make concrete some of the cryptographic ideas discussed in this book, we focus briefly on a specific arena in which it is possible to view the action of cryptographic software on text. In particular, we look at Pretty Good Privacy, a freeware program that combines encryption, decryption, digital signature generation, verification, and other information security tasks in a form convenient for use by people on single-user computers.

The implementation of PGP available through the MIT Web site has four basic functions that can be employed separately or together. It can be used as a plug-in to text editors and e-mail programs to encrypt, decrypt, sign, and verify. The way these functions are implemented is shown schematically in Figures 5.2 and 5.3. In addition, PGP generates block cipher, RSA, and

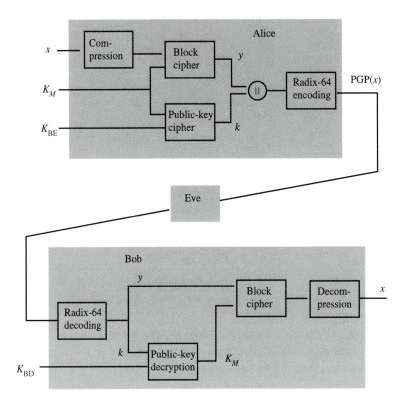

Figure 5.2 PGP encryption and decryption.

ElGamal keys.

Let's consider encryption in a little more detail first. The basic outline of this operation is that Alice has a message x, represented in binary form, to be encrypted using a block cipher (conventional cryptography), where the key for it is enciphered using a public-key algorithm and transmitted along with the encrypted message. Bob, the receiver, decrypts the message by first using her decipherment key for the public-key algorithm to decrypt the message key and then using this message key for the block cipher. More specifically,

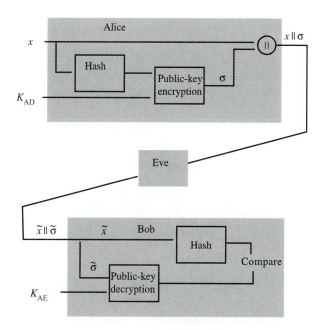

Figure 5.3 PGP digital signature generation and verification.

- **Setup**: Bob must generate a public and private key pair, K_{BE} and K_{BD}, for one of the public-key methods used in PGP, either RSA or ElGamal. He can do this by having the PGP software complete this operation. Bob's public encryption key K_{BE} must be made available to Alice.

- **Encryption**: Alice's message x is first compressed using some version of ZIP compression, a standard algorithm; this process preserves all of the message's information but reduces the number of bytes representing it. The software uses Alice's keystrokes and the times between them to generate a **message key** (sometimes referred to, as a session key), denoted K_M, for the specific block cipher being used (CAST-128, IDEA, or triple-DES in 64-bit CFB mode). This key is used only once, with the particular message x. Then x is enciphered with K_M to produce a pre-ciphertext, designated y in Figure 5.2. Alice uses Bob's public encryption key K_{BE} to encipher K_M with the public key encryption algorithm being used (RSA or ElGamal) to produce an encrypted key denote k in the figure. Then y and k are concatenated. These data are converted to **base**-64 (or **radix**-64) representation, which has a textual representation using only the symbols A, ..., Z, a, ..., z, 0, ..., 9, +, /. This ASCII text constitutes the final PGP ciphertext.

- **Decipherment** Receiving a PGP-enciphered e-mail, Bob first converts the radix-64 representation to binary and then takes the appropriate segment of bits for the enciphered block cipher key k. After that, he uses his private decryption key K_{BD} with the public-key algorithm to decrypt k and obtain the message key K_M. He then uses K_M in the block cipher to obtain the compressed plaintext. Finally he un-ZIPs the compressed plaintext to get the original plaintext from Alice.

When PGP generates the key for a public-key cipher, it prompts the user to select from either "RSA" or "Diffie-Hellman/DSS" for the public-key algorithm. It then uses a probabilistic prime searching algorithm to generate the public/private-key pair. Once the key pair is generated, the user can send the public encipherment key to a key server or hold onto it to distribute as he or she sees fit. The private decryption key is saved in encrypted form on the user's computer in a small file that is accessible by a passphrase chosen by the user. PGP also prompts the user for several keystrokes or mouse movements. The choice of the keys and the timing between the strokes is used as seed for a random number generator (itself based on the block cipher built into PGP). This random number generator produces the message key whenever a new message is encrypted.

Now let's consider an illustration of what the users of PGP experience. Suppose that Bob generated a 2048-bit key pair for RSA and that Alice has his public encryption key. If she wants to encrypt the e-mail message shown in Figure 5.4, then she selects Bob's encryption key from her "public-key

```
Dear Bob,

I hope your day is going well.

Alice
```

Figure 5.4 The plaintext of a message from Alice to Bob

ring," and PGP enciphers the message as shown in Figure 5.5.

This message contains two basic components. One is the message component, which, besides the actual characters of the note, includes a timestamp

```
-----BEGIN PGP MESSAGE-----
Version: PGPfreeware 6.5.1 for non-commercial use
<http://www.pgp.com>

hQEMA9i8brrFMQJhAQf9HZ0OfjwcgOA5vVnVZCkwfEb4sL2fbA9r3YdoMIk66MKU
r1TTF3Aq6aF9MbBkdNGF1i1SkkGlus7dau0IwkLXneaiaKerNnGqMiaApyqbihuJ
CV6yXRrDpZidojblC5byUImXZPC5bOqRxx9urmj+Fe/fKuGVUV1Fm1MOOPUxUi8F
iJ1iPhe7eCgFN27MZAhwN7ErVrayF9b3WiXwajaaDNyDKNoW3dFjqqZBCA1rkD49
Cz8UC3xpZvF/OhZ7NYVT1SNn89DhY9Cyva7JyT0m2FFIGZyMqZhyzYYebPCAFFVa
UW3A+QxBd/OB5ru4qWBJfk11/17DqZKKDoRV/h2h2aRK/45/QUjS4z2kUX5VKZHM
K0offXHC9cSMr2MZHgOXxbJlykSnFy5/32cCrdVlCQzqs+o1+4YLniu1Z1fR/HqY
dEeMiEKL+kqvR18=
=oCh2
-----END PGP MESSAGE-----
```

Figure 5.5 PGP encryption of the message in Figure 5.4.

and a filename. The other is the message key component, which includes the RSA-encrypted message key and a key identifier consisting of the rightmost (low order) 64 bits of the key Alice used to encrypt the message key. The identifier allows Bob's PGP program to use the correct key for decryption, as he may have several RSA key pairs in use at once.

Receiving this message, Bob uses PGP on it. The program uses the key identifier in the message itself to determine which private decryption key should be used, and it prompts Bob for the passphrase that will decrypt this key so that PGP can actually use it in the public-key algorithm. Using this private decryption key and the encrypted message key in the message from Alice, Bob's PGP computes the actual message key and then uses it in the block cipher algorithm to recover Alice's message.

Now we consider the signing and verification functions of PGP. Suppose Alice wants to affix a digital signature to the same message to Bob. Then she selects the signature option in PGP. It uses the Secure Hash Algorithm (SHA) to generate a 160-bit message digest. Then it prompts Alice for the passphrase that will decrypt her private RSA decryption key. Obtaining this key, PGP uses it in RSA decryption applied to the message digest. The result is the signature (Figure 5.6). The signature component here contains not only the encrypted message digest but also the leading 16 bits of the unencrypted message digest (to allow for checking that Bob's PGP is using the correct RSA encipherment key), the identifier of Alice's public key, and a timestamp.

When Bob receives this message-signature pair, his PGP program will

```
-----BEGIN PGP SIGNED MESSAGE-----

Dear Bob,

I hope your day is going well.

Alice

-----BEGIN PGP SIGNATURE-----
Version: PGPfreeware 6.5.1 for non-commercial use <http://www.pgp.com>

iQEVAwUBOce67Z/edPjnPHnzAQG1DAgAzFkjEWg7bOcFgbkMlmhxQMjlwHqFQWGX
/2aOkRrHahaPSbt16MMkoD+BYOHq97GClIjVXcOrjDmnrLuLRK5sAT3B3vo5I8y4
HuggOzQxd0ns8K+o/P6DphXSLzfdJpPEdY3ZIrw/ZbB8o/htAkBse65jF9n0PeAe
wHCGtiK2RiLSvntLaOz/DPRi9QDRHUHBZKaxxHl2HPafji0kocarHpddlfAtuVdd
q9EczAFVxeW0fROcXXBWq//Mty/PrMw/SAwfC4tg3En0ifrIYp1LyKAWNrmlWg73
obJ3Bbc4kwAeCi56vQfhdVMqK2yiGe8q2DBIJoXMwEGMJPl284yNBg==
=0VGU
-----END PGP SIGNATURE-----
```

Figure 5.6 The message in Figure 5.4 with a digital signature component.

find the key identifier in the signature component and look up Alice's public encryption key. It then applies RSA with this key to the encrypted message digest to obtain the digest itself. It also uses SHA to hash the message. If the decrypted digest and the hash value are the same, Bob's PGP gives the output shown in Figure 5.7.

```
*** BEGIN PGP SIGNED MESSAGE ***

*** PGP Signature Status: good
*** Signer: Alice <alice@here.edu>
*** Signed: 9/19/00 at 2:13 PM
*** Verified: 9/19/00 at 2:18 PM
Dear Bob,

I hope your day is going well.

Alice


*** END PGP SIGNED MESSAGE ***
```

Figure 5.7 Alice's signature verified.

Finally, PGP can be used to combine both the signing and encryption

```
-----BEGIN PGP MESSAGE-----
Version: PGPfreeware 6.5.1 for non-commercial use <http://www.pgp.com>

hQEMA9i8brrFMQJhAQgAjgCaWpN1Mp/q0n+yEV9vpzVMfCZ0GgqWGziBumDGry9v
nYi86nn1XxBivdiyYQv+Pm6U347dCCIFtX36zveAmICUTJ0ShqSwbFPBwoD9X34P
daUUtLYLf+CIIZlCmFqb/2AYmikQYrXMWvunQRF59RcSMt2ayT4tKKu9NyINtt46
UOly7pcRihfdLkdmC5lqmQKytrS0EI83BaCLPciAnkLmqMsTJfR4a/p4pZMY4tn+
Km4D+rOgYllJDjI/GGKRoVoPSUjusjuCPaUBIPjR32DV3rYmtHY9XacODfhgqK5g
USb5HAuD0XmYDq/6qMI+OlKs4AmyhIPnEuNGnNghS6UBZw61eG1vxHh5tn8Lom9x
TdjVkE5/cKEDPtnEzY8EPgBo6oIeKoYsrxN0C0HcgKHMSl2EWeIXUviuOANFvRsF
mH77XY4MiGWI7htavQoRFxAvsrHhBCpucOm0IWQKhXiG+Stb8ElnvkHLs419ng5C
rM2742Gflx28zbZI0gQ2FG5u6/k/gHOOK5jliqz/Qxb6s0/xZIhKWD0vQ6LlJYn4
Nl83Piq1+OaFvgAXUOyiJseWdAHw7G0wP+d/c4yszHSp+vjuWw+7v/FBiquOedSm
PaPaOpztC6w0kMG98d9+gqWNtP6Ol38fbfsNEXQBLgttt3CmurqGgQDxgY2E3p8e
o244SvERPZDNpXu3m931EQX5b2QjLX+JlmihrG+r1QaqMP15/pYI+GxVpp+105lO
88LsCY5osMrUMlq8/pMI9fnUz5GJcPyT/vlUZ32WWcYCGrihgcJpTtRkDkresMqS
wXkCuYLBvp7g
=YaBM
-----END PGP MESSAGE-----
```

Figure 5.8 Alice's signed and encrypted message to Bob.

functions. Say Alice wants to sign the example message and then encrypt it. Then she and her copy of PGP go through the signing steps, as in the earlier example, to produce the signature component shown in Figure 5.6. Then the message and signature components are concatenated and encrypted with a message key. The result is something like what is shown in Figure 5.8. Bob's PGP program decrypts as it did in the earlier example and then verifies the signature.

Even though the protocols described here seem complicated, they are not the whole story connected with PGP. There are, for instance, issues of managing private and public keys and revoking them. For instance, Bob may decide that his public key has been in use long enough, or he may think that the corresponding private key may have been compromised. Thus he would like to let those with whom he communicates in encrypted form that the old key has been "decommissioned" and that he is presenting a new one. But how could someone receiving such a revocation be sure that it really came from Bob and not instead from someone posing as him? Bob may need to send a **key revocation certificate**, which is a message bearing his digital signature and saying, in essence, "In the future, don't use the public key you're using to verify this signature."

Summary

Useful software, such as PGP, implementing methods discussed in this book is publicly available. From a purely technical viewpoint, it is interesting to see the functions of encryption and digital signature generation work.

EXERCISES

1. Do a search on the World Wide Web and find the MIT PGP site. Download PGP and try it out!

2. Encipher a short message two times to the same recipient. Study the resulting ciphertexts to see if you can identify the key and message components in the messages.

5.3   Public-Key Infrastructure

The use of public-key cryptography solves the key distribution problem—or so it seems. Let's take a look at an instance where a simple announcement of a public key is subject to attack.

A company called WSS (We Sell Stuff) maintains an online store. This Web site is set up so that when a customer is ready to check out by supplying address and credit card information, its software uses ElGamal encryption with the customer's computer to encrypt the credit card number.[3] To do this, WSS simply makes its public ElGamal key available to requesting clients.

Now suppose that Alice has been sending requests to and receiving responses from WSS over a channel (for instance an ethernet or optical cable network) that is monitored by Eve (Figure 5.9). Eve would like to obtain Alice's credit card number, and she devises the following plan. She will listen

---

[3]For simplicity, we are assuming that a public-key algorithm is used for the actual data encryption. In real implementations, a public-key method is used only to agree on a key for a symmetric encryption algorithm, such as triple-DES, which is then used to encrypt the actual data.

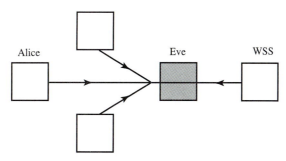

Figure 5.9 Alice and others conduct browsing and purchase transactions with WSS over a channel monitored by Eve.

to the transmissions between Alice and WSS, which are all in clear, up to the point when Alice will send her private information. When Alice presses the "ready-to-check-out" button, Eve intercepts the request for the information on WSS's secure page and does not relay it to WSS. She sends back to Alice a look-alike page that differs from WSS's only in that the ElGamal public key is one of Eve's own choosing. Alice then puts all of her information into the form and submits it. Once again, Eve intercepts this request and does not relay it to WSS. She decrypts the credit card number and can now use it to overextend Alice's credit limit or sell it to someone who will. In order not to arouse suspicion, Eve encrypts Alice's credit card number using WSS's ElGamal key and sends Alice's original request to WSS. Then WSS generates an "order received" response that Eve relays back to Alice. Throughout this process, from Alice's perspective, everything worked perfectly. Indeed, if Alice requested overnight delivery, then her package will arrive the next day. Unfortunately, Alice's credit card company may soon be alerting her that the card's limit has been reached.

In this scenario, Alice was a victim of what is sometimes termed a **man-in-the-middle (MIM)** attack.[4]   Eve has, without undue effort, forged the public key of a legitimate business. There is nothing special about the encryption method used in the example—the same thing could have been done with RSA. And there is nothing unusual about the assumption of the network connectivity among Alice, WSS, and Eve. Indeed, if the network is configured as shown in Figure 5.9, then Eve could engage in this sort of activity in a wholesale fashion, picking up credit card numbers from others such as Bob and Carol.

The example raises a serious issue:

---

[4]Of course, in this case it's a "woman-in-the-middle attack."

How can network entities (such as Alice in the example) that use
public-key cryptography be reasonably certain that the public
keys of other entities (such as WSS in the example) are the ones
they receive and use for encryption?

This is a wide-ranging concern because public-key cryptography is used not
only for data encryption, but also for symmetric-key exchange, digital signatures, and other protocols.

It is our purpose in this section to give a brief overview of measures that
can be taken to make such activities as Eve's much more difficult. In the current literature, this comes under the rubric of **public-key infrastructure
(PKI)**.

Public Announcement or Broadcast of Public Keys

If an individual wishes to place a copy of his or her public key on a Web
page on in a **finger file**[5] for others to use in sending encrypted e-mail, then
he may wish to assume that the likelihood is low that someone wishes to
forge his public key. For instance, there may be very little encrypted traffic
to him, and the information is not likely to be terribly valuable anyway.

For a business, however, the story is much different. If even one instance
such as we described with WSS occurs, then Alice would be justifiably out-
raged, not at Eve—whose existence she may be completely unaware of—but
at WSS, the entity that, from her perspective, let the credit card number get
into the wrong hands. The company could quickly have a public relations
nightmare and even go out of business if word of such disasters spread.

Trusted Public-Key Authority

The scenario for a business leads us to consider a more rigid key infrastructure in which the likelihood of such attacks as that just described is greatly
diminished. One solution is to create a centralized repository for public keys.
Then, either that authority disseminates a directory by means other than
the insecure network, or else mechanisms are set in place for the directory

---

[5]A finger file for Bob on a computer with the IP address name equivalent `there.edu`
would be a text file residing on `there.edu` that contains basic information such as Bob's
"real" name, his username on that computer (e.g., `bob@there.edu`), the time he last logged
in, and other information he chooses to place in the file. Whenever a user on another system
uses the Unix command `finger bob@there.edu` (or its equivalent in another operating
system), `there.edu` attempts to send the contents of the finger file back to the requester.

to be queried through the network. The latter approach entails the use of cryptographic protocols.

A Public-Key "Telephone Directory"

Somehow, potentail e-clients of companies would want assurance that real-time public-key forgeries could not happen. One way would be for there to be a public-key directory service that everyone could trust, a **public-key authority (PKA)**. This entity might be an organization that disseminates a list of public keys for network entities analogous to a printed telephone directory. Just as it would be harder to forge the phone book than to commandeer directory assistance at the telephone office and give out bogus numbers, so it would be harder to forge a widely distributed compact disk with a public key business directory on it than to forge than public keys transmitted through the network. While it would be expensive and cumbersome, such a scheme would thwart any attempt by Eve to do what she did in the example: Once Alice received the personal data form and putative public key information from WSS, she (her computer) could look up WSS's public key from the CD and compare it with that in the form. Any discrepancy would mean that Alice should not send sensitive information. Or Alice could use the public key on the CD to do the encryption and send the information. If the form she used was actually a forgery by Eve, then when Eve received the information and attempted to decrypt the credit card number, she would get garbage.

New e-businesses appear constantly, and with them grows the need for public keys to aid in making transactions secure. Also, existing e-businesses may wish or need to change public keys. These facts would make it important to produce public-key directories regularly and for network users to keep up with the latest directories.

Public-Key Distribution Authority

An alternative solution to the public key distribution problem relies on a protocol that is itself based on cryptographic components. Let the PKA database reside on the network. The organization maintaining it would still have to keep up with new and revoked public keys for businesses on the network, but these changes could be made quickly and the results of them available to users immediately. The assurance against fraudulent public keys would reside in a setup something like this: The PKA generates a public/private-key pair K_{PE} and K_{PD} for an asymmetric encryption function

F_k and gives out the public key to users over a channel not controlled by Eve. For instance, the PKA might give K_{PE} to (reputable) companies that make web browsers, and those companies in turn embed the key in the software they sell to users. Then, for instance, a protocol represented in Figure 5.10 can take place so that Alice can transmit securely to Bob. The steps in the

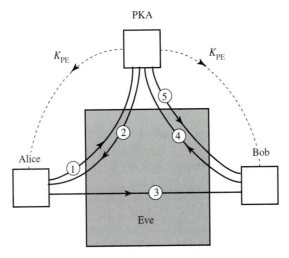

Figure 5.10 Public-key management with a network-based PKA. Setup: PKA distributes its public (encryption) key K_{PE} by some other means than through the network controlled by Eve.

protocol are given here.

1. Alice starts by forming a message consisting of her request R, Bob's identifier I_{B}, and the time T. She sends this message $R \,||\, I_{\mathrm{B}} \,||\, T$ in clear along the arrow labeled 1. Eve could alter the message or record it for use at some later time.

2. PKA receives a request $\tilde{R} \,||\, \tilde{I}_{\mathrm{B}} \,||\, \tilde{T}$, looks up $\tilde{I}_{\mathrm{B}}$'s public key in its database, concatenates this with Alice's original request, applies $F_{K_{\mathrm{PD}}}$ to this concatenation to "sign" it, and sends the resulting "certificate" along the arrow labeled 2. Assuming for a moment that Alice's original request went through unaltered (so that $\tilde{R} = R$, $\tilde{I}_{\mathrm{B}} = I_{\mathrm{B}}$, and $\tilde{T} = T$), we see that Eve can apply $F_{K_{\mathrm{PE}}}$ to the certificate and read it. However, if Eve seeks to manipulate the signed copy, the result going to Alice will be garbled when Alice applies $F_{K_{\mathrm{PE}}}$ to verify the certificate. If Eve seeks to alter the unencrypted copy, then she would have to use

PKA's private key to produce a "forged" certificate via $F_{K_{\mathrm{PD}}}$, but she does not know PKA's private key.

3. Alice receives the "certificate" and verifies it by applying $F_{K_{\mathrm{PE}}}$ to it and comparing to see that her request, Bob's ID, and the timestamp have come back unaltered. She can be confident that the public key in the certificate really does belong to Bob.

4. Alice encrypts her important information using Bob's public key and sends the cipertext to Bob. Since Eve does not know Bob's private key, it is not possible for her to read Alice's message.

5. If Bob needs to reply to Alice, he goes through the same procedure with the PKA as Alice did in order to obtain Alice's public key K_{AE}. He then encrypts sensitive information using this key and sends it on to Alice.

We examine the rationale for some of the arcane steps in this procedure.

Suppose that the protocol does not call for the certificate that PKA sends to Alice to contain Alice's original request: It just contains the requested public key and the timestamp. Then Eve can pretend to be Bob to Alice and Alice to PKA in a **masquerade attack**. She intercepts Alice's original request and changes it to read, "Please send me Eve's public encryption key K_{EE}." (We assume that Eve is herself registered with PKA.) PKA sends a certificate consisting of $F_{\mathrm{PD}}(K_{\mathrm{EE}} \,\|\, T)$, which Eve allows to pass on to Alice. Alice then applies F_{PE} and obtains a public key that she takes to be Bob's. Moreover, because of the timestamp, she is not suspicious of a replay attack, which we discuss in the next paragraph. Now when Alice encrypts data with the public key from the certificate and sends it, Eve intercepts and decrypts it with her private key.

Having the protocol include the requester's original request (or some sort of identifier generated for the particular request, sometimes called a **nonce**) makes it impossible in effect for Eve to masquerade as Bob to Alice.

Assume for a moment that the protocol does not call for the timestamp to be part of the certificate. Now suppose also that Eve has discovered Bob's *private* (decryption) key, but that he has become suspicious and has generated a new public/private-key pair and registered the new public key with PKA. At first glance, it appears that all is well since the decryption key that Eve possesses is no longer useful to decrypt messages to Bob. But this is not the case. Eve can mount a **replay attack**. When Alice sends a request to PKA for Bob's current public key, Eve intercepts the request and sends back to Alice an old "certificate" of Bob's public key that she recorded during a prior exchange between Alice and PKA. Alice is now using Bob's old public key, and when she encrypts a message with it, Eve intercepts and decrypts it with the old decryption key of Bob's.

We have seen an illustration of why the timestamp might be important. With it, old keys are no longer useful, for if the certificates sent by PKA contain a timestamp, then Eve cannot reuse an old certificate in effect to masquerade as PKA to Alice.

There is one more potential pitfall to the protocol paradigm we have described here. Return to the credit card encryption example with which we began this section, with WSS in the role of Bob. Alice has transmitted her encrypted credit card number to buy something, while Eve has been recording everything. Later, Eve wants to buy a bunch of really-cool-stuff from WSS, so she sends an order and merely uses the recorded encryption of Alice's credit card. WSS is none the wiser and so ships the stuff to Eve. To thwart this sort of attack, two more steps should be added to the protocol.

6. Alice concatenates a nonce n_A with her message before encrypting it with Bob's public key. When Bob receives this message, he generates a nonce n_B of his own and sends back to Alice $F_{AE}(n_A \,\|\, n_B)$. Since only Bob could decrypt Alice's message, the appearance of n_A in the message she receives is assurance that her message went to Bob.

7. Alice sends $F_{BE}(n_B)$ back to Bob, so now he is assured that it is actually Alice sending the message.

There is a certain amount of symmetry to these difficult-to-understand features of the public-key infrastructure. In each case, the effect is to prevent Eve from representing herself to other parties as someone else.

Public-Key Certificates

A modification of the PKA paradigm is for the public key authority to be replaced by a **certificate authority** (**CA**). Each participant generates its own public/private-key pairs and, by means other than over the network through which encrypted traffic will flow, applies to the CA for a certificate that consists of the participant's network identification, public key, and an expiration date for the certificate, all encrypted using the CA's private key. The CA gives this certificate to the registering participant.

In particular, say that Bob (whose identifier is I_B) has generated a public/private-key pair K_{BE} and K_{BD} and has agreed with the CA on an expiration date T_B. Then Bob's certificate C_B will be computed by the CA as

$$C_B = F_{K_{PD}}(T_B \,\|\, I_B \,\|\, K_{BE}),$$

where K_{PD} is the CA's private (decryption) key. Then any time Alice wants to send a message to Bob using his current public key, she requests his certificate. She verifies the certificate by computing

$$F_{K_{PE}}(C_B),$$

where K_{PE} is the CA's public (encryption) key. If the certificate has not been tampered with, since $F_{K_{PE}}$ and $F_{K_{PD}}$ are inverses, the result of this calculation will be

$$F_{K_{PE}}(F_{K_{PD}}(T_B \,\|\, I_B \,\|\, K_{BE})) = T_B \,\|\, I_B \,\|\, K_{BE}.$$

Alice can then compare the computed ID for Bob with the one from which she requested and obtained the certificate. She can also compare the expiration date with the current time to check that the certificate has not expired. This provides assurance that the quantity represented as Bob's public key really is his.

An advantage this scheme has over the centralized PKA scheme is that the CA is less likely to be a bottleneck.

You may have received a message from your Web browser at some point saying such-and-such certificate has expired. Chances are that you were accessing a site that sent your browser a certificate for which the expiration date had passed. Either that or else the clock on your computer was not set properly. This is a small indication of what goes on behind the scenes with such pieces of software.

The certificate authority scheme described here is but one of many that have been described in the literature and implemented. See [80] for detailed descriptions. The schemes described here are generic enough to give some genuine insight to the real potential weaknesses of the naive use of public-key cryptography. They also illustrate some of the potentially complex measures needed to shore up these weaknesses.

Public-key infrastructure, then, refers to the general issues of how to ensure that hardware and software interoperate properly in a fashion that is essentially independent of the particular protocol used.

Summary

While public-key infrastructure is ultimately a software and hardware issue, there are purely logical facets to it as well. These considerations are based on our general knowledge of how public-key encryption works and also on the way information flows in real computer networks. Using centralized public-key authorities or certificate authorities helps to prevent man-in-the-middle attacks on public-key exchanges. Including timestamps and nonces in protocols used by public-key distribution authorities helps to prevent replay and masquerade attacks.

EXERCISES

1. With two other people, agree on who will play the roles of Alice, Bob, and Eve. Then, have Alice and Bob communicate by e-mail, sending everything to Eve for forwarding. Agree that any encrypted portion of an e-mail message will be done by RSA and, to keep the computations manageable, that the moduli used by Alice and Bob will be three-decimal-digit numbers greater than 500. Have Bob generate a private/public RSA key pair, and have Alice come up with a three-digit "credit card number" whose first digit is no more than 4. Let Alice "purchase" something from Bob by sending that number encrypted in one of the messages. She will, of course, have to request his public encryption key. Have Eve do a man-in-the-middle attack to obtain Alice's credit card number. Reenact the scenario two more times, in each case with someone else playing Eve.

2. With three other people, agree on who will play the roles of Alice, Bob, Eve, and PKA. Arrange for e-mail communication between Alice and Bob through Eve as in Exercise 1, but have Bob send his enryption key directly to PKA, not forwarded through Eve. When Alice prepares to send her "credit card number" to Bob, have her request his key diretly from PKA. (Why would it not be wise for her to request Bob's public key through Eve?) Have Eve attempt to recover Alice's credit card number.

3. With three other people, agree on who will play the roles of Alice, Bob, Eve, and PKA. Have PKA choose a four-decimal-digit modulus greater than 5000, generate an encryption/decryption RSA key pair, and send

the encryption key to all the other participants. The PKA will record participant names as "1" for Alice, "2" for Bob, and "3" for Eve. Have Bob generate a public/private-key pair and deliver the public key to PKA withouth going through Eve. Then, with Eve being the conduit for subsequent communications among Alice, Bob, and PKA, have Alice request Bob's public key from PKA. Assume that PKA will encode a request for Bob's public key by prepending the digit "2" to the key before signing the "certificate." Have Eve attempt to foil this scheme in order to obtain Alice's credit card number.

5.4   Law and Issues Regarding Cryptography

Until the mid-1970s, cryptography was primarily the concern of diplomacy and the military. Confidentiality in message transmission in these arenas is essential to the very functions of these sorts of organizations. Between that time and the mid-1990s, there was, for instance, considerable growth in the use of automatic teller machines. Banks needed ways to ensure that communications between these devices and central recordkeeping computers would be secure. DES was one of various solutions. Other business entities began to need reliable encryption of communications among computers at remote sites. With the advent of the Internet, however, cryptography has become a matter of direct concern to many individual citizens. Electronic mail, a boon and convenience, operates in such a way that casual eavesdroppers, companies, or government agencies can record messages as they are relayed through computers on the Internet. The same principle applies to the messages sent and received by a home computer when its user employs a Web browser.

In the United States, privacy advocacy groups claim the federal government can too easily intrude on the privacy of individuals by archiving their e-mail and records of file transfers. Some claim that individuals' communications over the Internet should be placed in electronic "envelopes," that is, encrypted, so that the sender and the recipient can be reasonably certain that intermediaries have not snooped into the contents. This would be consistent with a deep-rooted notion in American democracy that whatever law-abiding citizens think, write, and do in the privacy of their own homes is nobody else's business. Some have made strong encryption freely available to anyone using the Internet as part of a cry for citizens to employ this form of privacy.

In [18], Diffie and Landau delve into the conflict between individual privacy and the use of technological innovations by government entities (such as law enforcement and intelligence) to conduct investigations. In a number of fascinating historical examples, they illustrate not only how the wiretap can be a tool for the greater public good but also how it has the potential for being abused for political or other purposes outside the scope enforcing law. Because digital "wiretaps" are much easier to mount than putting alligator clips on copper telephone lines leading into a building, and because it is not clear how current law applies to some newer telecommunication technology, the following question arises: What role does encryption play in preserving the privacy of citizens?

Companies increasingly conduct commerce electronically. Either to ensure secure financial transactions with their customers or to ensure that sensitive and proprietary data are transmitted without competitors acquiring it, they have a need for strong cryptography. Restrictions on the use of cryptography can hamper companies' attempts to conduct business, both domestically and internationally.

National governments have strong motives to outlaw or restrict the use of cryptography. These can be grouped into two general categories: concerns about criminal activity and concerns about national security. Criminals, especially organized crime, can use publicly available strong cryptography. The contents of their communications may remain hidden from law enforcement agencies monitoring them, thus allowing criminal activity to proliferate. There is little question that lawfully obtained orders for wiretaps have in the past assisted law enforcement in limiting or ending criminal activity. However, widely available strong cryptography makes an e-mail or cell-telephone wiretap technically almost impossible. More directly inimical to the national governments are the activities of spies and terrorists, who can also make use of strong encryption in their work.

Regulations in the United States

Prior to 1996, the Department of State administered the International Traffic in Arms Regulations (ITAR), which had a legislative basis in the Arms Export Control Act (AECA) of 1976. Under those federal regulations, cryptographic hardware and software were categorized as munitions, along with such items as tanks and guided missiles. These regulations specified severe penalties for exporting certain types of cryptographic hardware and software—fines of up to $250,000, 10 years in prison, or both.

In 1996, jurisdiction over cryptography not specifically for military use was transferred to the Department of Commerce. With this transfer, there came some easing in the ITAR restrictions: A company wishing to export software that employed encryption with a key no longer than 40 bits could do so after a one-time review by the Commerce Department. With review, a company could export encryption products with up to 56-bit keys provided that the company built and marketed key recovery products.

In 2000, technical restrictions were lifted, so that export of any type of cryptography to commercial and individual end-users in almost all countries in the world were permitted without a license. However, bans on export to terrorist states remained in place. The Bureau of Export Administration currently administers regulations regarding cryptography, and it generally requires a one-time review of products to be exported. These latest eased restrictions implement agreements reached in the Wassenaar Arrangement, which is discussed in the next subsection.

In 1993, controversy arose when the federal government proposed the **Clipper Chip**, a VLSI circuit designed by NSA that would be used for encryption of telephone transmissions. Actually, the controversy erupted over the Escrowed Encryption Standard (EES), of which Clipper was one implementation. EES called for each chip to be hard wired at the factory with its own unique **unit key**. This unit key would then be separated into two pieces, which were to be escrowed with two separate federal agencies (NIST and the Department of Treasury). Whenever the chip sends encrypted data to another receiving Clipper Chip using a key generated only for that session, it first uses the unit key to encrypt the session key and send that to the receiving chip. This 128-bit string is called the **Law Enforcement Access Field** (LEAF). If, for instance, the FBI has reason to believe that the conversants are engaged in an illegal activity, it could get a court order for NIST and Treasury to release to it the pieces of the unit key. Then the FBI can put these together, decrypt the LEAF on the receiving chip to obtain the session key, and finally use the session key to obtain the transmitted data. Many see the specter of Big Brother in this protocol and for that reason have opposed the entire concept of EES.

International Efforts in Establishing Cryptographic Standards

In 1996, through the Organization for Economic Cooperation and Development (OECD), the U.S. government proposed talks to establish guidelines for international cryptography policy. The organization's members—Australia, Austria, Belgium, Canada, the Czech Republic, Denmark, Finland, France, Germany, Greece, Hungary, Iceland, Ireland, Italy, Japan, Luxembourg, Mexico, The Netherlands, New Zealand, Norway, Poland, Portugal, South Korea, Spain, Sweden, Switzerland, Turkey, the United Kingdom, and the United States—began talks and drafted a document that calls on OECD members to fashion or revise cryptography policies to reflect its guidelines. The aims of the guidelines are to "promote the use of cryptography in order to foster confidence in networks and to help to ensure data security and privacy on global networks" and "to promote the use of cryptography without unduly jeopardizing public safety and national security" (see [4]). The eight guidelines of the OECD are listed here.

- **Trust in cryptographic methods** Cryptographic methods should be trustworthy in order to generate confidence in the use of information and communications systems.

- **Choice of cryptographic methods** Users should have a right to choose any cryptographic method, subject to applicable law.

- **Market-driven development of cryptographic methods** Cryptographic methods should be developed in response to the needs, demands, and responsibilities of individuals, businesses, and governments.

- **Standards for cryptographic methods** Technical standards, criteria, and protocols for cryptographic methods should be developed and promulgated at the national and international level.

- **Protection of privacy and personal data** The fundamental rights of individuals to privacy, including secrecy of communications and protection of personal data, should be respected in national cryptographic policies and in the implementation and use of cryptographic methods.

- **Lawful access** National cryptography policies may allow lawful access to plaintext, or cryptographic keys, of encrypted data. These policies must respect the other principles contained in these guidelines to the greatest extent possible.

- **Liability** Whether established by contract or legislation, the liability of individuals and entities that offer cryptographic services or hold or access cryptographic keys should be clearly stated.

- **International cooperation** Governments should cooperate to co-ordinate cryptography policies. As part of this effort, governments should remove, or avoid creating in the name of cryptography policy, unjustified obstacles to trade.

The full text of the recommendations and guidelines may be found on the OEDC Web page.

The guideline on lawful access received the most attention at the OECD talks. France, the United Kingdom, and the United States strongly support the notion of lawful access to encryption keys and plaintext, but many of the other member countries do not plan key-recovery systems. It is notable that this guideline alone contains the stronger verb *must* rather than *may*, thereby subordinating law enforcement's wiretapping authority to the other principles in the guidelines.

About the same time as the OECD talks, a 28-nation convention concluded a two-year effort to produce the **Wassenaar Arrangement on Export Controls for Conventional Arms and Dual-Use Goods and Technologies**. Named for Wassenaar, in the Netherlands, the city in which the negotiations took place, it went into effect in July of 1996. It classifies cryptography as a "sensitive (tier 2)" dual use material; that is, like an airplane, it can be used for civilian (commercial) or military purposes. By the agreement, the participants excluded from the dual use categorization such items as cable encryption, non-end-to-end cellular phone encryption, ATMs, point of sale devices, and MAC-generating equipment. They also agree to control dual use items "with the objective of preventing *unauthorized* transfers or re-transfers of these items," but they can nevertheless authorize exports at their discretion.

Summary

Widespread legal use of cryptography by individuals helps to ensure privacy in their telecommunications. Cryptography used by businesses streamlines their ability to operate at diverse sites and minimize the risks for interception of proprietary information. On the other hand, widespread availability of cryptographic hardware and software increases the likelihood that criminal entities may use it to impinge on the public welfare or that terrorist organizations may use it to subvert the state. Thus cryptography is an important issue in the formation and evolution of public policy. Currently, in the United States, there are essentially no restrictions on the use of cryptography and few constraints on its export. With the growth of international electronic communication and commerce, cooperation among nations in establishing cryptographic standards is important. Nations have made preliminary steps in this direction, in the form of the OECD Initiative and the Wassenaar Agreement.

EXERCISES

1. Suppose that all encryption hardware and software were illegal except for that meeting a standard such as the EES. Discuss the effects this might have on the balance among individuals' privacy, businesses' information security, and government's ability to ensure public safety.

2. Obtain pending legislation (at the federal or state level) that impinges directly on the use and distribution of cryptographic software. Write a brief essay in which you discuss the merits of the legislation.

Glossary

additive cipher a cipher in which a constant value is added (modulo the size of the alphabet) to the numerical equivalent of each plaintext letter to obtain the numerical equivalent of the corresponding ciphertext letter.

affine cipher a cipher in which plaintext numerical equivalent x is transformed into ciphertext numerical equivalent by a formula of the form $y \equiv ax + b \pmod{m}$, where a, b, and m are agreed upon by the correspondents.

algorithm a formal procedure for solving a mathematical problem. For example, "long division" is one algorithm for obtaining the quotient of two numbers.

anagram a word or phrase constructed by transposing the letters of another word or phrase.

ASCII acronym for American Standard Code For Information Interchange.

asymmetric cryptosystem a cryptosystem in which the decipherment key is not easily obtained from a knowledge of an encipherment key. Example: RSA, Merkle-Hellman knapsack.

attack an unintended recipient's attempts to read an encrypted message or obtain the key that was used to encipher it.

authentication a process by which communicating parties establish the identities of their correspondents.

block cipher a ciphersystem in which groups, or blocks, of symbols are encrypted. This is to be distinguished from a *stream cipher*. Examples: DES, Hill cipher.

Caesar cipher the particular shift cipher with a shift of 3.

Capstone chip microprocessor implementing the Skipjack algorithm.

checksum a number calculated from a block of transmitted digits that allows the recipient to check whether the digits have been altered during transmission.

chosen-plaintext attack an attack on a cryptosystem in which the cryptanalyst is able to choose plaintext that will be put through the encryption algorithm. The resulting ciphertext can then be compared with the chosen plaintext, and at least a portion of the key can be recovered. Example: The U.S. military, during World War II, was intercepting Japanese naval communications but did not know for certain the identity of a target to which they referred as "AF." American forces arranged for the garrison at Midway Island—the suspected target—to broadcast that they were low on fresh water. Shortly thereafter, the U.S. military intercepted Japanese radio transmissions saying that AF was low on water.

cipher a message or information concealment method in which individual letters of plaintext are transformed into letters of ciphertext. Contrast with a *code*, where letters, syllables, words, and phrases are the basic plaintext units that are enciphered.

cipher alphabet the letters of the alphabet listed in the order of their correspondence to the alphabet in its usual order. Example: For the Caesar cipher, the cipher alphabet is D, E, F, ..., Y, Z, A, B, C.

cipher block chaining (CBC) A form of block encipherment in which each block of ciphertext depends on both the corresponding cleartext block and the previous block of ciphertext.

ciphersystem (same as cryptosystem) a function that takes plaintext and a keyword or keystream as input and produces ciphertext as output.

ciphertext the text produced by an encryption algorithm.

class NP those mathematical problems for which there exists a polynomial-time algorithm that checks whether a given input is a solution to the problem. Class NP contains class P, and one of the central open questions in theoretical computer science is whether the two classes are in fact the same. It is generally believed that there are NP problems that are not P.

class P those mathematical problems for which there exists a solving algorithm that runs in an amount of time that is a **P**olynomial function of the size of the input. Example: If computational expense is counted as the number of divisions, then the Euclidean algorithm is in class P. (See also **class NP**).

code a symbol or group of symbols that represents a plaintext character, word, phrase, or number. Example: The ASCII code for the letter A is 65; the process of writing the ASCII codes corresponding to the letters of a text would be referred to as *encoding*, as opposed to encrypting or enciphering.

columnar transposition a cipher in which plaintext letters are written side by side in a fixed number of columns and then enciphered by transcribing them from the columns in some prescribed manner to produce ciphertext.

collision (1) in a substitution cipher, the encryption of a letter as itself. (2) a hash function hashing two different messages to the same hash value. (See *hash function.*)

computational complexity a measure of the amount of effort (time, computer storage, etc.) needed to solve a computational problem. Example: Finding the prime factorization of a 10-digit number has greater computational complexity than determining whether a 10-digit number is prime. Public-key cryptosystems rely on the general belief that the computational complexity of problems such as factoring and the discrete logarithm problem are such that they are not practically solvable in instances with large enough input.

computational security measures the security of a cryptosystem in terms of the computational complexity of the algorithms thought to be necessary to break the cryptosystem.

crib a portion of plaintext known to correspond to a particular piece of ciphertext.

cryptanalysis the activity of recovering plaintext or key from an enciphered message.

cryptography the design and analysis of cryptosystems.

cryptology term applied to designing, analyzing, and breaking cryptosystems.

cryptosystem same as *ciphersystem.*

Data Encryption Standard (DES) A symmetric cryptosystem established by the Federal Government in 1977 and widely used in nonclassified cryptographic applications. In effect, it is a simple substitution and transposition applied to messages in a 2^{64}-character alphabet. It is readily implemented in hardware and used in banking and commerce.

decipher, decipherment process by which a legitimate recipient of ciphertext obtains the corresponding plaintext. Example: Using the key SUMMER in the Vigenère method, a correspondent deciphers TODZMK as BURNIT. Usually, the term *decipherment* is applied when the intention of the ciphertext is concealment. This is distinguished from *decoding*, in which the message is represented in an alternative form for ease of transmission (e.g., one speaks of decoding a text message from a list of the ASCII codes for the individual letters).

decode process of translating encoded information into plaintext (See also *decipher*).

decrypt, decryption same as *decipher, decipherment.*

digital signature a group of symbols appended to a transmitted plaintext that provides the recipient a means of ascertaining the identity of the sender and authenticity of the message.

Digital Signature Algorithm (DSA) a standard algorithm, similar to the El Gamal algorithm, developed by NSA for producing a digital signature from data hashed by the Secure Hash Algorithm (SHA).

Digital Signature Standard (DSS) a Federal Information Processing Standard (FIPS) established by NIST for producing digital signatures. It is based on the Secure Hash Algorithm (SHA) and the Digital Signature Standard (DSA).

digraph two letters.

discrete logarithm for a given base b and modulus m, the discrete logarithm of a positive integer a is a number x satisfying $b^x \equiv a \,(\mathrm{mod}\, m)$.

encipher, encipherment to produce ciphertext from plaintext. (Same as *encrypt, encryption.*)

encrypt, encryption (same as *encipherment*) the process of producing ciphertext from plaintext.

Friedman test a method, developed by William Friedman in the 1920s, of estimating the keyword length from the index of coincidence for a polyalphabetic ciphertext.

grille a method of steganography in which plaintext words are hidden by some geometric means. The idea is used in the digital realm by so-called Mona Lisa ciphers, where messages are hidden in a designated pattern in an otherwise innocuous message (for instance, a digitized picture of Da Vinci's *Mona Lisa*).

hash function (or hashing algorithm) a function that takes plaintext as input and produces a much shorter output such that the output from different plaintexts are likely to be different. Example: The function h with inputs the first, middle, and last names of individuals and output the string consisting of the first letter of the first name, the first letter of the middle name, and the first four letters of the last name.

index of coincidence the probability that, in a given ciphertext, two randomly selected letters are identical. It is used to determine whether a ciphertext is produced by a polyalphabetic substitution and, if so, to estimate the keyword length.

Kasiski test a test for keyword length in a polyalphabetic cipher that rests on an analysis of the spacing between repeated groups of ciphertext letters.

Kerberos a centralized key distribution system on networks whereby users establish a session key from a centralized trusted authority in order to communicate via messages encrypted using the key.

key the secret (i.e., held by legitimate users of a cryptosystem) information supplied to a cryptosystem along with plaintext to produce ciphertext, or along with ciphertext to produce plaintext.

key agreement a protocol whereby two or more parties jointly establish a secret key by communicating over public channel. The key is determined as a function of inputs from both parties. Example: Diffie-Hellman key agreement protocol.

key distribution a mechanism whereby one party chooses a secret key and transmits it to other parties.

known-plaintext attack an attack in which a cryptanalyst attempts to recover the key used in encryption from a ciphertext and the plaintext that is known to have been encrypted to obtain it.

monoalphabetic substitution a cipher in which each occurrence of a symbol in plaintext is replaced by one other letter (compare with *polyalphabetic* substitution, where different occurrences of a plaintext letter are enciphered as various other letters).

National Institute of Standards and Technology (NIST) federal agency (formerly the National Bureau of Standards, NBS) responsible for establishing and regulating standards for industry and commerce.

National Security Agency (NSA) agency within the U.S. Department of Defense charged with maintaining communication security for the armed forces and with signals intelligence.

nomenclator a hybrid of code and cipher systems originating in the late fourteenth century in southern Europe. These evolved from simple substitution of code words to elaborate codebooks that included substitutions for letters, words, names, syllables, and phrases.

null a cipher symbol that conveys no information. It is either to confuse cryptanalysts or to pad cleartext so that complete blocks can be encrypted.

one-way function a mathematical function that is simple to evaluate but generally infeasible to invert. Example: Multiplication of two large prime numbers is easy to perform, but finding prime factors of a large number can take inordinate amounts of time.

password a short cryptographic key used by computer systems to authenticate users.

perfect security the property of a cryptosystem that a cryptanalyst, with knowledge of the probability distribution of plaintexts and in possession of a ciphertext, cannot do better than pure guesswork at recovering the original plaintext. Example: Vigenère encipherment with different random keys as long as the messages.

plaintext the original, unencrypted form of a message.

polyalphabetic substitution a cipher in which successive plaintext letters are replaced by corresponding letters chosen from two or more cipher alphabets in an agreed-upon fashion. Example: Vigenère encipherment with a keyword.

Pretty Good Privacy (PGP) a cryptographic protocol, hybrid between RSA and IDEA, that is used for electronic mail.

private-key cryptography (also called symmetric cryptography; compare with *public-key cryptography*). A cryptosystem in which both correspondents possess the same key and are able to encipher and decipher. The security rests on both parties keeping the key secret. Example: Monoalphabetic substitutions, polyalphabetic substitutions, transpositions, Hill cipher, DES.

protocol a procedure for the exchange of information between two parties. Example: Diffie-Hellman key exchange protocol.

pseudorandom numbers a sequence of numbers that passes one or more statistical tests for randomness but which is generated by a mathematical formula.

public-key cryptography (also called asymmetric cryptography) a cryptosystem in which the encipherment algorithm and key are made public but where it is not feasible to obtain the decipherment key from this information. The decipherment key remains in the possession of the message recipient. Example: RSA, Merkle-Hellman knapsack, ElGamal.

RSA acronym from the last names Ronald Rivest, Adi Shamir, and Leonard Adleman, who, in 1977, developed a public-key cryptosystem whose security depends on the general difficulty of factoring numbers into their prime factors.

Secure Hash Standard (SHS) an algorithm developed at NSA for a standard method of hashing messages encrypted by DES. This is part of the Digital Signature Standard.

Secure Hash Algorithm (SHA) a standard hash function designed by NSA.

shift cipher same as additive cipher.

shift register an electronic circuit, or a mathematical model for the circuit, that produces generally random-looking binary sequences. Shift register sequences are used as keystreams for certain cryptographic applications.

steganography the practice of hiding the existence of messages, such as with invisible ink, grilles, microdots, etc.

stream cipher a cipher in which each message character is enciphered just before its transmission and deciphered just after its receipt. Compare with *block cipher.*

substitution replacement of a symbol by another symbol.

symmetric cryptosystem (or private-key cryptosystem) a cryptosystem that uses a key held by both of the parties. All cryptosystems up to the invention of public-key cryptography are symmetric. Security rests on a private channel over which the key is transmitted.

transposition a cipher in which plaintext letters are rearranged (anagrammed) by some agreed-upon method to produce ciphertext.

trapdoor function (or sometimes a **one-way trapdoor function**) a function that is generally easy to evaluate and hard to invert without a small piece of special information.

trigraph a group of three letters.

trusted authority (TA) an entity on a network (typically a secure computer) that is responsible for verifying the identities of users, distributing cryptographic keys to users, etc.

Vigenère cipher a polyalphabetic cipher that uses the 25 shifts of the usual alphabet and a keyword or keystream.

Vigenère square the 26×26 table of the alphabet along with its 25 shifts.

Wheatstone-Playfair cipher digraphic cipher invented by Charles Wheatstone (1802–1875) and promulgated by Lyon Playfair. It consists of a small set of rules for transforming digraphs into other digraphs by using a square array of the alphabet.

zero-knowledge protocol a procedure by which an individual convinces another that he or she possesses some secret information without actually revealing it.

Bibliography

[1] W. R. Alford, Andrew Granville, and Carl Pomerance, "There are Infinitely Many Carmichael Numbers," *Annals of Mathematics*, (2) **139** (1994), 703–722.

[2] Robert Andrews, *Columbia Dictionary of Quotations*, Columbia University Press, New York, 1993.

[3] Robert Andrews, *Cassell Dictionary of Contemporary Quotations*, Cassell Wellington House, London, 1996.

[4] Stewart A. Baker and Paul R. Hurst, *The Limits of Trust: Cryptography, Governments, and Electronic Commerce*, Kluwer Law International, The Hague, The Netherlands, 1998.

[5] Wayne G. Barker, *Cryptanalysis of Shift-register Generated Stream Cipher Systems*, Aegean Park Press, Laguna Hills, CA, 1984.

[6] Friedrich L. Bauer, *Decrypted Secrets: Methods and Maxims of Cryptology*, Springer-Verlag, Berlin, 1997.

[7] Thomas Beth, "Confidential Communication on the Internet," *Scientific American*, December 1995, 88–91.

[8] Albrecht Beutelspacher, "Cryptology," Mathematical Association of America, Washington, DC, 1994.

[9] Gilles Brassard, "Quantum Computing: The End of Classical Cryptography?" *The Mathematical Intelligencer*, October 1994, 15–21.

[10] David M. Bressoud, *Factorization and Primality Testing*, Springer-Verlag, New York, 1989.

[11] K. Campbell and M. Wiener, "Proof that DES is not a Group," *Proceedings, Crypto '92*, Springer-Verlag, 1992.

[12] R. D. Carmichael, "On Composite Numbers P which Satisfy the Fermat Congruence $a^{P-1} \equiv 1 \,(\text{mod}\, P)$," *American Mathematical Monthly*, **19** (1912), 22–27.

[13] Betsy Carpenter, "Decoding the Electronic Future," *U.S. News & World Report*, March 14, 1994, 69–71.

[14] Center for Cryptologic History, *The Friedman Legacy: A Tribute to William and Elizebeth Friedman*, in a series United States Cryptologic History, *Sources in Cryptologic History, No. 3*, National Security Agency, 1992.

[15] William Cheswick, Warwick Ford, and James Gosling, "How Computer Security Works," *Scientific American*, October 1998, 106–109.

[16] W. Diffie and M. Hellman, "Exhaustive Cryptanalysis of the NBS Data Encryption Standard," *Computer*, 1997.

[17] W. Diffie and M. Hellman, "Privacy and Authentication: An Introduction to Cryptography," *Proc. of the IEEE*, **67** (1979), 397–427.

[18] W. Diffie and S. Landau, *Privacy on the Line: the Politics of Wiretapping and Encryption*, MIT Press, Cambridge, MA, 1998.

[19] Taher El Gamal, "A Public Key Cryptosystem and a Signature Scheme Based on Discrete Logarithms," *IEEE Transactions on Information Theory*, **31** (1985), 469–472.

[20] Howard Eves, *An Introduction to the History of Mathematics*, Holt, Rinehart, and Winston, Inc., New York, 1969.

[21] William F. Friedman and Lambros D. Callimahos, *Military Cryptanalytics*, parts I and II, Aegean Park Press, Laguna Hills, CA, 1985.

[22] *The Friedman Legacy: A Tribute to William and Elizebeth Friedman*, Center for Cryptologic History, National Security Agency, 1992.

[23] William F. Friedman and Elizebeth S. Friedman, *The Shakespearean Ciphers Examined*, Cambridge University Press, London, 1957.

[24] Helen Fouché Gaines, *Cryptanalysis, a Study of Ciphers and Their Solution*, Dover Publications, New York, 1939.

[25] Joseph A. Gallian, *Contemporary Abstract Algebra*, D.C. Heath and Company, Lexington, MA, 1990.

[26] Joseph A. Gallian, "The ZIP Code Bar Code," *The UMAP Journal*, **7** (1986), 191–195.

[27] Joseph A. Gallian, "Assigning Driver's License Numbers," *Mathematics Magazine*, **64:1** (1991), 13–22.

[28] Martin Gardner, *Codes, Ciphers and Secret Writing*, Dover Publications, Inc., New York, 1972.

[29] Simson L. Garfinkel, "Patented Secrecy," *Forbes*, Feb. 27, (1995), 122–124.

[30] Ralph P. Grimaldi, *Discrete and Combinatorial Mathematics*, 3rd edition, Addison-Wesley, Reading, MA, 1994.

[31] Alexander Hellemans and Bryan Bunch, *The Timetables of Science: A Chronology of the Most Important People and Events in the History of Science*, Touchstone, New York, 1988.

[32] Martin E. Hellman, "The Mathematics of Public-Key Cryptography," *Scientific American*, **241** (1979), 146–157.

[33] M. E. Hellman and R. C. Merkle, "Hiding Information and Signatures in Trapdoor Knapsacks," *IEEE Transactions on Information Theory IT-24* (1978), 525–530.

[34] Lester S. Hill, "Cryptography in an Algebraic Alphabet," *American Mathematical Monthly*, **36** (1929), 306–312.

[35] Lester S. Hill, "Concerning Certain Linear Transformation Apparatus of Cryptography," *American Mathematical Monthly*, **38** (1931), 135–154.

[36] F. H. Hinsley and Alan Strip, *Codebreakers—Story of Bletchley Park*, Oxford University Press, 1994.

[37] T. W. Hungerford, *Abstract Algebra—An Introduction*, Saunders College Publishing, Philadelphia, PA, 1990.

[38] David Kahn, *The Codebreakers, The Story of Secret Writing*, Macmillan, New York, 1972.

[39] David Kahn, *The Codebreakers: The Comprehensive History of Secret Communication from Ancient Times to the Internet*, Scribner, New York, 1996.

[40] Donald Knuth, *The Art of Computer Programming, v. 2, Seminumerical Algorithms*, Addison-Wesley, Reading, MA, 1981.

[41] Neal Koblitz, *A Course in Number Theory and Cryptography*, Springer-Verlag, New York, 1994.

[42] Neal Koblitz, *Algebraic Aspects of Cryptography*, Springer-Verlag, Heidelberg, 1998.

[43] Alan G. Konheim,*Cryptography: A Primer*, John Wiley & Sons, Inc., New York, 1981.

[44] T. W. Körner, *The Pleasures of Counting*, Cambridge University Press, Cambridge, U.K., 1996.

[45] Ramanujachary Kumanduri and Cristina Romero, *Number Theory with Computer Applications*, Prentice Hall, Upper Saddle River, NJ, 1998.

[46] Frances Lake and J. Newmark, *Mathematics as a Second Language*, Addison–Wesley, Reading, MA, 1977.

[47] Susan Landau, "Standing the Test of Time: The Data Encryption Standard," *Notices of the American Mathematical Society*, **47** (2000), 341–349.

[48] Susan Landau, "Communications Security for the Twenty-First Century: the Advanced Encryption Standard," *Notices of the American Mathematical Society*, **47** (2000), 450–459.

[49] Henry B. Laufer, *Discrete Mathematics and Applied Modern Algebra*, Prindle, Weber & Schmidt, Boston, 1984.

[50] Peter H. Lewis, "Between a Hacker and a Hard Place," *The New York Times*, April 10, 1995, C1.

[51] William Mendenhall and Richard L. Schaeffer, *Mathematical Statistics with Applications*, Duxbury Press, North Scituate, MA, 1973.

[52] Alfred Menezes, Paul van Oorschot, and Scott Vanstone, *Handbook of Applied Cryptography*, CRC Press, Boca Raton, FL, 1997.

[53] Carolyn P. Meinel, "How Hackers Break In...and How They Are Caught," *Scientific American*, October 1998.

[54] Meyer, Carl H. and Stephen M. Matyas, *Cryptography: A New Dimension in Computer Data Security*, John Wiley and Sons Inc., New York, 1982.

[55] S. Brent Morris, *The Folger Manuscript*, Ft. George G. Meade, MD, 1992.

[56] David E. Newton, *Encyclopedia of Cryptology*, ABC-CLIO, Inc., Santa Barbara, CA, 1997.

[57] Oystein Ore, *Number Theory and Its History*, Dover Publications, Inc., Mineola, NY, 1988.

[58] Ivars Peterson, "Bits of Uncertainty: Blazing a Quantum Trail to Absolute Secrecy," *Science News* (February 10, 1996), 90–92.

[59] Ivars Peterson, "Computing a Bit of Security: Zero Knowledge Proofs in Data Encryption," *Science News* (January 16, 1988).

[60] Ivars Peterson, "Encrypting Controversy," *Science News*, **143** (1993), 394–396.

[61] Ivars Peterson, "Hiding in Lattices: an Improved Mathematical Strategy for Encrypting Data," *Science News*, **152** (1997), 12–13.

[62] Ivars Peterson, "Quick Cracking of Secret Code," *Science News*, **154**, August 1998.

[63] Simon J. D. Phoenix, "Quantum Cryptography: How to Beat the Code Breakers Using Quantum Mechanics," *Contemporary Physics* (May/June 1995), 165–195.

[64] Edgar Allan Poe, "The Gold Bug," from *The Gold Bug and Other Tales*, Dover Publications, Mineola, NY, 1991.

[65] J. J. Quisquater, M. Guillou, and T. Berson, "How to Explain Zero-Knowledge Protocols to your Children," *Advances in Cryptology— Crypto '89 LNCS 432*, 1990, 628–631.

[66] Ronald L. Rivest, "The Case against Regulating Encryption Technology," *Scientific American*, October 1988, 116–117.

[67] R. L. Rivest, "Cryptography," in *Handbook of Theoretical Computer Science, Volume A: Algorithms and Complexity*, ed., Jan Van Leeuwen, Elsevier Science Publishers, B.V., Amsterdam, The Netherlands, and The MIT Press, Cambridge, MA, 1990, 71– 755.

[68] R. L. Rivest, A. Shamir, and L. Adleman, "A Method for Obtaining Digital Signatures and Public-Key Cryptosystems," *Communications of the A.C.M.*, **21** (1978), 120–126.

[69] Shawn Rosenhiem, *The Cryptographic Imagination: Secret Writing from Edgar Poe to the Internet*, Johns Hopkins University Press, Baltimore, MD, 1997.

[70] Edward Schaefer, "A Simplified Data Encryption Standard Algorithm," *Crytpologia*, 1996.

[71] Bruce Schneier, *Applied Cryptology: Protocols, Algorithms, and Source Code in C*, 2nd ed., John Wiley and Sons, Inc., New York, 1996.

[72] Adi Shamir, "A Polynomial Time Algorithm for Breaking the Basic Merkle-Hellman Cryptosystem," *Proceedings of Crypto 82*, Springer–Verlag, 1983.

[73] Claude E. Shannon, "Communication Theory of Secrecy Systems," *Bell System technical Journal*, **28** (1949), 656–715.

[74] Joseph H. Silverman, *A Friendly Introduction to Number Theory*, Prentice Hall, Upper Saddle River, NJ, 1997.

[75] Gustavus J. Simmons, "Cryptology: The Mathematics of Secure Communication," *Mathematical Intelligencer*, *1* (1979), 233–246.

[76] Simon Singh, *The Code Book: The Evolution of Secrecy from Mary Queen of Scots to Quantum Cryptography*, Doubelday, New York, 1999.

[77] Abraham Sinkov, *Elementary Cryptanalysis: A Mathematical Approach*, Mathematical Association of America, Washington, DC, 1966.

[78] Laurence Dwight Smith, *Cryptography, the Science of Secret Writing*, Dover Publications, New York, 1943.

[79] Richard E. Smith, *Internet Cryptography*, Addison-Wesley, Reading, MA, 1997.

[80] William Stallings, *Cryptography and Network Security: Principles and Practice*, 2nd ed., Prentice Hall, Upper Saddle River, NJ, 1999.

[81] Ian Stewart, "Proof of Purchase on the Internet: Zero-Knowledge Protocols," *Scientific American* (February 1996), 124–125.

[82] Ian Stewart, "What a Coincidence!", *Scientific American*, **278** (June 1998), 95–96.

[83] Douglas R. Stinson, *Cryptography: Theory and Practice*, CRC Press, Boca Raton, FL, 1995.

[84] Andrew S. Tanenbaum, *Computer Networks*, 3rd ed., Prentice Hall PTR, Upper Saddle River, NJ, 1996.

[85] Thomas M. Thompson, *From Error-Correcting Codes Through Sphere Packing to Simple Groups*, Mathematical Association of America, Ithaca, NY, Carus Monograph #21, 1983.

[86] Philip M. Tuchinsky, "International Standard Book Numbers," *The UMAP Journal* **5** (1985), 41–54.

[87] Dominic Welsh, *Codes and Cryptography*, Oxford University Press, Oxford, U.K., 1988.

[88] Fred B. Wrixon, *Codes and Ciphers*, Prentice Hall General Reference, New York, 1992.

[89] Corinna Wu, "Private Eyes: Biometric Identification is Set to Replace Passwords and PINs," *Science News*, **153** (April 1998), 216–217.

[90] Herbert O. Yardley, *The American Black Chamber*, Aegean Park Press, Laguna Hills, CA, 1931.

[91] Philip R. Zimmermann, "Cryptography for the Internet," *Scientific American*, October 1998, 110–115.

Table of Primes

2	179	419	661	947	1229	1523	1823	2131	2437	2749
3	181	421	673	953	1231	1531	1831	2137	2441	2753
5	191	431	677	967	1237	1543	1847	2141	2447	2767
7	193	433	683	971	1249	1549	1861	2143	2459	2777
11	197	439	691	977	1259	1553	1867	2153	2467	2789
13	199	443	701	983	1277	1559	1871	2161	2473	2791
17	211	449	709	991	1279	1567	1873	2179	2477	2797
19	223	457	719	997	1283	1571	1877	2203	2503	2801
23	227	461	727	1009	1289	1579	1879	2207	2521	2803
29	229	463	733	1013	1291	1583	1889	2213	2531	2819
31	233	467	739	1019	1297	1597	1901	2221	2539	2833
37	239	479	743	1021	1301	1601	1907	2237	2543	2837
41	241	487	751	1031	1303	1607	1913	2239	2549	2843
43	251	491	757	1033	1307	1609	1931	2243	2551	2851
47	257	499	761	1039	1319	1613	1933	2251	2557	2857
53	263	503	769	1049	1321	1619	1949	2267	2579	2861
59	269	509	773	1051	1327	1621	1951	2269	2591	2879
61	271	521	787	1061	1361	1627	1973	2273	2593	2887
67	277	523	797	1063	1367	1637	1979	2281	2609	2897
71	281	541	809	1069	1373	1657	1987	2287	2617	2903
73	283	547	811	1087	1381	1663	1993	2293	2621	2909
79	293	557	821	1091	1399	1667	1997	2297	2633	2917
83	307	563	823	1093	1409	1669	1999	2309	2647	2927
89	311	569	827	1097	1423	1693	2003	2311	2657	2939
97	313	571	829	1103	1427	1697	2011	2333	2659	2953
101	317	577	839	1109	1429	1699	2017	2339	2663	2957
103	331	587	853	1117	1433	1709	2027	2341	2671	2963
107	337	593	857	1123	1439	1721	2029	2347	2677	2969
109	347	599	859	1129	1447	1723	2039	2351	2683	2971
113	349	601	863	1151	1451	1733	2053	2357	2687	2999
127	353	607	877	1153	1453	1741	2063	2371	2689	3001
131	359	613	881	1163	1459	1747	2069	2377	2693	3011
137	367	617	883	1171	1471	1753	2081	2381	2699	3019
139	373	619	887	1181	1481	1759	2083	2383	2707	3023
149	379	631	907	1187	1483	1777	2087	2389	2711	3037

151	383	641	911	1193	1487	1783	2089	2393	2713	3041
157	389	643	919	1201	1489	1787	2099	2399	2719	3049
163	397	647	929	1213	1493	1789	2111	2411	2729	3061
167	401	653	937	1217	1499	1801	2113	2417	2731	3067
173	409	659	941	1223	1511	1811	2129	2423	2741	3079
3083	3433	3733	4073	4421	4759	5099	5449	5801	6143	6481
3089	3449	3739	4079	4423	4783	5101	5471	5807	6151	6491
3109	3457	3761	4091	4441	4787	5107	5477	5813	6163	6521
3119	3461	3767	4093	4447	4789	5113	5479	5821	6173	6529
3121	3463	3769	4099	4451	4793	5119	5483	5827	6197	6547
3137	3467	3779	4111	4457	4799	5147	5501	5839	6199	6551
3163	3469	3793	4127	4463	4801	5153	5503	5843	6203	6553
3167	3491	3797	4129	4481	4813	5167	5507	5849	6211	6563
3169	3499	3803	4133	4483	4817	5171	5519	5851	6217	6569
3181	3511	3821	4139	4493	4831	5179	5521	5857	6221	6571
3187	3517	3823	4153	4507	4861	5189	5527	5861	6229	6577
3191	3527	3833	4157	4513	4871	5197	5531	5867	6247	6581
3203	3529	3847	4159	4517	4877	5209	5557	5869	6257	6599
3209	3533	3851	4177	4519	4889	5227	5563	5879	6263	6607
3217	3539	3853	4201	4523	4903	5231	5569	5881	6269	6619
3221	3541	3863	4211	4547	4909	5233	5573	5897	6271	6637
3229	3547	3877	4217	4549	4919	5237	5581	5903	6277	6653
3251	3557	3881	4219	4561	4931	5261	5591	5923	6287	6659
3253	3559	3889	4229	4567	4933	5273	5623	5927	6299	6661
3257	3571	3907	4231	4583	4937	5279	5639	5939	6301	6673
3259	3581	3911	4241	4591	4943	5281	5641	5953	6311	6679
3271	3583	3917	4243	4597	4951	5297	5647	5981	6317	6689
3299	3593	3919	4253	4603	4957	5303	5651	5987	6323	6691
3301	3607	3923	4259	4621	4967	5309	5653	6007	6329	6701
3307	3613	3929	4261	4637	4969	5323	5657	6011	6337	6703
3313	3617	3931	4271	4639	4973	5333	5659	6029	6343	6709
3319	3623	3943	4273	4643	4987	5347	5669	6037	6353	6719
3323	3631	3947	4283	4649	4993	5351	5683	6043	6359	6733
3329	3637	3967	4289	4651	4999	5381	5689	6047	6361	6737
3331	3643	3989	4297	4657	5003	5387	5693	6053	6367	6761
3343	3659	4001	4327	4663	5009	5393	5701	6067	6373	6763
3347	3671	4003	4337	4673	5011	5399	5711	6073	6379	6779
3359	3673	4007	4339	4679	5021	5407	5717	6079	6389	6781
3361	3677	4013	4349	4691	5023	5413	5737	6089	6397	6791
3371	3691	4019	4357	4703	5039	5417	5741	6091	6421	6793
3373	3697	4021	4363	4721	5051	5419	5743	6101	6427	6803
3389	3701	4027	4373	4723	5059	5431	5749	6113	6449	6823
3391	3709	4049	4391	4729	5077	5437	5779	6121	6451	6827
3407	3719	4051	4397	4733	5081	5441	5783	6131	6469	6829
3413	3727	4057	4409	4751	5087	5443	5791	6133	6473	6833
6841	7211	7573	7927	8293	8681	9013	9391	9739	10103	10463
6857	7213	7577	7933	8297	8689	9029	9397	9743	10111	10477

6863	7219	7583	7937	8311	8693	9041	9403	9749	10133	10487
6869	7229	7589	7949	8317	8699	9043	9413	9767	10139	10499
6871	7237	7591	7951	8329	8707	9049	9419	9769	10141	10501
6883	7243	7603	7963	8353	8713	9059	9421	9781	10151	10513
6899	7247	7607	7993	8363	8719	9067	9431	9787	10159	10529
6907	7253	7621	8009	8369	8731	9091	9433	9791	10163	10531
6911	7283	7639	8011	8377	8737	9103	9437	9803	10169	10559
6917	7297	7643	8017	8387	8741	9109	9439	9811	10177	10567
6947	7307	7649	8039	8389	8747	9127	9461	9817	10181	10589
6949	7309	7669	8053	8419	8753	9133	9463	9829	10193	10597
6959	7321	7673	8059	8423	8761	9137	9467	9833	10211	10601
6961	7331	7681	8069	8429	8779	9151	9473	9839	10223	10607
6967	7333	7687	8081	8431	8783	9157	9479	9851	10243	10613
6971	7349	7691	8087	8443	8803	9161	9491	9857	10247	10627
6977	7351	7699	8089	8447	8807	9173	9497	9859	10253	10631
6983	7369	7703	8093	8461	8819	9181	9511	9871	10259	10639
6991	7393	7717	8101	8467	8821	9187	9521	9883	10267	10651
6997	7411	7723	8111	8501	8831	9199	9533	9887	10271	10657
7001	7417	7727	8117	8513	8837	9203	9539	9901	10273	10663
7013	7433	7741	8123	8521	8839	9209	9547	9907	10289	10667
7019	7451	7753	8147	8527	8849	9221	9551	9923	10301	10687
7027	7457	7757	8161	8537	8861	9227	9587	9929	10303	10691
7039	7459	7759	8167	8539	8863	9239	9601	9931	10313	10709
7043	7477	7789	8171	8543	8867	9241	9613	9941	10321	10711
7057	7481	7793	8179	8563	8887	9257	9619	9949	10331	10723
7069	7487	7817	8191	8573	8893	9277	9623	9967	10333	10729
7079	7489	7823	8209	8581	8923	9281	9629	9973	10337	10733
7103	7499	7829	8219	8597	8929	9283	9631	10007	10343	10739
7109	7507	7841	8221	8599	8933	9293	9643	10009	10357	10753
7121	7517	7853	8231	8609	8941	9311	9649	10037	10369	10771
7127	7523	7867	8233	8623	8951	9319	9661	10039	10391	10781
7129	7529	7873	8237	8627	8963	9323	9677	10061	10399	10789
7151	7537	7877	8243	8629	8969	9337	9679	10067	10427	10799
7159	7541	7879	8263	8641	8971	9341	9689	10069	10429	10831
7177	7547	7883	8269	8647	8999	9343	9697	10079	10433	10837
7187	7549	7901	8273	8663	9001	9349	9719	10091	10453	10847
7193	7559	7907	8287	8669	9007	9371	9721	10093	10457	10853
7207	7561	7919	8291	8677	9011	9377	9733	10099	10459	10859

Answers to Selected Exercises

1.1

1. ZMW ZUGVI GSVN GSV PRMT LU HSVHSZXS HSZOO WIRMP

3. JUST AS WATER REFLECTS THE FACE, SO ONE HUMAN HEART REFLECTS ANOTHER.

5. THE SCYTALE WAS AN EARLY EXAMPLE OF A TRANSPOSITION CIPHER

6. (a) IULHQGV URPDQV FRXQWUBPHQ OHQG PH BRXU HDUV

   (c) PNA JR RIRE UNIR GBB ZHPU BS N TBBQ GUVAT

7. I k m c & m i c l T z v v g x g z t h A f m a n e o k o L x & q f k c y d I a k

9. XWLEXV IRLPMON ISZVTY LHPBCEQ HH SRTRLNQ IWFA MMQVZKC

11. YOU BROKE IT

13. (a) KNOWLEDGE IS MORE THAN EQUIVALENT TO FORCE

15. This would implement a simple shift cipher. Once the shift amount was discovered by a cryptanalyst, the message would be easily obtained.

17. WE ARE NOT INTERESTED IN THE POSSIBILITES OF DEFEAT

19. AFGVFF GFVAAG VAXGVG AVXDXX VVAXVA GVGDGG

21. BETWEEN FRIENDS THERE IS NO NEED OF JUSTICE

22. (a) Blocks of b letters are rotated r letters to the right.

(c) GIVE THE PEOPLE A NEW WORD AND THEY THINK THEY KNOW A NEW FACT

23. (a) When the sum of the digits is divided by 10, the remainder is 5, so there is a digit in error.

(c) The postal address code 14850 1000 30 8 is correct, and so is 15840 1000 30 8.

24. (a) $M = 1033$, $e = 11410$, $d = 5187$, and $n = 57293$.

(c) $d = 52135$, PIN $= 2000$

1.2

1. (a) $f(\text{A}) = \text{M}$, $f(\text{V}) = \text{R}$

(c)

x	A	B	C	D	E	F	G	H	I	J	K	L	M
$f^{-1}(x)$	G	M	N	O	L	P	Q	I	B	R	S	K	A

x	N	O	P	Q	R	S	T	U	V	W	X	Y	Z
$f^{-1}(x)$	T	J	F	U	V	W	D	E	X	H	C	Y	Z

2. ATHEMATICSMAY ISAY ETHAY ANGUAGELAY OFAY ECRETSAY ITINGWRAY

3. If x is the numerical plaintext, then the ciphertext is $y = 25 - x$. Applying this twice gives $25 - (25 - x) = x$, so Atbash is an involution.

5. The composition is also a simple substitution.

6. (a) $P(s(\text{ARITHMETIC})) = P(\text{RATIMHTECI}) = 42114424322344151324$, but $s(P(\text{ARTHMETIC})) = s(11422444233315442313) = 11244244323351443213$, so in general $P(s(x)) \neq s(P(x))$.

2.1

1. (a) ELVIS WAS SIGHTED AT MAIN AND UNION

3. (a) $127 = (18)7 + 1$, (c) $1024 = (64)16 + 0$, (e) $-43 = (-11)4 + 1$

4. (a) 2, (c) 4

5. (a)

x	0	1	2	3	4	5	6	7
$(x + 2)$ MOD 8	2	3	4	5	6	7	0	1

(c)

x	0	1	2	3	4	5	6	7	8	9
$(x + 5)$ MOD 10	5	6	7	8	9	0	1	2	3	4

(e)

x	0	1	2	3	4	5	6	7	8	9	10	11
$(x+2)$ MOD 11	1	2	3	4	5	6	7	8	9	10	11	0

6. (a) 9, 35, 61, 87, 113, 139;

7. (a) 5; (c) 3; (e) 5

8. $a \equiv b \,(\mathrm{mod}\, m)$ means that $a = b + km$ for some integer k. Now the number $r = b$ MOD m satisfies $b = qm + r$, where $0 \le r < m$, so $a = qm + km + r = (q + k)m + r$. This says that $a \equiv r \,(\mathrm{mod}\, m)$, that is, $a \equiv b$ MOD $m \,(\mathrm{mod}\, m)$. The same reasoning shows that $b \equiv a$ MOD $m \,(\mathrm{mod}\, m)$.

9. AOLMB SSULZ ZVMSP MLPZP UAOLO HGHYK ZVMSP ML

11. IF YOU CAN'T BE KIND, AT LEAST BE VAGUE

13. TRUE WORTH IS IN BEING NOT SEEMING

15. PROSPERITY IS NOT WITHOUT MANY FEARS AND DISTATES, AND ADVERSITY IS NOT WITHOUT COMFORTS AND HOPES

2.2

1. Multiplication modulo 8 is, e.g.,

$\times$	0	1	2	3	4	5	6	7
0	0	0	0	0	0	0	0	0
1	0	1	2	3	4	5	6	7
2	0	2	4	6	0	2	4	6
3	0	3	6	1	4	7	2	5
4	0	4	0	4	0	4	0	4
5	0	5	2	7	4	1	6	3
6	0	6	4	2	0	6	4	2
7	0	7	6	5	4	3	2	1

The numbers having no factor (other that 1) in common with 8 have an inverse.

2. (a) 17; (c) 5

3. (a) 4; (c) 2; (e) 7

4. $a = 19, b = 13$

5. (a) $x = 17(y - 10) \text{ MOD } 26$

    (c) $x = 5(y - 8) \text{ MOD } 9$

6. (a)
x	1	3	7	9
$x^{-1} \pmod{10}$	1	7	3	9

    (c)
x	1	5	7	11	13	17	19	23
$x^{-1} \pmod{24}$	1	5	7	11	13	17	19	23

7. ZLZGB GZROZ DGWND ZOHNA NDGQ RALRQ QIBGG

9. $a = 11, b = 6$. Plaintext: IF YOU BOW AT ALL BOW LOW

11. $a = 39x, q = 34x$

12. (a) An affine cipher is of the form $y \equiv ax + b$. There are 12 possible values for a that have multiplicative inverses and 26 possible values for b. Thus there are $12 \cdot 26 = 312$ different affine ciphers. For the choice $a = 1$ and $b = 0$, the cipher does nothing. So there are $312 - 1 = 311$ nontrivial affine ciphers on a 26-letter alphabet.

13. Note that $(n - 1) \cdot (n - 1) \equiv n^2 - 2n + 1 \equiv 0 - 0 + 1 \equiv 1 \pmod{n}$.

15. (a) i. 1, 7, 10, 5, 9, 11, 12, 6, 3, 8, 4, 2, 1, ...

    ii. 1, 3, 9, 1, ...

    iii. 1, 7, 10, 6, 4, 3, 8, 5, 9, 0, 1, ...

    iv. 1, 1, ...

    (c) $a = 17, b = 1$

2.3

1. (a) ABCDEFGHIJKLMNOPQRSTUVWXYZ
       NATURLSECIOBDFGHJKMPQVWXYZ
       Ciphertext: C ENVR TNBRU PECM HKCFTCHBR AY WECTE RNTE MBCDEP
       VNKCNPCGF CL MRLOB CM HKRMRKVRU FNPQKNB MRBRTPCGF

2. (a)   plain   ABCDEFGHIJKLMNOPQRSTUVWXYZ
         cipher PAKYRBLZICOMDQEFUNGVSHWTJX

   (b) APREC EDENT EMBAL MSAPR INCIP LE

3. (a) THREE MAY KEEP A SECRET IF TWO OF THEM ARE DEAD

   (c) WE MUST ALL HANG TOGETHER OR ASSUREDLY WE SHALL ALL HANG
       SEPARATELY

   (e) LIFE IS ALWAYS A RICH AND STEADY TIME WHEN YOU ARE WAITING
       FOR SOMETHING TO HAPPEN OR HATCH

5. I KNOW NOT WHAT COURSE OTHERS MAY TAKE; BUT AS FOR ME, GIVE
   ME LIBERTY OR GIVE ME DEATH

7. A SHORT SAYING OFT CONTAINS MUCH WISDOM

10. $26! = 403291461126605635584000000 \equiv 4.03 \times 10^{26}$, so the time is
    $4.03 \times 10^{26}/19^9$ sec $= 4.03 \times 10^{17}$ sec $= 1.28 \times 10^{10}$ years.

2.4

1. EUCLID ALONE HAS LOOKED ON BEAUTY BARE

3. ITWMA ONAW ITEOH FADKH AMRST ONNHS RITSO NIKAE EIKOG EENNH TNOCE
   NCRVN TOPNO GETOW HSMOV EOHFR TTOPT

5. GIVE ME SOMEWHERE TO STAND AND I WILL MOVE THE EARTH

7. (a) 8, 7, 6, 4, 1, 8

   (b)

x	1	2	3	4	5	6	7	8	9	10
$p^{-1}(x)$	4	3	6	1	10	2	9	5	7	8

   (c) NEVER HELP A CHILD WITH A TASK AT WHICH HE FEELS HE CAN
       SUCCEED

2.5

1. (a) RSJVE SAVBV OKNFC IEIZT ICRRU XRFCR ESIIN IJKS

2. (a) MATHEMATICS IS ONLY THE ART OF SAYING THE SAME THING IN
       DIFFERENT WORDS

3. (a) PXTVMSUC

   (c) EYNUZCUB

5. THE TRUTH IS ALWAYS SOMETHING THAT IS TOLD, NOT SOMETHING THAT
   IS KNOWN. IF THERE WERE NO SPEAKING OR WRITING, THERE WOULD
   BE NO TRUTH ABOUT ANYTHING. THERE WOULD ONLY BE WHAT IS

6. (i) is the polyalphabetic substitution; (ii) is the transposition; (iii) is the monoalphabetic substitution

7. $x_i = (y_i - k_{i \text{ MOD } n}) \text{ MOD } 26$

9. (a) $x_i = (y_i - k_i - m_i) \text{ MOD } 26$

   (c) The effective length is the least common multiple of p and q.

2.6

1. $P(6, 3) = 120$, $P(10, 2) = 90$, $P(365, 4) = 1.74586 \times 10^{10}$

2. $C(6, 3) = 20$, $C(10, 2) = 45$, $C(365, 4) = 727\,441\,715$

3.

```
              1       6      15      20      15       6       1
          1       7      21      35      35      21       7       1
      1       8      28      56      70      56      28       8       1
  1       9      36      84      96      96      84      36       9       1
1      10      45     120     180     192     180     120      45      10      1
```

5. (a) $P(15, 10) = 1.089729 \times 10^{10}$

6. (a) $C(15, 10) = 3003$

7. (a) $17\,576\,000$ (c) 5.680024×10^{10}

8. (a) 1/6   (c) 1/3   (e) 2/3

9. (a) 1/36   (c) 1/12   (e) 5/18

10. (a) 0   (c) 1   (e) 0.683

11. (a) 0.066   (c) 0.0816   (e) 0.897

12. (a) 239, 410

13. (a) about 5

15. (a) 0.0745, 0.106, 0.35

   (b) 0.0023, 0.00183

2.7

1. (a) $7.07005 \approx 7$

   (c) $1.17222 \approx 1$

3. The index of coincidence is .071 and the keyword length is $.813 \approx 1$. On the basis of the Friedman test alone, we would conjecture that this is a monoaplhabetic subsitiution.

4. If $I = .03850001$. The keyword length estimate is

$$k \approx 0.0265n/(.026499 + .0000001n).$$

If n is large, on the order of $10\,000$, then this number is about $9\,636$. In general, if the index of coincidence is close to 0.0385, the estimated keyword length is about n, the length of the message itself.

6. HOPE IS DEFINITELY NOT THE SAME THING AS OPTIMISM. IT IS NOT THE CONVICTION THAT SOMETHING WILL TURN OUT WELL, BUT THE CERTAINTY THAT SOMETHING MAKES SENSE, REGARDLESS OF HOW IT TURNS OUT. Keyword is PEACE.

7. (a) A 1100-letter sample of French gives an s value of 0.0889644.

   (b) Using the given keyword estimation formula, we obtain $k \approx (0.0889644 - 0.0385) \cdot 523/((0.0889644 - 0.0531) + 523 \cdot (0.0531 - 0.0385)) = 3.43393 \approx 3$.

8. The keyword length is 6. Indeed, the keyword is in the footnote to this quotation.

2.8

1. Keyword length is 4.

3. (a) Plaintext in both cases is GENIUS IS NO MORE THAN CHILDHOOD RECAPTURED AT WILL, CHILDHOOD EQUIPPED NOW WITH MAN'S PHYSICAL MEANS TO EXPRESS ITSELF, AND WITH THE ANALYTICAL MIND THAT ENABLES IT TO BRING ORDER INTO THE SUM OF EXPERIENCE, INVOLUNTARILY AMASSED.

5. The keyword is MATH.

2.9

1. (a) $\begin{bmatrix} 5 & 5 \\ 5 & 3 \end{bmatrix}$;   (c) $\begin{bmatrix} 1 & 0 \\ 1 & 1 \end{bmatrix}$;   (e) $\begin{bmatrix} 22 & 14 \\ 8 & 4 \end{bmatrix}$;   (g) $\begin{bmatrix} 8 & 3 \end{bmatrix}$

2. (a) $\begin{bmatrix} 0 & 0 \\ 3 & 6 \end{bmatrix}$;   (c) $\begin{bmatrix} 13 & 0 \\ 0 & 13 \end{bmatrix}$

3. (a) 1,   (c) 0,   (e) 18

4. (a) $\begin{bmatrix} 1 & 0 \\ 1 & 1 \end{bmatrix}$;   (c) not invertible;   (e) not invertible;   (f) $\begin{bmatrix} 0 & 1 \\ 1 & 0 \end{bmatrix}$

5. OQZKLUVYDW

7. (a) $A^{-1} = \begin{bmatrix} 9 & 10 \\ 10 & 9 \end{bmatrix}$; ciphertext = IUWCWKPSYZ

    (b) GO AHEAD

9. $A = \begin{bmatrix} 24 & 23 \\ 19 & 0 \end{bmatrix}$

11. (a) is the Hill ciphertext; (b) is the monoalphabetic substitution.

13. 678-953-2900

14. (a) $A^{-1} = \begin{bmatrix} 1 & 2 & 2 \\ 3 & 3 & 0 \\ 0 & 3 & 3 \end{bmatrix}$ (c) $A^{-1} = A$

15. (a) AAA YOC VWSHQG

17. 16, 6

19. If A_i is the ith row of A and B_j is the jth column of B then the ijth entry of AB is $A_i B_j$, so the ijth entry of $k(AB)$ is $k \cdot (A_i B_j)$. This, in turn, is equal to $(k \cdot A_i)B_j$, by the distributive law of arithmetic and the definition of kA_i. This last expression is the ijth entry of the matrix product $(kA)B$.

3.1

1. (a) 33, (c) 171

2. (a) 1 000 000, (c) 11 101

3. (a) 17

5. STAY CALM

6. (a) 676, (c) 2398, (e) 8 943 601

7. (a) BB, (c) CAAA, (e) SPHERE

8. (a) 4

9. MEMPHIS, MEMPHIT, MEMPHIU, MEMPHIV, MEMPHIW, MEMPHIX, MEMPHIY, MEMPHIZ, MEMPHJA, MEMPHJB, MEMPHJC, MEMPHJD, MEMPHJE, MEMPHJF, MEMPHJG, MEMPHJH

10. (a) 110 000, 110, (c) $a = 1 110 100$, $b = 10$

11. (a) $a + b =$ CPQ, $a - b =$ OE

    (c) $a + b =$ OUT, $a - b =$ IN

13. (a) TWUTH MBHSE VTQCW

    (b) LOOSE LIPS SINK SHIPS

15. The number of base twenty-six digits in n is $\lfloor \log_{26}(n) \rfloor + 1 = \lfloor \ln(n)/\ln(26) \rfloor + 1$. So the number of base twenty-six digits in 1234567890 is 7.

3.2

16. (a) $f(x_1 x_2) = ((1 + x_1) \cdot (1 + x_2) + x_1 \cdot x_2)$ MOD 2

    (c) $h(x_1 x_2 x_3) = ((1 + x_1) \cdot (1 + x_2) \cdot (1 + x_3) + (1 + x_1) \cdot x_2 \cdot x_3 + x_1 \cdot (1 + x_2) \cdot (1 + x_3) + x_1 \cdot x_2 \cdot x_3)$ MOD $2 = (1 + x_2 + x_3)$ MOD 2

17. (a) 11101

18. If $y_1 y_2 y_3 y_4 = f(x_1 x_2 x_3 x_4)$, then $x_1 = y_4$, $x_2 = y_2$, $x_3 = y_1$ and $x_4 = y_3$, so $f^{-1}(y_1 y_2 y_3 y_4) = y_4 y_2 y_1 y_3$.

7. (a) 4, (c) 11, (e) 0, (g) 0.693147, (i) 2.00432, (k) -6, (m) 5, (o) 16/15

8. (a) all reals; 64, 128, 256, 1/2, 1/16, 11.471641984126618, 0.033261568201667494
   (c) 0, 1, 2, 3, -2, -5, 1.1447
   (d) 0, 1, 3, 8
   (f) 0, 0.45, -0.4, 4743.32

10. (a) 616094.4; (c) 23

12. (a) $f(x) = (-1)^x$; (c) $w(n) = 26^n$; (e) $u(m\,n) = n^m$

13.

n	3	4	5	6	7	8	9	10	11	12	13	14	15	16	17	18
$\pi(n)$	2	2	3	3	4	4	4	4	5	5	6	6	6	6	7	7

n	19	20	21	22	23	24	25	26	27	28	29	30	31	32	33	34
$\pi(n)$	8	8	8	8	9	9	9	9	9	9	10	10	11	11	11	11

n	35	36	37	38	39	40	41	42	43	44	45	46	47	48	49	50
$\pi(n)$	11	11	12	12	12	12	13	13	14	14	14	14	15	15	15	15

15. Since p and q are distinct we can list all the numbers in the range 1 to pq that have a factor in common with p and q: $p, 2p, 3p, \ldots, qp$, and $q, 2q, 3q, \ldots, (p-1)q, pq$. These lists contain, respectively, q, and p numbers, but pq appears in each list so the total number of values relatively prime to pq is $pq - (p+q-1) = pq - p - (q-1) = p(q-1) - q - 1 = (q-1)(p-1)$.

3.3

1. (a) At worst, n comparisons; at best, 1.

   (b) At best n comparisons will be needed.

3. Pick a positive a and a positive C. Then, for all sufficiently large values of n, $\ln(C) + n\ln(a) \le n\ln(n)$. That is, $\ln(C \cdot a^n) \le \ln(n^n)$, or $C \cdot a^n \le n^n$ for all sufficiently large n. This means that $n^n \notin \mathcal{O}(a^n)$ for any a.

5. $\mathcal{O}(10^{100}) \subset \mathcal{O}(\ln(n)) = \mathcal{O}(\log_{10}(n)) \subset \mathcal{O}(n^3) = \mathcal{O}(n^3 + n^2) \subset \mathcal{O}(n^{100}) \subset \mathcal{O}(1.1^n) \subset \mathcal{O}(3^n) \subset \mathcal{O}(n2^n) \subset \mathcal{O}(n!)$

7. (b) one multiplication is performed at each pass through the "while" loop; one division (with MOD) is performed whenever "if" is executed; three comparisons are performed. Counting each of these operations as a step, there are five steps in each pass throught the "while." At most $\lfloor\sqrt{n}\rfloor + 1$ passes through "while" will occur, so $\mu_{\text{trial division}}(n) = 5(\lfloor\sqrt{n}\rfloor + 1)$.

(c) Since $5(\lfloor\sqrt{n}\rfloor) \le 5\cdot(\sqrt{n}+\sqrt{n}) = 10\sqrt{n}$, for all $n \ge 1$, $\mu_{\text{trial division}} \in \mathcal{O}(n^{1/2})$.

(c) We know $x = \lfloor\log_2 n\rfloor = 1$, so, $x - 1 \le \log_2 n < x$, and $2^{x-1} \le n < 2^x$. Thus

$$5(\lfloor 2^{x-1}\rfloor + 1) \le \mu_{\text{binary}}(x) \le 5(\lfloor 2^x\rfloor + 1).$$

It follows that $\mu_{\text{binary}} \in \mathcal{O}(2^x)$.

3.4

2. SELL STOCK

3. (a) 10101110110001111100110100010000

   (c) 00000100101100111110001101110101

4. (a) $b_4 = b_3 + b_1$, (b) $b_4 = b_3 + b_2 + b_1$

6. (a) $b_5 = b_4 + b_1$, period 15, (b) $b_5 = b_3 + b_1$, period 31

7. No for 3, 4, 5; zero initial state implies zero forever.

8. $C(9, 2) = 36$

9.
```
1 0 1 1
0 1 1 0
1 1 0 1
1 0 1 0
0 1 0 0
1 0 0 1
0 0 1 0
0 1 0 1
1 0 1 1
```

period 8

3.5

1. AH in binary ASCII and subdivided into 4-bit blocks is 0, 1, 0, 0, 0, 0, 0, 1, 0, 1, 0, 0, 1, 0, 0, 0. Enciphering with $k = 001$ gives 0, 1, 1, 0, 0, 0, 1, 1, 0, 1, 1, 0, 1, 1, 0, 0.

3. (a) $y_0 = F_k(iv \oplus x_0)$, $y_i = F_k(y_{i-1} \oplus x_i)$, $i = 1, 2, \ldots$

(b) $x_0 = iv \oplus F_k^{-1}(y_0)$, $x_i = y_{i-1} \oplus F_k^{-1}(y_i)$, $i = 1, 2, \ldots$

4. $z_0 = I$, $x_i = y_i \oplus L_m(F_k(z_{i-1}))$, $z_i = S(F_k(z_{i-1}), y_i)$, $i = 1, 2, 3, \ldots$

5. $F_{k_1 k_2}^{-1}(y_1 y_2 y_3 y_4) = ((y_3 + k_1 k_2 y_1 + k_1 y_2^2)$ MOD $2)((y_4 + k_1 y_1 y_2 + k_2 y_1 y_2)$ MOD $2)(y_1)(y_2)$

3.6

1. VWNLB

2. (a) is likely uncorrupted; (c) is likely uncorrupted

3. HELLO WORLD (a) 26^5; $26^5/26^{10} = 1/26^5$. (c) 26^{5n-5}; $26^{5n-5}/26^{5n} = 1/26^5$.

4. The messages 00000000 00000000 10110101 and 00000000 01111010 10110101 hash to the same value.

4.1

1. See the table of primes.

3. $n!$ is divisible by 2, 3, $\ldots$, n, so $n! + 2$, $n! + 3$, $n! + 4$, $\ldots$, $n! + (n-1)$, $n! + n$ are all divisible by 2, $\ldots$, n.

6. (a) $2310 = 2 \cdot 3 \cdot 5 \cdot 7 \cdot 11$, (c) $961 = 31^2$

7.

n	$n!$	factorization
2	2	2
3	6	$2 \cdot 3$
4	24	$2^3 \cdot 3$
5	120	$2^3 \cdot 3 \cdot 5$
6	720	$2^4 \cdot 3^2 \cdot 5$
7	5040	$2^4 \cdot 3^2 \cdot 5 \cdot 7$
8	40320	$2^7 \cdot 3^2 \cdot 5 \cdot 7$
9	362880	$2^7 \cdot 3^4 \cdot 5 \cdot 7$
10	3628800	$2^8 \cdot 3^4 \cdot 5^2 \cdot 7$
11	39916800	$2^8 \cdot 3^4 \cdot 5^2 \cdot 7 \cdot 11$
12	479001600	$2^{10} \cdot 3^5 \cdot 5^2 \cdot 7 \cdot 11$
13	6227020800	$2^{10} \cdot 3^5 \cdot 5^2 \cdot 7 \cdot 11 \cdot 13$

8. (a) 25; no; $73 \cdot 137$

10. $23981204798221 = 15485863 \cdot 15485867$

11. (a) 15; (c) 61

12. (a) $17^{-1} \equiv 53 \,(\text{mod}\,60)$; (c) $3^{-1} \equiv 44 \,(\text{mod}\,131)$;
    (e) $1006^{-1} \equiv 3918816 \,(\text{mod}\,7233631)$

13. (a) $x = 17$; (c) $x = 48$

14. (a) $x = 12y \;\text{MOD}\; 13$; (c) $x = 9y \;\text{MOD}\; 17$

15. (a) $(2-1)! \equiv 1 \equiv -1 \,(\text{mod}\,2)$, $(3-1) \equiv 2 \equiv -1 \,(\text{mod}\,3)$, and so on.

    (b) $(n-1)! = [2 \cdot 3 \cdot 4 \cdot \ldots (n-3) \cdot (n-2)] \cdot (n-1)$, and by the exercise mentioned in the hint, each of the factors in the brackets has an inverse modulo n distinct from itself. So, somewhere in the product is the inverse of 2, somewhere else is the inverse of 3, and so on. Each number in the range 2 to $(n-2)$ is multiplied by its multiplicative inverse, so when this product is reduced modulo n, the quantity in brackets reduces to 1. Thus $(n-1)! \equiv 1 \cdot (n-1) \equiv -1 \,(\text{mod}\,n)$.

    (c) (i) If $n = 4$, then $(n-1)! = 6$, which is not congruent to -1 modulo 4. (ii) If n factors into distinct factors, then $n = r \cdot s$, where $r \neq s$. Since both r and s are less than $n-1$, they both appear as factors in $(n-1)!$, so n divides $(n-1)!$. (iii) If n is a square of a prime p at least 3, then $(n-1)! = 1 \cdot 2 \cdot \cdots \cdot p \cdot (p+1) \cdot \cdots \cdot (2p-1) \cdot 2p \cdot (2p+1) \cdot \cdots (n-1)$. Since the factors p and $2p$ appear in $(n-1)!$, this number is divisible by p^2, which is n.

17. (a) 3, 7, 31, 127

    (b) and (c) If $n = r \cdot s$, where r and s are greater than 1, then $2^n - 1 = 2^{rs} - 1 = (2^r)^s - 1 = (2^r - 1) \cdot ((2^r)^{s-1} + (2^r)^{s-2} + \cdots + 1)$, which is a factorization of $2^n - 1$ into nontrivial factors.

4.2

1. (a) 12, 13, 27, 55, 111, 219, 450 is superincreasing.
   (c) 17, 18, 39, 69, 180, 331 is not.

2. (a) 2725; (c) 7179

3. (a) 310 cannot be written as a sum of a subset of the sequence.

(c) 127 cannot be written as a sum of a subset of the sequence.

(e) 1, 1, 1, 1, 1, 1, 1, 1

5. 20, 40, 75, 145, 305, 625, 226, 482

7. 1, 1, 1, 0, 0, 1, 0, 1

9. 00110110

11. 9584, 11616, 9584, 1824, 1824, 7760, 9584, 9424, 1824, 11616, 1824, 15104, 1824, 15104, 1824, 3488

12. The pattern of sum representations is $1, 2, 3, \ldots, n, n+1, n+2, \ldots,$ $n+(n-1) = 2n-1, n+(n-1)+1 = 2n, n+(n-1)+2 = 2n+1,$ $\ldots, n+(n-1)+(n-2) = 3n-3, n+(n-1)+(n-2)+1 = 3n-2,$ $\ldots.$ The largest possible number representable by a subset sum is $1+2+3+\cdots+n = n(n+1)/2.$

13. Use the identity that $r^n - 1 = (r-1)(r^{n-1} + r^{n-2} + \cdots + r^3 + r^2 + r + 1).$

4.3

1. (a) 3   (c) 25

2. (a) 99   (b) 1   (c) 1   (d) 1   (e) 1   (f) 100

3. $56 = 3 \cdot 16 + 8$, so by Fermat's little theorem, since 17 is prime,

$$
\begin{aligned}
2^{56} + 3^{56} &\equiv 2^{3 \cdot 16 + 8} + 3^{3 \cdot 16 + 8} \\
&\equiv (2^3)^{16} \cdot 2^8 + (3^3)^{16} \cdot 3^8 \\
&\equiv 1 \cdot 2^8 + 1 \cdot 3^8 \\
&\equiv 2^8 + 3^8 \pmod{17}.
\end{aligned}
$$

Now $2^2 \equiv 4 \pmod{17}$, $2^4 \equiv 4^2 \equiv 16 \equiv -1 \pmod{17}$, and $2^8 \equiv (-1)^2 \equiv 1 \pmod{17}$; $3^2 \equiv 9 \pmod{17}$, $3^4 \equiv 9^2 \equiv 81 \equiv 13 \pmod{17}$ and $3^8 \equiv 13^2 \equiv 169 \equiv 16 \pmod{17}$. So

$$
\begin{aligned}
2^{56} + 3^{56} &\equiv 2^8 + 3^8 \\
&\equiv 1 + 16 \\
&\equiv 17 \equiv 0 \pmod{17}.
\end{aligned}
$$

4. (a) $a \equiv b \,(\mathrm{mod}\,m)$ means that $a - b = rm$ for some integer m. Multiplying by k gives $ka - kb = km$, which means that $ka \equiv kb \,(\mathrm{mod}\,km)$.

5. Let $r_1, r_2, \ldots, r_{\phi(n)}$ be the numbers in the range $1, \ldots, n-1$ that are relatively prime to n. For a relatively prime to n, all of the numbers $a \cdot r_1$ MOD n, $a \cdot r_2$ MOD n, $\ldots$, $a \cdot r_{\phi(n)}$ MOD n are distinct from one another, so they are just a reordering of $r_1, \ldots, r_{\phi(n)}$. Thus $(a \cdot r_1$ MOD $n) \cdot (a \cdot r_2$ MOD $n) \cdots \cdot (a \cdot r_{\phi(n)}$ MOD $n) \equiv r_1 \cdots \cdot r_{\phi(n)} \,(\mathrm{mod}\,n)$. This becomes $a^{\phi(n)} \cdot (r_1 \cdot r_2 \cdots r_{\phi(n)}) \equiv (r_1 \cdot r_2 \cdots r_{\phi(n)}) \,(\mathrm{mod}\,n)$. Cancel the quantity in parenthese from both sides to yield the desired identity.

7. (a) First note that $\phi(15) = (5 - 1)(3 - 1) = 8$. Then (a) $D(E(x)) = (x^3)^3)$ MOD $15 = x^9$ MOD $15 = x^{9 \text{ MOD } 8}$ MOD $15 = x^1$ MOD $15 = x$ for all x relatively prime to 15, by the previous exercise.

9. a is relatively prime to pq, so it has an inverse a^{-1} modulo pq. By definition, a^{-t} means $(a^{-1})^t$. In the proof of part (2), if a is not relatively prime to pq, then it has no inverse modulo pq.

10. (a) Multiply $a^{p-1} \equiv 1 \,(\mathrm{mod}\,p)$ by a^{-1}.

11. $561 = 3 \cdot 11 \cdot 17$, $1105 = 5 \cdot 13 \cdot 17$, $1729 = 7 \cdot 13 \cdot 19$, $2465 = 5 \cdot 17 \cdot 29$, $2821 = 7 \cdot 13 \cdot 31$, $6601 = 7 \cdot 23 \cdot 41$, $8911 = 7 \cdot 19 \cdot 67$, $10585 = 5 \cdot 29 \cdot 73$

4.4

1. (a) 329 236 (c) 035 450

2. (a) TELL (c) FIRE

3. TAKE TWO

4. (a) 22 681 (c) 05 589

5. (a) 10 164=PAY; (b) 05 118=HOW

7. DONT WORRY BE HAPPY

9. (a) $n = pq - p - q + 1$, so $p + q = pq - n + 1$; that is, $p + q = m - n + 1$
    (c) $m = 2039 \cdot 2617$

10. (a) By the theorem, there exist s and t, which are found by the extended Euclidean algorithm, such that $1 = se_a + te_z$. Thus $x \equiv x^1 \equiv x^{se_a + te_z} \equiv (x^{e_a})^s \cdot (x^{e_z})^t \pmod{m}$.

(b) $1 = 43 \cdot 47 - 20 \cdot 101$, so $x = 2467^{43} \cdot 2664^{-20} \equiv 1000 \pmod{m}$

4.5

1. (a)

x	2^x	3^x	4^x	5^x	6^x	7^x	8^x	9^x	10^x
1	2	3	4	5	6	7	8	9	10
2	4	9	5	3	3	5	9	4	1
3	8	5	9	4	7	2	6	3	10
4	5	4	3	9	9	3	4	5	1
5	10	1	1	1	10	10	10	1	10
6	9	3	4	5	5	4	3	9	1
7	7	9	5	3	8	6	2	4	10
8	3	5	9	4	4	9	5	3	1
9	6	4	3	9	2	8	7	5	10
10	1	1	1	1	1	1	1	1	1

(c) 2, 6, 7, 8

2. (a) $x = 6$; (c) $x = 10$

3. 6, 36, 31, and 1 are the only numbers that turn up as powers of 6, modulo 37. Since 36 is its own inverse, modulo 37, raising it to any even power will give 1. Raising 6 to an even exponent will then give either 36 or 1. It would be better to choose s relatively prime to 36 (e.g., $s = 11$).

5. Bob calculates 21^6 MOD 23, which is 18. This is the shift amount used to encipher the text, so he will use an 8-shift to decipher: STAYAWAKE.

6. (a) $(t, y) = (49, 25)$

7. (a) $x = 33$

8. (a) $(t, y) = (908, 989)$

9. (b) $x = 529$; (c) $x = 421$

10. (a) (11359, 6319), (7829, 10369), (514, 69)

11. By Fermat's little theorem, $t^{p-1-a} \equiv t^{p-1}t^{-a} \equiv 1 \cdot t^{-a} \equiv t^{-a} \pmod{p}$.

12. $s = p - 1$ would make s^a take either the value 1 or $p - 1$.

4.6

1. (a) $\sigma = 70$

   (b) He regards the pair as likely to be authentic since 54^7 MOD $91 = 89$.

2. (a) (185, 21)

   (b) $\tilde{x} = 44$, $\tilde{\sigma} = 86$. Signature is valid because $\tilde{\sigma}^{e_A}$ MOD $91 = 86^7$ MOD $91 = 44$.

3. The first is valid; the second is not.

5. 525

4.7

4. $(n - x)^2 \equiv n^2 - 2nx + x^2 \equiv 0 - 0 + x^2 \pmod{n}$

5.

Round	r commitment	$w \equiv r^2$ witness	e challenge	$y \equiv r \cdot s^e$ response	$z \equiv y^2$ comparison 1	$z' \equiv w \cdot v^e$ comparison 2
1	26	676	1	2938	2604	2604
2	519	1557	0	519	1557	1557
3	1040	2945	1	5935	560	560
4	2804	6832	1	4414	655	655
5	5991	6345	1	34	1156	1156
6	6263	6761	0	6263	6761	6761
7	1118	172	1	7310	1763	1763
8	4309	7176	0	4309	7176	7176

5.1

1. The cryptographic application stored on a computer disk can be modified by an opponent from a remote site. The modified application could leak key information or do other damaging work. If the cryptographic application is implemented in circuitry, then the opponent must mount a more daring attack of finding the physical device and either replacing or modifying it.

3. (a) Taking the base 10 logarithm of Stirling's formula and using properties of logarithms, we obtain $\log_{10}(n!) \approx ((n+.5)\ln(n) - n + \ln(2\pi)/2)/\ln(10)$. Substituting $n = 2^{64}$, we get $\log_{10}(2^{64}) \approx 3.474 \times 10^{20}$, which says that

$$2^{64}! \approx 10^{3.474 \times 10^{20}} = 2.951 \times 10^{10^{20}-3} \approx 2.951 \times 10^{10^{20}};$$

there are on the order of

$$10^{20} = 100000000000000000000$$

digits in the decimal representation of this number!

(b) It is about $2^{56}/2.951 \times 10^{10^{20}} = 7.2 \times 10^{16}/2.951 \times 10^{10^{20}} = 2.779 \times 10^{16-10^{20}} \approx 2.779 \times 10^{-10^{20}}$, an unimaginably small number.

(c) Highly unlikely.

4.
$$\begin{bmatrix} 1 & 0 & 0 & 0 & 0 & 0 & 0 & 0 & 0 & 0 \\ 0 & 0 & 0 & 0 & 0 & 0 & 1 & 0 & 0 & 0 \\ 0 & 0 & 0 & 0 & 0 & 0 & 0 & 0 & 1 & 0 \\ 0 & 0 & 0 & 1 & 0 & 0 & 0 & 0 & 0 & 0 \\ 0 & 0 & 0 & 0 & 0 & 0 & 0 & 1 & 0 & 0 \\ 0 & 0 & 1 & 0 & 0 & 0 & 0 & 0 & 0 & 0 \\ 0 & 0 & 0 & 0 & 0 & 0 & 0 & 0 & 0 & 1 \\ 0 & 0 & 0 & 0 & 0 & 1 & 0 & 0 & 0 & 0 \end{bmatrix} \text{ and } \begin{bmatrix} 0 & 0 & 0 & 0 & 0 & 0 & 0 & 1 & 0 & 0 \\ 0 & 0 & 1 & 0 & 0 & 0 & 0 & 0 & 0 & 0 \\ 0 & 0 & 0 & 0 & 0 & 1 & 0 & 0 & 0 & 0 \\ 0 & 0 & 0 & 0 & 1 & 0 & 0 & 0 & 0 & 0 \\ 0 & 0 & 0 & 0 & 0 & 0 & 0 & 0 & 0 & 1 \\ 0 & 1 & 0 & 0 & 0 & 0 & 0 & 0 & 0 & 0 \\ 0 & 0 & 0 & 0 & 0 & 0 & 0 & 0 & 1 & 0 \\ 1 & 0 & 0 & 0 & 0 & 0 & 0 & 0 & 0 & 0 \end{bmatrix}$$

5. $\text{IP}^{-1}(x_1x_2x_3x_4x_5x_6x_7x_8) = x_4x_1x_3x_5x_7x_2x_8x_6$

7. (b) 1011101110 is the key.

Index